FRANCIPLEGIUS

Francis P. Magoun Jr.

FRANCIPLEGIUS

MEDIEVAL AND LINGUISTIC
STUDIES IN HONOR OF
FRANCIS PEABODY MAGOUN, JR.

Edited by

Jess B. Bessinger, Jr. and Robert P. Creed

 New York University Press 1965

The frontispiece is a portrait photograph
of Francis Peabody Magoun, Jr. by
Robert Gardner.

FOREWORD

When Francis Peabody Magoun, Jr., became Emeritus Professor of English at Harvard University in 1961, he retired from only one area of his distinguished scholarly career, to revisit Finland and continue there the linguistic and literary studies which have lately been crowned by an epochal translation of the *Kalevala*, and honored by his appointment as Commander of the Order of the Lion of Finland. In celebration of his seventieth birthday (he was born in New York City on 6 January 1895) his students, colleagues, and friends present this "frankpledge," therefore, to hail his uninterrupted endeavors.

His list of publications will suggest that Professor Magoun's academic work and play have from the outset been marked by a strenuous variety of application not surprising in a lawn tennis enthusiast and member of the American Ambulance Corps (1916–17) and Royal Flying Corps (1917–18), to whom the Military Cross was awarded in 1918. Nor was his characteristic energy exhausted by the making of many books and articles. After study at Harvard University (A. B. 1916, Ph.D. 1923) and Trinity College, Cambridge (1919), he served at Harvard in the departments of English and Comparative Literature, and on occasion lectured abroad, at Paris and Strasbourg (1931–32) and University College, London (1951). He was one of the founders and Managing Editor of *Speculum* (1926–30) and Editor of *Harvard Studies and Notes in Philology and Literature* (1935–36). During 1955–56 he held a fellowship from the John Simon Guggenheim Memorial Foundation.

The present essays will recall some of his interests in selected areas, chiefly medieval—Old Germanic studies, early English and British language, literature, history, folklore, and textual criticism. There has not been room, of course, for all who would have liked to contribute to the book; the unattainable Festschrift for this wide-ranging man would swell to encyclopedic size. No volume, moreover, could properly convey the esteem of his students for Professor Magoun's teaching, which seems to us to have been carried on, in a pertinent Old English formula, *ellne miċele*, with immense zeal, with a special blend of urbanity and adventure both in Harvard Yard, and, with many a hospitable gesture from Margaret Boyden Magoun, in his own study, a room which has long been an intellectual and all but familial center for numberless

v

234523

students and friends on both sides of the Atlantic. The editors join his other well wishers, to very many of whom they are grateful for assistance of all kinds, in a general friendly salute, but with particular affection and gratitude.

J. B. B., Jr.
R. P. C.

CONTENTS

FOREWORD   v

BOOKS, ARTICLES, RECORDINGS, AND
   BOOK REVIEWS   3

WILLIAM ALFRED
Dedicatory Poem: A Translation of Alcuin's
"Debate of Spring with Winter"   17

BJÖRN COLLINDER
Remarks on the Origin of Speech   19

RENÉ DEROLEZ
Scandinavian Runes in Continental   30
   Manuscripts

C. L. WRENN
Some Earliest Anglo-Saxon Cult Symbols   40

A. H. SMITH
The *Hwicce*   56

ROBERT L. KELLOGG
The South Germanic Oral Tradition   66

FREDERIC G. CASSIDY
How Free Was the Anglo-Saxon Scop?   75

ALBERT BATES LORD
Beowulf and Odysseus   86

H. M. SMYSER
Ibn Faḍlān's Account of the Rūs, with Some
   Commentary and Some Allusions to
   Beowulf   92

KEMP MALONE
Some *Beowulf* Readings — 120

NORMAN E. ELIASON
The "Thryth-Offa Digression" in *Beowulf* — 124

G. N. GARMONSWAY
Anglo-Saxon Heroic Attitudes — 139

ALAIN RENOIR
Wulf and Eadwacer: A Noninterpretation — 147

JOHN C. POPE
Dramatic Voices in *The Wanderer* and *The Seafarer* — 164

LAURENCE K. SHOOK
Old English Riddle No. 20: *Heoruswealwe* — 194

FREDERICK NORMAN
Problems in the Dating of *Deor* and its Allusions — 205

DOROTHY WHITELOCK
Wulfstan at York — 214

ROGER SHERMAN LOOMIS
The Strange History of Caradoc of Vannes — 232

E. P. HAMP
Welsh *chwarddaf, chwerthin,* and *gwên* — 240

CHARLES W. DUNN
Havelok and Anlaf Cuaran — 244

TAUNO F. MUSTANOJA
Chaucer's *Manciple's Tale*, Lines 311–13 — 250

HOWARD R. PATCH
The Subjects of Chaucer's Poetry — 255

ARTHUR BROWN
The Study of English Medieval Drama — 265

BARTLETT JERE WHITING
A Collection of Proverbs in BM Additional
  MS. 37075   274

ANGUS McINTOSH
Some Linguistic Reflections of a   290
  Wycliffite

HELGE KÖKERITZ
Dialectal Traits in Sir Thomas Wyatt's Poetry   294

FRANCIS LEE UTLEY
Hic Jacet Lincoln, Rex Quondam Rexque
  Futurus   304

ILLUSTRATIONS

PLATES

Francis Peabody Magoun, Jr.   Frontispiece
Loveden Hill (Lincolnshire) Runes:
    Urn rim; detail   *page*   51

FIGURES

Runes: Caistor N 59   *page*   44
Loveden Hill Urn with runic inscription   51
The English Settlement of
    the South Midlands   57
Territory of the *Hwicce*   60

FRANCiplEGiUS

BOOKS, ARTICLES, RECORDINGS,

AND BOOK REVIEWS

by

Francis Peabody Magoun, Jr.

1924

REVIEW

John Beresford, *Poems of Charles Cotton, 1630–1687*, in *The Christian Science Monitor*, Eastern Seaboard edition, 25 June 1924, p. 9, cols 1–2.

1925

"Harvard Miltoniana," *Harvard Alumni Bulletin*, XXVII, 875–78.
"Two Lexicographical Notes," *Modern Language Notes*, XL, 408–12.
"Miltoniana," *Harvard Library Notes*, No. 15, 49–56.

1926

With C. C. Coulter. "Giraldus Cambrensis on Indo-Germanic Philology," *Speculum*, I, 104–109.
"Chaucer and the *Roman de la Rose*, vv. 16096–105," *Romanic Review*, XVII, 69–70.
"An *Index* of Abbreviations in Miss Alma Blount's Unpublished *Onomasticon Arthurianum*," *Speculum*, I, 190–216.
"The *Compilation of St Albans* and the Old-French Prose Alexander Romance," *Speculum*, I, 225–32.

REVIEWS

A. S. Cook and C. B. Tinker, *Select Translations from Old English Poetry*, in *Speculum*, I, 460–61.
J. H. Pitman, *The Riddles of Aldhelm: Text and Translation*, in *Speculum*, I, 357–59.
J. R. Reinhard, *Amadas et Ydoine, roman du xiiie siècle*, in *Speculum*, I, 359–60.
G P. Krapp, *The English Language in America*, in *The Saturday Review of Literature*, II, 856.

1927

"The Burning of Heorot: An Illustrative Note," *Modern Language Notes*, XLII, 173–74.
"Hermus vs. Hormuz," *PMLA*, XLII, 670–72.
"The Chaucer of Spenser and Milton," *Modern Philology*, XXV, 129–36.
"The Source of Chaucer's *Rime of Sir Thopas*," *PMLA*, XLII, 833–44.

REVIEWS

Stanley Rypins, ed., *The Old English Prose Tracts in MS. Cotton Vitellius A.xv*, in *Modern Language Notes*, XLII, 67–70.
E. C. Armstrong, *The Authorship of the Vengement Alixandre and of the Venjance Alixandre*, in *Speculum*, II, 228.
Bateman Edwards, *A Classification of the Manuscripts of Gui de Cambrai's Vengement Alixandre*, in *Speculum*, II, 228–29.
Robert Priebsch, *The Heliand Manuscript Cotton Caligula A.vii in the British Museum*, in *Speculum*, II, 229–30.

1928

With S. H. Thomson. "*Kronika o Alexandru Velikém:* a Czech Prose Translation of the *Historia de Preliis*, Recension J³," *Speculum*, III, 204–17.
"Harvard MS. Latin 34: *Historia de Preliis* (J³ Recension)," *Harvard Library Notes*, No. 20, 172–75.
"Anmerkungen zum Glossar des Tolkien-Gordonschen *Sir Gawain and the Green Knight*," *Anglia*, LII, 79–82.
With B. I. Jarcho. "Eine russische Handschrift der *Historia de Preliis* (Rezension J³)," *Archiv für slavische Philologie*, XLII, 262–74.

REVIEWS

E. P. Hammond, *English Verse between Chaucer and Surrey*, in *Speculum*, III, 269–70.
H. V. Routh, *God, Man, and Epic Poetry*, Vol. II, in *Speculum*, III, 124–27.

1929

The Gests of King Alexander of Macedon (Cambridge, Mass.: Harvard University Press. x + 261 pages.)
" 'Muchel *broken* harm,' C.–T., E 1425," *Anglia*, LIII, 223–24.
"Football in Medieval England and in Middle-English Literature," *American Historical Review*, XXXV, 33–45.
"Recurring First Elements in Different Nominal Compounds in *Beowulf*

and in the *Elder Edda*," *Studies in English Philology: A Miscellany in Honor of Frederick Klaeber*, edd. Kemp Malone and Martin B Rudd (Minneapolis), pp. 73–78.

"Medieval Literature," in "American Bibliography for 1928," *PMLA*, XLIV, 2–9.

REVIEWS

M. M. Bašić, ed., *Iz stare srpske Knjidzevnosti*, in *Speculum*, IV, 136–37.

Olga Dobiache-Rojdestvensky, *Analecta Medii Aeui*, in *Speculum*, IV, 135.

Bateman Edwards, ed., *Gui de Cambrai: Le Vengement Alixandre*, in *Speculum*, IV, 229–31.

Margaret Schlauch, *Medieval Narrative: A Book of Translations*, in *Speculum*, IV, 129–31.

1930

F. B. Gummere, *Founders of England . . . with Supplementary Notes by Francis Peabody Magoun, Jr.* (New York). A revised edition of Gummere's *Germanic Origins* (1892).

"Medieval Literature," in "American Bibliography for 1929," *PMLA*, XLV, 2–11.

"Word-Formation in Old English," in Milton H. Turk, *An Anglo-Saxon Reader*, 2d ed. (New York), pp. 48a–48m.

REVIEW

Margaret Wattie, ed., *The Middle English "Lai le Freine*," in *Speculum*, V, 239–41.

1931

"Place-Names: British," in L. J. Paetow, *A Guide to the Study of Medieval History*, rev. ed. (New York), pp. 46–53. Also contributor to smaller sections on Old and Middle English language and literature.

"General Section" in "American Bibliography for 1930," *PMLA*, XLVI, 2–13.

"Scottish Popular Football, 1424–1815," *American Historical Review*, XXXVII, 1–13.

"Shrove Tuesday Football," *Harvard Studies and Notes in Philology and Literature*, XIII, 9–46.

"Reading-List for the History, Culture and Literature of Pre-Conquest England (to 1066)," *Bulletin de la Faculté des Lettres de Strasbourg*, IX, 272–74.

REVIEWS

Anton Blanck, *Konung Alexander, Bo Jonsson Grip och Albrekt av Mecklenburg*, in *Speculum*, VI, 475−76.

Stefan Gaevskii, *"Aleksandrija" v Davnii Ukrainskoi Literature*, in *Speculum*, VI, 308−10.

A. R. Nykl, *A Compendium of Aljamiado Literature*, in *Speculum*, VI, 489−90.

1932

"The Harvard Epitome of the *Historia de Preliis* (Recension I²)" *Harvard Studies and Notes in Philology and Literature*, XIV, 115−34.

REVIEWS

W. J. Entwistle *et al.*, edd., *The Year's Work in Modern Language Studies*, in *Speculum*, VII, 127−28.

J. R. C. Hall, *A Concise Anglo-Saxon Dictionary*, 3d ed., in *Speculum*, VII, 286−89.

A. H. Heusinkveld and E. J. Bashe, *A Bibliographical Guide to Old English*, in *Speculum*, VII, 286−89.

G. P. Krapp, *The Anglo-Saxon Poetic Records: A Collective Edition*, Vol. I: *The Junius Manuscript*, in *Speculum*, VII, 286−89.

J. J. Parry *et al.*, *A Bibliography of Critical Arthurian Literature for the Years 1922−29*, in *Speculum*, VII, 127−28.

1933

"Cynewulf, Cyneheard, and Osric," *Anglia*, LVII, 361−76.

"A. N. Wesselofsky on the Old-French Romance of *Florimont*," in Alfons Hilka, *Aimon von Varennes: Florimont* (Gottingen), pp. cviii−ix.

REVIEWS

J. H. Cockburn, *The Battle of Brunanburh and its Period elucidated by Place-Names*, in *Speculum*, VIII, 85−87.

Ferdinand Holthausen, *Altenglisches etymologisches Wörterbuch*, in *Speculum*, VIII, 94−96.

1934

"A Prague Epitome of the *Historia de Preliis Alexandri Magni* (Recension I²)," *Harvard Studies and Notes in Philology and Literature*, XVI, 119−44.

With Alfons Hilka. "A List of Manuscripts containing Texts of the

Historia de Preliis Alexandri Magni, Recensions I¹, I², I³," *Speculum*, IX, 84–86.

"Whence 'Dulcifal' in *Göngu-Hrólfs Saga?*," *Studia Germanica till-ägnade E. A. Kock* (Lund), pp. 176–91.

REVIEWS

R. W. Chambers, *On the Continuity of English Prose from Alfred to More and his School*, in *Modern Language Notes*, XLIX, 477–80.

Albrecht Wettwer, *Englischer Sport im 14. Jahrhundert*, in *Speculum*, IX, 346–47.

1935

"Territorial, Place-, and River-names in the Old-English Chronicle, A-Text (Parker MS.)," *Harvard Studies and Notes in Philology and Literature*, XVIII, 69–111.

1936

REVIEWS

Lucienne Meyer, *Les Légendes des matières de Rome, de France et de Bretagne dans le "Pantheon" de Godefroi de Viterbe*, in *Speculum*, XI, 144–46.

Federico Olivieri, ed. and trans., *Beowulf*, in *Speculum*, XI, 304–305.

Margaret Schlauch, *Romance in Iceland*, in *Speculum*, XI, 151–53.

A. H. Smith, ed., *The Parker Chronicle (852–900)*, in *Speculum*, XI, 307–309.

1937

"Colloquial Old and Middle English," *Harvard Studies and Notes in Philology and Literature*, XIX, 167–73.

"Kleine Beiträge zu *Sir Gawain*," *Anglia*, LXI, 129–35.

"Zu den ae. Zaubersprüchen," *Archiv für das Studium der neueren Sprachen*, CLXXI, 17–35.

"*Ancrene Wisse* vs. *Ancren Riwle*," *ELH: A Journal of English Literary History*, IV, 112–13.

"*Sir Gawain* and Medieval Football," *English Studies*, XIX, 208–209.

"Strophische Überreste in den altenglischen Zaubersprüchen," *Englische Studien*, LXXII, 1–6.

REVIEWS

R. H. Hodgkin, *A History of the Anglo-Saxons*, in *Modern Language Notes*, LII, 510–15.

Werner Klett, *The Vision of William concerning Piers the Plowman by William Langland (14. Jahrhundert) unter dem Titel Peter der Pflüger aus dem Mittelenglischen ins Deutsche übersetzt*, in *Speculum*, XII, 125.

The Place-Names of Warwickshire (English Place-Name Society, Vol. XIII, 1936), in *The New England Quarterly*, X, 400–401.

1938

"Territorial, Place- and River-Names in the Old-English Annals, *D*-text (Ms. Cotton Tiberius B.iv)," *Harvard Studies and Notes in Philology and Literature*, XX, 147–80.

History of [British] Football from the Beginnings to 1871 (Kölner Anglistische Arbeiten, Vol. 31. ix + 151 pp.)

1939

"Aldhelm's Diocese of Sherborne *Bewestan Wuda*," *Harvard Theological Review*, XXXII, 103–14.

"Zum heroischen Exorzismus des Beowulfepos," *Arkiv för nordisk Filologi*, LIV, 215–28.

1940

With Sydney Fairbanks. "On Writing and Printing Gothic," *Speculum*, XV, 313–30.

"The Rome of Two Northern Pilgrims: Archbishop Sigeric of Canterbury and Abbot Nikolás of Munkathverá," *Harvard Theological Review*, XXXIII, 267–89.

"An English Pilgrim-Diary of the Year 990," *Mediaeval Studies*, II (Toronto), 231–52.

"Fífeldor and the Name of the Eider," *Namn och Bygd*, XXVIII, 94–114.

"On Six Old-Icelandic Words," *Modern Language Notes*, LV, 596–98.

"Zu *Etzeln Burc, Finns Buruh* und *Brunan Burh*," *Zeitschrift für deutsches Altertum und deutsche Literatur*, LXXVII, 65–66.

REVIEW

E. V. K. Dobbie, *The Manuscripts of Cædmon's Hymn and Bede's Death Song*, in *Englische Studien*, LXXIV, 110–12.

1941

"Additional Note on Printing Gothic," *Speculum*, XVI, 122.

With H. M. Smyser, trans. *Survivals in Old Norwegian of Medieval English, French and German Literature, together with the Latin Versions of the Heroic Legend of Walter of Aquitaine* (Connecticut College Monograph No. 1, Baltimore. xii + 163 pp.).

REVIEWS

A. M. Ryan, *A Map of Old English Monasteries and Related Ecclesiastical Foundations: A.D. 400 – 1066*, in *Modern Language Notes*, LVI, 306 – 308.

H. A. Rositzke, ed., *The C-Text of the Old English Chronicles*, in *Speculum*, XVI, 505 – 506.

1942

"Norman History in the 'Lay of the Beach' (*Strandar ljóð*)," *Modern Language Notes*, LVII, 11 – 16.

"Scottish History in the 'Lay of Gurun' (*Guruns ljóð*)," *A Philological Miscellany presented to Eilert Ekwall* (*Studia Neophilologica*, XIV – XV), I, 1 – 24.

"Il Gioco del Calcio Fiorentino," *Italica*, XIX, 1 – 21.

"The Italian Itinerary of Philip II (Philippe-Auguste) in the Year 1191," *Speculum*, XVII, 367 – 76.

With Roland Blenner-Hassett. "The Italian Campaign of Belin and Brenne in the Bruts of Wace and of Lawman," *Philological Quarterly*, XXI, 385 – 90.

"King Alfred's Naval and Beach Battle with the Danes in 896," *Modern Language Review*, XXXVII, 409 – 14.

"*Deors Klage* und *Guðrúnarkviða I*," *Englische Studien*, LXXV, 1 – 5.

REVIEWS

Helge Kökeritz, *The Place-Names of the Isle of Wight*, in *Speculum*, XVII, 302 – 304.

E. M. Metzenthin, *Die Länder- und Völkernamen im altisländischen Schrifttum*, in *Speculum*, XVII, 432 – 35.

The Place-Names of Middlesex apart from the City of London (English Place-Name Society, Vol. XVIII), in *Speculum*, XVII, 436 – 38.

Robert Steele, ed., *The English Poems of Charles of Orleans*, in *Modern Language Review*, XXXVII, 510 – 11.

1943

"OE Charm A 13: *būtan heardan bēaman*," *Modern Language Notes*, LVIII, 33 – 34.

"The Haddeby and Schleswig of Nikulás of Munkaþverá," *Scandinavian Studies*, XVII, 167 – 73.

"Otfrid's *Ad Liutbertum*, ll. 105 – 11, and the OHG *Tatian*," *Modern Language Notes*, LVIII, 357 – 61.

"Nikulás Bergsson of Munkaþverá and Germanic Heroic Legend," *Journal of English and Germanic Philology*, XLII, 210 – 18.

"Some Notes on Jónsson's *A Primer of Modern Icelandic:* Corrigenda and Addenda," *Scandinavian Studies,* XVII, 259–64.

"Otfrid's *Ad Liutbertum*," *PMLA,* LVIII, 869–90.

REVIEW

Sigurdur Nordal, *Hrafnkatla, mit einem Auszug auf Deutsch,* in *Speculum,* XVIII, 140–44.

1944

"The Iceland Voyage in the *Nibelungenlied*," *Modern Language Review,* XXXIX, 38–42.

"*Hymselven lik a pilgrym to desgise: Troilus,* v, 1577," *Modern Language Notes,* LIX, 176–78.

"Stojan Novaković on the so-called 'Serbian Alexander,'" *Byzantion,* XVI (American Series II), fascicle 1 for 1942–43, 315–38.

"The Pilgrim-Diary of Nikulas of Munkathvera: The Road to Rome," *Mediaeval Studies,* VI, 314–54.

"King Alfred's Hálgoland and Old Norwegian Syncope," *Scandinavian Studies,* XVIII, 163–64.

REVIEWS

Agapito Rey and A. C. Solalinde, *Ensayo de una Bibliografía de las Leyendas Troyanas en la Literatura Española,* in *Journal of American Folklore,* LVII, 93.

Gabriel Turville-Petre and E. S. Olszweska, trans., *The Life of Gudmund the Good, Bishop of Holar,* in *Journal of English and Germanic Philology,* XLIII, 107–10.

V. E. Hull and Archer Taylor, *A Collection of Welsh Riddles,* in *California Folklore Quarterly,* III, 245–46.

E. V. K. Dobbie, ed., *The Anglo-Saxon Minor Poems* (The Anglo-Saxon Poetic Records, Vol. VI), in *Modern Language Notes,* LIX, 497–502.

1945

"The Long-Lost *Instruzione del Modo del Giuocare il Calcio a i Giovani Nobili Fiorentini* of 1739," *Italica,* XXII, 14–20.

"The Domitian Bilingual of the *Old-English Annals:* The Latin Preface," *Speculum,* XX, 65–72.

"*Noþðæs sweoster*: 'Need's' sisters," *Arkiv för nordisk Filologi,* LX, 98–106.

"A Note on Old West Germanic Poetic Unity," *Modern Philology,* XLIII, 77–82.

"*The Owl and the Nightingale* and the Tale of the Cat and the Fox," *California Folklore Quarterly,* IV, 390–92.

"Geographical and Ethnic Names in the *Nibelungenlied*," *Mediaeval Studies*, VII, 85–138.

"The Domitian Bilingual of the *Old-English Annals:* Notes on the F-Text," *Modern Language Quarterly*, VI, 371–80.

"Some Additions to Blöndal's *Islenzk-Dönsk Orðabók:* Linguistic Terms," *Arkiv för nordisk Filologi*, LX, 159–68.

REVIEWS

Douwe Kalma, *Kening Finn* and *De Pearel*, in *Modern Language Notes*, LX, 353–54.

H. M. Chadwick, *The Study of Anglo-Saxon*, in *Speculum*, XX, 245–47.

M. M. Long, *The English Strong Verb from Chaucer to Caxton*, in *Speculum*, XX, 250–51.

Halldór Hermannsson, ed., *The Vinland Sagas*, in *Speculum*, XX, 355–57.

G. R. Stewart, Jr., *Names on the Land*, in *The New England Quarterly*, XVIII, 544–45.

1946

"Jóhann Sigurjónsson's *Fjalla-Eyvindur:* Source, Chronology, and Geography," *PMLA*, LXI, 269–92.

With M. R. Brown. "Tyrkir, First German in North America," *Modern Language Notes*, LXI, 547–51.

1947

"On Some Survivals of Pagan Belief in Anglo-Saxon England," *Harvard Theological Review*, XL, 33–46.

"Brutus and English Politics," *ELH: A Journal of English Literary History*, XIV, 178–80.

"On Writing and Printing Gothic, II," *Speculum*, XXII, 621–25.

With Helge Kökeritz. *A Short History of the Swedish Language, by Gösta Bergman . . . translated and adapted* (Stockholm, Swedish Institute, 106 pp.)

"Photostats of the *Historia de Preliis Alexandri Magni* (I³)," *Harvard Library Bulletin*, I, 377–79.

"*Annales Domitiani Latini:* An Edition," *Mediaeval Studies*, IX, 235–95.

REVIEW

Guðni Jónsson, ed., *Íslendinga sögur*, Vols. I–XIII, in *Speculum*, XXII, 471–73.

1948

"OE *ealle þráge*," *Modern Language Notes*, LXIII, 127–28.

"The Middle-Swedish *Konung Alexander* and the *Historia de Preliis Alexandri Magni* (Recension I²)," *Études germaniques*, III, 167–76.

"The *Praefatio* and *Versus* Associated with Some Old-Saxon Biblical Poems," *Mediaeval Studies in Honor of J. D. M. Ford*, edd. U. T. Holmes and A. J. Denomy (Cambridge, Mass.), pp. 107–36.

"Some Notes on King Alfred's Circular Letter on Educational Policy Addressed to His Bishops," *Mediaeval Studies*, X, 93–107.

With J. A. Walker. *An Anthology of Old-English Prose and Verse represented in J. W. Bright and J. R. Hulbert, An Anglo-Saxon Reader*, mimeographed preliminary edition. (Cambridge, Mass. x + 223 pp.)

REVIEW

Piter Sipma, *Fon alra Frêsena Frîdôme: in Ynlieding yn it Aldfrysk*, in *Speculum*, XXIII, 507–508.

1949

"King Alfred's Letter on Educational Policy According to the Cambridge Manuscripts," *Mediaeval Studies*, XI, 113–22.

"Danes, North, South, East, and West, in *Beowulf*," *Philologica: The Malone Anniversary Studies*, edd. T. A. Kirby and H. B. Woolf (Baltimore), pp. 20–24.

"On the Old-Germanic Altar- or Oath-Ring (*Stallahringr*)," *Acta Philologica Scandinavica*, XX, 277–93.

An Anthology of Old-Norse Prose and Verse represented in E. V. Gordon, An Introduction to Old Norse. Trial mimeographed translation (Cambridge, Mass., Department of English, Harvard University. ix + 200 pp.).

REVIEWS

Johannes Hedberg, *The Syncope of the Old English Present Endings: a Dialect Criterion*, in *Word*, V, 91–92.

Alarik Rynell, *The Rivalry of Scandinavian and Native Synonyms in Middle English*, in *Speculum*, XXIV, 140–41.

Archer Taylor, *The Literary Riddle Before 1600*, in *Journal of American Folklore*, LXII, 333–34.

1950

With W. P. Giddings. "Sucking Wounds at the Battle of Stiklestad," *Études germaniques*, V, 31–34.

With J. A. Walker. *An Old-English Anthology: Translations of Old-English Prose and Verse* (Dubuque, Iowa. x + 108 pp.)

With H. M. Smyser. *Walter of Aquitaine: Materials for the Study of his Legend* (Connecticut College Monographs, No. 4. viii + 62 pp.)

"Readings from Old English Prose and Verse" (Side 1) and "Readings from the *Beowulf*" (Side 2), *Harvard Vocarium* LP record L 6000–01 (released September 1950).

"*Cursor Mundi*," *Collier's Encyclopedia*, VI (New York), 182.

"*Héliand*," *ibid.*, IX, 628.

"Layamon or Lawman," *ibid.*, XII, 219.

"Mannyng, Robert," *ibid.*, XIII, 114.

"*Waltharii poësis*," *ibid.*, XIX, 323.

REVIEW

Stefán Einarsson, *Icelandic*, rev. ed., in *The Amateur Book Collector*, I, 7, col. I.

1951

"King Æthelwulf's Biblical Ancestors," *Modern Language Review*, XLVI, 249–50.

"A Brief Plea for a Normalization of Old-English Poetical Texts," *Les Langues modernes*, XLV, 63–69.

REVIEW

Cyril Fox and Bruce Dickins, edd., *The Early Cultures of North-West Europe* (H. M. Chadwick Memorial Studies), in *The Modern Language Review*, XLVI, 259–60.

1952

"Chaucer's Sir Gawain and the OFr. *Roman de la Rose*," *Modern Language Notes*, LXVII, 183–85.

"Víga-Glúmr's Equivocal Oath," *Neuphilologische Mitteilungen*, LIII, 401–408.

REVIEWS

Gust Johansson, *Beowulfsagans Hrones-Næsse: Lekmannafunderingar angående det Gamla Götland*, in *Speculum*, XXVII, 225–26.

Jacob Hammer, ed., *Geoffrey of Monmouth: Historia Regum Britanniae*, in *Speculum*, XXVII, 386–87.

Bertil Thuresson, *Middle English Occupational Terms*, in *Speculum*, XXVII, 431–32.

1953

"Oral-Formulaic Character of Anglo-Saxon Narrative Poetry," *Speculum*, XXVIII, 446–67.

"The Geography of Hygelác's Raid on the Lands of the West Frisians and the Hætt-ware, *ca.* A.D. 530," *English Studies,* XXXIV, 160 – 63.

"*Inwlatide < Onfunde,*" *Modern Language Notes,* LXVIII, 540 – 41.

"Chaucer's Ancient and Biblical World," *Mediaeval Studies,* XV, 107 – 36.

REVIEWS

A. W. Brøgger and Haakon Shetelig, *The Viking Ships: their Ancestry and Evolution,* trans. K. John, in *Speculum,* XXVIII, 135 – 38.

Kemp Malone, ed., *The Thorkelin Transcripts of Beowulf in Facsimile* (Early English Manuscripts in Facsimile, Vol. I), in *Speculum,* XXVIII, 194 – 95.

Godfrid Storms, *Anglo-Saxon Magic* in *Speculum,* XXVIII, 203 – 12.

Adolphe van Loey, *Introduction à l'Étude du Moyen-néerlandais,* in *Speculum,* XXVIII, 218.

Dorothy Whitelock, *The Beginnings of English Society,* in *Speculum,* XXVIII, 220 – 22.

Norman Davis, ed., *Sweet's Anglo-Saxon Primer,* 9th rev. ed., in *Speculum,* XXVIII, 876 – 77.

1954

"The Sutton Hoo Ship-Burial: A Chronological Bibliography," in *Speculum,* XXIX, 116 – 24.

"Béowulf and King Hygelác in the Netherlands Lost Anglo-Saxon Verse-Stories about this Event," *English Studies,* XXXV, 193 – 204.

With J. F. Madden. *A Grouped Frequency Word-List of Anglo-Saxon Poetry* (Cambridge, Mass., Department of English, Harvard University. First, second corrected printings, 1957, 1960. xi + 52 pp.).

"Chaucer's Great Britain," *Mediaeval Studies,* XVI, 131 – 51.

"Chaucer's Ancient and Biblical World: Addenda," *ibid.,* pp. 152 – 56.

Reader for *Middle English Dictionary, Plan and Bibliography* (Ann Arbor, Mich.), p. xi, col. 2.

REVIEWS

R. H. Hodgkin, *A History of the Anglo-Saxons,* 3d ed., in *Speculum,* XXIX, 125 – 26.

J. H. G. Grattan and Charles Singer, edd., *Anglo-Saxon Magic and Medicine,* in *Speculum,* XXIX, 564 – 69.

C. A. Mastrelli, trans., *L'Edda: Carmi norreni,* in *Speculum,* XXIX, 579 – 82.

1955

"Bede's Story of Cædman: The Case History of an Anglo-Saxon Oral Singer," *Speculum,* XXX, 49 – 63.

"*Canterbury Tales*, F 1541–44," *Modern Language Notes*, LXX, 173.

"*Canterbury Tales*, A II," *ibid.*, 399.

"Orwell Haven in the 'Anglo-Saxon Chronicle'?" *Modern Language Review*, L, 44–45.

With Gretchen Paulus. "Readings from Anglo-Saxon Poetry," *Harvard Vocarium* LP record L 7000–01 (Cambridge, Mass.)

"The Theme of the Beasts of Battle in Anglo-Saxon Poetry," *Neuphilologische Mitteilungen*, LVI, 81–90.

"Abbreviated Titles for the Poems of the Anglo-Saxon Poetic Corpus," *Études anglaises*, VIII, 138–46.

"Chaucer's Mediaeval World outside of Great Britain," *Mediaeval Studies*, XVII, 117–42.

"Chaucer's Summary of Statius' *Thebaid* II–XII," *Traditio*, XI, 409–20.

1956

The Anglo-Saxon Poems in Bright's Anglo-Saxon Reader: Done in a Normalized Orthography (Cambridge, Mass., Department of English, Harvard University. First, second corrected printings, 1960, 1961. [iii] + 49 pages.)

"*Canterbury Tales* B 1761–63, 1839," *Modern Language Notes*, LXXI, 165–66.

REVIEWS

E. V. K. Dobbie, ed., *Beowulf and Judith*, in *Modern Language Notes*, LXXI, 209–11.

H. C. Matthes, *Kampfrune und Buchschreibersymbole*, in *English Studies*, XXXVII, 73–75.

1957

With T. J. Heiskanen, ed. *Graded Finnish Readers*, Nos. 1–3 (Helsinki).

1. Daniel Defoe, *Robinson Crusoe*, abridged by Signe Kantele.
2. Erkki Koivusalo, *Pilviä taivaanrannalla*, a radio play.
3. T. J. Heiskanen, *Three Short Stories and a Familiar Essay*.

REVIEW

E. S. Duckett, *Alfred the Great*, in *The Saturday Review*, XL (29 June 1957), 18–19.

1958

"*Béowulf* A'": A Folk-Variant," *Arv: Tidskrift för nordisk Folkminnesforskning*, XIV, 95–101.

"Two Verses in the Old-English *Waldere* Characteristic of Oral Poetry," *Beiträge zur Geschichte der deutschen Sprache und Literatur* (Tübingen), LXXX, 214–18.

Kalevala: Song 33, ed. with Introduction and Glossary. Trial hecto-graphed edition (Cambridge, Mass. 20 pp.)

1959

Béowulf and Judith: Done in a Normalized Orthography and Edited (Cambridge, Mass., Department of English, Harvard University. [ii] + 107 pages.)

"*Béowulf* in Denmark: An Italo-Brazilian Variant," *Mélanges de Linguistique et de Philologie. Fernand Mossé in Memoriam* (Paris), pp. 247 – 55.

1960

The Vercelli Book Poems: Done in a Normalized Orthography and Edited (Cambridge, Mass., Department of English, Harvard University. [i] + 118 pp.)

With A. H. Krappe, trans. *The Grimms' German Folk Tales* (Carbondale, Ill. viii + 674 pp.)

"Conceptions and Images Common to Anglo-Saxon Poetry and the *Kalevala*," *Britannica: Festschrift für Hermann M. Flasdieck,* edd. Wolfgang Iser and Hans Schabram (Heidelberg), pp. 180 – 91.

1961

A Chaucer Gazeteer (Chicago. 173 pp.)

"Some Notes on Anglo-Saxon Poetry," in *Studies in Medieval Literature in Honor of Professor Albert Croll Baugh,* ed. MacEdward Leach (Philadelphia), pp. 273 – 82.

1963

The Kalevala or Poems of the Kaleva District Compiled by Elias Lönnrot: A Prose Translation with Foreword and Appendices (Cambridge, Mass. xxiv + 410 pp.)

"*Béowulf* B: A Folk-Poem on Béowulf's Death," in *Early English and Norse Studies Presented to Hugh Smith,* edd. Arthur Brown and Peter Foote (London), pp. 127 – 40.

1964

REVIEW

E. J. Moyne, *Hiawatha and Kalevala: A Study of the Relationship between Longfellow's "Indian Edda" and the Finnish Epic,* in *American Literature,* XXXVI, 369 – 70.

Dedicatory Poem: A Translation of Alcuin's "Debate of Spring with Winter"

WILLIAM ALFRED
Harvard University

All of a sudden the shepherds came down from the mountain pastures
And met in the fluttering shade of the spring-lit branches,
Graciously capping each other's happy bursts of music.
Young Daphnis himself was at hand, and the old man Palæmon;
Spring came, his head wreathed with grass-braids threaded with
     flowers,
And winter giving off cold, his hair stiff as stubble.
Great was the contest between them about the song of the cuckoo.

Spring was the first to play the melodious game of three verses:

"I long for the cuckoo to come, the bird that I cherish,
Singing his good measures true from a beak that is golden,
Always proving the guest most wanted by men in their houses."

Icily Winter replied, in a voice that was harsh and forbidding:
"That he never may come, but sleep on in his cursed tree hollow.
It is his constant way to bring bad trouble with him."

"I long for the cuckoo to come with the blossoms in glory.
He drives the frost away; the sun is bosom-companion.
With ever-lengthening gaze, it looks with love on his singing."

"That he never may come. What can he cause us but trouble?
Starting up battles again, he shatters the rest we made love to.
Everything all at odds, both the sea and the land are set striving."

"What right have you, dim-witted Winter, to pile abuse on the cuckoo,
Passed out as you are for the most part, hid away in some shadowy
     cavern,
After your orgies with Venus, your cups with that idiot Bacchus?"

"Why, these are riches to me, good times which set the heart dancing.

Recreation is sweet, and the warmth of a fire within doors.
No sense of these has the cuckoo, but false-heartedly mars them."

"The flowering branch in his beak, he serves us with various honies.
He pitches his nest, and he coasts the waves he has gentled.
He brings us the new-born with joy, and dresses the fields to receive
    them."

"These things are loathsome to me which you seem to find joyous.
What raises my heart is to count through coffers of treasure I wanted,
Rejoicing in feasts to come and in not being bothered forever."

"Dim-witted that you are, always ripe for a bout with your pillow,
Who rakes in those treasures for you and piles them upon one another
When the Spring and the Summer have labored for nothing
    beforehand?"

"Now you are telling the truth. You are, since you do so much for me,
Both of you certainly bondsmen, enslaved by my power,
Serving me as your lord, whatever the tasks you may work at."

"You are no lord at all, but a bankrupt, arrogant pauper.
By your own means, you could not so much as put food in your belly,
Were it not for the cuckoo who comes and supplies you with victuals."

From his seat above them all, Palæmon, his heart leaping, answered
(And Daphnis' heart leapt as well, and the hearts of that band of good
    shepherds):

"Spare us the rest of it, Winter. You are brutally lavish with charges.
May the cuckoo come, who sweetens the lives of the shepherds;
May these brown hills of ours explode with buds in their glory;
May pasture be good for the flock, with sport and sweet times in the
    meadows,
And branches grow deep green with shade above the bones of the
    tired;
May the udders be full to dragging of goats come home to the milking,
And may the birds, voice by fresh voice, greet the sun at his rising.
That is the reason we say, O Cuckoo, come quickly.
Love in its fullness you are, the guest which all of us long for.
All that God made expects you, the sea and the earth and the heavens.
Welcome, sweet honor to men, Cuckoo, world without end, we cry
    welcome."

Remarks on the Origin of Speech

BJÖRN COLLINDER
Uppsala

THIS PAPER is what the Germans call a *Lückenbüsser:* it should fill a gap left in an article I published some years ago. Before I come to the heart of the matter, I must summarize that article.[1]

i

A WELL-KNOWN BOOK on the origin of the belief in God begins, "We do not know how belief in God originated; we were not present." At any rate, I do not think we should leave the psychologists and the philosophers alone with the riddle of the origin of speech, because we may know more about language than they do. A fruitful approach to this profound subject matter is that by Géza Révész in *Ursprung und Vorgeschichte der Sprache* (1946), who starts from what he calls *Kontaktlaute.* Just as we used to talk about primary interjections ("pooh") and secondary interjections ("dammit"), so we might talk of primary and secondary contact sounds. A typical secondary contact sound is "howdyedo," as uttered simultaneously by two British gentlemen who do not know each other and are not the least interested in each other's metabolism. Révész tries somehow to derive human speech from the utterances of sociable vertebrates, especially our closest relatives, the anthropoid apes. But he makes things difficult for himself by an assumption which he holds in common with Wilhelm von Humboldt and many others: he thinks that men have been able to talk to each other as long as there have been men, and women, in this world. He says explicitly, "Ohne Sprache kein Mensch." Now really, why not? One might think that the sentence just quoted might be taken for a formal definition of man. That would be, using the nomenclature of Linnaeus, "If there were prehistoric two-handed primates without a language, they could not be regarded as human beings." Everyone is entitled to coin those formal definitions he thinks appropriate; but the matter is not that simple. Révész goes on: "If diluvial man exercised such activities as are necessarily connected with the existence of language, let us say, the fabrication and improvement of tools, and traditions, then we must take it for granted that he had a language: *homo faber* can be identified with *homo loquens.*"

I do not agree. Why must we assume that *homo alalus*, the man without a language, could not have had inventions? Would it have been impossible for Thomas A. Edison, if he had been born before there was language, to make a flint knife or borer, because he was unable to speak? I think the most gifted *homines alali* may have been fully capable of making simple arms and tools.

Let us see what kind of language Révész imputes to primitive man. Basically language is, according to him, "Statements and communications which people make by the means of words and combinations of words in order to make themselves mutually understood." Having stated that there are in all known languages regular expressions for exhortation, indication, and question, he infers that "the primordial form of language was an acoustic language with imperative, indicative and interrogative forms of expression." Now, the interrogative state of mind is complicated. It may imply, first, that you know there is something you do not know; second, that you want to get rid of the feeling of uncertainty which this knowledge has called forth; third, that you think somebody can do that for you by telling you something; fourth, that you want him, and nobody else, to do this for you; and fifth, that you want to tell him so. We cannot admit that complicated expressions, Russian interrogative specifics, for example, must have belonged to primordial human speech; they simply cannot have existed then. It seems certain also that in primordial human speech there were no combinations of words, no contrast between word and sentence, only simple utterances, indivisible segments of speech, supplemented by nonacoustic context: gestures and expressions of the face, and the environmental situation. No theory that makes the connection between the exclamations of apes and sentences consisting of words can be taken seriously. The comparative method of diachronic linguistics cannot be applied to the problem of the origin of human speech, or it must be applied with the utmost care. The comparison of all the automobiles in the world cannot tell us much about the first man-made vehicles.

The origin of speech was a series of events, or several disparate series of events, in different parts of the globe. We should all like to know, as Leopold von Rancke put it, speaking of course about political history, "Wie es eigentlich gewesen." But, speaking of linguistic origins, Heymann Steinthal has said the question is rather about "Wie es gewesen sein muss." I believe we should try rather to find out how it *may* have been. Since, it seems, the problem cannot be solved by induction, we must apply a deductive method, starting from the structure of the human mind rather than from the comparative study of the three thousand languages of the world. As far as is known, all these languages have developed for hundreds of centuries and they have all attained a state of maturity. We can make the structure of any of them the subject of typological research, trying to sort out prehistoric strata to put them in a hypothetic chronological order according to psychological necessity or likelihood.

Admittedly, the so-called primary interjections generally are stereotyped and conventionalized cries or other vocal gestures. They stand out from the general pattern of expressions if a language is, as Aristoteles put it, a conventional system of communication, for the nexus of sound and meaning is here natural and obvious, not merely traditional. This is not true of all of them, of course. In Swedish, *hej* is an expression of mirth, more so than in English; in Hungarian, *hej* has a melancholic tinge. Insofar as a shout belongs to a system of expressions, it will have a meaning, and meaning has an active and a passive aspect. It is connected with an idea both in the mind of the speaker and in the mind of the hearer, although it is not always quite the same idea in both.

What does the snarl of a watchdog mean? Some think it means "Come nearer, and I'll bite you." Some think it is merely a symptom of the dog's frame of mind. There are also people who think with Descartes that dogs are machines, while human beings are regulated by their intellect. This opinion is an outgrowth of human conceit. Ecclesiastes tells us, "They all have the same breath, and man has no advantage over the beasts."

There is more common sense in the doctrine of the behaviorists, who believe that both men and beasts are machines. They think rightly that introspection is fallacious. Introspective understanding of utterances presupposes that the movements of the speech organs are caused by the ideas which the speaker connects with the words which he hears himself utter. But it may be that all physical and chemical processes are caused only and exclusively by other physical and chemical processes. If this is so, the ideas we connect with the words we hear are mere epiphenomena. If we think that they cause the utterances, which are material and not intellectual occurrences, we are victims of an illusion. The function of an utterance consists in the movements which it calls forth in human bodies. The ideas which accompany the utterance in the mind of the speaker cannot be observed by the hearer, and the speaker cannot afterwards know what he thought he wanted to say in the moment he started talking. Sometimes in excitement we may be surprised at what we suddenly hear ourselves say.

This argument seems difficult to refute. Let us accept it. We admit with Schopenhauer and Ludwig Büchner (*Kraft und Stoff*, 1855) that the human brain produces thoughts as the kidneys excrete urine. What people call "will" is merely the feeling of tension that accompanies the idea of two opposite motives of action, and these motives as well as the feeling of tension are only epiphenomena that accompany electric and chemical occurrences which we do not know anything about.

Having admitted this, we state that under such circumstances not even the most evident conclusion can convey any knowledge; no argument is apt to convince anybody of anything. Arguments are merely epiphenomena. The only thing we know is that the feeling of evidence often leads us astray. It may be postulated that there is a preestablished harmony between thoughts and feelings on the one hand and unknown material occurrences on the other. But we know that mental disorders sometimes correspond to anatomic disorders in the brain, which means that our postulate is not watertight. We cannot look into other people's brains to check the machinery; we can usually only judge the product.

J. B. Monboddo's *Origin and Progress of Language* (1773) stated that there were African languages so primitive that they could not function in darkness. This statement is misleading for more than one reason. Even the English language works better in daylight: "there" is a common word, but if you hear it spoken in the darkness it may mean to you only "at a place where the speaker is not," and if you do not know where the speaker is, the word tells you next to nothing. Such demonstrative words, however, or, to be more specific, deictic expressions, represent the second prehistoric stratum in our dictionaries. Semantically they are more advanced than the interjections; but a deictic expression does not wholly belong to acoustic language. The sound must be supplemented by a pointing gesture. This complex acoustic-optic sign is not beyond the capability of a chimpanzee, but a human baby cannot master it before having passed a toilsome course of orientation in its tridimensional environment. The acquisition of deictic expressions to indicate distance would seem to mark the third state in the development of speech and the first decisive step beyond the capability of other mammals. But I think we must distinguish between two different stages here. At the first, the primary tones, produced in the larynx, were the essential stuff of pronominal utterance. I suppose that *Pithecanthropus erectus*, when the situation did not compel him to speak very loudly, would talk *a bocca chiusa*. (The two kinds of whispering, school whispering and theater whispering, may be comparatively recent inventions.) The second stage could come only after the birth of music. Primitive man learned from singing birds to produce constant tones and create melodies with pure intervals, and this activity became a pastime which must have influenced the technique of speech. From the beginning, acoustic communication was so dependent on what gestures and miens could indicate that the acoustic element rather accompanied than dominated the act. The shout had the function of expressing the emotional attitude of the

speaker, but at the same time it conveyed an idea of the object of communication as being desirable or dangerous, big or small, near or distant. After people had learned to pay attention to the primary tones
and modulate them, the musical element of speech may have been
cultivated as an exclusive means of picturing the emotions of the
speaker; and the intellectual task of communication was taken over
by the resonances and overtones that are generated in the pharynx, the
mouth, and the nose cavities. The symbolic use of high and low vowel
sounds made way for the formation of articulate speech, which belongs
in all probability to a late stage in the prehistory of language. The
Lappish language gives evidence of the symbolic value which vowel
qualities may have in demonstrative pronouns. In Northern Lappish
there are five demonstrative stems: *tá-* 'this' (with *ich-Deixis*, to use
Karl Brugmann's terminology); *ta-* anaphoric; *tie-* 'this, that' (with
du-Deixis: nearer to the person spoken to than to the speaker); *tuo-*
'that, yonder (not far away)'; *tó-* 'that, yonder (far away).'

The fourth stage in the genesis of speech was name giving. Here, as
in the third stage, there could be no convention at the start, so there was
need of obvious symbols. I agree with Hugo Schuchardt that primitive
man cannot have avoided taking recourse to vocal imitation, onomatopoeia. Some scholars underrate the role onomatopoeia has played. It
may be true that in all known languages only a very small part of the vocabulary consists of obvious symbols like "ding-dong," but this proves
nothing. During many thousand years, some words have changed their
phonologic shape, some have changed their meaning, and some have
changed both. In whatever language, those words which still remain,
unchanged in sound and meaning, from a time when the language was
in a rudimentary state of development are certainly so few that an
argumentum e silentio on the basis of the actual vocabulary cannot be
conclusive.

The so-called *Lallwörter*—the type "papa," "mama"—are not easy
to place in our diachronic typology. The material of these words is time-
less; it is unceasingly furnished by all the babies of the world. The
babbling infant emits, when it neither cries nor is silent, a current of
sounding air, a vocalization, interrupted by frequent contractions of the
lips. If the soft palate or velum remains passive, the acoustic result is
m plus a vowel: *ma-ma-ma, mu-mu-mu*, or the like. The adults make a
word of conventional length from this chain pump: Latin *mamma*,
Chinese *mu*. If the velum is active, we get *ba-ba*. If the infant contracts
its tongue instead of its lips, we get, with passive velum, *na-na*, and with
active velum, *da-da*. Contraction of the lips and simultaneous interrup-
tion of the primary tone gives, with active velum, *pa-pa*. The meanings
of these words are chiefly supplied by the adults.

Figurative or metaphoric usage has come about because children and imaginative adults have made a virtue out of necessity. In our civilization, most people use only a small percentage of the vocabulary of their native language, and nobody masters all of it; but there is always a demand that exceeds supply and cannot be satisfied by the coining of new expressions. This is one of the main causes why words change their meaning, or rather, assume new meanings in addition to the old. Verbal insufficiency must have been felt strongly by primitive man. He had to extend and vary the meaning of the few expressions he possessed. He could use the expression for one visible thing to denote another visible thing: he could say "foot," meaning footstep or trace. He could take recourse more or less unconsciously to synaesthesia, or sense-analogy, as when we speak of "loud colors." As soon as the parts of the body had got their names, there were ways and means of designating psychic states and qualities and activities. "Gall" might be used for "wrath," "heart" for "intellect" or "courage" or even for "through," "hand" for "sway, domination," and so on.

What we call personal pronouns of the third person are demonstratives used of persons. Historically speaking, it may be the same with the personal pronouns of the second person. In common Fenno-Ugric, there were two sets of demonstrative pronouns, one beginning with *t*, the other with *n*; and there were two corresponding sets of personal pronouns of the second person. The distinction between the *ego* and everything else comes early in the intellectual development of the infant. But the acquisition of the corresponding pronoun belongs to an advanced stage, at which the child discovers that everybody else is, from his own point of view, an *ego*, just as I am myself, from other points of view, a *thou* or a *he*. I once asked one of my Lapp informants – an intelligent man, as all my informants were – to translate into Lappish the sentence "I am hungry," and he rendered it as "He is hungry."

When primitive man had acquired some hundred indivisible expressions, it became difficult to memorize them and keep them apart. Presumably there existed groups of expressions corresponding, as a class, to the roots of the Indo-European and Semitic languages. The alternation of symbolic vowels may have made way for a selective process, the outcome of which was a simple system of speech sounds that can form an infinite multitude of combinations. All languages are articulate, consisting, from the viewpoint of material, of some decades of different building stones. This similarity would seem to indicate that all languages have a common origin, or in other words, that the creation of language was a unique event or series of events. But this inference is not conclusive. It may well be that language has originated independently at many places and that articulate speech is the work of the rational human mind, which always and everywhere keeps, in the long run, to the principle of the least effort.

ii

I HAVE now given an account of my earlier views concerning the origin and prehistory of language. A reviewer has objected that any attempt to solve this problem must fail because there is in the development of the faculty of speech a gap which cannot be filled out by research work. He did not specify his statement, but I suppose he was thinking of the transition from proper names to words for generic notions, so I shall try to fill this gap as best I can.

I believe *homo alalus* may have had some generic notions, for it seems that even horses can distinguish men from women, occasionally mistaking a man for a woman, if he wears an apron. Viktor Rydberg comments:

The expert hunting dog undoubtedly has generic images of "man," "tree," "gun," "rabbit," but he has no generic images of such things of one and the same kind as cannot be pictured in a schematic image. Such generic images have a certain degree of abstraction, but they should be kept apart from those logical notions which take their place in more developed thinking. The dog forms his generic image of man from observations of the human shape, man's specific smell, etc.; the logical notion "man" is formed quite otherwise.[2]

It may be that at an early stage of the development of thinking the opposition between individual notions and generic notions was not established. What our senses convey directly to our consciousness are not things or beings, but sensations, which are worked up by the intellect. The notions of individual things are products of our intellectual activity. A two-months-old baby that sees, as by glimpses, something or somebody, but meanwhile does not seem to see anything, is at this stage in the midst of the intellectual activity through which it connects its visual impressions with its tactile and acoustic impressions, trying to orient itself in the surrounding world. At first the baby may not be able to distinguish between its own body and what is outside. Little by little, it forms, by combining its visual impressions with its tactile impressions, notions about one thing after the other. Through this process its field of vision is radically transformed. From the beginning it perceived only kaleidoscopic figures in one plane, when its eyes were open, and a faintly glimpsed *clair-obscur* when it shut its eyes; but these two different visual fields had not much to tell the baby. When the kaleidoscopic picture has become tridimensional and eyesight has become perspective, when the baby begins to perceive objects which it can identify by touching them, does it then have individual notions or generic notions of these objects? The question is too sharpened. We can answer that in the beginning the baby is quite sufficiently busy with the task of finding real

objects in the field of vision. This is the first stage of seeing things. The
next stage implies that the baby follows with its eyes an object that
moves in the field of vision, and identifies it in its different positions. The
third stage implies that the baby compares its actual field of vision with
its memory of another field of vision and identifies an object which it
sees with a more or less similar memory picture, for example, its mother
in another garment. Through this kind of identification the notions of
things acquire a stability which they henceforth will keep. We should
not forget that the disparate sensations are prior to the notions of things.
The formation of notions of things may have its starting point in the
baby's dawning notion of itself, especially in its own body, as a unit.
We leave alone the question as to when and how the baby begins to distinguish between things proper and beings. At this stage it would not
make sense to distinguish between individual notions and generic ones.
Pa is the word which the one-year-old child has learned to associate with
certain characteristics. The notion "thing" is somehow an auxiliary
notion, which we are so accustomed to that we take for granted that it
has contextual reality in every instance. We often apply it in an arbitrary way. Is a sandy desert a thing? Is a heap of sand a thing? Is a grain
of sand a thing? Is a silicon proton a thing? Granted that the generic
notion "grain of sand" has no counterpart in the domain of reality: in
the real world there are only individual grains of sand. But in that world
of notions where language belongs, generic notions are not secondary to
individual notions, and probably they never were. In a sand heap, where
all the grains are alike, there is nothing interesting about a single grain
of sand; the only individuality it has is that at a given moment it occupies
a given place to the exclusion of all the other grains.

When the notion of things is established and has become a corner-
stone in the conception of the real world, it inevitably brings with it the
notion of *qualities*. While the baby is still in the state of kaleidoscopic
seeing, the parts of the fields of vision frequently shift their position —
one could really say, with Herakleitos, that everything flows. But meanwhile everything in the field of vision rests unmoved; and sometimes it
partly moves and partly rests. When the child has become acquainted
with things which it can touch, it acquires, by combining the perception
of movement with the notion of things, the notion of *change*. Another
step is taken when the child sees a fire on an open hearth. A flame is
brought to the fuel, the flame expands, there rises smoke; little by
little, the fuel disappears. At last there remains something that in no
wise resembles the fuel. Now the chemist knows that combustion is
oxidation, setting free so much heat that it makes gases glow, that is,
causes a molecular movement swift enough to influence eyesight. In
his opinion not even the chemical elements are unchangeable. He
resorts to *matter* as the bearer of all the qualities of all the elements. In

itself, matter has no qualities except extension and gravitation, and indeed, according to recent theories, it has merely extension, which seems to imply nothing else than that two particles of matter cannot at the same time occupy exactly the same position in space. Thus, matter in itself has no qualities, but it is the bearer of all the qualities and all the changes in the world. So the scientist and the unlearned savage seem to share an untenable metaphysical conception. This conception of things and qualities has become fixed through language, and we cannot free ourselves from it in our common thinking and daily life.

If we had not a language, we would not be able to form and retain complicated trains of thought. We live and move in the world of language; we cannot get free of it. And in the world of language the generic notions are primary to the individual notions. The real grain of sand, unambiguously determined as to point of time and position in space, has no name. It has only a designation or denomination, and we designate it as a grain of sand, that is, we subsume the individual notion under a generic notion.

Everything that is real exists somewhere. It is obvious that at the very point in space that is occupied by a certain particle of matter, there cannot at the same time be another particle. When I direct my attention to a thing that is unambiguously determined as to space and time, I have an individual notion of it. But in this notion there are usually two constituents: the idea of what it is, for example, a cloud, and the idea of something that has a certain position just now. Often the latter idea comes first, and its indetermined nature can be expressed by a silent monologue question: What is that?

In the English language there are specific expressions to indicate individual notions: the definite article, the indefinite article, pronouns, adverbs, and proper names. Both the definite and the indefinite article are lacking in some languages, for example, Latin and Standard Finnish: *granum arenarium* or *hiekkajyvä* means "a grain of sand," or "the grain of sand," or just "grain of sand." This deficiency does not seem to cause any great inconvenience. In those languages where there is a definite article, it used to be, historically speaking, a demonstrative pronoun, and mostly it has, as far as I know, also a deictic or anaphoric function. It is a symptom of the limitations of human resources of expression that in some languages, German and French for instance, the definite article can be used to designate a whole class as well as a certain individual. In Sophocles' "Many things are mighty, and yet nothing is more mighty than man," the Greek counterpart of "man" is, as in English, put without an article: πολλὰ τὰ δεινὰ κοὐδὲν ἀνθρώπου δεινότερον πέλει. The Sophoclean sentence translated into French and German must render ἄνθρωπος by *l'homme* and *der Mensch*. But a generic class of things or beings is not the same as the class in its totality.

A correct statement about a class may prove false when it is applied to an individual of the class. Man is mighty and glorious, even if many a man is a burden to the soil. Ἄνθρωπος, in the Greek sentence, does not mean any real being, but denotes an idea, which has no equivalent in the real world. Words symbolize things only in an indirect way; immediately, they symbolize ideas. The meaning of a linguistic expression is the idea which calls it forth on the lips of the speaker and is called forth by it in the mind of the hearer—or rather, that which is common to the idea of the speaker and the idea of the hearer.

One may object that *meaning* can be defined as that which one is talking of, the referent. But too many words have a meaning without referring directly to any real thing or being—"usefulness," "probability," "or," "ever," "nevertheless." Therefore, if we maintain that every utterance normally has a meaning, then when speaking of the part of the real world to which a word relates, we should not use the word "meaning." I have defined the word thinking of the normal situation of oral communication; strictly speaking, the definition does not apply to an isolated word, spoken or written, that has no context whatever. (Cut out single letters of the alphabet from a printed card and throw them into a hat. Put out the light and take five letters from the hat and arrange them in a row on the table. Switch on the light; suppose you find that the letters form the word "sugar." Does this word then have a meaning? I would say it has a passive meaning, conveying a clear idea to everybody who knows English; but the meaning is deficient because the active requisite is lacking—the word has not been called forth by an idea—and it has no function.)

Let us return to the articles. The definite article is a pronoun not only diachronically but also synchronically, and it is a typical pronoun. Adolf Noreen distinguished between *expressive* and *pronominal* sememes; much later Karl Bühler made practically the same distinction in other terms. Pronominal sememes—adverbs like "here," "there," "now," "then" included—are the linguistic means of orientation in time and space, and consequently, in the world of real things and beings. From the viewpoint of diachronic typology, the pronominal sememes are primary to the expressive sememes, which denote, beside relations, qualities, states, changes, and attributes, classes of things and beings, not real individuals. (Pronominal meaning bearers may be *autosemantic* or *synsemantic*. The definite article is a synsemantic demonstrative pronoun.) Pronominal meaning bearers are the specific means of identifying individual things and beings by locating them in coordinate systems of space and time where the speaker marks the center, or point zero, the "here and now." The primordial system of pronouns, we will recall, is the deictic or pointing system that does not work in the dark; the anaphoric system that works by referring to the spoken or written context is a much more sophisticated means of identification. Pronouns are not substitutes for nouns. "I" is not simply a substitute for my name or any other. It has the generic meaning of "the person speaking"; the individual meaning is indicated by an extra-linguistic device. Pronouns are not substitutes for names. Pronouns and proper names represent two different ways of identifying individuals. Words like "John" and "Robertson" imply the idea of a human being, rather a male than a female. The combination "John Robertson" does not by itself unambiguously identify an individual human male, however. It is not the designation of a class of human males; it is an epitomizing designation of an indeterminate number of persons who have in addition to male sex the common characteristic that in a given context they can be identified by the expression "John Robertson." Historically, "John," "Robert," and "son" are designations of classes. Proper nouns like "John," which are not identifying by themselves, may be called *indefinite proper nouns*; unique, unmistakably identifying names may be called *definite proper names*, but these are not numerous. Historically, they are mostly appellative nouns, that is, class designations. *Kilimanjaro* and *Popocatepetl* are as limpid to some people as *Kebnekaise* and *Uludag* are to myself.

iii

THE VERBAL fixation of generic notions must have been the decisive point in the development of human speech. This acquisition transformed man into an historical being; it made way for oral tradition and infinite progress. The formation of concepts of classes of visible objects was well within the reach of primitive man. The formation of generic notions on a higher level of abstraction cannot have been more or less unreflective teamwork; it must have been the work of highly gifted individuals, capable of intellectual concentration. Every step on the path of intellectual progress is the product of one man's effort. The contribution of the community consists only in adopting that which the few have created.

NOTES

1. "Die Entstehung der Sprache," *Ural-Altaische Jahrbücher*, XXVIII (Göttingen, 1956).

2. *Skrifter*, Vol. XIV: *Varia* (Stockholm, 1899), p. 478.

Scandinavian Runes in Continental Manuscripts*

RENÉ DEROLEZ
Ghent

THE PRESENT brief survey of *runica manuscripta Scandinavica* is
limited to those found in continental manuscripts. I have not included
the runes in Scandinavian manuscripts, partly because they are as a rule
of a much later date, and partly because the most important specimens
have been very expertly edited by Dr. Anders Bæksted.[1] Neither have I
been able to include the Norse runic material found in Irish and English
codices. The former present the runes in an Ogham context that would
require a disproportionate amount of space to disentangle (Dublin,
Royal Irish Academy, Book of Ballymote; Brit. Mus., Addit. MS. 4783).[2]
A few of the English sources have been treated at some length in *Runica
Manuscripta* (Oxford, St. John's College, MS. 17; Brit. Mus., Cotton
MSS. Domitian A.ix, Galba A.ii, and Titus D.xiv), though with the accent
on the Anglo-Saxon runes found in the immediate vicinity of the Norse
ones;[3] some of the other Norse runic items in English manuscripts
are again fairly late (Cambridge, Trinity College, MS. R.14.34; Brit. Mus.,
Harley MS., 2399, Stowe MS. 57). Actually there is only one runic inscription in an English manuscript that has found favor in the eyes of
Scandinavian runologists, presumably because it is ultimately connected with the Sigtuna amulet: the runic charm of Brit. Mus., Cotton
MS. Caligula A.xv.[4] If the manuscript runes of Scandinavian origin do
not seem to have received all the attention they deserve, one is hardly
justified to put the blame on Scandinavian scholars, surrounded as they
are by an ever-growing number of authentic inscriptions. The manuscript runes look all too often like ragged and degenerate descendants
of those noble characters—but who will deny that hereditary features,
hardly noticeable in the ancestors, may sometimes become apparent in
such descendants? Without the secondary evidence provided by manuscripts, we should know little or nothing about such essential features of
the runic system as the names of the characters, or some of their uses in
magic and cryptography. This, with the early date and inherent cultural

significance of some of the continental runic items, is sufficient reason
for examining them here.

By the end of the eighth century, the original runic alphabet common to a number of Germanic tribes, if not to all, was being subjected
to a radical renovation in the Scandinavian area. The result of this
renovation was an alphabet of only sixteen characters, which replaced
the old twenty-four-character alphabet all over Scandinavia after what
seems to have been a very short transition period. So far no satisfactory
explanation has been offered for this runological revolution.[5] It resulted
at any rate in making runic inscriptions more difficult to decipher. At
about the same time we find the first traces of a scholarly interest in
runes on the Continent, and this interest is clearly directed to the runes
of the north. The unknown author of *De inventione litterarum*, a short
treatise on the various alphabets known in those days, devoted a paragraph to the runic alphabet.[6] He introduced it with the following text:

> Litteras quippe quibus utuntur Marcomanni, quos nos Nordmannos
> vocamus, infra scriptas habemus (a quibus originem qui theodiscam
> loquuntur linguam trahunt); cum quibus carmina sua incanta-
> tionesque ac divinationes significare procurant, qui adhuc pagano
> ritu involvuntur.

In another version of *De inventione litterarum*, the paragraph on the
runes has an even more authentic ring:

> Hae quoque litterarum figurae in gente Northmannorum feruntur
> inventae; quibus ob carminum eorum memoriam et incantationum
> uti adhuc dicuntur; quibus et runstabas [*late var.*: runstafas] nomen
> imposuerunt, ob id, ut reor, quod his res absconditas vicissim
> scriptitando aperiebant.

Those who expect to find a Scandinavian runic alphabet below the two
texts just quoted will, however, be disappointed. Under its German
garb – the names of the runes, and some of the sound values assigned to
the characters, show unmistakable German influence – the runic alphabet can easily be traced back to an Anglo-Saxon original. Only in the late
and much-trimmed version of Stowe MS. 57 (Peterborough s. XII[2]), does
the heading *Litterę norm[ann]orvm quę dicvntvr rvnstafes* introduce
an interesting collection of Scandinavian runes.[7] The presence of these
runes at Peterborough is not wholly unexpected. To nearby Thorney we
owe one of the most complete collections of *runica* and other alphabet
lore of that century (Oxford, St. John's College, MS. 17; 1110).[8]

If, as seems most likely, *De inventione litterarum* was compiled
toward the end of the eighth century, its origin coincides with the conquest of the Saxons by Charlemagne. This conquest extended the frontiers of the Frankish kingdom to the confines of Denmark. The

Marcomanni of *De inventione* have, of course, no direct (and hardly any indirect) connection with the *Marcomanni* of antiquity. They were the inhabitants of Denmark (cf. a letter of Otto I, dated 26 June 965: *in marca vel regno Danorum*; the oldest occurrences of the name Denmark are in King Alfred's Orosius) with whom Charlemagne concluded a peace treaty in 811.[9] The interest in the mysterious alphabet used by these pagan neighbors may have several roots. There existed no doubt a certain amount of antiquarian curiosity, which linked up with contemporary philological considerations, as in *De inventione* – though we can hardly assume with Baesecke that a runologist of the ninth century will have thought of reintroducing runic writing in Germany. Plans for the conversion of the north may have been equally decisive, if not more so. Between Willibrord's first missionary endeavors early in the eighth century and Ansgar's full-scale attempt in 826 and following years (initiated by Paul I and Louis the Pious, and supervised by Archbishop Ebbo of Rheims), there may have been other, less widely publicized initiatives. Any missionary contemplating working in Scandinavia would have found some knowledge of the runes a useful asset. Evidence of such a knowledge in Carlovingian times comes from two areas: South Germany and the Loire region.

I]   St. Gall MS. 878 has been known for almost 150 years now as the repository of perhaps the most puzzling of all manuscript runic items, the *Abecedarium Nordmannicum*.[10] Its importance has further grown since Bischoff has demonstrated that it was in all probability compiled by Walahfrid Strabo (809/10 – 849), the pupil of Hrabanus Maurus who became praeceptor of Charles the Bald and abbot of Reichenau.[11] Page 315 and following of the manuscript contain extracts from Isidore's *Etymologiae*, followed by a Hebrew and a Greek alphabet. After the latter, on page 321, there comes a remarkably correct Anglo-Saxon runic alphabet, entitled *Anguliscum*, and finally the *Abecedarium Nord[mannicum]*. The text of the *Abecedarium* was probably much faded as long ago as the beginning of the last century. About 1823 the St. Gall librarian Ildefons von Arx tried to restore its legibility by the application of a reagent, and probably succeeded up to a point, at least for the time being: the copies he made suggest that he could read most of the text.[12] But nowadays very little is visible in the dark brown to bluish black stains left by his reagent. If the runes can be made out with some certainty, part of the text at least seems to be irretrievably gone.

The *Abecedarium* is a poem, or rather, a poor piece of doggerel, enumerating the runes of the shorter Scandinavian alphabet, and their names. The text itself is a curious mixture of Low German and High German elements, but the runes are clearly of the ninth-century Danish type. Many of the rune names, too, point, or may point, to an Old Norse original: *hagal, is, ar, sol, yr, naut*, possibility also *ur* and *os* (ON *hagall, íss, ár, sól, ýr, nauþ, úr, ǫss/áss.*)[13] The name of þ, *thuris*, may go back to ON *þurs*, but perhaps also to OE *þyrs* (in English alphabets, however, this rune is regularly called *þorn*); *chaon* is a Germanized ON *kaun*, and *brica* points to ON *birca(n)* (cf. *biarkan* in the runic poems), rather than to OE *beorc, berc*. But the name of the *l*-rune, *lagu*, is the OE or OS equivalent of ON *lǫgr*, while the name of this rune seems to have been *laukr* in the north; and *rat* is much closer to OE *rād* than to ON *reiþ*. Nor are these the only traces of Anglo-Saxon interference. Below the first two words of the text we find the word wreat written in runes. Whatever its meaning, the runes w and ea can only come from an English alphabet. Similarly, above six of the Norse runes their English equivalents have been added (h, o, m, y, f, n; the last two runes have, of course, identical forms in the two alphabets, but the other four are sufficiently conclusive).[14] These traces of Anglo-Saxon influence are not so easy to interpret as one should like them to be. For one thing, the English runes in the *Abecedarium* may well have been derived from the preceding *Anguliscum* alphabet. And ultimately we shall be left with the question, where and when Walahfrid Strabo collected his runic material. A simple formula such as the one proposed by Baesecke and others for the *Abecedarium*, namely, "unknown Danish runemaster > Hrabanus Maurus,"[15] is tempting but dangerous, because it oversimplifies a complex situation and blinds us to the numerous other possibilities offered by that age. Neither should we overrate the value of the runological information conveyed by the poem, for it gives only what must have been available to the average "outsider": "f is the first rune, then comes u; þ is the third stave," and so on. It is, then, in no way comparable with the other runic poems, where each rune is given a meaningful (though perhaps not always authentic) explanation of the type "f = *feoh* is property," and so on. If it was really the compiler's intention to reintroduce runic writing into Germany (which I doubt),[16] we can easily understand why he was not successful. Without an introductory text explaining what these mysterious characters were and for what purposes they could be used, they must soon have become worthless *curiosa*.

2] The runic alphabet of Leiden MS. Voss. Lat. Q. 83 (s. x¹; from St. Benoît-sur-Loire) calls for a different approach. If the *Abecedarium* problem is complicated by a profusion of more or less divergent indications, it is rather the absence of clues that will make it difficult to sketch the cultural environment of the Leiden runes. To be sure, the codex in which they have been preserved has been known for a long time. The text covering the first twenty-three folios, namely, Plautus' *Aulularia*, was used as early as 1564 by Pierre Daniel for his edition of the comedy. The runic material itself, which happens to be written on

the last page of the manuscript (fol. 24^v), was examined by Hendrik Kern and Julius Zacher in 1872, and has been studied since by various scholars. It has suffered a lot from fading and rubbing, so much so that without the help of ultraviolet photographs I should not have been able at all to read some of the rune names (even so, I find that one or two of my readings are possible or, at best, probable, rather than certain). The word (or words) on the first line of the page in question seems to have been no more than a *probatio pennae*, but the text which at one time covered lines 3–8 has been erased almost completely. This happens also to be the case with the text of the three lines (15–17) immediately preceding the runic material. An attempt has been made at one time or other to improve the legibility by the application of a reagent, but apparently with little success (similar attempts on the text of lines 3–8 seem not to have been more successful). The arrangement of the runic material on lines 18–23 calls for some comment. The alphabet does not begin with **f u þ a̧ r k**, and so forth, as most editions of the Leiden runes imply.[17] The order is **t b m l ʀ f u þ/a̧ r k h n i a s**; in other words, the third *ætt* or group of runes has been placed at the head of the alphabet, an arrangement sometimes used in runic cryptography or magic. The final line of runes points in a different direction. There the Latin equivalents and the runes appear in the order *b k d t – f l m n r r* (that is, **ʀ**) *s – a e̜ i u – h*, which is clearly derived from a Latin grammar (for example, Priscian I, 8–10: *mutae, semivocales, vocales*, and *h=aspirationis nota*). The confrontation of runic and Latin lore has here gone beyond the stage of a simple rearrangement of the runes in the order of the Latin alphabet, as is mostly the case.

The runic information provided by the Leiden manuscript is unique in another way still. The names of the runes in the alphabet (ll. 19 and 21) are given twice, once in Latin minuscules above each rune (ll. 18 and 20) and a second time in runic characters, to the right of each rune. The latter way of presenting the rune names is fundamentally in contradiction with the runic system itself. Since each character could stand not only for its sound value but also for its name (f = *f*, or = OE *feoh*, ON *fé* 'property'), there was actually no point in writing the name in full with runes.[18] One might, of course, suppose that a "rune master" without knowledge of the Latin alphabet would resort to runes if asked to write the names in full, but some of the Leiden rune names hardly look as if they had been written by somebody with inside knowledge. That **þ** has the shape of a Latin *D* need not surprise us; this form of **þ** is well known from Danish inscriptions of the "second period."[19] But the fact that the *þ*-sound is transcribed **þh** in the rune name **þhurs**, and that **þ** is everywhere rendered by the Latin *d* in the transcriptions (*dhurs, reidu, naudr*) looks more suspicious; one may even suspect the scribe (if not his model) of having interpreted the *D*-shaped **þ** as a Latin *D*.

There are other discrepancies that seem to point to the existence of one or more intermediate stages between the Leiden material and the original: the name of the *a*-rune is **aR** in runes, but *ae* in Latin script, that of the *s*-rune **sulu** and *soulu*. If on the one hand we find no hint of an Anglo-Saxon or Continental Germanic background, we are entirely at a loss as to the actual link between St. Benoît-sur-Loire (supposing the runes were written there) and Denmark. Internal linguistic evidence is not promising either. The Leiden rune names themselves have often been used for dating phonological changes; hence the danger of our being caught in a vicious circle would by no means be imaginary.[20]

3]   The only other fuþark inscription in a Continental manuscript is of a much later date, but its environment is not unlike that of the *Abecedarium*. MS. Clm. 276 of the Bayerische Staatsbibliothek, Munich, contains a number of scientific works, among which there is a *liber astrologus ut videtur ignotus*, and, included in the latter, *Geomantia est vaticinatio terrenorum* and so forth. It is in this *geomantia* that a page of alphabets has been inserted (fol. 96[v]). The arrangement of the various alphabets seems to be unique: instead of starting the series with the Hebrew alphabet, to be followed by the Greek and the Latin letters, the runes are given pride of place. They are followed by a cryptic alphabet (also found in Clm. 641),[21] two Hebrew alphabets, two Greek alphabets, the second followed by the inscription *minores greci* (?); then come *litere cosmografi* (that is, the alphabet of Aethicus Ister),[22] and finally, three Hebrew alphabets added by later hands. In the left margin a list of Greek numerical symbols is given with their values in Latin numerals.

The runic material of Clm. 276 consists of (a) a fuþark with four additional characters (**c, e, p, d**) and, for each character, its sound value and its name (except for the last four, below which there is only the one word *solhengethe*); and (b) a runic alphabet with three additional characters; above each rune a Latin letter indicates its sound value (but there is no such indication above the last three). A number of characters, both in the fuþark and in the alphabet, would hardly be recognized as runic in other surroundings, distorted as they are for having gone through what must have been a fairly long series of intermediate stages.[23] This impression is confirmed when we examine the names of the runes. If *ur, os, ar, sol*, and even *madher* present no difficulties, the intrusion of *h* in *fhe, ihs*, and *thur* (= *týr*) is not so easy to explain. German influence may be responsible for the spirant in *biorchi* and *chon*, but one wonders how the þ-rune came to be transcribed by *z*, or why the *k*-rune was given the value *q* (and not *k* or *c*). And what does the last rune name *solhengethe* (?) stand for? Still, enough evidence remains by means of which to trace the origin of the runic material. For example, *au* is monophthongized to *o* in *chon* and *nodher* (ON *kaun*, *nauþr*), and *ei* to *e* in *rethet* (ON *reiþ*).[24]

The runic alphabet of Clm. 276 is not derived from the preceding fuþark. It goes ultimately back to another source, which had a dotted *k*-rune for *g*, but apparently no dotted *b*-rune for *p* (the *p* of the alphabet is simply a Roman P). The *d* of the alphabet is a poor imitation of þ, rather like that in the fuþark, but there the Latin equivalent is *z*. The runic symbol for *x* is of special interest. It is derived from the old *s*-rune (*knésól*) by crossing the two vertical strokes, and seems to occur only in two other inscriptions, a runic amulet found at Odense and an alphabet in Copenhagen MS. AM 175c, 4° (fol. 16*ᵛ*). Bæksted, who does not seem to have known the Munich alphabet, concluded that the similarity of the Odense and the Copenhagen *x*-runes was accidental.[25] This third occurrence rather points to these runes having had a common origin, which will be another good reason for examining the Munich manuscript more closely.

4] The three manuscripts discussed so far are no doubt the most important witnesses of the dissemination of Norse runic lore on the Continent, but they are not the only ones. Transmission via England seems to be implied by the runic alphabet of Paris Lat. MS. 9666 (Orosius, s. XI). On folio 181*ʳ*, after *Versus de provinciis* (covering part of 180*ᵛ* and the first twenty-one lines of 181*ʳ*) a contemporary hand has written a runic alphabet (a b k þ f h i l m n a̧ r s t u R) and two dotted runes (g, e), separated from the first sixteen by a division mark (a cross made of five dots). Above the first rune there is a reference mark, which is repeated in the left margin with the inscription "Danor*um*." The runes are followed by five more characters, written by the same hand and described as "Anglor*um*" in the right margin: the sign for *and*, *w*, ð, a crossed þ (= *þæt*) and the *a* + *e* ligature. Their presence, and the way in which they have been appended to the runic alphabet, remind one of the procedure followed by some English alphabetizers, who add such signs to their runic alphabets.[26] The use of R for *y* is said by Jacobsen and Moltke to be typical of their fourth period, that is, to be dated after 1100.[27] But the handwriting of the Paris codex, including that of the marginal inscriptions accompanying the runes, can hardly be of a much later date. In view of the many doubts that surround the chronology of runic inscriptions and the appearance of new types, it would probably be worthwhile examining the *runica manuscripta* (both Continental and English) from this angle.

5] A fuþark of a later type provided the material for a runic alphabet and an inscription on the first page of another Paris codex, MS. Grec 375 (*Officium Ecclesiasticum Graecorum*, 1022). These runes were first

described and copied by Bernard de Montfaucon, and his facsimile is the more valuable because the page has suffered much damage.[28] The alphabet is characterized by dotted runes for *d*, *e*, *g* and *p*. The sign for *x* is identical with the *h*-rune. There are two types of *s*, the old (*knésól*) type with the value *c*, and the short "dotted" type for *s*. Just below the alphabet, the same hand wrote *sanctus dionisius*. This inscription, together with the *lectio Actuum Apostolorum in die Sancti Dionysii recitari solita* at the end of the codex, connects the manuscript and the runes with the abbey of St. Denis. It remains an open question whether the use of runes on the front page was in some way prompted by the fact that the manuscript text was Greek. Runic and Greek alphabets are found together too often to exclude this possibility.

6] My last item comes from Karlsruhe MS. Aug. 163 (Priscianus maior, s. XI/XII). This *codex Augiensis* did not reach Reichenau until the fourteenth or the fifteenth century – it is supposed to have come from northern France or Italy – and its runes have no connection with the other Reichenau *runica*.[29] Folio 165 bears two inscriptions, one in Roman capitals (*PRISCIANUS. LIBER. ROT.*) and, just above it, one in runes, with dotted k and crossed i for *g* and *e* respectively: KONSTITIT: AR-GENTI: iii.÷.7s, that is, *constitit argenti tres dimidium et semis* (?).[30] The former inscription refers to the contents of the codex; the latter, probably written by a different hand, seems to indicate the price paid for it at one time. The use of the colon to divide the inscription into words reminds one immediately of the commonest division mark in Norse inscriptions[31] and seems to imply that the runes were written by a Scandinavian, and not by an ignorant scribe who took them from some or other runic alphabet. This need not mean, of course, that the manuscript was bought in Scandinavia, as Längin suggests.[32] But the Karlsruhe runes look no doubt more authentic than any of the other *runica manuscripta* in this survey.

7] To measure the full extent of the circulation of Norse runes on the Continent, we should perhaps also include stray runes of northern origin which have found their way into Anglo-Saxon *runica manuscripta*. A couple of instances are to be found in the mainly English alphabet of *De inventione litterarum*: there the *k*-rune (= *c* in the alphabet) is a Norse type, but its name (*chen*) points to England rather than to Scandinavia.[33] The characters of the "Arabic" alphabet in Clm. 14436 are Anglo-Saxon runes, but some of the names are Norse rather than English: *birca* (ON *biarkan*, OE *beorc*), *caon* (ON *kaun*, OE *cen*), *naut* (ON *nauþr*, OE *nead*), *sol* (ON *sól*, OE *sygil*).[34] These few instances will help to prove that the transmission of the Norse *runica manuscripta* must have been a far more complicated matter than appears at first sight. But this is only what we can expect if we keep in mind how numerous the potential channels of transmission must have been: does not the Reichenau *liber confraternitatis* contain the names of almost 700 Scandinavian pilgrims,[35] to whom we should add such famous travelers as the Nikulás of Munkathverá, to whose diary Professor Magoun has devoted an illuminating study?[36]

NOTES

*For the transliteration of runic inscriptions I have followed the systems used by Lis Jacobsen and Erik Moltke (cf. n. 4) and by Bruce Dickins, *A System of Transliteration for Old English Runic Inscriptions* (Norwich, 1950).

1. Anders Bæksted, *Islands runeindskrifter*, (Bibliotheca Arnamagnæana, II [Copenhagen, 1942]), pp. 26–28, 213–25.
2. George Calder, *Auraicept na n-Éces. The Scholars' Primer being the texts of the Ogham tract from the Book of Ballymote and the Yellow Book of Leccan*, etc. (Edinburgh, 1917), esp. pp. 311 and 313. René Derolez, "Ogam, 'Egyptian,' 'African' and 'Gothic' Alphabets," *Scriptorium*, V (1951), 3–20.
3. René Derolez, *Runica Manuscripta: The English Tradition* (Brugge, 1954), pp. 3 ff.; 26 ff.; 34 ff.
4. Ivar Linquist, *Religiösa runtexter. I. Sigtuna-galdern* (Skrifter utgivna av Vetenskaps-Societeten i Lund, 15 [Lund, 1932]). Lis Jacobsen and Erik Moltke, *Danmarks runeindskrifter* (Copenhagen, 1942), Text, no. 419, col. 488–90. Yet these authors include such very late inscriptions as the "alphabet stone" of Øster-Marie (no. 396, col. 455: "sen- eller efter-middelalderlig"). Is not this a too narrow interpretation of the term "inscription"?
5. Neither the phonological evolution of Old Norse nor the technical difficulties of carving runes suffice to explain this radical renovation. Cf. Anders Bæksted, *Målruner og troldruner*, (Nationalmuseets Skrifter, Arkæologisk-Historisk Række, IV [Copenhagen, 1952]), pp. 140 ff., and the English summary, p. 329: "Judging from the available material, there should be a period, not only for

Denmark but for all the Northern countries, during which the runes were out of use, though not entirely forgotten. Upon this assumption, the runes of the Viking Age should be regarded as a purely new creation, a conscious modernization of an old and well-known tradition, out of use over a long period of time . . . . It is likely that the Northern peoples cognizant of the contemporary renaissance-like trends of patriotic character in the Frankish domain, were impelled by a desire to recover their extinct, distinctly national system of writing, both for ordinary antiquarian gratification and as a means, among others, to emphasize a peculiar national feature."
6. Derolez, *Runica Manuscripta*, Ch. IV. See also my paper "Die 'Hrabanischen' Runen," *ZfdPh.*, LXXVIII (1959), 1–18.
7. N. R. Ker, *Catalogue of Manuscripts Containing Anglo-Saxon* (Oxford, 1957), p. 337.
8. Derolez, *Runica Manuscripta*, pp. 26 ff., 38 ff., 48 ff., 157 ff., 264 ff., and Plate III.
9. Peter Skautrup, *Det danske sprogs historie* (Copenhagen, 1944–53), I, p. 90.
10. Derolez, *Runica Manuscripta*, pp. 73 ff. (Bibliography: p. 74).
11. Bernhard Bischoff, "Eine Sammelhandschrift Walahfrid Strabos (Cod. Sangall. 878)," *Aus der Welt des Buches: Festgabe Georg Leyh = Zentralblatt für Bibliothekswesen*, LXXV (Leipzig, 1950), pp. 30–48.

12. Described by Georg Heinrich Pertz in his report "Italiänische Reise vom November 1821 bis August 1823," *Archiv der Gesellschaft für ältere deutsche Geschichtskunde*, v (1824), 462 f., 511.

13. On the ON rune names cf. Kristian Kålund, "Et gammel-norsk Runerim og nogle islandske Runeremser," *Småstykker udg. af Samfund til Udgivelse af gammel nordisk Litteratur* (Copenhagen, 1884–91), pp. 1–21, 100–13; Bruce Dickins, *Runic and Heroic Poems of the Old Teutonic Peoples* (Cambridge, 1915), pp. 24 ff.

14. The possibility of "old" and "new" runes being used side by side should perhaps not be excluded a priori (cf. the Rök and Sparlösa inscriptions), but the probability of the "old" runes being derived from the *Anguliscum* is much greater, especially in view of the ea in wreat.

15. Georg Baesecke, "Das Abecedarium Nordmannicum," *Runenberichte*, I (1941), 76–90; Helmut Arntz, "Runenkunde," in *Deutsche Philologie im Aufriss*, ed. Wolfgang Stammler (Berlin-Bielefeld-Munich, 1952–59), III, col. 1557.

16. Derolez, *Runica Manuscripta*, pp. xlix, 427 f.

17. For example, Helmut Arntz, *Handbuch der Runenkunde* (Halle/Saale, 1944²), p. 169 (the transcription too is inaccurate).

18. This seems to be overlooked by scholars, who argue that the *laukaR* inscriptions on a number of bracteates prove **laukaz*, *laukr* to have been the name of the *l*-rune.

19. Jacobsen and Moltke, col. 976.

20. For example, Adolf Noreen, *Altnordische Grammatik. I. Altisländische und Altnorwegische Grammatik* (Halle/Saale, 1923⁴), §80, p. 153; R. C. Boer, *Oudnoorsch Handboek* (Haarlem, 1920), §99; etc.

21. Bernhard Bischoff, "Übersicht über die nichtdiplomatischen Geheimschriften des Mittelalters," *Mitteilungen des Instituts für Österreichische Geschichtsforschung*, LXII (1954), 1–27 (p. 12, no. 65; p. 24).

22. Derolez, *Runica Manuscripta*, pp. 276 f.; Bischoff, "Geheimschriften," pp. 8 f., no. 31.

23. In the process of copying, the inscription "minores," in characters of the second Hebrew alphabet, has been shifted to a position after the second Greek alphabet, and a Greek numeral (*antisimma mille*) has been inserted between the *q* and the *s* of Aethicus Ister's alphabet.

24. Cf. the forms *reð, con, noð* in the second Norse fuþark of Oxford MS., St. John 17 (Derolez, *Runica Manuscripta*, Pl. III); and *can, noþer* in Cotton MS., Vespasian A. xviii.

25. Bæksted, *Islands runeindskrifter*, pp. 45 f., 222; fig. 122–23.

26. On the problem of alphabetization cf. Derolez, *Runica Manuscripta*, pp. 171 ff., 230, 265; "Die 'Hrabanischen' Runen," pp. 4 ff.

27. Jacobsen and Moltke, col. 980.

28. Bernard de Montfaucon, *Palæographia græca, sive de ortu et progressu litterarum græcarum* (Paris, 1708), pp. 292 f. The fuþark in the facsimile on p. 293 is Montfaucon's reconstruction.

29. Th. Längin, "Altalemannische Sprachquellen aus der Reichenau," in K. Beyerle *et al.*, *Die Kultur der Abtei Reichenau* (Munich, 1925), II, pp. 684–702 (esp. pp. 699 ff.); Derolez, *Runica Manuscripta*, pp. 320 ff., 360, 414.

30. The reading proposed by Preisendanz (Längin, p. 701), viz. *constitit: argenti*: III: *id est* [*tre*]*s* does not seem to fit the abbreviations in the manuscript.

31. See, for example, Jacobsen and Moltke, col. 997.

32. Längin, p. 701.

33. Derolez, *Runica Manuscripta*, p. 362.

34. Derolez, *Runica Manuscripta*, pp. 257 ff.

35. Skautrup, pp. 94 f.

36. Francis P. Magoun, Jr., "The Pilgrim-Diary of Nikulás of Munkathverá: The Road to Rome," *Mediaeval Studies*, VI (1944), 314–54.

Some Earliest Anglo-Saxon Cult Symbols

C. L. WRENN

Pembroke College, Oxford

i

IN A VERY fertile discussion of "Some Survivals of Pagan Belief in Anglo-Saxon England" in the *Harvard Theological Review* of 1947,[1] Professor Magoun has emphasized the very influential survival of the concept of *mana*, so widespread among primitive peoples, in the ancient Germanic cultures. This had already been treated, fairly fully for Old Norse, but only slightly for West Germanic (including Anglo-Saxon) by Jan de Vries in his famous *Altgermanische Religionsgeschichte*;[2] but I believe Magoun is the first to suggest anything like a full and illustrated exploration of mana among the Germanic inhabitants of Britain. He suggests the "verbalizing" of the mana concept in the Old Norse words for "strength," *megin* and *máttr*, and their OE cognates, *mægen* and *miht*, as in some of the *Charms* from England and the magical *megin-runar* of Scandinavia. No doubt, too, some of the implements and drinking vessels used by the neolithic inhabitants of Greece, and in England some of the Anglo-Saxon sixth- and seventh-century artifacts, such as hanging bowls[3] and some of the Sutton Hoo finds, are likewise at least in part to be regarded as cult symbols. Again, the decorative symbols on the incinerary urn in the Loveden Hill cemetery,[4] to be discussed later in this paper, with its runes followed by its rune-like yet non-runic symbols and its circles with their interior cruciform patterns, as well as parallel features on other cremation urns from the same cemetery are similarly to be interpreted.

In my detailed discussion of the runes on the sheep's astragalus found in the Caistor-by-Norwich cemetery among its earliest group,[5] I proposed that each of the six runes might best be looked at as cult symbols, and that perhaps the inscription read as a whole also made up a magical and sacral word implying divine or supernatural powers. This too carries with it the idea of mana. That cult was a dominant factor among the earliest users of the Loveden Hill cemetery is also suggested by evidences of some kind of deliberate ceremonial breaking of implements and weapons, such as a hanging bowl and a sword, parallel to similar evidences from the neolithic Greek period.

The two escutcheons with birds' heads with garnet eyes and shell-decorations in gilt bronze, seen at top and bottom of the Sutton Hoo harp as reconstructed, must again be, in some sort at least, partially cult symbols. These gilt bronze escutcheons have been recently discovered to be in every feature identical with the two escutcheons which Mr. R. Bruce-Mitford has lately reclaimed among forty-one fragments of a second seventh-century harp from hitherto unregarded scraps brought in 1883 from the Taplow barrow.[6] The Sutton Hoo harp was the property of an East-Anglian king whose treasures were given a ship burial, whereas the harp of the Buckinghamshire chief belonged to one who was inhumed. But such disparities between the Sutton Hoo ship burial and the Taplow barrow perhaps may rather emphasize in the identical harp escutcheons that these were indeed cult symbols.

The seventh-century Oghamic inscription on the Weeting horn knife haft described by the late Dr. Rainbird Clarke in 1952[7] suggests magic; and there may be some kind of cultic inheritance of magic in the incomprehensible runes and Oghams cut by the Hackness nuns on their stone cross commemorating their beloved abbess St. Ethelburga. The Christian use of runes throughout the Anglo-Saxon period frequently shows traces of magic and cult symbolism. The word *rūn* itself to the Indo-European etymologist suggests a murmur of magic; and it is significant that the word went into Finnish very early from Germanic as *runo*, originally a short incantatory poem and still surviving as the ordinary Finnish word for a short poem or lay. The explanation of the *t*-rune in the OE *Runic Poem* points the same way:

> *TIR* biþ tacna sum,   healdeþ trywa wel
> wiþ æþelingas.

Here the Germanic and most auspicious war god Tiw, the *Tuisco* of the manuscripts of Tacitus' *Germania*, is confused, naturally enough, with *tir* 'glory.'

It is well known that Old Norse tradition preserved in the *Edda* poems ascribes the invention of magic runes and of the art of communication by engraved symbols to the magician-god Óðinn. A similar Irish tradition would connect the invention of the Oghams with the god *Ogma mac Elathan (filius scientiae)* who is possibly to be identified with the Gaulish deity Ogmios. With Óðinn as the discoverer of runes, one might perhaps compare the reference by a late tenth-century Irish poet to God as *Rí rúine* 'king of mysteries.'[8] For though the Irish *rún* was commonly used in ecclesiastical writings for *Sacramentum*, it is clearly the same word as the Germanic, whether we regard it as a loan from Germanic to Celtic or vice versa. I have not found *rún* in the sense of an engraved symbol in Irish, though I am told it was so employed at least once. The survival of runes as cult symbols is strongly indicated by both the prose and the verse pieces in OE on *Solomon and Saturn*.

In the prose *Dialogues of Salamon and Saturn*, uniquely edited by John Kemble, Woden, under the name of Mercurius, is credited with the first use of runes:

> Saga me hwa ærost bocstafas sette?
> Ic ðe secge Mercurius se gigand.[9]

In the verse piece we find the rune R (*RAD*) as a "prince of writing-symbols" leading fiercely the forces of the Pater Noster against the devil:

> Ðonne hiene on unðanc R (*RAD*)   ieorrenga geseceð,
> *bocstafa brego,*   bregdeð sona
> feond be ðam feaxe.[10]

The OE *Runic Poem* quite definitely fixes the divine origin of writing in a way very much parallel to the Eddaic tradition. The O rune OS, etymologically the OE development of the Germanic *ansuz*, a god or divine power, the name of the *a*-rune in the original fuþark, is said to have been the originator of language:

> OS byþ ordfruma   ælcre spræce,
> wisdomes wraþu.

In the Preface to his learned and thorough, if highly speculative, study of the Germanic runes, *Die germanischen Runennamen*, Karl Schneider[11] makes what I take to be a basically important statement, which I believe should be the starting point for all such studies. The system of runic writing, he says, is primarily a cult script (*Kultschrift*), and only secondarily a means of communication. The Germanic runes must, therefore, be studied in the light of all the traditions and other traces of ancient Indo-European culture. They must be examined particularly with a view to digging up their roots in the ancient Germanic religion, in its historical background of Indo-European culture and cult myths. Furthermore, one may add, the runes must be explored in the light of evidences of prerunic and extrarunic symbols that may have cultic significance. I propose to look at some of the earliest Anglo-Saxon runic and other cult symbols in the light of the foregoing observations.

ii

IN MY discussion of the Caistor-by-Norwich inscription in the Tolkien Festschrift,[12] I have tried to show that it must now rank as clearly the oldest runic inscription known in Britain, probably belonging to the last years of the fifth century. A full report on the whole cemetery is being prepared for the Society of Antiquaries: and this will no doubt include the evidence for this dating from the scientific standpoint of current archeological methods. The runes on the Caistor astragalus thus definitely are earlier than the famous imitation of a gold solidus of Emperor Honorius, with its runic inscription *SCANOMODU*. The origin of this latter is quite unknown, as the coin is first heard of in the collection of King George III, from whom it passed to its present location in the British Museum. Dr. R. Page of Cambridge, in a recent paper, has sought to show that the Honorius inscription is in fact Frisian in origin and, therefore, not part of the British runic corpus.[13] But even if Frisian influence is discernible in the shapes of some of these runes, I would still regard them as of Anglo-Saxon provenance; for there are Anglo-Saxon areas of strong Frisian influence; and there is, too, Procopius' famous emphasis on the Frisians as one of the three groups into which the inhabitants of Britain were divided in the mid sixth century, according to his strange reckoning. The Loveden Hill area in Lincolnshire, for instance, shows marked Frisian influence in its place names, of which *Frieston* is a notable instance. Now attempts to explain *SCANOMODU* as a proper name have, I think, hitherto produced far from convincing results in view especially of the phonological difficulties. Since onomastic evidence suggests Frisian influence in the Loveden Hill area, and since the incinerary urns found there seem to show unparalleled and apparently symbolic decorations accompanying runes, I am inclined to believe that the Honorius *SCANOMODU* may in fact prove to be properly interpreted as a set of cult symbols from a Frisian Anglo-Saxon area, and not a proper name at all. If the Caistor runes should turn out to be cult symbols primarily, then of course the likelihood of a similar interpretation fitting the Honorius solidus would be increased. I do not, however, at this stage of tentative ignorance, propose to say anything more of *SCANOMODU*.

The Caistor-by-Norwich runic inscription, discovered some thirty years ago among the oldest group of that cemetery's cremations, and confidently dated not later than circa A.D. 500, I have discussed at some length in the *English and Medieval Studies* presented in 1962 to J. R. R. Tolkien. Figure 1 is a reproduction of the line drawing first published in that volume as kindly supplied to me by the late Dr. Rainbird Clarke, the curator of the Castle Museum at Norwich, where the astragalus on which the inscription is incised now rests. This is a sheep's astragalus, or ankle bone, of normal size, with the six runes rather unevenly spaced on the largest flat surface of the bone. Dr. Clarke provided an excellent photograph in his descriptive historical popular book *East Anglia* (Plate 43).[14] I incline to regard these runes as basically cult symbols connected with magic, though this is, of course, not their whole story. That traditional feelings of mana lying behind the use of runes in Christian inscriptions and graphic symbolism is indicated, for instance, by the use of runes by Cynewulf in his so-called "signed poems"; for it is clearly, I think, their value as lucky auspices that led the poet (or possibly a scribe)—though probably by no means consciously—to produce the runic passages.

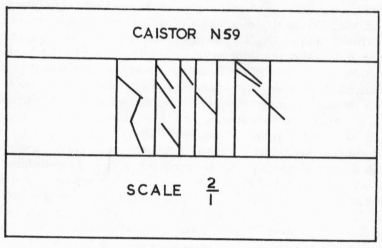

Figure 1

The Caistor runes are incised only on the one astragalus, though there were indications of some thirty others found in the same urn. This collection of astragali, on only one of which symbols are cut, naturally at first might suggest some game of chance played with the astragali as dice, as was done by the ancient Greeks and Romans: and the well-known keenness of the Germanic tribes on gambling with dice, as emphasized by Tacitus, would seem to encourage this view.[15] Or, more likely, one may be reminded of the Greek and Roman game of magic divination by sortilege, described by Pauly-Wissowa under *Astragalomanteia*, or astragalomancy. In this sport, only one side of the astragalus was marked, often with names like Eros, Alexandros, or Aphrodite, to symbolize good luck in love or war: so that the auspicious throw would be one which brought the symbolic name uppermost. This kind of sortilege, supported as a possible Anglo-Saxon practice by Tacitus' account of the Germani, who "auspicia sortesque ut qui maxime observant,"[16] may have been in some ways comparable to the Old Norse game of *hneftafl*. In this latter, only one piece, the *hnefi*, was marked: and van Hamel has shown how it was closely connected with magic.[17] Tacitus' account of this type of sortilege makes it clear that its performance, either in public by the *sacerdos civitatis* or in private by the *pater familias*, was essentially religious as well as magical. Indeed, the officiant carried out the sacramental ceremony only "precatus deos caelumque suscipiens."[18]

But whereas such a practice of astragalomancy, comparable with the later Norse *hneftafl*, would be quite credible among the pagan Anglo-Saxons as a Germanic inheritance, it seems far less probable that the dice game of the Roman astragalus would have been acquired by Anglo-Saxons of the late fifth century, unless a cultural continuity from Roman to Saxon eastern Britain is postulated far greater than is usually believed by historians.

However, the kind of game or ceremony in which the astragali were used at Caistor need not seriously affect the question of the meaning of the runes, so long as the interpretation arrived at is in some sort religious and magical. And if the word formed by the six runes is, as I think, RAH(W)HAN – a very sacred and numinous name of supernatural powers cognate with Norse *Regin* and OE *regn* – the view that here is a series of cult symbols together forming a mysterious term of deep religious and magical significance, that the inscription relates to some type of sortilege of the astraglomantic type, would be strengthened. It is pertinent here, too, to recall that along with the thirty astragali of the Caistor urn were found the clear remains of thirty-three of those cylindrical pieces of bone with metal spindles (apparently belonging to some game like draughts), almost exactly of the kind found among the belongings of the seventh-century chief buried in the famous Taplow barrow.

The six runes, reading from left to right, are to be taken at this very early date as: R A H (W) H A N, making the word *rah(w)han*.[19] I take the second and fifth rune to be *a* (the Germanic **ansuz* familiar from early runic inscriptions), for the Anglo-Frisian First Fronting, which raised *a* to *æ*, had probably scarcely taken place before circa A.D. 500, or even if it had, the memory of the traditional use of this rune would have persisted in such an inscription. The new use of this rune as *æsc* is first attested, as a result of the First Fronting, in the Honorius solidus in which the new rune for *a* (*āc*) apparently has been found necessary because the original use of the **ansuz* rune had been replaced by its employment for the new sound of *æ*, and its name therefore changed to *æsc*. It makes no difference whatever to the matter of its possible significance as a symbol whether we regard the third rune as to be transliterated *H* or *HW*, though it is most likely that at so early a date the yew-tree rune *ēoh* or *īh*, in historic times rendering *H* (sometimes *I*) had not yet lost the labial element in its pronunciation. The OE forms *eoh* in West Saxon, Anglian *ih*, and *eow*, *iow*, and *iw* as the name of the tree also (cf. *iuu* in the Corpus Christi Cambridge Glossary) all clearly look back to Germanic **ixwō*, the OE forms for the yew showing alternating *h* and *w* forms by *grammatische Wechsel*.

If the runes on the Caistor astragalus are read, as would be normal, then, from left to right, their names would be *RAD*, **ANSUZ* (the historical OE form of this word had become *ŌS* and had acquired the value

of *o*), *ĒOH* or *ĪH*, *HAGOL*, *A* (**ANSUZ*), and *NĒD*. If we take these runes
at the values suggested above, the resulting word is *RAH(W)HAN*. This,
which I assume to be of course a prehistoric form, may be thought of as
a cognate of the historical OE *regn* 'magical or supernatural power' of
Beowulf, *re(g)nian* 'to contrive magic against,'[20] the ON *regin* 'the gods,'
the Eddaic *ragna* 'to invoke by means of magic,' Gothic *raginon* 'to have
power over'; and ON *Ragn-* and OE *Ræg(e)n-* in proper names. One may
compare, too, such uses of ON *ragina-* in magical senses in runic inscriptions like the *RAGINARUNOR* of the Björketorp inscription. As
I have said, I would take this *rah(w)han* to be a word of mysterious and
sacred magical potency whose significance was known only to the
Germanic priests or their equivalents, and one especially appropriate
to death and the symbols of mortality indicated by the separate runes.

Reading the runes, on the other hand, as is not impossible, from right
to left, we only seem to get two groups of three runes, the two words
NÆH and *HWÆR*, 'near' and 'where,' taking *næh* as the Prim. OE for
West Saxon *nēah*. I can make nothing of these words. Nor have I been
in the least successful in interpreting the inscription as a cryptogram or
an exercise in the magical science of numerology as applied to runes. Let
us then consider the Caistor-by-Norwich inscription a little more in
detail from the point of view of cult symbolism.

iii

NO SENSE, it is clear, could be made by trying to evolve a continuous coherent passage of thought by taking each rune name as a complete word, after the manner of the epilogue to Cynewulf's *Elene*. *RĀD*
would, if this method were tried, stand for "riding," "chariot," or
"wagon," or possibly for "charioteer" or "wagoner." **ANSUZ* or OE
ŌS would be "a god," and possibly Woden, in view of evidence from
Sutton Hoo of the influence of the Woden cult in East Anglia as late as
the middle of the seventh century.[21] The rune *ĪH*, which occurs twice,
as third and fifth in the inscription, would mean "yew tree." *HAGOL* is
"a hailstorm" or "hail," simply; and the final rune *NĒD* would be "need"
or "necessity," or possibly might retain its earlier sense of "death." As
the dead man with whose ashes our astragalus was found was clearly
not an aristocrat, we are most unlikely ever to be able to know anything
whatever about him beyond what may be inferred from the finds in the
Caistor cemetery. If we reject the idea of a dice game, as I believe we
must, we can scarcely think of him as some sort of village "character,"
famed locally as an inveterate gambler, as the late Dr. Clarke once
suggested—perhaps not very seriously.[22] There is, therefore, no chance
of relating these rune names as words to facts or guesses about the
deceased.

If, however, we take these words in their traditional Germanic cultic significance, and in the light of their Indo-European historical and folkloristic background, they will, I suggest, be found to be generally meaningful and appropriate as symbolic reminders of mortality. Nor will this interpretation of the rune names as cult symbols conflict with the total impression got in the magic word *rah(w)han*, which was reached by taking the runes of the inscription at their phonetic values.

The cultic significance of the rune *RĀD* has been very fully and admirably treated by Professor Karl Schneider in his exciting, if extremely speculative, study.[23] From all the available evidence, it seems clear that this name is ultimately to be associated with the Indo-European cult of the sun and the sun god. Its primary sense was derived from the rising and falling action of riding, or of the sound of the wheels of a wagon. The form *RAEDA* in the Vienna Alcuin MS. fuþark indeed may suggest a noun of agent descended from Gmc. *RAIÐJŌ, with the sense of "wagoner" or "charioteer"; and one may then think of legends such as that of Apollo and Phaeton, of the sun god driving his chariot across the sky. The OE compound *swegl-rad* of the *Riming Poem* 29 refers to the rhythmic rise and fall of music, as does the phrase *swegles gong* in *Andreas* 869.[24] In an admirable exposition of compounds in *-rad*,[25] Dr. Caroline Brady has demonstrated that this word "imports a rising and falling movement typical of the movement of sound"; and *swegles gong* in *Andreas* definitely describes the rhythm of the song of the angels. The distant rising and falling of the murmur of wagon wheels as the wagoner, the *raiðjō (OE *ræda*) drives his vehicle along is again consonant with the concept of the supreme wagoner of the sky: and in view of the likelihood of the second and fifth runes of the inscription *ansuz (OE *ōs*) being Woden, the *RAD* may well imply a memory of this same god as master of the sun. The description of *RAD* as "prince of incised symbols," *boc-stafa brego*, already cited from *Salamon and Saturn*, as leading the attack on the devil, and the fact that *RAD* is placed first in this probably incantational inscription, supports this speculation. Moreover, a principal deity might be conceived as carrying the spirit of the dead man to his next world, as perhaps suggested too by the winged creature projecting from the Sutton Hoo shield. In *RAD* may be the joined concept of chariot and charioteer. Incidentally, it is now generally agreed that *RAD* of the *Runic Poem* expresses the rhythmic music of harp (or possibly flute): and in both such music and the distant roll of a wagon may be heard a *fractum murmur*.

If *RAD*, then, is the chariot of a god, as I would conjecture, it is much more probable that the two runes *ANSUZ* and *OS* refer to Woden. In the *Runic Poem*, *OS* as the originator of every kind of language (*ordfruma ælcre spræce*) and the support of wisdom (*wisdomes wraþu*) is clearly Woden, even if, as some think, the maker of this description also was influenced by the Latin *os* 'mouth.' The traces of a Woden cult in some of the Sutton Hoo artifacts, notably in the shield and helmet, have been referred to earlier: and like Sutton Hoo, Caistor-by-Norwich is in East Anglia, where the originally Swedish dynasty of the Wuffingas held sway in the seventh century, after leaving their earlier seat near Wodanistic Uppsala. The Wuffingas no doubt would have brought their Woden cult to East Anglia with them. One's first inclination to read these runes as forms of *æ* (*æsc*) should, however, probably be rejected, as indicated already, in view of the very early date of our inscription, in favor of the original god rune. But if *æsc* were in fact the correct name of the rune here, this being a late development, *æsc* could not have acquired a cult significance as the members of the original fuþark had done: so that it would be irrelevant to discuss it here. Now it would be natural to take this runic symbol **ANSUZ* $\overline{OS}$ as the Woden who conveyed the spirits of the dead from this world—again appropriate to an incantational inscription to accompany the ashes of a corpse. From Tacitus (*Germania*, cap. 9) we learn that Mercurius was the principal Germanic god: and here too, equating Mercury with Woden, the idea of Woden escorting the spirits of the dead finds some support. In the Scandinavian tradition Óðinn and Freyja looked after the spirits of warriors who fell in battle. There is, of course, no question that Old Norse poetic tradition employed the term *óss* or *áss* corresponding to **ansuz* and OE *ōs*, as a term for Óðinn, as may be seen, for instance, from the account of *óss* in the Icelandic *Runic Poem*:

> ÓSS er aldingautr ok asgarðs jöfurr,
> ok valhallar vísi.

The OE prose *Dialogues of Salamon and Saturn*, as cited early in this paper, certainly equates Mercury with Woden: for it is to "Mercury the giant" that the first use of letters is there attributed. Twice, then, it would now seem, is Woden as the god of the dead symbolized on our astragalus.

Whatever be its exact phonetic value, the third rune, *ÍH*, stands for the yew tree. Karl Schneider has made out a strong case, which I have followed in my own examination of the inscription, for taking this cult symbol as the great yew tree of life that supports the world.[26] This "world-yew" (*Welteibe*), he argues, was in some way replaced in the Eddaic tradition by the ash tree; for whereas the yew is a true evergreen, the ash, strangely described as "ever green" in stanza 18 of the *Völuspá*, is not:

> Ask veitk standa,   heitir Yggdrasill;
> hár baðmr ausinn   hvít auri;

þaðan koma döggvar   þærs í dala falla;
stendr æ of grœnn   Urðar brunni.

Schneider convincingly compares this strophe[27] with Adam of Bremen's account of a holy tree near a temple at Uppsala, "always green in both winter and summer," close to which is a fountain in which the pagans perform human sacrifices. Here it seems quite clear that this "arbor maxima late ramos extendens, semper viridis hieme et aestate" must be the sacred and magical yew: and the reference in this account to a nearby *fons* startlingly parallels the *Urðar brunni* of the *Völuspá*. The holy world-tree of life, ever green, could not originally have been the ash, as has usually been assumed of the Eddaic Yggdrasill, despite the word *ask*. One is reminded of Goethe's famous lines of the tree of life:

Grau, teurer Freund, ist all Theorie;
Und grün des Lebens goldner Baum.

With regard to the Eddaic Yggdrasill, Woden's horse and gallows, there is some attraction in the suggestion made by Rolf Nordenstreng in 1929[28] that the element *ygg*, instead of being the adjective *yggr* 'fearful,' and so forth, as is almost always accepted, might in fact be derived in this compound from the Germanic **ixwō* or *eixwō* 'yew.' He would assume a progression Gmc. **ixhwō* > Prim. N. **iggwa* or **iggva* > ýr, in which *ygg-* of Yggdrasill would be an early stage. The yew, still widely known as poisonous to cattle, has from time immemorial had associations with the supernatural and with magic, and also with death. As a cult symbol in our inscription, then, it may stand for the world yew tree of life: and it would thus again be appropriate in its place.

The rune *NĒD*, commonly signifying in OE "need," "distress," "trouble," and so on, must have had a long semantic pedigree in Indo-European culture. But its ultimate connection with the process of making a fire by rubbing a stick in the hollow of a second one, and hence a symbolic sense of coitus in the Germanic **nauþiz* (OE *nēd*, ON *nauð*, and so on) as confidently argued by Schneider,[29] cannot well be accepted on linguistic grounds. The ultimate meaning of *nēd*, as the best etymological dictionaries show, is "death."[30] Its Indo-European root is *nāu nǝu nū*, and its cognates in historical Germanic languages are seen in Gothic *naus*, ON *nár* 'corpse,' and in OE *nē-* and *nēo- nīo-* in compounds like *nēfugol* 'carrion-bird' and *nēobed* 'bed of death.' The confusion in late OE of *nēd* 'necessity' with *nēod* 'desire' might seem to lend some support to Schneider's case, but I believe that a study of all the forms and their probable etyma will confirm the usual view that the Indo-European and early Prim. Gmc. ancestors of *nēd* meant "death" or "killing." The semantic development from "death" to "trouble," "necessity," and so on, is not difficult to imagine. In such an incantational use of cult symbols as that on the Caistor astragalus of the close of the fifth century, we should expect the memory of this sense of death to have remained in the rune *NĒD*.

I take *NĒD* then as "death." Perhaps something of this ancient sense of the word may be seen in the use of the compound *neidfær* in the oldest manuscript of *Bede's Death-Song*; for this *faru* or journey is not merely one which is compulsive, as Symeon of Durham rendered it with his *necessarium exitum*, but looks back also to the journey of death in the meaning of *neid*. Furthermore, one might even link the second element of *neidfær* with the word *fær* 'ship,' and so think of the Germanic ship which conveys the dead hence.

To summarize now my speculations as to the basic significance of the inscription. The whole forms the deeply sacred and mysterious word *RAH(W)HAN*, meaning "divine power," and cognate with ON *regin*. No doubt this word was fraught with mana. The separate runes as cult symbols suggest Woden's chariot, the god himself who escorts the dead from this world, the world yew tree of life associated also with death (probably again a name with much of mana in it), a hailstorm whose symbolic force we may not yet perceive, and finally death, with a preceding repetition of the **ansuz*-rune to remind us again of Woden's special relation with the dead.

iv

THE PROBABLE connection of the rune *RAD* with the Indo-European cult of the sun god has already been mentioned. It is this cult which manifests itself in the symbolism of the ancient Greek sun god *Helios*, with his chariot or wagon and two horses, and in the parallel implications for *Sūrya* in the hymns of the Ṛgveda. A clear link between this cult and the cult symbols of pagan Anglo-Saxon England is suggested not only by the associations of *RĀD* (and of course the OE *SIGEL* and the ON *SÓL* of the *Runic Poems*) but also, I think, vividly by the cruciform symbols surrounded by circules, mentioned at the beginning of this paper, from an incinerary urn in the large Anglo-Saxon cemetery at Loveden Hill in Lincolnshire, excavated by Mr. Kenneth Fennell some few years ago. This small, black, squat incinerary urn, a photograph of which, kindly supplied by Mr. Fennell, appears in Figure 2, has a series of seven recognizable runes incised on its middle portion, with a series of these esocyclic cruciform symbols in its upper section running the whole way round the urn. These latter can only be seen in part from the larger photograph: but the new method of "periphotography" provides us with a sight of the whole urn in one view, as reproduced in Figure 3. Following on continuously from the seven rune-like symbols just mentioned is a series of so far unrecognizable symbols which cannot all be runes. They

Figure 2

Figure 3

Figure 4

may be merely decorative devices of no special significance (as we often see on Anglo-Saxon monuments), or they may also be cultic symbols whose meaning remains entirely mysterious. But the esocyclic cruciform series of identical symbols running all around the upper part of the urn are obviously, I think, simple representations of the sun's rays, and at the same time, of wagon wheels (presumably of the sun god). They remind us a little, too, of the cruciform patterns on the silver bowls of the Sutton Hoo ship cenotaph. It may well be that this kind of symbolism or decoration, like the esocyclic crosses, pertained in some way to the same cult. In view of the considerable onomastic Frisian elements in this district—in such names as Friesthorpe and Frieston—this cult may have been especially strong in areas originally colonized by Frisians; and it may perhaps be thought of as an Anglo-Frisian cult of the sun god.

Mr. Fennell has provided me with a drawing of the runes and the unrecognizable symbols which follow them, together with some of the crosses (Fig. 4). In the top lefthand corner of this drawing is a rough thumbnail sketch of the urn itself, from which the reader will be able to get a fairly clear picture of what the urn looks like as a whole. The first seven runic symbols of the urn, though very irregularly formed, may be recognized as S I Þ Æ (or A) B Æ (or A) G, of which I can make nothing if they are to form a word, nor with any certainty if taken separately as cult symbols, though they may, nevertheless, have cult significance. If they were cult symbols, the symbolic words then would probably be SIGEL 'the sun,' ĪS 'ice,' ÞORN 'thorn,' but probably with something of its older Germanic sense of "thunder,"[31] *ANSUZ or ŌS 'a god,' BEORC 'birch,' *ANSUZ (or ŌS) again "a god," and GEOFU 'gift.' Of these words ÞORN, with its earlier connotations of thunder, might easily be taken as a cult symbol in itself, as could also SIGEL. The remaining symbols, which are scarcely recognized as runes, though they are often rune-like, I must leave undiscussed. They could all be possibly explained as runes oddly shaped of varying types and periods; but they seem more probably to be symbols which are not runes proper.

Other urns of similar type have been found in Loveden Hill: and this fact only strengthens the probability of the existence of an influential religious cult, relating to the disposal of the dead, of pagan Anglo-Frisian origin in this area.

v

IN THE TWO pre-Christian inscriptions discussed above, we have echoes of prehistoric Indo-Eurpoean religious cults inherited through Germanic culture by pagan Anglo-Saxons in Norfolk and in Lincolnshire.

That of Caistor-by-Norwich, with its especially magical implications, probably owes a good deal to the proximity of its cemetery to the mysterious stone remains, those

> orþanc enta geweorc,   þa þe on þysse eorðan sindon,
> wrætlic weallstana geweorc

of MS. Brit. Mus., Cotton Tiberius B.i,[32] the so-called Cotton Gnomic verses. For Caistor-by-Norwich, within sight of which this vast cemetery grew up from the late fifth century, was the capital of the Roman British *civitas* of the Iceni, known as *Venta Icenorum*: and its surviving deserted ruins must have strengthened the sense of awe in the Saxon settlers. The Loveden Hill cemetery, on the other hand, scarcely likely to have been influenced by the proximity of Roman British inheritance, was near probable centers of Swedish-inherited cults such as that of Woden, and Anglo-Frisian religious sun cults. My speculations about these inscriptions are, of course, quite tentative; but I have brought them forward in the belief that there is yet a chapter to be written by scholars of Germanic and Anglo-Saxon historical anthropology to the making of which this kind of stimulus might be helpful. This age of dark riddles of culture, the English fifth to seventh centuries, may yet be much illuminated as the excavations of hitherto only primordially investigated Anglo-Saxon cemeteries advance; for such excavations are even now only in their relatively beginning stages. Chance seemed suddenly to revolutionize our archeology in 1939 with the almost accidental finding of the Sutton Hoo ship cenotaph, which suddenly illuminated so much of the most obscure period of Anglo-Saxon life and thought: and the series of lucky accidents has continued, as the foregoing should have illustrated. Again, the discovery lately of authentic remains of King Eadwine's palace at Yeavering has thrown sudden light. The material which may lead to an authentically vivified picture of "dark-age" Anglo-Saxon civilization has indeed begun to accumulate. Not alone for the archeologist are such finds of immense significance; for from full excavation and interpretation of Anglo-Saxon grave finds we may hope to be able to construct portraits in some sort of the men who were cremated or inhumed in them, of their religious feelings and aspirations as well as their material possessions – of the kind of mana which lies behind their cult symbols. But this new section of historical anthropological science cannot, even when and if the requisite material becomes available, be devised by the anthropologists alone – nor yet by the archeologists. An uncomparative separation of the specialists in the various disciplines has generally hitherto rather increasingly prevailed since the days of the relatively encyclopedic antiquarians of the Renaissance, such as Camden, Dugdale, and Sumner. Only by some kind of sympathetic collaboration of archeologists, anthropologists, philologists, and historians could the hoped-for material be rightly interpreted and made to yield its entire fruit.

Such a collaboration might have enabled me to answer several puzzles which arise from the inscriptions I have discussed. For instance, what is the connection between the apparent suggestion of sortilege of the thirty astragali, with only one marked with cult symbols of the Caistor inscription, and the funerary or cremation rites implied by all the circumstances? Or again, what conception of the human spirit and its *post mortem* future is implied in our inscriptions? And how does such a belief relate to the motives of the Sutton Hoo ship cenotaph? And is there any connection between the Mithraic cult known to have been prevalent in later Roman Britain and the esocyclic cruciform symbols of the Loveden Hill urn? Then, one might ask how far there are common European or even world elements in the religious cults of pre-Christian Saxon England. Here one may call to mind Tacitus' observation that the Suevi sacrificed to the originally Egyptian deity Isis: "Pars Suevorum et Isidi sacrificat"[33] for the Isis symbolism of a sun disc surrounded with horns might be related to that on the Loveden Hill urn. The goddess Isis, in later Roman times the protectress of ships, was often symbolized in the figureheads of ships: and Tacitus, though regarding it as an indication of foreign importation, tells in the immediately following passage of Isis venerated by the Suevi in "signum ipsum in modum liburnae figuratum." But I have said enough to make my point.

NOTES

1. Vol. XL, No. I, 33–46.
2. Vol. I (Berlin, 1935); only pp. 315–17 treat of the South Germans, and pp. 244–50 cover the Anglo-Saxons: but in Vol. II (Berlin, 1937) over fifty pages (32–74) are devoted to the North Germanic peoples.
3. Cf. K. R. Fennell's discussion of a Loveden Hill bowl in "Hanging-bowls with pierced Escutcheons," *Medieval Archaeology*, IV (1960).
4. No. 61 (251) A. II. I owe all information on the Loveden Hill cemetery to Mr. Kenneth Fennell, who has for long been excavating it. He has placed also drawings and photographs at my disposal.
5. "Magic in an Anglo-Saxon Cemetery," *English and Medieval Studies*, *Essays Presented to J. R. R. Tolkien on his 70th Birthday*, edd. Norman Davis and C. L. Wrenn (London, 1962), pp. 306–20. Cf. also my paper "Anglo-Saxons and Celts in South-West Britain," *Trans. of the Honourable Society of Cymmrodorion* for 1959, esp. pp. 39–43.
6. See my essay "Two Anglo-Saxon Harps" in *Comparative Literature*, XIV (1962), 116–28.
7. See "An Ogham-inscribed Knife-handle from South-West Norfolk," *The Antiquaries Journal*, XXXII, 71–73.
8. Quoted in the late Gerard Murphy's *Early Irish Lyrics* (Oxford, 1956), No. 30, stanza 5, a poem wrongly attributed to St. Columcille.

9. Ed. John M. Kemble for the Aelfric Society (London, 1847), Part 2, p. 192, ll. 58-59.

10. Ed. E. V. K. Dobbie, *Anglo-Saxon Poetic Records*, Vol. vi, ll. 98-100.

11. *Die germanischen Runennamen, ein Beitrag zur idg. Kultur- und Religionsgeschichte* (Meisenheim am Glan, 1956).

12. See n. 5.

13. See "The Old English Rune EAR," *Medium Aevum*, xxx (1962), 72-74.

14. (London, 1960). There is a good summary account of the Anglo-Saxon cemetery on pp. 132-52, and useful further references on pp. 188-89.

15. See *Germania*, cap. 24.

16. *Germania*, cap. 9, *ad fin.*

17. *Arkiv för nordisk Filologi*, L (1934), 218 f.

18. See *Germania*, cap. 10.

19. For an attempt to justify the equation of this *rah(w)han* with ON *regin* 'divine powers,' OE *regn-* in the phrase *regnhearde randas* of *Beowulf* 326, etc., on phonological grounds, see the detailed exposition of the inscription in the Tolkien Festschrift (n. 5, above).

20. *Beowulf*, l. 2168.

21. See my paper "Sutton Hoo and Beowulf," *Mélanges de linguistique et de philologie: Fernand Mossé in Memoriam* (Paris, 1959), pp. 495 and

501. There is a valuable, though speculative, detailed study of the Woden cult at Sutton Hoo by Karl Hauck in "Herrschaftszeichen eines Wodanistischen Königtums," *Festschrift Anton Ernstberger* (Erlangen, 1954), pp. 9-65.

22. Clarke, p. 137.

23. Pp. 116 f.

24. Cf. my R. W. Chambers Memorial Lecture, "Anglo-Saxon Poetry and the Amateur Archaeologist" (London, 1962), pp. 9-11.

25. "The Old English Nominal Compounds in −RAD," *PMLA*, LXVII (1952), 538-71.

26. Pp. 277 f.

27. P. 277.

28. "Studier tillägnade Axel Kock," *Arkiv för nordisk Filologi*, XL (1929), 194 f.

29. See pp. 136-42. He relies largely on a very free exposition of the account of NYD in the OE *Runic Poem*, and derives this word from Indo-European *neu* 'rub.'

30. On the Indo-European etymology of this rune name see Pokorny's revision of Walde-Pokorny, s.v. 2 *nāu nǝu nū*.

31. Cf. Schneider, pp. 392 f.

32. *The Anglo-Saxon Poetic Records*, Vol. vi, ed. E. V. K. Dobbie (London, 1942), p. 55.

33. *Germania*, cap. 9.

The *Hwicce*

A. H. SMITH

University College, London

THE OLD ENGLISH folk known as the *Hwicce*[1] occupied territory in the southwest Midlands; their immediate neighbors were the West Saxons on the south and southeast, various peoples grouped as the Middle Angles on the east and northeast, the Mercians on the northeast and north, and the *Magonsætan* on the west beyond the Severn, all of these except the West Saxons being of Anglian origin and ultimately forming the kingdom of Mercia.[2] Something is known historically about the political relations of the *Hwicce* with the kingdom of Mercia under Penda, who, Sir Frank Stenton thinks,[3] may have been "a landless noble of the Mercian royal house fighting for his own hand"; in 628 (ASC) when Penda came to terms with the West Saxons at Cirencester (Gl), he may simply have been the leader, perhaps the usurping leader, of the *Hwicce*; he had in the first instance brought the rulers of the *Hwicce* under his authority, for it was not until 632 that he succeeded to the kingdom of Mercia; thereafter the *Hwicce* always appear as a large but dependent subkingdom of Mercia.[4] In the southern part of the region which eventually emerged in historical times as the territory of the *Hwicce*, there had been a late sixth-century West Saxon campaign against the Britons; in 577 (ASC) the West Saxons defeated three British kings at Dyrham in south Gloucestershire and captured the three towns of Bath, Cirencester, and Gloucester. But any interest the West Saxons had, at least in the Cotswolds, was terminated by Penda in 628 (ASC). Very early Mercian historical traditions are comparatively meager, and it is perhaps the absence of this kind of information which has obscured the origin of the *Hwicce*, while the clear statement about the 577 campaigns has given undue emphasis to a Saxon element in the composition of the folk who eventually occupied the territory of the *Hwicce*.

Place names of an early type[5] and, more particularly, numerous heathen English cemeteries[6] show that the West Saxons were by the early sixth century established in the middle and upper Thames valley as far west as Fairford (Gl). The Saxon victories in 556 (ASC) at *Beran*

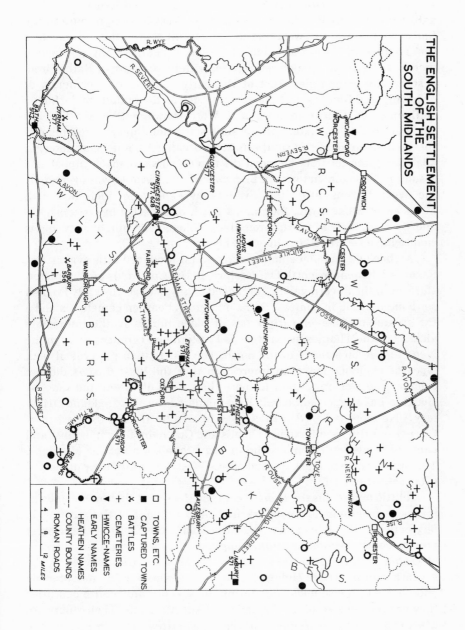

THE ENGLISH SETTLEMENT
OF THE
SOUTH MIDLANDS

□	TOWNS, ETC.
■	CAPTURED TOWNS
✕	BATTLES
+	CEMETERIES
▲	HWICCE-NAMES
●	EARLY NAMES
○	HEATHEN NAMES
─ ─ ─	COUNTY BOUNDS
────	ROMAN ROADS

byrg, now Barbury (W 278), and in 571 (ASC) at the unidentified *Bedcan-forda*, when *Lygeanburg* (Limbury, Bd 155), *Ægelesburg* (Aylesbury, Bk 145), *Bænesingtun*, and *Egonesham* (Benson and Eynsham, O 116, 258) were captured, indicate considerable West Saxon pressure in the Salisbury Plain to the west and in the central south Midlands north of the Thames in the second half of the sixth century. The 577 Saxon victory at Dyrham, already referred to, with the capture of Bath, Ciren-cester (only eight miles west of the early sixth-century cemetery at Fairford), and Gloucester, has been regarded as the prelude to the Saxon settlement of Gloucestershire and Worcestershire (Wo xiv ff.), but Hodgkin doubts the extent of any such settlement and Stenton regards the area secured as the southern Severn valley.[7] Some years later, in 584 (ASC), the territory between the two regions already occupied as a result of the Saxon victories of *Bedcanford* and Dyrham was overrun by the West Saxons after their victory at *Feþanleag*, identified with *Fethelee* in Stoke Lyne, four miles north of Bicester in Oxfordshire,[8] and Ceawlin their king captured many villages and much booty and is said to have returned "in anger" to his own land.[9]

Archeology and place names have so far produced little evidence of Saxon settlement in north Oxfordshire, in the Cotswolds of Gloucester-shire, or in the Severn valley,[10] or indeed of any noteworthy early English settlement at all, in contrast to the numerous heathen cemeteries and a far greater number of early types of place names in the immediate vicinity of the Thames as far west as Fairford and Cirencester, or in the Nene and Avon valleys to the north. The distribution patterns of both types of evidence leave an impression that the West Saxons did not colonize the western region to more than a small extent and may, as Hodgkin has suggested, merely have rendered the captured lands tribu-tary.[11] No more is heard of the Cotswold area until 628 (ASC), when at Cirencester the West Saxons Cynegils and Cuichelm fought against and came to terms with Penda, who in 632 became king of the Mercians. This would seem to mark the end of any West Saxon authority in most of Gloucestershire.

A little before this the *Hwicce* come on the scene, their name appear-ing as a geographical landmark in Bede's account of the meeting in 603 between the missionary Augustine and the bishops of the nearest province of the Britons at *Augustinaes Ác . . . in confinio Huicciorum et Occidentalium Saxonum.*[12] Later, the *Hwicce* are included in the seventh-century Tribal Hidage (see n. 4) as a considerable folk of some 7000 hides or households, and during the seventh and eighth centuries they are recognized as a subkingdom of the Mercians. Their rulers are described chiefly as *reguli, subreguli, comites,* or *ministri* of the Mercian kings,[13] but Oshere is styled *rex* in 678–93 (BCS 51), Ailric as *Oser[i] regis filius* in 706 (BCS 117), and Osric as *rex* in Bede (iv, 23).

Other evidence also points to at least a noble, if not a royal, origin for these rulers; the same Osric and his brother Oswald are *nobilis generis in provincia Huicciorum* in 681 (BCS 60), and about the same time Eabae, queen of the South Saxons, was after the conversion of her kingdom baptized among her own people *in prouincia Huicciorum* (Bede iv, 13); in 716–43 (BCS 165) Osred is described as *de stirpe non ignobili prosapia regali gentis Huicciorum*. The pattern of naming of some of these rulers of the *Hwicce* does not fall in with that of the West Saxon royal family, but it may fall in with that of the Northumbrian (Bernician) royal family.[14]

Some time after Penda's death in 654 and the conversion of the Mercian kingdom, the *Hwicce* were one of the Midland peoples who received a bishop, with his see at Worcester, the others being a group of Middle Anglian folk, with a see at Leicester, and the *Magonsætan*, with the see at Hereford beyond the Severn. The bishops of the *Hwicce* continued to call themselves *episcopi Hwicciorum* and the like as late as the tenth century.[15] But the significance of this episcopal foundation lies in its identity with the bishopric of Worcester, which like other ancient sees is unlikely to have changed its traditional boundaries in later medieval times. These (and hence probably those of the *Hwicce* themselves in the seventh and eighth centuries) can be determined from the *Taxatio Ecclesiastica* of 1291;[16] the bishopric then included the whole of Worcestershire except for the northwestern tip of the modern county, the southwest of Warwickshire, and all Gloucestershire, except for the Forest of Dean and other lands west of the river Severn and the river Leadon (which were in the diocese of Hereford and therefore had presumably been in the territory of the *Magonsætan*).[17]

Of similar territoral importance are the places named from the *Hwicce* or stated to be in their land. On the periphery of the bishopric are Wichenford in northwest Worcestershire (Wo 179), Whichford in southwest Warwickshire (Wa 301), and Wychwood Forest, just over the boundary in west Oxfordshire (O 386), whilst in the Cotswolds the *mons Hwicciorum*[18] of BCS 236 can be identified with Cutsdean Hill, five miles east-northeast of Winchcomb (Gl ii, 8).[19] Winchcomb itself was said to be *in provincia Wictionum* (BCS 338), and Bredon in south Worcestershire was *Breodun in Huic'* (BCS 209, cf. also 236). In 800 (ASC), the aldorman Æþelmund is stated to have ridden across from the *Hwicce* at Kempsford (in south Gloucestershire) to meet the men of Wiltshire, and later in the ninth century Asser described Cirencester (nine miles northwest of Kempsford) as in *meridiana parte Hwicciorum*.[20] In 825 (BCS 384–85) a meeting between Uulfred, Archbishop of Canterbury, and Cwoenðryð, daughter of the Mercian king Coenwulf, was held at *Oslafeshlau* in *provincia Hwicciorum*, and Dr. Finberg identifies this place with Oswaldslow in White Ladies Aston

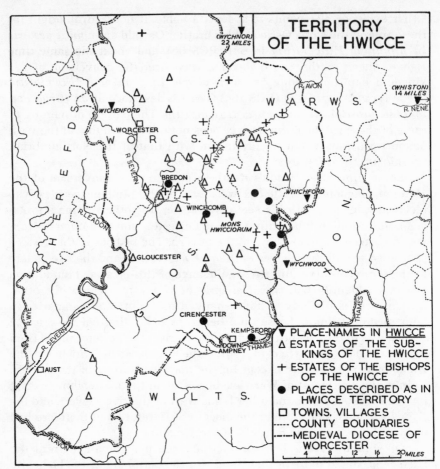

(Wo 89), four miles east of Worcester.[21] Some of the later references doubtless embody traditional lore about the *Hwicce* and may have no administrative implications about the region in later times, but it should be remembered that Gloucestershire as a separate shire does not seem to have existed before the end of the tenth or beginning of the eleventh century,[22] and *Hwicce* may have continued in use as the name of the region as well as the diocese. In addition to such localized allusions to the *Hwicce*, the places where grants were made by the Mercian kings as overlords, by the underkings of the *Hwicce*, and by their bishops are numerous, and all are within the limits of the ancient diocese of Worcester, chiefly in the Cotswolds, in the Avon valley in all three shires which came within the see, and in the vicinity of Worcester itself.[23]

The distribution of places associated in one way or another with the *Hwicce* gives a picture of a compact and not insignificant territorial unit, and geographically at least, suggests that the *Hwicce* could have

been an Anglian folk who had migrated from Middle Anglia into the
Avon valley, from which they spread northward into Worcestershire and
southward into the Cotswolds of Gloucestershire. But in two respects
this simple view of their origin has been questioned. In the first place,
the presence of artifacts in the Avon valley cemeteries, like applied,
disc, and saucerbrooches, usually associated with Saxon cemeteries
and found here by the side of more characteristically Anglian objects,
like annular, cruciform, and open-work swastika brooches, has been
interpreted as a mixed culture showing the presence of Saxons as well
as Angles in the region.[24] But precisely the same kind of mixed culture
is to be found in the Nene valley cemeteries of Middle Anglia and even
further east in Cambridgeshire.[25] So far as the *Hwicce* territory is
concerned, this mixed culture could most certainly have been imported
direct from Middle Anglia and need owe nothing of its supposed Saxon
element to the West Saxon occupation of the southwestern part of the
region after the battle of Dyrham in 577.

The second difficulty in regarding the *Hwicce* as a purely Anglian
folk lies in the suggestion that certain place names of West Saxon
origin are to be found in Worcestershire. Chauson (Wo 307) has, for
instance, been derived from a West Saxon broken form **Cealf*, but
another explanation is possible,[26] and some Old English personal names
thought to occur in the place names and suggested (Wo xx) to have a
West Saxon provenance, like **Ambre* in Ombersley (Wo 268), **Ceatwe*
in Chaceley (Wo 192), **Cifa* in Chevington (Wo 219), and so on, are too
imperfectly evidenced to warrant such localization; or they occur outside the Saxon area, like **Cifa* found as far away as Northumbria (in
Chevington and Cheveley, Nb 44); or they may, like the first element of
Chaceley, be better explained as of Celtic origin. Even allowing in Old
English times for the predominance of standard West Saxon ortho-
graphy in the place-name forms of the region and in Middle English for
the increasing use of Chancery spellings of East Midland origin, the
dialect pattern of place names in Worcestershire and all but the south
of Gloucestershire is that of the Midlands and not the south;[27]
Dr. Margaret Gelling has noted (O xix) distinctively Anglian forms in
Oxfordshire on its western border in Wychwood Forest, and here too
Charlbury (O 415) was said to be in the region of the *Feppingas*, a
Middle Anglian people who, like the folk of Phepson, had probably migrated from the Northamptonshire region (cf. Wo xviii note).

Although in the time of Penda the population of the territory of the
Hwicce could have included some Saxon settlers from the short-lived
Saxon occupation of Gloucestershire and must have included Celtic
people who survived the West Saxon conquest, the linguistic evidence
of place names, the possible name links of the rulers of the *Hwicce* with
the Northumbrian royal dynasty, the appearance of the folk name or

personal names derived from it in other midland place names, the emergence in historical times of the *Hwicce* as a large and territorially coherent though dependent folk, and the parallels of other Anglian folks moving into the region – all these make it likely that the *Hwicce* were essentially of Anglian origin; it may well be that at the dawn of their recorded history, when their own rulers had become subject underkings, the adventurer Penda found in them the power to create a great Mercian kingdom out of a large number of minor Anglian peoples. It is in the Midlands rather than the south that the origins of the *Hwicce* should be sought.

NOTES

1. The name of the *Hwicce* is obscure; it would seem to be a very early type of folk name, perhaps, in view of its lack of etymological connections in Old English, of pre-Migration origin. A possible, though by no means certain, suggestion is a Germanic root *xwik-, which survived only in Old Icelandic *hvik* 'a quaking, a wavering,' *hvika* 'to quail, to shrink, to waver,' and *hvikari* 'coward' (cf. A. Jóhannesson, *Isländisches etymologisches Wörterbuch* [Bern, 1956], p. 260); if so, the name would be of the pejorative kind, like *Quadi* or *Ubii* 'the evil ones' (F. Solmsen [ed. E. Fraenkel], *Indogermanische Eigennamen als Spiegel der Kulturgeschichte* [Heidelberg, 1922], pp. 104–105).

In this paper the following abbreviations are used: ASC: *Two of the Saxon Chronicles Parallel*, ed. C. Plummer (Oxford, 1892, 1899); BCS: W. de Gray Birch, *Cartularium Saxonicum* (London, 1885); Bd: A. Mawer and F. M. Stenton, *The Place-Names of Bedfordshire and Huntingdonshire* (EPNS iii); Bk: A. Mawer and F. M. Stenton, *The Place-Names of Buckinghamshire* (EPNS ii); EPNS: publications of the English Place-Name Society (Cambridge, 1924 and in progress); Finberg: H. P. R. Finberg, *The Early Charters of the West Midland* (Leicester, 1961); Gl: A. H. Smith,

The Place-Names of Gloucestershire (EPNS xiii); Wo: A. Mawer, F. M. Stenton, and F. T. S. Houghton, *The Place-Names of Worcestershire* J. K. Wallenberg, *The Place-Names of Kent* (Uppsala, 1934); KCD: J. M. Kemble, *Codex Diplomaticus Aevi Saxonici* (London, 1839–48); Nb: A Mawer, *The Place-Names of Northumberland and Durham* (Cambridge, 1920); O: Margaret Gelling, *The Place-Names of Oxfordshire* (EPNS xxiii, xxiv); St: W. H. Duignan, *Notes on Staffordshire Place-Names* (London, 1902); Stenton: F. M. Stenton, *Anglo-Saxon England* (Oxford, 1943); W: J. E. B. Gover, Allen Mawer, and F. M. Stenton, *The Place-Names of Wiltshire* (EPNS xvi); Wa: J. E. B. Gover, A. Mawer, and F. M. Stenton, *The Place-Names of Warwickshire* (EPNS xiii); Wo: A. Mawer, F. M. Stenton, and F. T. S. Houghton, *The Place-Names of Worcestershire* (EPNS iv). It may be added that the material used in this paper will be found in the foregoing volumes and that some of the linguistic problems are explored in more detail in Gl IV, pp. 38–43.

2. OE *Merce*, *Mierce* 'the border people,' is probably a folk name which arose locally in Old English times to denote the Anglian people living on the Welsh border, which at the time the name was first used

may well have been the Cannock Chase area of south Staffordshire (cf. F. M. Stenton, *Anglo-Saxon England* [Oxford, 1943], p. 40). In that volume Sir Frank deals comprehensively with the growth of the Mercian kingdom.

3. Stenton, p. 45.
4. The Tribal Hidage (BCS 297, 297A, 297B) lists the tributary folks of the Mercian kingdom, and the *Hwicce* in the somewhat corrupt texts are called *Hwinca* in 297, *Hynica* (v. l. *Hynita, Hinta*) in 297A, and *Hwynca* in 297B.
5. In particular, folk names formed with *-ingas* from personal names, like Hastings (Sussex), Reading (Berkshire), or *Stoppingas* (Wa xvii), and place names formed from such folk names, like Buckingham (Bk 60), but excluding those folk names formed from older place names, like Avening (Gl i, 86), from a river name *Avon*, or Twyning (Gl ii, 71), from the OE place name *Tweoneaum* (cf. A. H. Smith, *English Place-Name Elements* [EPNS xxv], i, pp. 298–301); archaic elements, like **gē* 'district,' in Ely (Cambridgeshire) or Surrey, and archaic usages recorded only in heroic literature, like the word *drihten* 'a man's overlord' (as distinct from the later OE meaning "the Lord God"), as in Drigsell (Sussex) or *drihtnes dene* (Gl i, 29), and personal names recorded only in heroic contexts, like the *Wudia* and *Becca* of Withington and Beckford (Gl i, 186, ii, 43), both names of places with heathen burial sites; names originating in heathen religion, like Arrowfield and Weoley (Wo 333, 350), named from heathen temples, and Tysoe (Wa 284) and *Thunresfeld* (W 341), from the gods *Tīg and Þunor*, and so on. On archaic names see E. Ekwall, *The Oxford Dictionary of English Place-Names* (Oxford, 1960), pp. xiii, xv–xvi, xxx, xxxv; *English Place-Names in -ing* (Lund, 1960): A. H. Smith, "Place-Names and the Anglo-Saxon Settlement" in *Proceedings of the British Academy*, XLII (1957), 67–88. Such early names in the south Midlands are noted on Map 1, and details of

the names will be found in the introductions to the appropriate county volumes of the English Place-Name Society.
6. These are listed in G. B. Brown, *The Arts in Early England* (London, 1915), IV, pp. xxxi ff. There are other sites like those at Beckford (Gl) and Stratford (Wa) which have been discovered since 1915, but a catalog of sites has been prepared by Dr. Audrey Meaney and is now published, 1964, by Allen and Unwin (London) as *A Gazetteer of Early Anglo-Saxon Burial Sites.*
7. Hodgkin, I, p. 191; Stenton, pp. 29–30.
8. Stenton, p. 29; M. Gelling in O 238–39.
9. This phrase in ASC (all manuscripts except E), 7 *ierre* [corrected to *erre* in A; *yrre* in B, C] *he hwearf þonan to his agnum*, is usually rendered in this way, *ierre* being taken as an adjective in apposition to *he*. But the significance is obscure; Ceawlin's anger and action seem strange after his great success. Professor Magoun might care to sport with an emendation *ierfe* 'patrimony,' which Professor Quirk and I have done but not to our liking. In a paper "Wansdyke Reconsidered" in *The Archaeological Journal*, CXV (1960), 43, Aileen and Cyril Fox regard the battle of *Fethanleag* and the death of *Cutha* as a serious defeat for the West Saxons and the capture of many villages as an act of vengeance, after which Ceawlin "in anger returned to his own." In a note (p. 46) Dr. Kenneth Sisam has called attention to the difficulty of *ierre*, which is "quite as much out of style as out of time" and regards its use here as possibly a vestige of a lost English verse source.
10. The locations of both types of evidence are set out in Map 1.
11. Hodgkin, p. 191.
12. *Venerabilis Baedae Historia Ecclesiastica Gentis Anglorum*, ed. Charles Plummer (Oxford, 1896), pp. ii, 2. Unfortunately the oak has not been identified. The Oak (in Down Ampney) and Aust (Gl i, 51, iii, 127) have been suggested, but

from a place-name point of view without conviction.

13. The terms occur in Gloucestershire and Worcestershire documents: *regulus* BCS 183, 187, 202–204; *subregulus* BCS 204–205, 217, 223, 231, 238, 246, 278; *minister* BCS 60, 165; *comes* BCS 156, and so on.

14. Especially the names beginning with *ōs-* (*Oshere, Osric, Osred,* and so on). Cf. Hodgkin, p. 192, and especially H. P. R. Finberg, *The Early Charters of the West Midlands* (Leicester, 1961), pp. 167–80.

15. In 985, cf. KCD 649.

16. *Taxatio Ecclesiastica* (Record Commission, London, 1802), 216–40.

17. Map 2 shows the 1291 boundary of the Worcester diocese, as well as the places named in the following paragraph. In Warwickshire just on the eastern boundary of the diocese with that of Lichfield, the field name Martimow in Radway, eight miles east-southeast of Stratford on Avon (Wa xvii, 272), is the *mercna mere* of 969 BCS 1234, that is, "boundary of the Mercians," presumably opposite the *Hwicce.* The western boundary, which marches with that of the Hereford diocese, is confirmed in an eleventh-century document (in M. Förster, *Der Flussname Themse und seine Sippe* [Munich, 1941], p. 769) and is discussed in Finberg, Ch. XII. In this area west of the Severn there is ample evidence in the place names of such characteristically West Midland forms as *wælla* for *wella* 'spring,' *worðign* 'enclosure,' etc.

18. The *monte Wiccisca* 'the Hwiccean hill' of 964 BCS 1135, p. 379, on the other hand, denotes the eastern part of the Cotswolds, and the places named in the charter as being in that area are Daylesford, Evenlode, and Dorn and Northwick in Blockley, all in the east of Gloucestershire (Gl i, 217, 219, 235).

19. Outside the Worcester diocese three other place names may be connected with the *Hwicce* – Witchley Green (Rutland) from a personal name *Hwicc*, Whiston near the Nene in Northamptonshire from a personal name *Hwicca* (Nth

152), and Wichnor (St 171) from the same personal name or the folk name itself; the personal names must be derived from the folk name (cf. Wo xv, and E. Ekwall in *Namn och Bygd* xli.). These places are far outside the area of West Saxon influence, and Witchley and Whiston would suggest a line of penetration of the *Hwicce* from the Nene valley to the Avon valley. Two close parallels to the migration of Anglian folks into Worcestershire have often been noted in Phepson (Wo xviii, 137), named from a group of the *Færpingas* from Middle Anglia, and Whitsun Brook (Wo xix, 16) from the *Wixna* of the Fens, both folks named in the Tribal Hidage.

20. Asser's *Life of King Alfred*, ed. W. H. Stevenson (Oxford, 1904), *s.a.* 879.

21. Finberg, p. 169. Oswaldslow (now Low Hill) was the meeting place of a hundred and was renamed Oswaldslow in 964 after Bishop Oswald (BCS 1135, p. 380); Spetchley and Spechull (Wo 165) from OE *spǣc* 'speech' and Stoulton (Wo 166) from OE *stōl* 'throne' are within a mile or two of this important and ancient assembly place on the road from Evesham on the Avon to Worcester. The personal name *Oslaf* in the older name of the mound may be that of a member of the ancient ruling family of the *Hwicce* (see n. 14).

22. Cf. H. P. R. Finberg, *Gloucestershire Studies* (Leicester, 1957), pp. 17–51, and Gl i, 1. Worcestershire is first named as a shire c. 1040 (Wo 1) and Warwickshire c. 1016 (ASC).

23. These are located on Map 2. A list of the relevant charters where specific reference is made to the rulers and bishops of the *Hwicce* making the grants is given in Gl, Part IV, p. 33, n.

24. G. Baldwin Brown, pp. 622–26.

25. E. T. Leeds, *Archæology of the Anglo-Saxon Settlements* (Oxford, 1913), pp. 37, 68; and *A Corpus of Anglo-Saxon Square-headed Brooches* (Oxford, 1949), pp. 104 ff. Leeds considered that another possible line of ingress of the Saxons to the middle Thames valley was by way of Icknield Street from Middle

Anglia (cf. R. G. Collingwood and J. N. L. Myres, *Roman Britain and the English Settlements* [Oxford, 1936], pp. 407–10, for an assessment of this problem).

26. Chauson (like Chelfridge, Gl iii, 236, which is in the Forest of Dean across the Severn and certainly outside the area of West Saxon influence) would from its spellings be derived from an OE (Anglian) *i*-mutated by-form *celf* (Mercian *cælf*, West Saxon **cielf*) 'calf'; a parallel to an initial palatal in this case can be found in OE (Anglian, Kentish) *celde*, West Saxon **cield*, 'spring,' an *i*-mutated derivative of OE *cald, ceald* 'cold,' as in such place names as Bapchild, Honeychild (K 242, 481). See further Gl iv, p. xiii (addendum to p. 39). A recent account of some of the ME dialect problems of Wo is Bertil Sundby, *Studies in the Middle English Dialect Material of Worcestershire Records* (Bergen-Oslo, 1963).

27. Some of the linguistic problems of the place names and the West Midland charters have been analyzed by David Mills in an unpublished thesis, "A Linguistic Study of Gloucestershire Place-Names," University of London Library (1960). There are, in fact, very few traces of southern influence in any Gloucestershire place names. West Saxon broken forms are infrequent, but may occur sporadically as in Chalford and Chalkley from West Saxon *cealc* (Gl i, 127, iii, 29), *Eldermanstile* in Lechlade (Gl i, 44) from *ealdormann*, Barnsley Wold (Gl i, 25), which has a single spelling *Weldam* from West Saxon *weald*; the normal type even in the south is the Anglian unbroken form, as in Aldsworth (Gl i, 23) or Alderton (Gl ii, 48), while the single spelling *Eldeberge*, which has been derived from West Saxon *eald* (E. Ekwall, *Contributions to the History of Old English Dialects* [Lund, 1917], p. 22) is to be identified with Hillborough in Alderton (Gl ii, 50) and could be more appropriately derived from OE *helde* 'slope.' A few examples of OE (West Saxon) *filiðe* 'hay' (as in Feltham or Filton, Gl iii, 58, 103), and *hlyp-geat* 'leapgate' (as in Lypiatt, Gl i, 119), etc., as well as the supposed West Saxon form of Cirencester (Gl i, 60), are all in the south of the county.

The South Germanic Oral Tradition

ROBERT L. KELLOGG
University of Virginia

PROFESSOR MAGOUN'S essay on the "Oral-Formulaic Character of Anglo-Saxon Poetry" will, if his thesis is correct, leave much criticism of Old English poetry obsolete.[1] Our usual notions of literary influence, of date of composition, of poetic originality, and of the significance of textual nuances must in many cases be radically revised if we are to follow the implications of his argument to their utmost conclusions. Thirty years ago Milman Parry advanced the principle that "literature falls into two great parts not so much because there are two kinds of culture, but because there are two kinds of *form: the one part of literature is oral, the other written.*"[2] The literary critic must from the first proceed from the assumption either that such poems as *Beowulf* are oral compositions or that they are literary compositions. He can hardly avoid taking a stand. If there are two kinds of literature and two kinds of form, there must be two kinds of literary analysis and evaluation—one of which is relevant to an orally composed *Beowulf* and the other of which is relevant to a literary *Beowulf*.

Unfortunately there seems to be no ground upon which the critic who would imagine a "transitional" form—half oral and half literary—may stand. As in the case of Parry's demonstration that the Homeric epics were orally composed, the most convincing arguments for the oral composition of Anglo-Saxon poetry proceed from analogy between the diction and construction of Anglo-Saxon poems and that of the South Slavic oral epics recorded by Parry and Lord.[3] Few reservations to the acceptance of Magoun's thesis can not be met by comparing the performances of Yugoslav singers to the surviving Anglo-Saxon texts. By now the arguments are familiar.[4] Even the vexing questions raised by the preservation of oral compositions in written texts can be most conveniently approached through observing the experience of modern singers who either dictate to scribes or, like Milovan Vojičić in Nevesinje, Hercegovina, write down their own compositions.[5] Perhaps most relevant to the study of Anglo-Saxon poetry is Professor Lord's observation that in the South Slavic epic tradition the alternative to oral composition is not a literary continuation of the tradition; it is the death of the tradition altogether. For this reason, an experienced scholar like Lord, who knows a large oral tradition well, can distinguish between orally composed texts and literary texts without admitting a dubious class of transitional texts.[6] His experience confirms Parry's principle of *"either literary or* oral."

Although the presence of a large number of traditional formulas and themes is the formal characteristic that distinguishes oral from written literature, the individual fixed formulas are, according to Professor Lord, of somewhat limited importance to the skillful singer. If he controls a large stock of fixed formulas, he will be able to rely on them in meeting the many restrictions governing the construction of verse in his tradition. But as we do not learn to speak our native language by memorizing fixed formulas or paradigms, so the accomplished oral poet must learn how – while performing before an audience – to invent phrases that will, like the fixed traditional formulas he uses as models, also meet the restrictions of his tradition. Professor Lord maintains that "in studying the patterns and systems of oral narrative verse we are in reality discovering the 'grammar' of the poetry, a grammar superimposed, as it were, on the grammar of the language concerned."[7] To continue his analogy with language, we might add that the fixed formula is to the abstract pattern of which it is a manifestation as the phone-type is to the phoneme.[8] Both the fixed traditional formulas and the phrases invented by the singer during a performance will conform to a given number of abstract patterns. And it is an elaborate set of these patterns, rather than merely the stock of fixed formulas conforming to the patterns, that constitutes the verse-making tradition of oral-formulaic poetry. Lord summarizes: "I believe that we are justified in considering that the creating of phrases is the true art of the singer on the level of line formation, and it is this facility rather than his memory of relatively fixed formulas that marks him as a skillful singer in performance."[9]

As the analogy with the South Slavic oral tradition has led students to seek fixed formulas in Anglo-Saxon poetry, it must also lead them to study the morphology and syntax of the poetic "grammar" superimposed on the normal grammar of Old English, thus making possible a description of the abstract patterns or formulaic systems governing the production of phrases in oral composition. Professor A. G. Brodeur argues, for example, in his admirably thorough study of compound words in *Beowulf* that because the poet aptly employed a large number of compounds not found elsewhere in Anglo-Saxon poetry, and because he chose not to employ common compounds available to him, he could not have been composing orally.[10] This argument seems to assume that the patterns governing the formation of new compound words could not have been a part of an oral singer's verse-producing grammar. If we can grant that an oral singer can—indeed must—continually use new phrases constructed according to traditional patterns, then perhaps we must also grant that in the case of the Germanic languages, compound-word formation was an active element of every singer's poetic grammar. Certainly the formation of compound words would be much closer to the level of syntax in everyday spoken Old English than it is in Modern English. The unfortunate truth is, however, that we do not possess a corpus of poetry large enough to encompass and to illustrate adequately a complete poetic tradition, that is, in terms of verse construction, a complete poetic grammar. Whether the large number of *hapax legomena* in Old Icelandic as well as in Anglo-Saxon poetry reflects the paucity of the surviving records or the freedom with which poets could invent compounds, we cannot say with certainty. We can say, however, that if Anglo-Saxon poetry was orally composed, the *normal* expectation would be that it would contain unique phrases and perhaps some unique compounds—all constructed, however, within the set of patterns that made up its traditional poetic grammar.

Without an extensive body of texts, we must continue to speculate about whether given elements in the diction of Anglo-Saxon poems are traditional or not. The vastness of the collection of texts from the living South Slavic tradition provides Professor Lord with an adequate basis for making such distinctions. Even so, we now know that the really relevant elements, in analysis as in composition, are not the verbatim repeats within the corpus, but rather they are the abstract patterns governing the construction of lines and verses. The appearance of formulas is still the best demonstration of oral composition. Given a large enough corpus, the next stage in analysis ought to be the arrangement of formulas into formulaic systems.[11] When the abstract patterns of the tradition have been thoroughly described, the description should have some prediction value. We should be able, in other words, to compose. But at least we should be able to judge whether or not a given verse were "formulaic," even though it appeared nowhere else in the corpus. With only a small corpus, we are forced too soon into the necessity to generalize (if only implicitly) about the nature of formulaic systems in the hope of demonstrating the traditional or nontraditional status of a particular phrase, compound, or poem.

There is, in fact, one way in which our knowledge of both the fixed formulas and the formulaic systems of the Anglo-Saxon poetic tradition may be enlarged significantly. A glance at the "Formelverzeichnis" appended to Sievers' edition of *Heliand* (Halle, 1878) suggests the richness of the Old Saxon poem in traditional South Germanic formulas. Sievers identified and analyzed thousands of them. In addition, he noted several thousand parallels between *Heliand* and Anglo-Saxon poems.

There are more than three hundred references to *Beowulf* alone. The vast majority of these parallels are commonplaces in Anglo-Saxon tradition. Occasionally, however, one comes across a phrase in *Heliand* that could not have been recognized as formulaic in an Anglo-Saxon poem because it occurs only once in Old English. *The Seafarer*, for example, the formulaic character of which has recently been the subject of discussion, contains at least two formulas that are not recognizable except by comparison with *Heliand*.[12] *Bitre breostceare* (*Sfr* 4a) is matched by *bittra breostkara* (*Hel* 4033a),[13] and *wið feonda niþ* (*Sfr* 75b) is matched by *endi uuið fiundo nîð* (*Hel* 4116b). In addition to finding fixed formulas through the comparison of the two poems from the two dialects, we also notice the similarity in the positions of the verses within the line. As often as not, this comparative method demonstrates the formulaic nature of both the Old Saxon phrase and the Old English phrase, thereby increasing our knowledge of the stock of traditional formulas in the two dialects as well as suggesting such information as restrictions on the position of the phrase that might contribute to our knowledge of the system of which it is a member.

Heliand provides two formulas out of which a familiar passage of *Beowulf* could be composed. *Sô lioht ôstene quam* (*Hel* 4241b) combines with *berht bôcan godes* (*Hel* 661a) to form

> Leoht eastan com,
> beorht beacen Godes.
>
> [*Bwf* 559b–560a]

Again, the formulas occupy the same halves of lines in the two poems. Although the *billes bite* of *Bwf* 2060a, *æfter billes bite*, is a common enough looking formula, I believe that it is not found elsewhere in Anglo-Saxon poetry. *Heliand*, however, uses the formula in 4903a, *thes billes biti*. Only a few of the more or less commonplace correspondences between *Heliand* and *Beowulf* a-verses can be given here. There are, for example[14]

æþele ordfruma	[*Bwf* 263a]	adalordfrumo	[*Hel* 31a]
feorran gefricgean	[*Bwf* 2889a]	ferrene gifrugnun	[*Hel* 3752a]
fuse to farenne	[*Bwf* 1805a]	fûsa to faranne	[*Hel* 650a]
hæleðum to helpe	[*Bwf* 1709a]	helidun te helpu	[*Hel* 1719a]
leode gelæsten	[*Bwf* 24a]	liudiun gilêstean	[*Hel* 1052a]
sefa wið sorgum	[*Bwf* 2600a]	seƀo mid sorgun	[*Hel* 608a]
self(a) mid gesiðum	[*Bwf* 1313a, 1924a]	selƀo mid is gesiðon	[*Hel* 4013a]
wið wrað werod	[*Bwf* 319a]	uuið that uurêðe uuerod	[*Hel* 4904a]
se þe his wordes geweald	[*Bwf* 79a]	ni habda is uuordo geuuald	[*Hel* 4978a]

Of the literary and religious culture underlying *Heliand* there can
be little doubt. The parallels between the poem and the pseudo-Tatian
harmony of the Gospels are too close to be denied. The commentaries of
Hrabanus Maurus on Matthew, Bede on Luke and Mark, and Alcuin on
John are also probably to be counted as influences.[15] At the same time,
Sievers' "Formelverzeichnis" is testimony of the poem's conventional
diction. *Heliand* constitutes, therefore, an ideal locus for examining the
questions of (1) the degree to which a learned literary poem may employ
traditional formulas, or (2) the degree to which an orally composed poem
may use learned literary sources. I believe that the latter is the relevant
question. By analogy with the South Slavic oral epic, the evidence of
extremely formulaic diction points unmistakably to oral composition.
Regardless of how learned or unlikely the sources of a South Germanic
alliterative poem turn out to be, the traditional and formulaic character
of the diction must outweigh all other evidence in determining oral
composition. With the example of *Heliand* before us, it is pointless to
argue that this or that supposed echo of classical antiquity or Biblical
commentary in a poem like *Beowulf* argues in any way convincingly
against oral composition. As Parry pointed out, it is the form, not the
matter, that characterizes oral in contrast to literary composition. Because of the rather awkward arrangement of the "Formelverzeichnis,"
I will illustrate the formulaic character of *Heliand* by citing a short
passage with solid underlining to indicate formulas and broken underlining to indicate phrases that may form part of a formulaic system without actually appearing verbatim elsewhere in the South Germanic poetic
corpus. The passage is a paraphrase of Matthew 2:7−8 and Hrabanus
Maurus' commentary on Matthew 2:8. Sievers also notes the similarity
to a passage from Gregory's tenth homily.[16]

> Thô gifragn ic that sân aftar thiu   sliðmôd cuning   630
> thero uuârsagono uuord   them uurekkiun sagda,
> thea thar an elilendi   erlos uuârun
> ferran gifarana,   endi he frâgoda aftar thiu,
> huan sie an ôstaruuegun   êrist gisâhin
> thana cuningsterron cuman,   cumbal liuhtien   635
> hêdro fon himile.   Sie ni uueldun is im tho helen eouuiht,
> ac sagdun it im sôðlîco.   Thô hêt he sie an thana sîð faran,
> hêt that sie ira ârundi   al undarfundin
> umbi thes kindes cumi,   endi the cuning selƀo gibôd
> suîðo hardlico,   hêrro Iudeono,   640
> them uuîsun mannum,   êr than sie fôrin uuestan forð,
> that sie im eft gicûðdin,   huar he thana cuning scoldi
> sôkean at is selðon;   quað that he thar uueldi mid is gisîðun tô,
> bedon te them barne.   Than hogda he im te banon uuerðan

uuâpnes eggiun.   Than eft uualdand god   645
thâhte uuið them thinga: he mahta athengean mêr,
gilêstean an thesum liohte: that is noh lango skîn,
gicûðid craft godes.   Tho gengun eft t hiu cumbl forð
uuânum undar uuolknun.   Thô uuârun thea uuîson man
fûsa te faranne: giuuitun im eft forð thanan   650
balda an bodskepi: uueldun that barn godes
selbon sôkean.

Supporting Evidence[17]

[630a] thô (thar) gifragn ic that 367, 510, 3347, 3883, 3964, 4065; so
gifragn ik that 288, 2621, 3780, 4452; sân aftar thiu 192, 214, 699, 995,
1596, 2100, 2947, 3108, 4342, 4545, 4970, 5041, 5659, 5867, 5907. [630b]
slîðmôd cuning 703; cf. *Dan* 100, 161, 269, 529 swiðmod cyning. [631a]
uuârsagono uuord 3399, 4935. [633a] *Bwf* 3113 feorran feredon; *SmS*
178, *Gen* 498 feorran gefered. [633b] (tho) gifrang aftar thiu 715, 800.
[635a] *Exo* 175 cumbol lixton. [636a] hêdro fon himiles tunglun 600;
MBo 6.4 hadrost of heofone; *MBo* 20.230 hadre on heofonum; *Bwf* 1571
efne swa of hefene/hadre scineð; *Hárbarðsljóð* 19 á þann inn heiða
himin; *Völuspá* 57 hverfa af himni/heiðar stjörnur. [636b] hêlag an
himile/huuand imu nis beholan neouuiht 1577. [637a] sagda sôðlîco
494, 581; seggean sôðlîco 565, 1361; *Bwf* 141 gesægd soþlice; *Chr* 203
sægde soþlice. [637b] Nu hiet he me an thesan sîð faran 122; *Gen* 499
Þa het he me on þysne sîð faran; *And* 795 Het hie to þam siðe gyrwan.
[638a] Cf. Nu sculum gi an thana sîð faran/an that ârundi 1888b–1889a.
[639b] endi (thô) X selbo gibôd (*always in a b-verse*) 1843, 2897, 3423,
4209, 4502; *Bwf* 29b swa he selfa bæd. [640b] heriscipi Iudeono 5481;
(thiu) heri Iudeono 5057, 5368, 5409, 5413; cf. *the shorter formula*
hard heritoga *which forms an a-verse at* 5314, 5476, 5558. [641] that
uuârun thea uuîson man/uueston gihuuorban 717. [643a] sôkeas min
seliða 2106, 2123. [643b] Thô gengun is gesîðos tuelibi. [644a] Cf. bedos
te minun barma 1104. [644b] *Edda* at bana verða *eight times as a b-
verse; see note* 19, *below*). [645a] uuâpnes eggion 742, 3530, 5135, 5243,
5506; *And* 71, *SmS* 260 wæpna ecgum; *Gen* 1830, *SmS* 165 wæpnes ecge.
[645b] *The following lines end a b-verse with* uualdand god 20, 98,
1402, 1614, 1618, 1622, 1659, 1665, 1907, 1959, 2533, 2634, 2790, 3613,
3650, 3831, 4408, 4440, 5048. [646a] thenkean thero thingo 314; thenkean fora themu thinge 4376. [647a] gilêstead an thesumu liohte 1626,
gilêstid an thesumum liohte 3457. [648a] cûðian thia craft godes 5869.
[648b] Thô geng imu thar Iudas forð 4478. [649a] uuânum thurh thiu
uuolcan 392; *Bwf* 651 wan under wolcnum; *Bwf* 1374 won to wolcnum.
[649b] that uuârun thea uuîson man 717. [650a] fûs te faranne 4782,
5656; *Bwf* 1805 fuse to farenne. [650b] giuuitun im thô eft thanan 832,

5910; giuuet imu thô at (up) thanan 4628, 5974; tho giuuet imu waldand forð 3033; tho giuuet imu use drohtin forð 4185. [651] them bodon baldlîco:/'ni bium ic,' quað he, 'that barn godes,' 915; giboren that barn godes,/si ni uueldun is gibodskepi thoh 2666; bêðea is gibodskepies,/thô habda sie that barn godes 2264. [652a] *Chr* 524 sylfa gesecan.

The close similarity between the formulas of *Heliand* and those of the Anglo-Saxon corpus reflects the extreme conservatism of the South Germanic alliterative tradition well into the ninth century. The Old High German *Muspilli* and the *Hildebrand* are as highly formulaic as *Heliand* and share many formulas in common with the other poems in the South Germanic dialects. And even the Eddic poems that survive from the North Germanic alliterative tradition share enough formulas in common with the South Germanic poems to establish the formulaic nature of rare Old English words and phrases. Six of the compounds that occur in *Beowulf* but in no other Anglo-Saxon poem do occur in Icelandic poetry: *beadu-serce:böð-serke*; *earm-beag:arm-baugr*; *eormen-grund:jörmun-grund*; *hand-bona:hand-bani*: *here-wæd:herváð*; and *medo-ærn:mjöðrann*. At least in the cases of these six words we find a demonstration either that the compounds themselves were in fact very old elements of the Germanic poet's tradition or that the patterns according to which they were formed were old elements that remained productive in both the Icelandic and the Anglo-Saxon sub-traditions.[18] Furthermore, two of the compounds appear to be parts of traditional formulas. *Ofer eormengrund* (*Bwf* 859) is matched by *jörmungrund yfir* in *Grímnismál* 20.

> Wearþ he Heaþolafe   to handbonan   [*Bwf* 460]

and

> wearð him on Heorote   to handbanan   [*Bwf* 1330]

are matched by

> an thia hêlogun tîd   te handbonan
> uuerthan mid uuâpnon   an them uuîhdage   [*Hel* 5199, f.].

In addition to these three examples in which *to handbonan* forms a b-verse, the expression forms an a-verse in *Bwf* 2502. A shorter form of the idiom, *at bana verða*, occurs in eight Eddic poems, always as a b-verse.[19]

We can safely assume that the many poetic elements common to Anglo-Saxon, Old Icelandic, Old Saxon, and Old High German alliterative poetry reflect the common usage of a more or less unified and indisputably oral tradition stretching back in time to the early centuries of the Christian era, and perhaps much further.[20] All but the minor details of the separate poetic "dialects" developed and spread during times when anything but oral composition was out of the question. The whole poetic "grammar" was invented by oral poets. If a Germanic poet should recite a poetically "grammatical" passage of verse slowly enough for someone to write it down, or to write it down himself, he would presumably have the same difficulty keeping his thoughts and rhythm straight that such cooperative singers in the South Slavic oral tradition experience. Like his Yugoslav counterparts, he would presumably tend to lapse into prose.[21] His whole poetic apparatus was perfectly suited to oral composition. For centuries it had served and been perfected by oral poets. The very restrictions of the superimposed poetic grammar that made it poetry were at the same time the valuable patterns by which the poets constructed verses and episodes. In orally composed poetry there is little tension between "rules" and the patterns that satisfy the rules. The formulaic systems and themes both define the poetic and provide for its realization. The continuity and unity of the Germanic alliterative tradition would point unmistakably to oral composition even had writing materials been available to the early poets. But the unified body of formulas does not simply bolster the case for oral composition. It means, further, that no statement about the traditional or nontraditional status of a poetic element found in one South Germanic dialect can be valid without consulting the poetic tradition in its entirety. Our knowledge of the formulas—and even more importantly, the formulaic systems—of Anglo-Saxon poetry depends upon a knowledge of the formulas and formulaic systems of *Edda*, *Heliand*, *Muspilli*, and *Hildebrand*.

NOTES

1. *Speculum*, XXVIII (1953), 446–67.
2. "Whole Formulaic Verses in Greek and Southslavic Heroic Song," *Transactions and Proceedings of the American Philological Association*, LXIV (1933), 180.
3. For a full account of Parry's work and a most significant analysis of oral poetry, see A. B. Lord, *The Singer of Tales* (Cambridge, Mass., 1960).
4. Wayne A. O'Neil, "Another Look at Oral Poetry in *The Seafarer*," *Speculum*, XXXV (1960), 596, 2, gives a bibliography, to which should now be added R. P. Creed, "On the Possibility of Criticizing Old English Poetry," *TSLL*, III (1961), 97–106; Robert E. Diamond, "Theme as Ornament in Anglo-Saxon Poetry," *PMLA*, LXXVI (1961), 461–68; Francis P. Magoun, Jr., "Conceptions and Images Common to Anglo-Saxon Poetry and the *Kalevala*," *Britannica: Festschrift für Hermann M. Flasdieck* (Heidelberg, 1960), pp. 180–91; and "Some Notes on Anglo-Saxon Poetry," *Studies in Medieval Literature: In Honor of Professor Albert Croll Baugh* (Philadelphia, 1961), pp. 273–83; R. D. Stevick, "The Oral-Formulaic Analyses of Old English Verse," *Speculum*, XXXVII (1962), 382–89 (skeptical); and William Whallon, "The Diction of *Beowulf*," *PMLA*, LXXVI (1961), 309–19.
5. Lord, p. 129 and n.

6. Lord, pp. 129–38.

7. Lord, pp. 35–36.

8. See O'Neil, p. 598, for a statement of the possibility of describing with precision "those semantic and metric equals which are in complementary distribution with respect to alliteration."

9. Lord, p. 43.

10. *The Art of Beowulf* (Berkeley and Los Angeles, 1959), pp. 1–38.

11. As has been done by Creed in his study of "The *andswarode*-System in Old English Poetry," *Speculum*, XXXII (1957), 523–28.

12. J. J. Campbell, "Oral Poetry in *The Seafarer*," *Speculum*, XXXV (1960), 87–96, and O'Neil, *op. cit.*

13. Anglo-Saxon poems are cited from *Anglo-Saxon Poetic Records*, edd. G. P. Krapp and E. V. K. Dobbie (New York, 1931–53). The *Heliand* text cited is that of Otto Behaghel, *Heliand und Genesis*, 3d ed. (Halle-Salle, 1922).

14. These are in addition to the common formulas cited by Fr. Klaeber, *Beowulf and the Fight at Finnsburg*, 3d ed. (New York, 1950), p. lxvi. The community of diction among Germanic alliterative poems, like the formulaic nature of the diction, has long been a critical commonplace. The significance of this unified, formulaic tradition was not understood, however, until Parry and Lord's work on the oral poetry of Yugoslavia. Nor did the older critics seem to realize how thoroughly formulaic Germanic alliterative poetry is.

15. Sievers conveniently prints the parallels at the foot of the page in his edition of *Heliand* (Halle, 1878).

16. Sievers, p. 47.

17. Numbers following phrases given as supporting evidence refer to lines of *Heliand*. Anglo-Saxon and Old Icelandic citations precede the parallel phrases.

18. For further parallels in diction between Eddic and South Germanic poetry, see Jón Helgason, "Norges og Islands Digtning," *Litteraturhistorie*, ed. Sigurður Nordal (*Nordisk Kultur*, VII B, Copenhagen, 1953), pp. 6–7.

19. *Baldars draumar* 8, 9; *Völundarkviða* 33; *Helgakviða Hundingsbana I* 36; *Grípisspá* 11; *Reginsmál* 5; *Guðrúnarkviða I* 21; *Guðrúnarhvöt* 10; and *Völuspá* 45.

20. For the dating and unity of Germanic alliterative tradition, see W. P. Lehman, *The Development of Germanic Verse Form* (Austin, Tex., 1956), pp. 8, 29.

21. Lord, p. 127.

How Free was the Anglo-Saxon Scop?

FREDERIC G. CASSIDY
University of Wisconsin

THAT OLD ENGLISH POETRY was in some sense of the phrase "oral-formulaic" has now become an accepted fact, thanks to the writings of Professor F. P. Magoun, Jr.,[1] and those whom he has aroused to re-examine this literature. Yet as we must agree, the phrase, and the word "formula" itself, can easily be misunderstood or misapplied.[2] One basic area of uncertainty has to do with the structure of the formula, the degree of its fixity. Admitting that the scop used formulas in composing (or recomposing) his song as he presented it, just how adjustable or inflexible were they? How much did the oral-formulaic method limit the poetic creation, both action and product? In short, in what respects and to what extent did the scop have any freedom or poetic scope?

Milman Parry defined the formula in the first place as "a group of words which is regularly employed under the same metrical conditions to express a given essential idea,"[3] and this definition has generally been accepted. Though he applied it initially to Homeric verse, he found it applicable also to Serbocroatian; Albert B. Lord has further used it of Old English, Old French, and eighth-century Greek verse.

The key to the identification of a verbal formula as such has always been repetition; so the word itself implies. Ideally, when the singer is known, as with the Serbocroatian songs collected by Parry and Lord, the repetitions are sought only within the corpus of his recorded performances. But when, as in Old English, singers are unknown or the authorship of works is uncertain, one must rely on repetition of the phrase or word within the larger corpus of the surviving poetry. The dangers of this procedure are obvious. For example, it begs the question whether all Old English poetry is of the oral-formulaic type, or whether some may not have been composed by writers in imitation of the oral compositions. A related danger is that we may unwittingly use such a writer's repetition or imitation to "prove" that a phrase is an oral formula.[4] But these unavoidable dangers must be risked at the beginning in the hope that refinements in analysis and interpretation may later remove them.

It is now generally understood that the scop was relatively free as regards the larger parts of his composition. The "same" story could be told in expanded or contracted versions depending on the time available, the response of an audience, and the like.[5] So long as he held pretty well to the traditional narrative sequence (as required by history, logic, and so on) the scop was free to add or to elaborate themes or episodes, to digress in descriptive, sententious, or even lyrical passages.[6] Or he might reduce it to the bare essentials. All such alterations could be made without disturbing the formula; thus if any feature of the poetry brought a serious limitation to the scop, it was this: he had freedom to choose, but not greatly to change, formulas.

Opinions differ, however, as to how inflexible the formula was. Conceived as a fixed verbal unit which the scop fits together with others into a sort of mosaic,[7] the formula is a mere precut tessera, and the activity of composition seems largely mechanical. Seen in evolutionary terms, the formula, used and reused with small changes by generations of scops, tends to approach static perfection drained of individuality: "To the extent that a language is formulaic its individual components must be regarded as no more distinguished than other clichés."[8] Use of the oral formula limits the scop's freedom considerably: "The epic language was not entirely the servant of the poet; it was partly his master."[9]

Yet all students of the oral formula in Old English recognize that the repeated words that compose it need not be identical in every detail. If the stressed bases are repeated, the unstressed (that is, weakly stressed) morphemes, bound or free, may be varied without destroying the formula.[10] Thus *nap nihtscua* (*Seafarer* 31a) and *nipeð nihtscua* (*Wanderer* 104a),[11] despite the inflectional difference (which, however, does not change the verse type) are the "same" and support each other in proving this a formula. So *þæt wæs god cyning*, used repeatedly without change, is certainly a formula; preceded by *ac* it is still the same formula, and so would it be if *ond* were used rather than *ac*, *is* rather than *wæs*, or some other unstressed word were slipped in—say *ond þa ðæt wæs god cyning*.

We go from the small differences within the "same" formula to a larger kind of variation, that existing within a "formulaic system,"[12] when one of the *stressed* words is varied—for example if the synonymous *til* were used instead of *god*; or if *hlaford* took the place of *cyning*. How many such alterations can be made before one feels that it is no longer the "same" system? Is *þæt wæs til hlaford* in the same system with *þæt wæs god cyning*, or are we now in a different system? Or, since the first does not recur, must it be rejected as a formula despite its close similarity to the second? Is the repetition of words, even stressed words, all that makes the formula? Does the similarity among members of a formulaic system depend merely on word substitution, or is there some other feature of structure involved?

There is, of course, the stress, a prosodic feature, a part of the structure of the poetic verse. This is recognized when another kind of variation is admitted as not basically altering the formula: when the sequence of the stressed words can be reversed without changing the verse type. Thus *sawle minre* and *minre sawle* are used in the same poem and both are Sievers' verse type A1.[13] Yet what are we to say about *fela feorhcynna* (*Beowulf* 2266a) and *feorhcynna fela* (*Maxims* I, 14a), verse types D and E respectively? Which is more decisive, the repetition of the words in the same syntactic relation or the alteration of word order and rhythmic pattern? Must we find recurrences of each of these verses before it can be considered a formula, or do they support each other?

The borderline examples which have just been cited are by no means unique; the definition of the formula must take them into account. We are most certain we have a formula when the stressed words (a single compound word or a group) recur (a) identically or (b) with only changes in affixes or (c) with additional unstressed small words (prepositions, conjunctions, pronouns, and so on); we are less certain when (a) one of the stressed words recurs but the other is replaced by a synonym, (b) the same stressed words recur but in reversed word order, or (c) the changed word order also involves an altered verse type. But there is a more fundamental structural layer yet, which, once recognized for what it is, carries us toward a firmer concept of the formula.

It is a commonplace that a native but naïve speaker of a language knows its structural rules without knowing that he knows them. The proof that he knows them is that he obeys them constantly in using the language; what he does not know is the grammarian's way of stating these rules. Similarly, though the unlettered scop certainly could not have set forth Sievers' or any other articulated system to explain his prosodic practice, he too knew its rules. The proof is in his singing. Like the grammarian, the student of Old English poetry seeks to discover and to state the tacit rules by which the scop sang his songs.

As we are already aware, the scop's prosodic practice included two distinct sets of interacting rules. The first concerned the alliterative and stress system: the places where alliteration was required, where optional, and the verse types with their permitted variations. The scop knew that a verse with a single alliterating sound could go in either half of the line but that one with double alliteration could go only in the first half. He knew that he could use any type of verse in either half of the line, but convention and experience had shown him which fitted best together for particular uses.

The second distinct set of rules, as we now realize more clearly, concerned the formulas that must be fitted to the alliterative and stress system, ready-made for the scop's use when he had to compose. Scholars have necessarily approached these first in their most obvious form: as groups of specific words like those already cited. And the only way to recognize their formularity was by their actual recurrence. But this has left uncertain the status of the "borderline cases," and further, it leaves many probable formulas at the mercy of a fragmentary corpus. It has been frequently and ruefully remarked that if only we possessed a fuller body of Old English poetry, many verses that now appear unique would turn up again and, therefore, be proved to be formulas. As it is, we can never show that more than about eighty percent of verses were formulaic; we must resign ourselves to admitting an unprovable residue.

Recent investigation has shown, however, that the verbal formula rests upon one or another of a limited number of archetypal syntactic patterns, each furnishing a "frame" by means of which a very large and theoretically unlimited number of differently worded verbal formulas may be produced. This fact was sensed, though not fully worked out, by those who recognized the validity of the "formulaic system."[14] But now a large body of Old English poetry, consisting of the Elegies (709 lines) and all of *Beowulf* (3182 lines), has been examined with rather remarkable results; for it turns out that Old English verse is built upon only twenty-five syntactic patterns, six of which are noun-centered and nine verb-centered frames of frequent occurrence, five adjective-centered and five adverb-centered frames of less common occurrence, and five other minor types.[15] These were arrived at by classifying the syntactic patterns of the verses (half-lines); the verbal formulas provable by recurrence in the usual way were then observed in their relationship to the syntactic frames. Especially it was found that those verses unprovable as verbal formulas through lack of repetition nevertheless turned out to fit into these frames. In short, the syntactic frame gives us a new means of identifying as probable formulas some word groups that do not recur in the surviving body of poetry.[16]

Before considering further implications of the syntactic frame it would be well to give examples of the main types. They are presented in descending order of frequency; the number and percentage of occurrences are tabulated below.

1]   The AN frame: a stressed adjective or past participle qualifies a stressed noun:

> *hæþene sawle*   [*Bwf* 852a]
> *guðrinc goldwlanc*   [1881a]
> *wea widscofen*   [936a]

Since this frame permits stressed or unstressed beginnings, it may be realized through any of the verse types; its word order can also be reversed.

2] The N frame: one noun, normally a compound, receives both metrically heavy stresses:

> *breostgewædu*   [1211a]
> *of brydbure*   [921a]
> *to þæm heahsele*   [647a]
> *we synt gumcynnes*   [260a]

It may be realized through all verse types except E, most often through C; it is not reversed.

3] The N1N2 frame: a stressed noun in the genitive case qualifies another stressed noun or a nominal; the latter can be in any case:

> *wuldres wealdend*   [17a]
> *sceaþena þreatum*   [4b]
> *þær wæs madma fela*   [36b]

It has stressed or unstressed beginnings, hence may be realized through any of the verse types. It may be reversed, the genitive noun then following the other:

> *Geata dryhten*   [2991b]
> *dryhten Geata*   [2402a]

4] The OV frame: primary stresses fall upon a direct object and a verb:

> *sundwudu sohte*   [208a]
> *Heo þa fæhðe wræc*   [1333b]
> *niðwundor seon*   [1365b]

It is realized through all verse types, and with reversals.

5] The SV frame: primary stresses fall upon subject and verb:

> *deað oferswyðeð*   [1768b]
> *deaðfæge deog*   [850a]
> *Him wæs ful boren*   [1192a]

It is realized through all verse types, and with a few reversals.

6] The N/V frame: a stressed noun in an oblique case (dat. or gen.) precedes a stressed verb:

> aldrum neþdon   [510a]
> siðes getwæfde   [1908a]

It is realized through all verse types, and with a number of reversals.

7] The AdV frame: the primary stresses fall on an adverb which modifies a verb:

> ær gemette   [757b]
> oftost wisode   [1663b]
> innan healde   [2719b]

It is realized through all verse types; reversal is not uncommon.

8] The PV frame: primary stresses fall upon the object of a preposition and upon a verb:

> He æt wige gecrang   [1337b]
> ofer sæ sohtan   [2380a]

It is realized through all verse types except D; reversals are frequent.

9] The N(A3) frame: one noun in the second foot of the a-verse carries the alliteration:

> wæs min fæder   [262a]
> ðe me se goda   [355a]

10] The CV frame: a stressed complement appears with a stressed verb:

> colran weorðað   [2066b]
> gegyred hæfde   [1472b]

It is realized through all verse-types and with a few reversals.

These ten most frequent syntactic frames account for fully three-fourths of the verses in the poetry so far examined. The other fifteen, though less common, are all supported by enough examples to prove their reality as recurrent types. Space will be taken here to tabulate the numbers and percentual figures for only the first ten, as they occur in *Beowulf* and in the Elegies:

Frame	No. in Beow.	Percent in Beow.	No. in Eleg.	Percent in Eleg.
AN	932	14.6	226	15.9
N	830	13.0	126	8.9
N1N2	801	12.6	150 *	10.6 *
OV	527	8.2		
SV	479	7.5	166	11.7
N/V	352	5.5	*219	*15.4
AdV	335	5.3	76	5.4
PV	295	4.6	55	3.9
N(A3)	221	3.5	35 *	2.5 *
CV	209	3.3		

*Figures for the Elegies were grouped together; the combined numbers and percentages are given under N/V.

It may be noted that three very common noun-centered frames account for over 40 percent of the verses of *Beowulf*, of the Elegies over 35 percent. The next seven frames, each of which is used at least 200 times, are mostly verb-centered, and they together count for another almost 38 percent of the verses of *Beowulf*, of the Elegies almost 39 percent. In short, more than 78 percent of the verses of *Beowulf*, and more than 74 percent in the Elegies fall into only ten syntactic frame classes. It may be readily understood, therefore, how much a scop could depend on these to carry the burden of formulaic composition.[17]

If the ontogeny of the formula recapitulates the phylogeny of Old English verse,[18] it may be not entirely fanciful to reconstruct theoretically the origin of that verse from the nature and use of the oral formula. Each of the latter is a species of which the syntactic frame is the genus; and the genera are the survivors of a process of natural selection. The first scop, if we can imagine him, having something important to express and to communicate, feels the need of a language more emphatic or elevated than that of every day. Using special qualities of voice and rhythmic stress, more or less isochronous, he pulls into elliptical prominence only those words or phrases which his meaning requires. The result is a sort of incantation; not, however, to make something happen—rather, to make something heroic that has happened happen again in the telling, to establish it in memory, to beat out a place for it in history. The ictus of the hero's sword stroke is echoed in the verse itself. The beat is strengthened by alliteration, which also serves to yoke the verse units and, by its discontinuance, to mark the end of each line, or two-verse unit.

This kind of discourse is necessarily built with the words of fullest semantic value, the stress and alliteration increasing their force and reducing by contrast the relational role and the variety of syntactic morphemes. It lifts out of ordinary prosaic expression the nouns and verbs, adjectives and adverbs, with the syntactic frames that hold them together, and centers the verse units upon them. The phrases thus formed are gradually refined by repeated use, those features which prove effective and which aid the singer in his performance being retained. So the formulaic units evolve: a limited number of syntactic frames, and a much larger number[19] of conventional word groups fitting these frames, the formulas.

In the well-developed stage of the art, the singer has consciously learned, and if experienced can use with ease, a large number of these verbal formulas, suited to the songs he has to sing. But, realizing it or not, he also knows the syntactic frames (just as he knows the ordinary grammatical patterns of his language) which allow him on occasion— whether he is attempting a slightly different type of song, or is prompted by imagination to some unconventional wording, or even more, perhaps, if he has used a first verse with an alliterating sound which must be matched in the second verse but for which he knows no existing verbal formula—to make new wordings strictly analogous to the established ones and therefore safely within the system. In short, the syntactic frame, very much like Saussure's *langue*, underlies the verbal formula, the *parole*, and furnishes the scop a certain area of freedom within the patterned realm of his discipline.

Before leaving such a theoretical reconstruction, it is necessary to remind ourselves of certain hard facts. First, and ironically, no single exact record of an Old English scopic song as it was sung remains to us. We have only written records, which do not represent performances accurately,[20] and some of which will probably prove, once our methods of discrimination have been refined, to be imitations of scopic songs, made with a pen in the first place and perhaps never performed by a scop. However good these written records and imitations may be, we cannot see clearly through them. The veil may be thin but it is there. It was the hope of tearing away this veil from Homeric song that sent Milman Parry in the first place to study living Serbocroatian song.

Secondly, we should ever be aware that under normal conditions it would have taken about four times as long for a scribe to write down a song as for the scop to sing it. *Beowulf* could conceivably have been orally presented in one evening; to dictate it for writing would have taken many days.[21] The essence of the scopic song, as we understand it, was that it had no fixed text in the modern sense, but was remade on the spot every time with variations of one sort or another.[22] Lengthen out the time so that a scribe can write it down and one removes the very pressure which produced and preserved the formulaic method. While the scop is waiting, what is his mind doing? He is able to compose the next bit in a flash, choosing appropriate formulas. But now we may find him changing the words, perhaps from having lost the thread, or from quickly revising before he has to speak the next lines.[23] It is only plausible that this will produce differences other than those normal to oral presentation. And if this is true for a dictated song, how much truer for one written down by a lettered scop,[24] or, most of all, one originally composed in writing in imitation of the scopic method! Not only is there time to alter the larger parts, but to experiment with diction, to play with the formula, and ultimately to change its nature altogether.[25]

Returning finally to our original question, we may say that, so far as the situation of the unlettered Anglo-Saxon scop may be plausibly reconstructed, his oral performance of the "same" song, though never twice alike in detail, probably had a fairly stable narrative sequence and probably some essential episodes identifying the hero and telling of the actions that made him one.[26] But he had freedom to elaborate or to abbreviate. As to details, he had a stock of conventionalized verbal formulas to draw upon, some suited to specific points in the performance — introductory and concluding formulas, patronymic and genetonymic formulas, kennings and other tropes — but others too which were free to be used wherever appropriate.[27] It is these that have proved less rigid than some had thought, because, as we now see, all verbal formulas were referable to archetypal syntactic frames: the verbal details could change, not only unstressed elements but even stressed ones as in formulaic systems, within the steadying patterns of the syntax. Most fundamental of all, of course, was the structure of the poetic line with its two alliteratively linked halves, each built on a limited number of established stress patterns. Yet even here the syntactic frame beneath permitted the scop to choose among synonyms for alliteration and to adjust the verse types in various ways.[28] The Anglo-Saxon scop, like any other poet, had to work within the restrictions of his medium. But these were more flexible, less confining, than the "formulaic" idea has seemed to suggest.

NOTES

1. "Oral-Formulaic Character of Anglo-Saxon Narrative Poetry," *Speculum*, XXVIII (1953), 446–67, was the first article to be printed.
2. R. D. Stevick, "The Oral-Formulaic Analyses of Old English Verse," *Speculum*, XXXVII (1962), 382–89, points out ambiguities in terminology and calls for clarification. In the present paper "scop" always means a singer who performs orally, "song," the composition he sings on a single occasion; other definitions are given in the text and notes.
3. Quoted from A. B. Lord, *The Singer of Tales* (Cambridge, Mass., 1960), p. 30.
4. Stevick, pp. 388–89. One might count something, nevertheless, for the contemporary imitator's knowledge of oral singing.
5. Magoun, p. 447. See also Lord, Ch. 5, and the parallel tabulations in Ch. 4 and App. 2 of different performances of Serbocroatian heroic songs.
6. There is still a question whether *Beowulf* was typical of the extended

heroic song, and whether its mixture of poetic types was a by-product of its length or perhaps an indication that it was not exclusively the production of an oral singer.

7. This figure goes back to W. W. Lawrence, *Beowulf and Epic Tradition* (Cambridge, Mass., 1928), p. 4, "The art of the singer was coming to resemble that of a worker in mosaic, placing in combinations pieces ready to his hand." William Whallon, "The Diction of *Beowulf*," *PMLA*, LXXVI (1961), 309–19, considers this remark a fair one to make about Homeric poetry but not very accurate about *Beowulf*, which he considers "far from being totally formulaic" (p. 319).

8. Whallon, p. 310.

9. Whallon, p. 311. Whallon is quoting from Frederick M. Combellack, "Milman Parry and Homeric Artistry," *CL*, XI (1959), 193–208, but presents the idea of the rigidity of the formula only to oppose it. Magoun (pp. 447–48) quotes Parry concerning the growth of the formulaic phrase: "In time the needed number of such phrases is made up: each idea to be expressed in the poetry has its formula for each metrical need, and the poet, who would not think of trying to express ideas outside the traditional field of thought of poetry, can make his verses easily by means of a diction which time has proved to be the best."

10. The structure of the verse type limits the number and positions of such additional morphemes.

11. These examples are taken from Wayne A. O'Neil, "Oral-Formulaic Structure in Old English Elegiac Poetry," Univ. of Wisconsin diss. (1960), p. 30.

12. The recognition of the existence of the "formulaic system" goes back at least to Milman Parry, whom Magoun quotes (pp. 450–51): "Any group of two or more such like formulas makes up a system, and the system may be defined in turn as a group of phrases which have the same metrical value and which are enough alike in thought and words to leave no doubt that the poet who used them knew them not only as a single formula but also as formulas of a certain type." The term has been adopted generally.

13. These examples are from *Resignation*, ll. 11 and 61. (Quoted from O'Neil, p. 32. The next two examples: *Ibid.*, p. 30.)

14. Parry's definition (n. 12 above) does not mention syntax. Magoun's discussion (p. 452) of the "large number of verses consisting of a compound present participle, of which there are many in *Beowulf*," which tend "to break down into various semantic systems such as the idea of 'seafarer' expressed by *brim-* and *sæ-liðende*" take us close to the N frame (see below). R. P. Creed in "The Making of an Anglo-Saxon Poem," *ELH*, XXVI (1959), 445–54, comes to the very edge of the concept: "To be useful to the singer every phrase or word which is metrically significant should also be a syntactic entity. . . . It should be, for example, an article and its noun, or a noun or pronoun and its verb, or a verb and its object, or a preposition and its noun, not such syntactically meaningless groups as, for example, an adverb and a preposition" (p. 446). Lord also came close to stating the basic role of the syntactic frame when he discussed the singer's manner of learning his craft (pp. 35–37).

15. O'Neil made the first classification of types (pp. 134–35), his corpus being the whole body of Old English elegiac verse (listed pp. 13–14). In "The Syntactic Basis of the Poetic Formula in Beowulf," Univ. of Wisconsin diss. (1962), Godfrey L. Gattiker took *Beowulf* as his corpus and based his statement of types (Chs. II and III) on O'Neil's, but with some small differences.

16. The rest of the Old English poetic remains should now be examined for the syntactic frames underlying the provable formulas. Though some details of O'Neil's and Gattiker's studies may then need to be revised, the considerable body of data they have examined leaves no doubt that the syntactic frame was a functioning structural reality.

17. O'Neil's definition is as follows:

"By a syntactic pattern is meant a recurrent morphemic and relational frame into which the words of a verse fit" (p. 83). He discusses the implications for literary study (pp. 119–22), especially with respect to the "Riming Poem" (pp. 122–27), which turns out to be less anomalous than is usually thought. Gattiker alters O'Neil's definition slightly, defining the syntactic frame as "a recurrent morphemic and relational pattern into which the word or words bearing primary stress fit" (p. 150). He discusses the technique of composition of the *Beowulf* poet in this light (pp. 151–66).

18. Old English as a type of Germanic versification, of course. Magoun discusses the origins of this from what Tacitus and others have written, which leads us to believe in the existence of a long tradition going back to Continental sources (p. 447).

19. Magoun visualizes "a vast reservoir of formulas" which would fill virtually every need of the scop (p. 446). Their number would be limited, one would guess, less by the scop's powers of memory than by the limitations of his subject matter.

20. This point is discussed by Mac-Edward Leach, "Problems of Collecting Oral Literature," *PMLA*, LXXVII (1962), 335–40. We are forced to assume that our written remains are basically similar to the performed scopic songs, correcting ourselves as best we can by such excellent studies as Lord's. Cædmon's song is a fragment.

21. Lord has heard Serbocroatian songs much longer than *Beowulf* performed in a single evening. He estimates that it would take "undoubtedly more than one day of dictating and writing" (p. 200) to get *Beowulf* written down. I estimate it

at from four to five days under the conditions of the time.

22. Magoun, p. 447; Lord, p. 5.

23. Highly instructive in this regard are Lord's parallel versions (see n. 5). The dictated version in his Chart IV differs more from the recorded versions than the latter differ among themselves, but the portion given is too short to be trusted, and the complete versions have not yet appeared in the Parry-Lord series of *Serbocroatian Heroic Songs*, 1953, 1954.

24. No such holographs survive in Old English. One would expect the writer to edit them well.

25. O'Neil's discussion (see n. 17) of the "Riming Poem," an experimental composition from late in the OE period, probably a product of the cloister, though it breaks away markedly from formulaic style, nevertheless holds to the syntactic frames. Though unorthodox, it thus keeps touch with the tradition. (It may be noted here that though the syntactic frame can help to distinguish a good formulaic verse from a defective one, it cannot help to distinguish verse of oral origin from that of written origin imitating it.)

26. Such components, in Lord's experience (p. 71), vary with both the singer and the song.

27. Some OE verbal formulas were rather unadaptable, others protean, usable in quite different situations. This difference in degrees of adaptability deserves more attention by scholars. A related point about the scop's originality is made by S. B. Greenfield in *Speculum*, XXX (1955), 205.

28. Whallon furnishes useful lists of synonyms which the scop had at hand and which he could vary systemically within the frames according to need (pp. 316–17).

Beowulf and Odysseus

ALBERT BATES LORD

Harvard University

ORAL TRADITION leaves its mark not only in the formulaic style of verse making and the presence of repeated themes but also in the persistence of certain basic narrative patterns, in spite of sea changes and rein-terpretations. There seems to be evidence that one of the patterns found in Odysseus' story also underlies a section of the first half of *Beowulf*.

Friedrich Panzer's study of the relationship of the Bearson folktale to the story of Beowulf focuses on the struggles of the hero with two monsters, the second of which is in the "other world."[1] There are surely many similarities both in essence and in detail between the folktale and this part of the Old English epic. Rhys Carpenter has reviewed the adventures of Odysseus as told by the hero, concentrating especially on the incident of the Cyclops, and has found a parallel between them (or it) and the folktale of the Bearson.[2] According to the work of these two eminent scholars, Beowulf and Odysseus have much in common. They share at least one traditional story pattern.

It is frequently pointed out that the taunting of Beowulf by Unferth is reminiscent of the challenge and insult to Odysseus by Euryalus at the court of Alcinous on Phaeacia.[3] In this case the parallel is between themes, incidents in a story, namely, calumny of a stranger at a feast, whereas in the previous instance the parallel was between narrative conglomerates.

So far as I am aware, no attempt has been made to place the events leading up to the Unferth episode against those leading up to the taunt of Euryalus in the *Odyssey* to see if the parallelism goes beyond the single theme to include the larger complex.

In the Old English poem we have the following sequence: (A) Beowulf has a ship built, (B) crosses a body of water, (C) is met by the coast guard on the opposite shore, and (D) after identification is led to Heorot, (E) where he is graciously received and entertained, except that (F) during the entertainment he is, without provocation, insulted by Unferth, but (G) after he has proven himself by the long story of his adventures with Breca, (H) the entertainment continues and is ended (I) when all go to bed. In the *Odyssey* the pattern is as follows: (A) Odysseus builds a raft on the island of Ogygia, where he is being detained by Calypso, (B) crosses a body of water, on which he loses his ship but is provided a substitute for one by Ino, (C) encounters Nausicaa and her maidens on the shore, and (D) is directed to the palace of Alcinous, (E) where he is graciously received and entertained, except that (F) during the games he is, without provocation, insulted by Euryalus, but (G) after he has proven himself, (H) the entertainment continues, including his identification and story of his adventures, and is ended (I) by all going to bed. It is clear that the two sections have the same basic pattern of narrative. It will be worthwhile to examine the subdivisions in more detail.

A] Both Beowulf and Odysseus are presented as having neither means of transportation nor companions at the beginning of this section. They both acquire a new ship by building it or having it built. Beowulf at this same time acquires companions. These companions are, however, not a necessary element in the section of story that we are considering. Only when one of them is destroyed by Grendel before the attack on Beowulf himself do the companions enter the essential plot. At the moment of which we are speaking, the sequence of events from the departure of Beowulf from home to the end of the banquet, the companions are not necessary. On the other hand, in the *Odyssey*, although the companions do not appear at the moment we are studying, they are a significant element in Odysseus' complete story. He sets out at the beginning of the war with comrades, he leaves Troy with comrades, and they are destroyed in the course of his wanderings. The sequence within sequences that we are examining, partial microcosm of the macrocosm, finds the hero situated at the point where his comrades have all been lost.

B] Beowulf's sea voyage is uneventful. As indicated above, Odysseus suffers shipwreck, loss of raft, and acquires Ino's wimple to assist him. This loss is possibly the remains of the theme of loss of comrades and/or ship, which seems to be part of the *Beowulf* story also; for Beowulf loses one comrade to Grendel. As a matter of fact, the presence of the shipwreck in the *Odyssey* pattern under consideration is accounted for by Odysseus' previous shipwreck, in which the remnant of his companions was finally lost. This occurred just before his arrival at Ogygia. Thus the sea voyage between Ogygia and Phaeacia and the method of landing, that is, swimming to shore with a log or a wimple, are in reality a duplication of the journey from the Isle of the Sun to Ogygia. This is a peculiarity of the form of the theme in the *Odyssey*.

c]   In both *Beowulf* and the *Odyssey* the traveler is met by someone.
The coast guard fits well the stark Germanic heroic scene; Nausicaa and
her maidens on the shore of Phaeacia are meaningful in their setting
also. Indeed, the comparative absence of female figures in *Beowulf*
contrasts strikingly with their important role in the *Odyssey*. When
Odysseus lands on Ogygia, it is to be with Calypso; on Phaeacia,
Nausicaa and the queen, Arete, take much of his attention. There is
some evidence to show that the journeys have a woman as their object.
Although the basic frame is the same in the Old English poem and in the
Greek one, the outward form is different.

d]   Identification is present at this point in the northern song, but not
in Homer. This element is delayed in the *Odyssey* until after the gracious
reception of the stranger. It is present, but occurs at a different point in
the sequence. In both poems, however, the person who meets the hero
conducts him to the abode of the leader, although Nausicaa, for reasons
of propriety, does not take Odysseus all the way into town, but gives him
directions.

e]   The correspondences in the theme of entertainment are transparent and do not need to be commented on further here.

f]   This theme (the insult) and the next (the reply) are the most
distinctive in our sequence, because they mar the joy and peace of the
banquet and entertainment. There is an interesting sequel to the relationship between Beowulf and Unferth and between Odysseus and
Euryalus which is found later in each poem. It has been pointed out
before, of course,[4] but cannot be omitted here. Unferth gives to Beowulf
his sword for use in the mere, in spite of the fact that Beowulf has a
sword of his own. This incident is outside of our sequence in *Beowulf*,
but it has a parallel within the sequence in the *Odyssey*. During the
entertainment that continues after the insult to Odysseus, Euryalus
approaches and gives to our hero a beautiful sword and an apology.
    Another element associated with the theme of Unferth's taunt is
the flashback related by Beowulf in answer to Unferth's insult, the
relating of a past adventure. It is in the continuation of the entertainment at the court of Alcinous that Odysseus relates his wanderings at
such great length. In other words, the telling of a story from the past is
a constant, and hence very probably significant, element in our sequence.
It has reached the ultimate in expansion in the *Odyssey*.

i]   All go to bed. Is it significant that in *Beowulf* the most important
woman in the poem appears in our sequence for the first time and special
mention is made that Hrothgar at the end of the feasting left the hall on

his way to bed with Wealhtheow? Perhaps so, but we shall have to analyze more material before reaching even a tentative decision.

There is, therefore, a real parallelism between the sequence in *Beowulf* distinguished by the Unferth incident and the sequence in the *Odyssey* distinguished by the taunting by Euryalus. What follows in *Beowulf*, namely the fight with Grendel, has a parallel in the *Odyssey*, as Carpenter has pointed out, in the blinding of the Cyclops, but it does not occur at the same point in the story. The subsequent events in the *Odyssey* are the equipping of Odysseus for his return to Ithaca after he has recounted all his adventures.

As a matter of fact, the same pattern of equipping, sailing over the sea, landing, being met by someone, being entertained and reviled, is repeated in Odysseus' return to Ithaca. The ship provided by the Phaeacians is a special ship, but its crew could not by any means be called companions for Odysseus on his voyage to Ithaca. Like the journey of Beowulf, that of Odysseus in this case is uneventful, but far more mysterious. As for a possible vestige of the loss of both ship and companions, it should be noted that the ship of the Phaeacians was turned to stone on its return, but of its crew nothing was said.

It is typical of the *Odyssey* that the hero is met on the shore by a female figure, and that a goddess, Athena. Straightway the question of identity arises between Odysseus and Athena, in a scene which is almost a parody.

From here to the end of the poem the sequence is not always clear because of the tendency of the *Odyssey* to duplication and ornamentation, but what does stand out is that the poem contains the distinctive elements of entertainment, vilification, acquiring of weapons (cf. Unferth), the long flashback (Odysseus to his wife), and finally bed. The elements are all there. Identification is repeated a number of times, but it is still identification. Vilification also takes several forms. But in this final instance of the sequence in the *Odyssey* the hero meets and slays those who are haunting the house, namely the suitors of Penelope. The events in Phaeacia have been a duplication of events that are to happen in Ithaca up to the end of the banqueting, when the story takes the same turn as in *Beowulf*. In the *Odyssey* the sequence of the narrative goes from release from detention (Calypso on Ogygia, Arete on Phaeacia; an element common to these two examples in the *Odyssey*, but missing in *Beowulf*) to the end of feasting, in which the hero is taunted, and all retire for the night. The parallel in *Beowulf*, then, is to the homecoming of Odysseus *and* the slaying of the suitors, the disturbers of the peace and order of Odysseus' halls.

We might carry the comparison still further. The slaying of the suitors begins a feud with their families and the relatives set out to take revenge upon Odysseus and Telemachus, who have gone off to Laertes' farm. Can this be parallel to the desire for revenge on the part of Grendel's dam? In the *Odyssey* the theme is abortive, because the *deus ex machina* stops the feud. Yet, it should be noted that the story persists in describing a descent to the lower world (the so-called Second Nekyia) at this point in the sequence where in *Beowulf* the hero goes down into the mere.

At the other end of the story there are correspondences that are, at least, suggestive. In both *Beowulf* and the *Odyssey* considerable point is made of the fact that a "time of troubles" has lasted for twelve (*Beowulf*) or twenty (*Odyssey*) years. During this period a monster has killed the inhabitants, or suitors have devoured the substance, of a kingdom. The return of Odysseus and the arrival of Beowulf have the same salutary effect. Evil doers are punished and order is restored.

Does this mean that the story of the first part of *Beowulf* is a "return story"? Not necessarily. It does mean that the narrative frame of part of the return story is similar to, if not identical with, the sequence of narrative in another kind of adventure tale. There is still another example in the *Odyssey* of the pattern "ship journey – taunting at banquet or games – bed." This section of narrative, it would seem, is distinctive or separate enough to have an existence of its own.

In the early books of the *Odyssey* Telemachus, who even before this has had his share of vilification and taunting, at last is able, with the help of Athena, to equip a ship and to cross the sea to Pylos, where he is entertained by Nestor. In the course of the conversation with Nestor, there is very probably the vestige of a taunt. Nestor has expressed the pious hope that Athena may show the same care of Telemachus that she did of Odysseus. Telemachus, ever the defeatist, says that this is too much to be hoped for. He dare not expect such happiness. Athena rounds on him with

> Telemachus, . . . What a thing to say! However far a man may have strayed, a friendly god could bring him safely home, and that with ease. And for myself, I would rather live through untold hardships to get home in the end and see that happy day, than come back and die at my own hearth, as Agamemnon died by the treachery of Aegisthus and his wife.[5]

Certainly not a strong taunt, but this upbraiding does take place at the proper point in the frame, and it should be remembered that taunting has been a characteristic of the story of Telemachus up to this point, taunting both at banquet and at assembly. When the exact sequence is not kept in oral traditional narrative, often the elements all occur in the story but in different order. After the banqueting and entertainment, during which Nestor tells a long story (like Odysseus' tale of his wanderings), all go off to bed.

This example of the pattern occurs not as "return" but on the outward journey, as the young hero goes forth on his first adventure. In the *Odyssey* the story of Telemachus is abortive. *Beowulf* shows the heroic conclusion with its slaying of monsters. But I wonder if the story of the rescue of the maiden in some Yugoslav oral songs is not both older and more typical. The hero finds himself in disguise in the city of the enemy whither he has gone, after various degrees of vilification, in order to rescue a girl whom he has already accepted as his betrothed.[6] His journey, which is overland, has been uneventful, and on arrival in the enemy city he betakes himself to a tavern, where he is cared for by the tavern keeper, a woman. The question of identification arises, because the tavern keeper thinks that she recognizes the hero. In the course of recognition she recounts a long history of their previous encounter many years before. Then she leads him to his betrothed and advises how the escape may be managed. After the slaughter of those who hinder the girl's marriage, including a suitor, the wedding takes place.

The examples of the narrative sequence which we have been investigating seem to indicate that it is useful and has meaning both on the return of the hero to his home to set everything in order and to remarry his wife and on the outward journey of the young hero to win a wife. In *Beowulf* the pattern has remained in spite of the loss in this heroic Germanic society of the purpose of winning a wife or returning to one. Perhaps Wealhtheow's role is vestigial. Further study may also reveal the function of vilification in this narrative pattern. That it is a necessary element is demonstrated by its constant appearance.

The *Odyssey* of Homer had no direct influence on *Beowulf*; the Old English poet did not borrow from Homer. But they both belonged, as the present-day Yugoslav singer of tales does also, to an Indo-European oral epic narrative tradition. The story patterns in such a tradition are very old, amazingly stable, surprisingly alive, whether we observe them in the eighth century B.C., the eighth century A.D., or in our own time.[7]

NOTES

1. *Studien zur germanischen Sagengeschichte, I. Beowulf* (München, 1910).
2. *Folk Tale, Fiction and Saga in the Homeric Epics* (Berkeley, 1946), pp. 136 ff., 184 ff.
3. *Beowulf and the Fight at Finnsburg*, ed. Fr. Klaeber (Boston, 1941), pp. 149–150.
4. Example, J. A. Work, "Odyssean Influence on the *Beowulf*," *Philological Quarterly*, IX (1930), 399–402.
5. Book III, ll. 229 ff., trans. E. V. Rieu.
6. See Milman Parry and A. B. Lord, *Serbocroatian Heroic Songs* (Cambridge, Mass., and Belgrade, Vol. I, 1954, Vol. II, 1953), No. 24.
7. For another aspect of comparison of elements in *Beowulf* with elements in the Homeric poems see R. P. Creed, "The Singer looks at his Sources," *Comparative Literature*, XIV (1962), 44–52.

Ibn Faḍlān's Account of the Rūs with Some Commentary and Some Allusions to *Beowulf*

H. M. SMYSER

Connecticut College

In 921, Ibn Faḍlān set out as secretary of an embassy from the Calif of Bagdad to the king of the Bulgars of the Middle Volga, a Turkish people with a remote and more or less nominal relationship to the Bulgars of the Balkans.[1] Of this mission he wrote an account, called a *Risāla*,[2] in which he described, among the various peoples with whom the embassy came into contact, a tribe of Swedish Rūs Vikings, or, more accurately, Rūs armed merchants, and among the events of the expedition the witnessing of a funeral which these Rūs accorded one of their chief men, a cremation within a ship, preceded by ceremonies nowhere else described nor inferrable from any literary allusions or grave finds. This extraordinarily interesting travel history has until recently been known to the modern world not in its entirety but only through generous excerpts preserved by the Arab Yāqūt, who lived from 1179 to 1229. These excerpts appear under various headings in Yāqūt's Geographical Dictionary, one of the headings being "Rūs."[3] In 1923, however, the Turkish scholar Ahmed Zeki Validi Togan discovered at Meshed in Iran a manuscript, probably of the eleventh century,[4] of the complete *Risāla*, and in 1939 he brought forth an edition for the Deutsche Morgen-ländische Gesellschaft,[5] with an introduction in German, a translation into German, copious and vastly learned *Exkurse* on a multitude of topics, and footnotes to the translation concerned with textual and other matters and including an interesting and previously neglected epitome of Ibn Faḍlān by the sixteenth-century Persian geographer Amīn Rāsī, to which we shall return shortly.

Zeki Validi was not alone in the fruitful exploitation of his discovery; other important editions and translations followed.[6] Among these is to be mentioned especially the richly annotated translation into French by Marius Canard, to whom, along with Zeki Validi, the present writer is most heavily and gratefully indebted. In my Englishing (*i*), I have used Canard's and Zeki Validi's translations alike, noting significant variations and discussing them in my commentary (*ii*). Canard makes a judicious and selective use of Zeki Validi and of all the works listed in my note 6 except the earlier (1939) edition and translation into Russian by Kovalevsky, which was not available to him. Zeki Validi, copious to the point of unwieldiness, runs true to form in his discussion of the Rūs, concerning whom he has consulted several Germanists, including the noted Rudolf Meissner and the noted Heinrich Heimpel. I have drawn on this material somewhat more fully than did Canard and have supplemented it in places. It is my hope that this little compendium may be of interest to students of *Beowulf*.

Before we turn to the translation, a word about the *Risāla* and its author and about the possible role of Amīn Rāzī as a witness to an earlier version than that of Meshed.

The route which the embassy took from Bagdad to the Bulgar settlement on the Middle Volga was circuitous: it swung far out to the east to Bokhara, then turned west through the Oxus towns of Kath and Ǧurǧānīya,[7] then north over the Ust-Ürt plateau between the Caspian and Aral seas, and on north to Bulgar,[8] south of the modern city of Kazan, on the great Volga bend a few miles below where the Kama flows into it. The embassy, which started on 2 April 921, reached its destination on 12 May 922, having waited out a bitterly cold three months at Ǧurǧānīya.[9] It was there, at the Bulgar capital, that Ibn Faḍlān was to come into contact with the Rūs.

Ibn Faḍlān's descriptions of the peoples encountered on the way — Khwarizmians, Oghuz (Ghuzz Turks), Pechenegs, Bashkirs — with details of dress, daily customs, burial rites, and religious beliefs, are fascinating and no doubt a veritable gold mine for students of the history and ethnology of this gateway region between East and West.[10] The greater part of the *Risāla* is devoted to this journey and to a description of the Bulgars and of the so-called Jewish Khazars,[11] about whom Ibn Faḍlān learned from his Bulgar hosts. The remainder of the *Risāla* (at least of what survives: there is no account of the return to Bagdad) is devoted to the Rūs. This is about one fifth of the *Risāla*. The other four fifths do not concern us here except insofar as they can be used in coming to a judgment as to the accuracy and veracity of the author as a reporter.

Although Ibn Faḍlān had had the religious training of a *faqīh*, that is, an expert in canon law and casuistry, he was attached to the embassy as secretary; the embassy also had a *faqīh*, who was to instruct the king of the Bulgars in the orthodox Muslim rite of Bagdad. This *faqīh*, however, remained timidly behind in Ǧurǧānīya, and Ibn Faḍlān performed his duties. He did so so well that he won from the redoubtable king of the

Bulgars—"a voice issuing from a barrel," he calls him—the grudging and cryptic but obviously laudatory appellation of "Abū Bekr the Truth-ful."[12] A number of modern orientalists have felt that this judgment was merited.

Two of these, the late R. P. Blake and R. N. Frye, jointly speak of Ibn Faḍlān as an eyewitness "whose general reliability as a reporter is vouched for by the accuracy of his observations of the manners and customs of the tribes through whom he passed."[13] Marius Canard speaks of his "vive curiosité" and his "faculté d'observation étonnante," and comments that if, in giving us a rich fund of information, he picks up a number of more or less legendary details such as one finds in other Arabian geographical works, "le contenu concret de son exposé est considérable et donne l'impression d'avoir été puisé dans la réalité."[14] Zeki Validi is stronger in his praise. Modern travelers in the regions concerned, he says, well might envy Ibn Faḍlān "die lakonische, aber glänzende Beschreibung der Länder, die bewundernswerte Aufmerk-samkeit und Beobachtungsgabe in der Beschreibung der Sitten und Gebräuche fremder Völker bis ins kleinste Detail."[15] Ritter quotes Kovalevsky as commenting that Ibn Faḍlān gives us practically none of the commonplace fables of travel literature, and himself adds that this is perhaps attributable to the small role played by literature in the training of a *faqīh*.[16] It will not do, however, to say that all extravagances in the *Risāla* come in descriptions which Ibn Faḍlān is repeating at secondhand, for in the land of the Bulgars (ZV § 49) he explicitly "saw" a display of northern lights that presented a battle scene with accompanying, awe-inspiring sound effects, and in the same land (§ 52) he "saw" a forest of which the trees were thickly draped with serpents, sometimes a dozen to a branch, and he "saw" among them a particular serpent with the thickness of a large tree trunk. Similarly disconcerting are a few repetitions, of which the following may serve as an example:

§ 20, end, concerning the Oguz (Ghuzz Turks): They do not wash either after defecation or urination, nor do they bathe because of pollution from orgasm, nor in other circumstances.
§ 83, concerning the Rūs: They are the filthiest of God's creatures. They have no modesty in defecation and urination, nor do they wash after pollution from orgasm, nor do they wash their hands after eating. They are thus like wild asses.

In the main, however, Ibn Faḍlān's *Risāla*, as presented in the Meshed MS., like the excerpts given by Yāqūt, is sober enough and self-consistent enough to invite consideration as history. I shall give a close summary of it based on the translations both of Zeki Validi and Canard. I shall also reproduce the aforementioned abridgment of Ibn Faḍlān offered by the sixteenth-century Persian geographer Amīn Rāzī,

which both Zeki Validi and Canard translate, but a word of explanation
at this point is in order, for the question of what authority to grant
Amīn Rāzī is a perplexing one.[17]

Amīn Rāzī was first brought into consideration in connection with
Ibn Faḍlān by Zeki Validi (1939), but he was taken up also by Kovalevsky
in the latter's second edition (1956), and he is treated very seriously by
Canard. It must be granted, of course, that although Amīn Rāzī wrote
in 1593, some 671 years after Ibn Faḍlān, his source may have been an
older and better one than that preserved in the Meshed MS. or in the
various MSS. of Yāqūt (d. 1229). When both Zeki Validi and Canard say
that the original *Risāla* must have been more detailed than the *Risāla*
of the Meshed MS.[18], it is chiefly or solely the variants in Amīn Rāzī
that move them to this opinion. After studying these variants, and also
Zeki Validi's arguments based on them (pp. xi–xii and *Exk.* § 91a and
§ 91c), I have come to the conclusion that it would be wrong not to consider Amīn Rāzī a witness to an older text of Ibn Faḍlān than Meshed or
Yāqūt.[19] What makes the problem of Amīn Rāzī's independence hard to
judge is the fact, as it seems to me, that he is a *rationalizer*; for example,
in describing the "breast boxes" (large convex brooches) worn by Rūs
women, he adds the rather improbable explanation that they were worn
from infancy to prevent the breasts from growing large. Unlike the
Meshed text and Yāqūt, he sees the sexual performances preceding the
cremation as celebration of a posthumous marriage. Nothing could be
more plausible, but one wonders whether it is a keen mind in Amīn Rāzī[20]
or his use of a better manuscript of Ibn Faḍlān that contributes this
plausibility. Nevertheless, there is a residue of data, some of which fit
neatly into the account, that can hardly have been inference even of the
keenest mind, and on the basis of these I think we must view Amīn Rāzī
as offering independent testimony as to the original *Risāla*.[21] For this
reason I reproduce him in full.

i

THE FIRST ALLUSION to the Rūs comes (in ZV § 77) toward the close
of the description of the Bulgars: when the Rūs or people of another race
come with slaves (for sale), the king of the Bulgars has a right to choose
one slave in each ten (for himself).

The full description begins:

§ 80. I have seen the Rūs as they came on their merchant journeys
and encamped by the Atil [i.e., Volga]. I have never seen more
perfect physical specimens, tall as date palms, blond and ruddy;
they wear neither *qurtaqs* [tunics] nor caftans, but the men wear a

garment which covers one side of the body and leaves a hand free.

§ 81.   Each man has an axe, a sword, and a knife and keeps each by
him at all times. The swords are broad and grooved, of Frankish sort.
Every man is tattooed from finger nails to neck with dark green (or
green or blue-black) trees, figures, etc.

§ 82.   Each woman wears on either breast a box [*Buchse, boite*] of
iron, silver, copper, or gold; the value of the box indicates the wealth
of the husband. Each box has a ring from which depends a knife.
The women wear neck rings of gold and silver, one for each 10,000
dirhems[22] which her husband is worth; some women have many.
Their most prized ornaments are green glass beads (corals) of clay,
which are found on the ships [so ZV; Canard: are beads of green
glass of the same make as ceramic objects that one finds on their
ships]. They trade beads among themselves and pay a *dirhem* for a
bead [Canard: they pay an exaggerated price for them, for they buy
them for a *dirhem* apiece]. They string them as necklaces for their
women.

(AR [two passages given in the following order by ZV, pp. 83 f.]:

1. *In place of gold [i.e., coins] the Rūs use sable skins. No standard
measure is known in the land; they buy and sell by dry measure
(?). They are very fond of pork and many of them who have assumed the garb of Muslimism miss it very much.   2. The Rūs are
a great host, all of them red haired; they are big men with white
bodies. The women of this land have boxes made, according to
their circumstances and means, out of gold, silver, and wood. From
childhood they bind these to their breasts so that their breasts will
not grow larger. Each man puts a chain around his wife's neck
for each thousand dinars of his wealth.*)

§ 83.   This section opens with the "filthy creatures" passage quoted
on page 94 and then continues:
When they have come from their land and anchored on, or tied up at
the shore of, the Atil [Volga], which is a great river, they build big
houses of wood on the shore, each holding ten to twenty persons
more or less. Each man has a couch on which he sits. With them are
pretty slave girls destined for sale to merchants; a man will have
sexual intercourse with his slave girl while his companion [*sic*] looks
on. Sometimes whole groups will come together in this fashion, each
in the presence of the others. A merchant who arrives to buy a slave
girl from them may have to wait and look on while a Rūs completes
the act of intercourse with a slave girl.

§ 84.   Every day they must wash their faces and heads and this
they do in the dirtiest and filthiest fashion possible: to wit, every
morning a girl servant brings a great basin of water; she offers this
to her master and he washes his hands and face and his hair—he
washes it and combs it out with a comb in the water; then he blows
his nose and spits into the basin. When he has finished, the servant
carries the basin to the next person, who does likewise. She carries

the basin thus to all the household in turn, and each blows his nose, spits, and washes his face and hair in it.

§ 85. When the ships come to this mooring place, everybody goes ashore with bread, meat, onions, milk and *nabīd* [an intoxicating drink, perhaps beer²³] and betakes himself to a long upright piece of wood that has a face like a man's and is surrounded by little figures [idols], behind which are long stakes in the ground. The Rūs prostrates himself before the big carving and says, "O my Lord, I have come from a far land and have with me such and such a number of girls and such and such a number of sables," and he proceeds to enumerate all his other wares. Then he says, "I have brought you these gifts," and lays down what he has brought with him, and continues, "I wish that you would send me a merchant with many dinars and *dirhems*, who will buy from me whatever I wish and will not dispute anything I say." Then he goes away.

If he has difficulty selling his wares and his stay is prolonged, he will return with a gift a second or third time. If he has still further difficulty, he will bring a gift to all of the little idols and ask their intercession, saying, "These are the wives of our Lord and his daughters and sons [Canard omits "and sons"]." And he addresses each idol in turn, asking intercession and praying humbly. Often the selling goes more easily and after selling out he says, "My Lord has satisfied my desires; I must repay him," and he takes a certain number of sheep or cattle and slaughters them, gives part of the meat as alms, brings the rest and deposits it before the great idol and the little idols around it, and suspends the heads of the cattle or sheep on the stakes.²⁴ In the night, dogs come and eat all, but the one who has made the offering says, "Truly, my Lord is content with me and has consumed the present I brought him."

§ 86. An ill person is put in a tent apart with some bread and water and people do not come to speak to him; they do not come even to see him every day, especially if he is a poor man or a slave. If he recovers, he returns to them, and if he dies, they cremate him. If he is a slave, he is left to be eaten by dogs and birds of prey. (AR: *When one of them is ill, he is brought from the settlement and left with bread and water. If he recovers, he returns again to their midst; if he dies, beasts of prey eat him. If he is a personage, with friends and servants, people come out many days to learn how he is; if he dies, they cremate him.*) If the Rūs catch a thief or robber, they hang him on a tall tree and leave him hanging until his body falls in pieces.

§ 87. I had heard that at the deaths of their chief personages they did many things, of which the least was cremation, and I was interested to learn more. At last I was told of the death of one of their outstanding men. They placed him in a grave and put a roof over it for ten days while they cut and sewed garments for him.

If the deceased is a poor man they make a little boat, which they lay him in and burn. If he is rich, they collect his goods and divide them into three parts, one for his family, another to pay for his

clothing, and a third for making *nabīd*, which they drink until the
day when his female slave will kill herself and be burned with her
master. They stupify themselves by drinking this *nabīd* night and
day; sometimes one of them dies cup in hand.

(AR: *They burn him in this fashion: they leave him for the first
ten days in a grave. His possessions they divide into three parts:
one part for his daughters and wives; another for garments to
clothe the corpse; another part covers the cost of the intoxicating
drink which they consume in the course of ten days, uniting sexually with women and playing musical instruments. Meanwhile,
the slave girl who gives herself to be burned with him, in these
ten days drinks and indulges in pleasure; she decks her head and
her person with all sorts of ornaments and fine dress and so
arrayed gives herself to the men.*)

When a great personage dies, the people of his family ask his
young women and men slaves, "Who among you will die with him?"
One answers, "I." Once he or she has said that, the thing is oblig-
atory; there is no backing out of it. Usually it is the girl slaves who
do this [i.e., volunteer].

§ 88.   When the man of whom I have spoken died, his girl slaves
were asked, "Who will die with him?" One answered, "I." She was
then put in the care of two young women, who watched over her and
accompanied her everywhere, to the point that they occasionally
washed her feet with their own hands. Garments were being made
for the deceased and all else was being readied of which he had
need. Meanwhile the slave drinks every day and sings, giving herself over to pleasure.

§ 89.   When the day arrived on which the man was to be cremated
and the girl with him, I went to the river on which was his ship. I
saw that they had drawn the ship onto the shore, that they had
erected four posts of birch wood and other wood, and that around it
[the ship] was made a structure like great ships'-tents out of wood
[Canard: and that around these posts they had arranged some kind
of great scaffolding of wood]. Then they pulled the ship up until it
was on this wooden construction. Then they began to come and go
and to speak words[25] which I did not understand, while the man was
still in his grave and had not yet been brought out. (AR: *The ninth*
[ZV; Canard: tenth] *day, having drawn the ship up onto the river
bank, they guarded it. In the middle of the ship they prepared a
dome or* pavillon à coupole (kunbad)[26] *of wood and covered this with
various sorts of fabrics.*) Then they brought a couch and put it on
the ship and covered it with a mattress of Greek brocade.[27] Then
came an old woman whom they call the Angel of Death, and she
spread upon the couch the furnishings mentioned. It is she who
has charge of the clothes-making and arranging all things, and it
is she who kills the girl slave. I saw that she was a strapping old
woman, fat and louring.

When they came to the grave they removed the earth from above
the wood, then the wood, and took out the dead man clad in the
garments in which he had died. I saw that he had grown black from
the cold of the country. They had put *nabīd*, fruit, and a pandora[28] in

the grave with him. They removed all that. The dead man did not smell bad[29] and only his color had changed. They dressed him in trousers, stockings (?), boots, a tunic [*qurtaq*], and caftan of brocade with gold buttons. They put a hat of brocade and fur on him. Then they carried him into the pavilion [*qubba*][30] on the ship. They seated him on the mattress and propped him up with cushions. They brought *nabīd*, fruits, and fragrant plants, which they put with him, then bread, meat, and onions, which they placed before him. Then they brought a dog, which they cut in two and put in the ship. Then they brought his weapons and placed them by his side.[31] Then they took two horses, ran them until they sweated, then cut them to pieces with a sword and put them into the ship.[32] They took two cows, which they likewise cut to pieces and put in the ship. Next they killed a rooster and a hen and threw them in. The girl slave who wished to be killed went here and there and into each of their tents, and the master of each tent had sexual intercourse with her and said, "Tell your lord I have done this out of love for him."

(AR: *The tenth day, they brought the deceased out of the ground and put him inside the pavilion* [qubba] *and put around him different kinds of flowers and fragrant plants. Many men and women gathered and played musical instruments, and each of his kinsmen built a pavilion* [qubba] *around his pavilion* [qubba] *at some distance.*[33] *The slave girl arrayed herself and went to the pavilions of the kinsmen of the dead man, and the master of each had sexual intercourse once with her, saying in a loud voice,*[34] *"Tell your master that I have done the duty* [or *exercised the right*[35]] *of love and friendship." And so, as she went to all the pavilions to the last one, all the men had intercourse with her. When this was over, they cut a dog in two halves and put it into the boat, then, having cut the head off a rooster, they threw it, head and body, to the right and left of the ship.*)

§ 90.   Friday afternoon they led the slave girl to a thing that they had made which resembled a door frame. She placed her feet on the palms of the men and they raised her up to overlook this frame. She spoke some words and they lowered her again. A second time they raised her up and she did again what she had done; then they lowered her. They raised her a third time and she did as she had done the two times before. Then they brought her a hen; she cut off the head, which she threw away, and then they took the hen and put it in the ship. I asked the interpreter what she had done. He answered, "The first time they raised her she said, 'Behold, I see my father and mother.' The second time she said, 'I see all my dead relatives seated.' The third time she said, 'I see my master seated in Paradise and Paradise is beautiful and green; with him are men and boy servants. He calls me. Take me to him.'" Now they took her to the ship. She took off the two bracelets which she was wearing and gave them both to the old woman called the Angel of Death, who was to kill her; then she took off the two finger rings which she was wearing and gave them to the two girls who served her and were the daughters of the woman called the Angel of Death. Then they raised her onto the ship but they did not make her enter into the pavilion.

Then men came with shields and sticks. She was given a cup of *nabīd*; she sang at taking it and drank. The interpreter told me that she in this fashion bade farewell to all her girl companions. Then she was given another cup; she took it and sang for a long time while the old woman incited her to drink up and go into the pavilion where her master lay. I saw that she was distracted; she wanted to enter the pavilion but put her head between it and the boat [*sic*; see p. 109 below]. Then the old woman seized her head and made her enter the pavilion and entered with her. Thereupon the men began to strike with the sticks on the shields so that her cries could not be heard and the other slave girls would not be frightened and seek to escape death with their masters.[36] Then six men went into the pavilion and each had intercourse with the girl. Then they laid her at the side of her master; two held her feet and two her hands; the old woman known as the Angel of Death re-entered[37] and looped a cord around her neck and gave the crossed ends to the two men for them to pull. Then she approached her with a broad-bladed dagger, which she plunged between her ribs repeatedly, and the men strangled her with the cord until she was dead.

(AR: *After that, the group of men who have cohabited with the slave girl make of their hands a sort of paved way whereby the girl, placing her feet on the palms of their hands, mounts onto the ship. After that, they give her a hen, which she throws into the ship after tearing off its head. Then she drinks a cup of an intoxicating drink and pronounces many words, and, thrice standing on the palms of the men, she comes down and mounts again to the ship and recites many things* [Canard: sings some snatches]. *She goes into the pavilion* [qubba] *in which her husband* [Mann; mari] *has been put, and six of the relatives of her husband go into the pavilion and unite sexually with this wife in the presence of the dead man. When they have finished these duties of love,*[38] *the old woman who, according to the belief of these people, is the Angel of Death arrives*[39] *and lays the wife to sleep beside her husband. Of the six men, two seize the legs of the slave girl, and two others her hands, and the old woman, twisting her veil, puts it around her neck and gives the ends to the two other men so that they can pull it so tight that the soul escapes from her body.*[40])

§ 91.   Then the closest relative of the dead man, after they had placed the girl whom they have killed beside her master, came, took a piece of wood which he lighted at a fire, and walked backwards with the back of his head toward the boat and his face turned (toward the people),[41] with one hand holding the kindled stick and the other covering his anus, being completely naked, for the purpose of setting fire to the wood that had been made ready beneath the ship.[42] Then the people came up with tinder and other fire wood, each holding a piece of wood of which he had set fire to an end and which he put into the pile of wood beneath the ship. Thereupon the flames engulfed the wood, then the ship, the pavilion, the man, the girl, and everything in the ship. A powerful, fearful wind began to blow so that the flames became fiercer and more intense.

(AR: *After the girl is slain, two relatives of the dead take brands and set the ship on fire, so that the dead man and the ship*

are shortly burned to ashes. If in this moment a wind blows and the
fire is strengthened and the ashes are dispersed, the man is accordingly one who belongs in Paradise; otherwise they take the dead to
be one unwelcome at the threshold of bliss or even to be condemned. When two people among them quarrel and the dissension
is prolonged and the king is unable to reconcile them, he commands that they fight with swords; he who wins is right.)

§ 92.   One of the Rūs was at my side and I heard him speak to the
interpreter, who was present. I asked the interpreter what he said.
He answered, "He said, 'You Arabs are fools.'" "Why?" I asked
him. He said, "You take the people who are most dear to you and
whom you honor most and you put them in the ground where insects
and worms devour them. We burn him in a moment, so that he enters
Paradise at once." Then he began to laugh uproariously. When I
asked why he laughed, he said, "His lord, for love of him, has sent
the wind to bring him away in an hour." And actually an hour had
not passed before the ship, the wood, the girl, and her master were
nothing but cinders and ashes.
   Then they constructed in the place where had been the ship
which they had drawn up out of the river something like a small
round hill, in the middle of which they erected a great post of birch
wood, on which they wrote the name of the man and the name of the
Rūs king and they departed.

§ 93.   It is a custom of the king of the Rūs to have with him in his
palace four hundred men, the bravest of his companions and those
on whom he can rely. These are the men who die with him and let
themselves be killed for him. Each has a female slave who serves
him, washes his head, and prepares all that he eats and drinks, and
he also has another female slave with whom he sleeps. These four
hundred men sit about the king's throne, which is immense and
encrusted with fine precious stones. With him on the throne sit
forty female slaves destined for his bed. Occasionally he has intercourse with one of them in the presence of the companions of whom
we have spoken, without coming down from the throne. When he
needs to answer the call of nature he uses a basin. When he wants
to ride out, his horse is brought up to the throne and he mounts. If
he wishes to dismount, he rides up so that he can dismount on to the
throne. He has a lieutenant who commands his troops, makes war
upon his enemies, and plays his role vis-à-vis his subjects.
   (AR: *Their king spends his time in a very high palace and four
hundred men of his army are always in his service, sleeping by
night under his throne. Each of these four hundred men has a girl
slave. Each of them, whenever he pleases, has intercourse with
his girl slave in the presence of the king. The king also has four
hundred [for forty] maidens for his bed. He has a great throne
studded with precious stones. He sits with those forty concubines
on this throne, makes merry with them, and whenever he feels like
it has intercourse with them in the presence of his courtiers and
does not consider this anything wrong. Their king never descends
from this throne, but when he wants to ride out, his horse is*

*brought to the throne and he mounts him from the throne, and
when he dismounts, he dismounts on to the throne. He has no other
occupation than having sexual intercourse with the women,
drinking wine, and enjoying himself. Outstanding men among
them are inclined to occupy themselves with tanning and are
not ashamed of this lowly occupation. The cloth of these lands
and localities is famous, especially that of their capital, which
is called Kyawh. Famous and noted cities of the Rūs are Crsk and
Hrqh.*[43])

ii

THE LAST SECTION of Ibn Faḍlān's description of the Rūs, § 93,
comes as a sort of appendix to the rest, which reaches its climax in the
cremation scene. This section is certainly wholly based upon hearsay:
Ibn Faḍlān does not claim ever to have been anywhere near the court
he is describing. Taken as a whole it is perhaps the most extravagant
part of the description of the Rūs.[44] For this reason we might do well
to look at it first, to see what kernels of truth, if any, it contains, as a
preliminary to examining the generally more plausible earlier sections.

Zeki Validi and his German consultants do not find much that is
basically Germanic in this chapter. Meissner points to the *Yngvars saga*
for an instance of warriors riding into a hall and up to the throne of a
king, and Heinz Graf hesitantly cites a passage in *Rígsþula* (27), where
a man and wife are shown sitting together, presumably on a throne.
Heimpel spurns the picture of a Germanic king as delegating the command of his armies to a subordinate. In the Germanic *Waltharius*,
Attila deputizes Walter to lead in the field, but this Heimpel sees as
"fast komisch" — a picture of what a Hunnish king would do, not a
Germanic one. Zeki Validi notes that the king of the Rūs behaves in
this respect like the king (Khaqan) of the Khazares and other Turkish
tribes (see *Exk.* § 100a), who delegated war-making to a bey, but by
implication defends the accuracy of the text, since he makes this
passage a point of departure for a learned excursus on the length of
time that the Rūs had been in contact with oriental peoples (while remaining, however, "im Grunde immer Normannen").[45] We are left not
knowing whether in this respect Ibn Faḍlān was misled, or whether, as
Zeki Validi seems to think, we have an account of a Rūs court much
influenced by contact with oriental peoples. I should like, however, to
point out one significant and truly Germanic detail in the section, at the
very beginning. The most conspicuous institution of Germanic society,
stressed by historians and poets from Tacitus on, is the comitatus: the
chieftain is surrounded by a small number of men, his bravest and most
reliable, an elite of "hearth companions," who are expected to fight to

the death in his defense or in defense of a field on which he has been killed. That the number in Ibn Faḍlān is 400, and the manner of death mass suicide rather than death in battle, is due to oriental influence either on the Rūs or on Ibn Faḍlān's account of them: Zeki Validi (*Exk.* § 93a) and Canard (n. 357) offer oriental parallels for the number 400 and for mass suicide.[46] The institution of a core of chosen warriors, however, is characteristically Germanic.

We turn now to the beginning of the description. We find in the dress and armor some details that seem verifiably Germanic. When Ibn Faḍlān says that the Rūs wear neither *qurtaqs* nor caftans (§ 80), he is evidently thinking of their daily garb during the time he saw them; he later tells us that a *qurtaq* and a caftan (as well as shoes and some sort of under-breeches and over-breeches) were put on the dead man before he was placed in the ship (§ 89). On the basis of the sort of garment known as a *qurtaq* in the orient, Zeki Validi would identify the Rūs *qurtaq* as an ON *kyrtill*, a sort of knee-length tunic; Shetelig and Falk tell us that the *kyrtill* was belted and had sleeves.[47] The word "caftan" designates a heavy woolen overgarment; a similar Norse garment is described by H. Falk in his *Altnordische Kleiderkunde*;[48] it is known as an *ólpa* (cf. ZV, *Exk.* § 89d). Ibn Faḍlān's "garment which covers one side of the body and leaves a hand free" suggests a kind of ON cloak – to Zeki Validi an ON *mǫttull* or *skikkja*, to Shetelig and Falk a *feldr*, that is, a cloak of doubled cloth which "was fastened with a clasp over the right shoulder so that the right arm remained free."[49] (ZV remarks in *Exk.* § 81b that the sleeveless *mǫttull* would permit the tattooed arms to be seen.) In other words, if these identifications are correct, Ibn Faḍlān has said that the Rūs whom he observed wore *feldir* (or *mǫtlar* or *skikkjur*)[50] but that later the dead man was clad in a *kyrtill* and an *ólpa*.[51]

As Canard remarks, the arms of the Rūs (§ 81), which they are never without, remind us that the Rūs were at once merchants and warriors; the ax and knife at least also served on occasion as handy tools on expeditions (n. 283). The Frankish sword is described in Zeki Validi's translation as "platt (breit), mit Blutrinnen versehen," and Canard cites Zeki Validi as authority for his own words "à large lame, striée de rainures."[52] Shetelig and Falk tell us that the one-edged sword had deep grooves, usually three, along the back of the blade, which accords well enough with Zeki Validi's translation. The battle-ax is a very characteristic Germanic weapon; Gedeonov holds that it was unknown to the Slavs (ZV, *Exk.* § 81a). The Norse cross of Middleton, Yorkshire, of the mid-tenth century, shows a warrior in his grave with a sword, knife, battle-ax, and spear.[53] The spear, too, seems to have been a very basic weapon to the Norse in warfare and ritual, favored perhaps because in very early times the Germanic warriors were unarmored.[54] If the Rūs had spears they would presumably not be going about with them but only with weapons that would be worn, not carried in the hand. The weapons put into the ship with the dead man are not particularized.

The "breast-boxes" of the women (§ 82) refers possibly to oval, convex brooches, frequently found in graves of women. These are as much as 4½ inches long and 3 inches wide. A pair were sometimes connected by a "luxurious set of beads or chains which lay as a necklet across the breast" (Shetelig and Falk), each end of the necklet being attached to a ring set in the bottom of the brooch. No brooches seem to have been found with a knife depending from such a ring (as described in Meshed but not in Amīn Rāzī), though knives have been found in graves of women of this era.[55] Notable examples of brooches have been found in Gotland, sometimes thought to have been the original home of the Rūs.[56]

We do not know how big were the "big houses of wood" constructed on the shore (§ 83). In the Danish city of Haddeby, which was ruled by Swedes at about the time of Ibn Faḍlān's journey, the buildings — warehouses and small workshops as well as dwellings — ranged in size from 22 feet by 54 feet to 10 feet by 10 feet.[57] Since the buildings on the Volga were temporary, it seems likely that the ten to twenty occupants "more or less" of each probably did not have much space per capita. Crowded living conditions, to cite an axiom of social anthropologists, are the enemy of decent reticence. If there is any basis whatever besides national and religious prejudice to Ibn Faḍlān's report of a total lack of that preference for seclusion during sexual intercourse found even among such gaily unselfconscious people as Malinowski's Trobrianders, this lack would be congruous with crowded living quarters. But we must note that public copulation is also reportedly practiced in the king's palace in § 93. Rudolf Meissner refers Zeki Validi to a picture of slave traffic by a Russian (Scandinavian) merchant in the *Laxdæla saga*, Ch. XII (Thule, *Altnordische Dichtung und Prosa*, VI, 43 ff.). In a market place, Hǫskuld bought a female slave from Gilli, a Russian merchant. In a resplendent tent sat twelve salable women behind a curtain. Gilli invited Hǫskuld to step behind the curtain and see the women. They sat in a row across the tent. A poorly dressed one on the end of the row was attractive to Hǫskuld; but she was also attractive to Gilli, who set her price at three marks and urged Hǫskuld to take one of the other girls for a single silver mark. (Apparently Gilli kept his favorite poorly dressed in hopes that she would not be bought.) Of the market it is said that it was a scene of much gaiety, carousing, and pleasure of all sorts. The slaves in Ibn Faḍlān and the *Laxdæla saga* are presumably Slavic, but Germanic peoples, for example, the Frisians, sometimes sold other Germanic people into slavery, and one recalls lines 3016b — 3021a of

Beowulf, where slavery is anticipated for women of the conquered Geats:

né mæʒeþ scíene
habban on healſe   hring-weorðunge;
ac sceal ʒeómor-mód,   golde beréafod,
oft, nealles ǽne,   ell-land tredan.[58]

[No fair maiden shall have the ring-adornment on her neck, but, sad in heart, deprived of gold, shall walk not once but often in foreign lands.]

Zeki Validi cites a passage in Ibn Rusta on the cleanliness of the clothing of the Rūs and points out that the daily hair washing of the Rūs (§ 84) makes them in that particular more hygienic than the Arabs, who wash their hair only when they bathe. Ibn Faḍlān's disgust at the "filthiness" of the Rūs stems at least in part from the revulsion he feels as a pious Mohammedan at washing in still water: an Arab washes only in running water or water poured from a container; he will not wash in his own rinsings, so to speak. Hair washing among Germanic people is well attested, and the courtly custom of the wash basin and towel brought by a servant before and after meals is conspicuous down through the Middle Ages. (For evidences concerning the Rūs, see ZV, *Exk.* § 84a.)

To the modern reader who is accustomed to thinking of Norse religion chiefly in terms of short, dramatic scenes and haunting allusions in the Elder Edda, Ibn Faḍlān's account of sacrifices to a circle of wooden idols (§ 85) comes as rather a shock. It is more reminiscent of some of the stories in Yule's *Hobson-Jobson* (for example) than of Wagner's *Götterdämmerung.* But the use of *trémenn* – wooden men – by road sides and perhaps beside harbors is well attested. Meissner calls attention to *Hóvamǫl,* where we read (49):

Vápir mínar   gaf ek velli at
tveim trémǫnnum;
rekkar þat þóttusk   es þeir ript hǫfþu:
neiss es nøkkviþr halr.

[My garments I gave in a field to two wooden men; heroes they seemed when they had clothes: the naked man is nought.]

R. L. Rasmussen, commenting on this passage in Ibn Faḍlān, enumerates Odin's wives as Frigg, Hertha, and Skade, and his mistresses as Gunlada, Rinda, and Grida.[59] It is perhaps worth noting that the first men, Ash and Embla, who, Snorri tells us, were carved out of two trees found on the seashore (*Gylfaginning,* IX) are represented in *Vǫluspǫ́* (17) as wooden men.[60]

The suspending of the heads of cattle and sheep on stakes echoes a statement made in § 31, where the Oguz are said to suspend on stakes the heads, feet, skins, and tails of horses which they sacrifice at funerals; the opening of our next section (§ 86), telling how the Rūs isolate their ill, echoes § 30, where the Oguz are said to do the same thing. The passage at the close of § 86, to the effect that a criminal is hanged and left hanging until his body falls to pieces, echoes § 64, where the Bulgars are said so to treat those among them convicted of involuntary manslaughter, and also echoes § 65, where they are said so to treat any man of such extraordinary spirit and wisdom as to be a fit gift for their god. Perhaps it is significant that repetitions accumulate at this point in the text. Ibn Faḍlān is ready now to embark on the account of the funeral, the longest narrative of the whole *Risāla* and the one which must have been the most interesting to him, as it is to us — he says he had heard of such funerals and was interested to learn more. It may be that he racked his memory a bit too hard as he cleared the board preparatory to embarking on his climactic narrative. Or, the text may be faulty. This is not to deny, however, that these data may not be coincidentally applicable to Oguz and Bulgars as well as Rūs, or that they may not be properly applicable only to Rūs and have been mistakenly inserted in the text where it deals with Oguz and Bulgars. Especially does the hanging datum seem peculiarly Germanic, the custom that is the forerunner of the sickening "hanging in chains" of so many later centuries. Hanging is the mode of sacrifice to Odin (often with simultaneous stabbing, as we shall see later) and the hanged were left to dangle from the rope. Twice in *Beowulf* we read of hanged men being left as prey to ravens: once in the allusion to the hypothetical old man whose son is hanged *hræfne to hróðre*, "a joy to the raven" (see ll. 2444 — 49), and once when Ongentheow is threatening his enemies at Ravenswood that "some on the gallows-tree [will be] sport for the birds" (*sume on ʒealg-tréowum/[fugolum] to gamene* — see ll. 2940 — 41). Such sacrifices were sometimes wholesale; Thietmar of Merseburg tells us that ninety-nine men were sacrificed to Odin at Lejre in Denmark — the site of Hrothgar's Heorot! — every ninth year, and such ritual massacre is thought to have continued there until about 930.[61] Indeed, Ibn Faḍlān's story (§ 65) of how the Bulgars sacrificed their best and wisest, though circumstantial to the extent that a case is cited of a visiting Sind (from Northwest India) who was so dealt with by the Bulgars, would fit in very well with what we know of Odin worship — better, in fact, than it fits in with what is known of the customs of the Bulgars, to judge from Zeki Validi's *Exk.* § 65a.

It is not surprising that Ibn Faḍlān had heard of Rūs burial rites (§ 87). Although ship burials, with or without burning, were all but unknown in Denmark[62] and were rare in Viking settlements of the

West,[63] the number is estimated at 550 in Norway and more than a thousand in Sweden. These date chiefly from the seventh to tenth centuries, and in the latter part of this period, ship or boat burial was accorded not only to the very great but also to relatively humble persons, women as well as men.[64] It is notable that the subject of the lavish rites which Ibn Faḍlān witnessed, while not a humble person, is nowhere described as *the* chief of the tribe—he is only "one of their outstanding men," and his rites are of the sort usually accorded to their "chief personages." The Swedes seem to have been the most conscientious of the North Germanic peoples in observing the obsequies of their religion, and the piety of the Swedish Rūs in this respect is reported by numbers of Arabian writers. One such report is particularly interesting. It does not have to do with ship burial or cremation, but it is eloquent evidence of the importance which the Rūs attached to ritual burial. In the year 943, a group of Rūs made an overambitious invasion deep into Armenian territory. There, as reported by Ibn Miskawaïh,[65] they ate some fruit which gave them dysentery, and while suffering from this malady they were surrounded and besieged. Whenever one of their number died, they interred him with his arms "and garments and tools, and likewise they interred with him his wife or another of his women and his servant if he had been fond of him, and all this according to their custom." After they managed to break away (they were later annihilated) their enemies dug up the graves for the sake of the swords, which they prized for their excellent quality. Piety can go no further than this, even though the form it takes may not be exactly to modern taste.

The funeral of the Rūs chief begins with the placing of his body in a grave where it is to remain until the tenth day. Ibn Faḍlān was present on the tenth day and saw the grave opened (§ 87, § 89). With the body were drink, fruit, and a stringed instrument. This last will remind us of the harp found at Sutton Hoo.[66] The temporary burial, it will be noted, was not purely a matter of preserving the dead man's body in a cold place: provision is made for his entertainment, as for that of his fellow-Rūs, until the day of his "departure."[67] Here we have the idea of continued existence in the grave such as is implied by the kind of burial given by the Rūs in Armenia (and often elsewhere). Incidentally, even in ship burials where there is no cremation, the idea of continued, stationary existence in the grave-ship seems sometimes to have predominated over the idea of a journey to another world, for some grave-ships are securely anchored to great rocks.[68] But the Rūs chief's ten-day sojourn in a grave is, of course, only preliminary to what is most explicitly a journey by fire to another world.

Ibn Faḍlān does not see the ship until it has been drawn up on the shore and made ready for the ceremony (§ 89), and his description of it is not clear, to judge by the varying translations and annotations of Zeki Validi and Canard. Four posts have been erected, and there follows the statement that *anābīr* (pl.) have been constructed. Zeki Validi translates this passage: "around it [the ship] was made a structure like great ship's tents [*anābīr*] of wood." Canard reads: "and around these posts were made some sort of scaffoldings [*anābīr*] of wood." Then both agree that the ship was drawn up and placed *on* this construction. Amīn Rāzī is simpler: "In the middle of the ship they prepared a dome or domed tent [ZV: *Kuppel*; Canard: *pavillon à coupole*] of wood and covered this with all sorts of fabrics." The Persian word in Amīn Rāzī which Zeki Validi and Canard translate respectively as *Kuppel* and *pavillon à coupole* is transliterated by Canard as *gunbâdh*[69] and identified by him with the Arabic word *qubba*, which appears later in the text to designate the grave chamber and which ordinarily denotes, according to Zeki Validi (*Exk.* § 90b), the dome-topped felt tent or *jurte* of the Turks. It would be fruitless to pursue this textual problem in greater detail, but we may hazard a guess as to what the antecedent probabilities may have been.

In the first place, it would seem that what the ship was set *on* was a heap of firewood. When later the torch is applied (§ 91), it is applied to wood *under* the ship, about which we have not been told before. In one of the graves at Old Uppsala, stakes driven into the clay and burned at the upper end are assumed once to have held a boat upright for burning,[70] and this could well have been the function of the four posts, two on a side. We know from the course of the ritual as later described that an enclosure, a grave chamber of some sort, a *qubba*, was already on the ship when the body of the dead man was carried aboard. As we have just seen, Amīn Rāzī mentions this enclosure at this point, a *qubba*, or, in his Persian, a *gunbādh*, made of wood; the Meshed text instead here makes the confusing account of *anābīr* and only later reveals that there is (also?) a *qubba* on the ship. The *anābīr*, whether "ship's tents" or "scaffoldings," are of wood; both Zeki Validi and Canard speak of the *qubba* as a tent, though ZV remarks that it may have been made of wood to burn better. We get a hint as to the possible cause of the confusion when we look at the grave chambers of ship burials known to archeology.

The grave chambers of the Oseberg ship and of the Sutton Hoo ship may be taken as typical. They were of wood; they were ridge-roofed and gable-ended; and they were not meant to represent the house of the deceased but to represent a ship's tent. The eaves of this wooden "tent" rested inside the gunwales of the ship. The roof of the Sutton Hoo grave chamber collapsed, but the original angle of the roof was marked by discoloration of the sand, and the sides of the Sutton Hoo ship were sprung slightly outwards from the pressure which the eaves had once exerted.[71] For what reason I do not know, Bruce-Mitford thinks that the grave goods were laid in the Sutton Hoo ship before the grave chamber was erected over them (there never was a body in the Sutton Hoo ship, it will be remembered), but we have already noted that the grave chamber was prepared on Ibn Faḍlān's ship before the body and grave goods were placed aboard, and it is tempting to think that the wooden *anābīr* made up this grave chamber, constituted indeed a wooden structure like a ship's tent, and that Zeki Validi and we may as well identify this structure with the *qubba* later mentioned, as does Amīn Rāzī. I would not wish to push this too far, however.[72] It must be confessed that, whether the *qubba* was a wooden-gabled roof or a felt or cloth tent pitched on the bottom of the ship, it is hard to see how the slave girl in § 90 got her head between the *qubba* and the side of the ship.

There is ample evidence of human sacrifice in early Germanic funerals. When it appears in literature it is sometimes disguised or mentioned obliquely, as in the account of Balder's funeral in Snorri's Edda, when Balder's wife, Nanna, who is burned on the pyre with Balder, is said to have died of grief, and the dwarf Litr is kicked into the flames by Thor in a moment of rage; sometimes it is directly stated, as in the *Sigurþarkviþa en skamma* and *Vǫlsunga saga*, where Brynhildr takes her place beside Sigurðr on the pyre with the bodies of slain servants. Among these last, according to the *Sigurþarkviþa*, are serving women who volunteer (like the slave girl in the *Risāla*): "I will not," says Brynhildr, "that anyone reluctant or slow to obey should give up life for my sake."[73] These and a number of other very striking examples are discussed by H. R. Ellis in her *Road to Hel* (pp. 50–58). Archeological evidence of human sacrifice is likewise copious. In 1910 Haakon Shetelig listed forty-four graves in Norway which offered evidence of human sacrifice, and especially suttee, through having the bones of two and/or a mixture of men's and women's grave goods, though he remarks that it was Sweden, rather than Norway, "where Paganism was longest and most strictly preserved."[74] Bones of a young woman and an old were found in the Oseberg ship, thought by some to be those of a queen and her serving woman.[75] We have noted Ibn Miskawaïh's account of the burials of Rūs in Armenia, each with a wife or a concubine and sometimes a man servant. The fact of a sacrificed slave girl in Ibn Faḍlān is in no way surprising.

The Angel of Death does not have any clear parallel, as far as I can find, elsewhere in Germanic lore, though the priestess-prophetess, the *vǫlva*, shadowed forth as early as Tacitus' *Germania*, and the valkyries or (OE) *walcyrge*, as Chadwick and others have shown, have had a very broad, though elusive, role in Germanic religion—much broader than the classic role assigned them as "choosers of the slain" on the battlefield.[76]

H. R. Ellis cites a record of suttees in Bali in the seventeenth century in which old women attended those who were to die, "to instruct and encourage them."[77] In both of the cremation funerals in *Beowulf* we have a woman figuring prominently: at the pyre of Hnæf "The lady lamented, mourning with songs" (*ides gnornode,/ʒeómrode ʒieddum*—ll. 1117b–1118a), and at Beowulf's own pyre, "So a Geatish woman, a Weder woman sang, with braided (or wound up) hair, sorrowful, sang a mournful song about Beowulf, said very often (or earnestly) that she sorely dreaded heavy days to come" (*swelće ʒeómor-ʒiedd Ʒéatisc méowle,/ Weder-cwǽn awræc, wunden-heorde/sang sorg-cariʒ swíðe ʒeneahhe/ þæt hío hire héofung-dagas hearde ondréde, . . .*—ll. 3150–53). In the first passage the context indicates that the lady is Hildeburh, Hnæf's sister, whose son is also on the pyre. In the second passage, no identification of the mourning lady is at hand; some editors have gone to the rather extreme length of supposing that Beowulf must have had a widow and in order to give him one have conjectured that he has married Hygd after the death of Hygelac. But her prophecies suggest a ritualistic role, and though she is not explicitly old—unless her hair-style indicates age rather than marital status—it is just possible that she may be analogous in some fashion to the Angel of Death in Ibn Faḍlān.

The object like a door frame over which the slave girl sees into Paradise (§ 90) has no clear parallel. It would seem to represent the wall of the other world. Immediately after looking over it, the girl decapitates a hen, which is then put into the ship. A story in Saxo Grammaticus is suggestive in this context: Hadingus is conducted by a witch woman on a journey down under the ground since, as Saxo infers, "the nether gods purposed that he should pay a visit in the flesh to the regions whither he must go when he died." When the two reach a wall, the woman tries to jump over it, but it is too high for her; she strangles a cock which she is carrying and throws it over the barrier; the bird comes to life immediately, for they can hear it crowing.[78] That the hen or cock played a role in the funeral rites more symbolic than that played by the other animals put into the grave is the implication not only of Ibn Faḍlān's and Saxo's accounts as noted but by the fact that the Middleton cross depicts the Norse warrior entombed not only with his arms but also with a bird-like object—perhaps a chicken or head of one.[79]

The "beautiful and green Paradise" of Ibn Faḍlān's account may, as Arbman remarks, have meant something very different to Ibn Faḍlān from what it meant to the Rūs,[80] but it is more than doubtful that it meant Valhalla, if only because of the "motley throng" (as Major puts it) that the slave girl expects to meet there;[81] it is not the place where Odin's *einherjar* fight daily as they await Ragnarǫkr. Meissner calls attention to the "green meadows of the gods" in the *Hákonarmál* (ZV, *Exk*, § 90a). Probably Norse conceptions of the other world were varied and somewhat confused, as are no doubt modern Christian conceptions of heaven, but there seems to have been from a very early day the idea that "men and women, whatever the manner of their deaths, had a chance of admission to the dwelling of the gods pending the day of doom."[82]

The representation in the Meshed text of the sexual orgy involving the slave girl with, first, the master of each of the tents on the ground beside the ship, and, later, with six kinsmen of the deceased in the grave chamber on the ship differs from the representation in Amīn Rāzī in two important particulars: (1) In Meshed it is an orgy *per se*, with no particular meaning. In Amīn Rāzī it is consistently the celebration of a posthumous marriage. (2) In Meshed it is interrupted by the enactment of the dramatic ritual of the door frame in front of which the girl is thrice lifted up on the palms of some men; thereafter, she kills the hen which is put into the ship. In Amīn Rāzī, for the door frame ritual is substituted a ritual in which the men make a paved way of their palms up to the ship and the girl walks over this way; she then kills the hen and throws it into the ship; thereafter she descends and reascends twice more over the way of palms.

The implication of posthumous marriage appears in Amīn Rāzī in such facts as these: when the girl has intercourse with the master of a pavilion, the master is referred to as a kinsman of the dead and he says in a loud voice, "Tell your master that I have done the duty," and so on: the "kinsman" expects his "loud voice" to be overheard by the dead man. She goes into the pavilion (grave chamber) where her *husband* has been put and the six men who unite with her there are explicitly *relatives* of her husband; the woman is then laid beside her *husband*. She is strangled not by just a cord but by her bridal *veil*, which is twisted round her neck. Canard, who, relying in part on Kovalevsky, makes these points very clear in his translation and notes, is, however, somewhat baffled by the use in Amīn Rāzī of the word for "veil" where Meshed has "cord," and he asks (n. 350) if this veil can refer to the *mouchoir-serre-tête*, that is, the *babushka*, which, among Russian women, distinguished the married woman from the unmarried. But the case is simpler: among the Norse, brides wore veils. Thor wore a bridal veil (*brúðar lín*) when he went disguised as a bride to the hall of Thrym (*Þrymskviða*). The paved way of palms is less dramatic than the scene of the door frame, but the paved way fits the folklore of a marriage ceremony and is quite possibly not merely a distortion of the door frame episode:[83] in many wedding ceremonies throughout the world the bride must not be allowed to touch the earth lest she be contaminated – such a belief may lie at the back of the modern custom of carrying the bride over the threshold of her new home.[84] I have said that I think we must suspect Amīn Rāzī of having rationalized his account in a fashion that might make it seem to be older than it is. On this account, the next two (and last) items seem to me particularly noteworthy, because they appear only in Meshed and not in Amīn Rāzī, yet fit into the scheme of the posthumous marriage. In the first place, as Canard points out (n. 336), following Kovalevsky, when the slave girl, looking over the door frame, sees her family in Paradise, we may have the suggestion that she, as the wife of her lord, now has the status of a free woman and that her family are therefore participators in the marriage. In the second place, there is the beating of sticks on shields (not mentioned in AR) "so that the slave girl's cries could not be heard." The noise-making begins as the girl enters the grave chamber to lie with the six kinsmen before being strangled, and, as Canard says, is actually for the purpose of driving away evil spirits "qui pourraient venir troubler la seconde cérémonie de consommation du mariage, la plus réelle, celle qui a lieu en présence du mort" (n. 340).[85]

The classic method of sacrifice to Odin was, of course, hanging, but there is also a tradition of stabbing or "marking for Odin," that is, consecrating the ill to Odin by a spear wound, probably a relic of an older custom of spearing the ill to death by way of assuring them acceptance by the god. Chadwick cites, too, two instances of simultaneous hanging and stabbing, one, of Odin in *Hóvamǫl*, 139: "I know that I hung full nine nights on the windy tree, wounded by the spear and offered to Odin, myself to myself," and the other of Vikar in *Gautreks saga*, 7, and says that in the latter "the combination of hanging and stabbing [is] parallel to the combination of strangling and stabbing in Ibn Faḍlān's story."[86] There is no reason to suppose that Ibn Faḍlān was deceived, or has deceived us, as to what sort of execution took place in the grave chamber. In this connection, it may be interesting to look at that passage in *Beowulf* (ll. 1936–39) which describes the fate of any man so bold as to look openly upon Offa's terrible queen: "[Such a one] accounted the hand-woven deadly bonds destined for him; quickly after being seized, the sword was appointed for him, so that the patterned blade might settle the matter, make known his death."[87] Here one normally supposes that the man is seized, that his hands are bound behind his back, and that he is decapitated. Perhaps such a supposition is necessitated by the word "bonds" (a.p. [*wæl*] *benda*), but is it not possible that his execution was of the type described in Ibn Faḍlān?

To the ceremonial lighting of the pyre (§ 91) – the closest relative of the deceased walks backwards, naked, with a brand and kindles the fire and after him others come, each with a brand to feed the flames – I know of no analogies save the general analogy that Germanic cremations were traditionally lavish and ceremonial. Tacitus tells us (27) that the Germanic dead "certis lignis crementur"; he implies that the ritual was simple. His editor R. Much cannot say what these kinds of wood were but points out that, as we have seen, grave finds and literary references such as those in *Beowulf* and the Eddas refute any idea of simplicity at a later date.[88] Perhaps Tacitus is once again using his plain and noble Germanic savages as a stick with which to hit his Roman contemporaries. One would suppose that the Rūs had had some sort of ceremonial preparation of the pyre onto which the ship had been drawn, but Ibn Faḍlān, who was not present until the ship was in place on the shore, tells us of none.[89] In the account of the actual conflagration of the ship and its freight of human and animal corpses (§ 92), Amīn Rāzī again deviates from Meshed in a fashion by now familiar. Meshed tells us that a wind sprang up, that a Rūs laughed heartily and, being asked why, explained that the Lord had sent the wind to hasten the dead man on his journey. Amīn Rāzī does not give the vivid anecdote but instead a general statement: if, when the pyre has been lighted, "a wind blows and the fire is strengthened and the ashes are dispersed, the man is accordingly one who belongs in Paradise; otherwise [the Rūs] take the dead to be one unwelcome at the threshold of bliss or even to be condemned." Whether AR found this generalization in his source or deduced it from the anecdote of the laughing Rūs, the generalization is probable enough, and it received a somewhat oblique confirmation from Snorri Sturluson, who tells us in the *Ynglinga saga*, 9, of the belief in ancient Sweden "that the higher the smoke rose in the air, the loftier would his position be in heaven whose burning it was."[90] Both these omens— a rising smoke and a quickening wind—are found together in the description of the burning of Beowulf, most interestingly in that the wind is no necessary or expected part of the description: "The warriors began then to kindle the greatest of funeral fires on the barrow; the wood-smoke arose black over the fire, the resounding fire surrounded by weeping—*the tumult of winds subsided*—until, hot in the breast, it had destroyed the body":

> Ongunnon þá on beorge   bǽl-fýra mǽst
> wíȝend weććan;   wudu-ríeć ástág
> sweart ofer sweoloðe,   swógende líeȝ,
> wópe bewunden   —wind-bland ȝelæȝ—,
> oþ-þæt hé þá bán-hús   ȝebrocen hæfde,
> hát on hreðere.   [ll. 3143—48a]

In the middle of the mound which the Rūs construct over the ashes is placed a great post of wood—a wooden counterpart of the *bautarsteinar* found so frequently in Scandinavia. On this is written the name of the deceased and of the Rūs king. Unfortunately, Ibn Faḍlān, for all his training as a *faqīh* and his eager interest, does not describe this writing.

In the foregoing commentary I have tried to overlook no possible point of relevance in Ibn Faḍlān to *Beowulf* and have consequently cited in *Beowulf* the prophecy of exile of Geatish women, references to hanging men "as prey to birds," mourning women at the funerals of Hnæf and Beowulf, the execution of the man so bold as to look on Offa's queen, the selection of householders to gather wood for Beowulf's funeral pyre (in n. 89), and the mention of wind in the description of the burning of this pyre. But the impression which Ibn Faḍlān's account of the Rūs makes on the reader of *Beowulf* is certainly on the whole not one of congruence or kinship but on the contrary one of deep contrast. Like so many other monuments and documents which portray Germanic peoples of the earlier Middle Ages, Ibn Faḍlān's account makes the *Beowulf* stand out like a sunlit peak above a valley. That an eighth-century poet could have the sense of order and of human dignity implicit in *Beowulf* and could portray a court such as Heorot must argue some happy conjunction of the genius of a poet on the one hand and on the other a realm somewhere in Britain of prosperity and security, if only for a generation or two – an island in a world enduringly and universally barbarous, of which Ibn Faḍlān's engrossing description is characteristic.

NOTES

1. Ibn Faḍlān calls the Bulgars "Ṣaqāliba," a name often applied to other tribes and groups of tribes. See Zeki Validi's *Exkurs* Ia, and "Anhang über Ṣaqāliba," pp. 104 f. and 295–331, respectively, in the edition cited in n. 5.

2. The word means "writing" or "scripture," and was first applied, perhaps ineptly, by the Arab Yāqūt (see n. 3).

3. Ed. and translated into German by C. M. Frähn, *Ibn-Foszlan's und anderer araber Berichte über die Russen älterer Zeit* (St. Petersburg, 1823). The portion having to do with the Rūs has been translated in its entirety by A. S. Cook, "Ibn Faḍlān's Account of Scandinavian Merchants on the Volga," *Journal of English and Germanic Philology*, XXII (1923), 54–63, and in part by Charis Waddy, "A Scandinavian Cremation Ceremony," *Antiquity*, VIII (1934), 58–62, and A. F. Major, "Ship Burials in Scandinavian Lands and the Beliefs That Underlie Them," *Folk-Lore*, XXXV (1924), 113–50. See also Hilda Roderick Ellis, *The Road to Hel* (Cambridge, 1943), pp. 45–47.

4. The date is from Blake and Frye (as cited in n. 6), p. 28. For further description of the Meshed MS. and its discovery, see Zeki Validi's Introduction to his edition as cited in n. 5 and his remarks in the *Geographische Zeitschrift*, XL (1934), p. 368 and n. 1. Other manuscript data are offered by Paul Kahl in the *Zeitschrift der deutschen Morgenländischen Gesellschaft* (ZDMG), LXXXVIII (1934), 12, 43–45.

5. *Ibn Faḍlān's Reisebericht*, Abhandlungen für die Kunde des Morgenlandes, XXIV, 3, of the DMG (Leipzig, 1939).

6. The year 1939 also saw an edition and translation into Russian by A. P. Kovalevsky, published at Leningrad by the Russian Academy of Sciences. Subsequently there have appeared: an acute criticism of the Zeki Validi and Kovalevsky editions by Helmut Ritter ("Zum Text von IF's Reisebericht," *ZDMG*, XCVI [1942], 98–126); a photo-

graphic edition with a valuable Introduction in German and textual notes by the Hungarian K. Czeglédy ("Zur Meschheder Handschrift von Ibn Faḍlān's Reisebericht," *Acta Orientalia Hungarica*, I, fasc. 2–3 [Budapest, 1951], pp. 217–60); a translation into English of such parts of Ibn Faḍlān as do not appear in Yāqūt (the Rūs description appears in Yāqūt, as noted above), with some comments, by R. P. Blake and R. N. Frye ("Notes on the Risāla of Ibn-Faḍlān," *Byzantina Metabyzantina*, I, Pt. II [1949], 7–37); a new edition and translation by Kovalevsky, with a study and very full commentary (Editions de l'Université nationale Gorki de Kharkov [Kharkov, 1956]); and an annotated translation into French by Marius Canard ("La relation du voyage d'Ibn Faḍlān chez les Bulgares de la Volga," *Annales de l'Institut d'Études Orientales* of Algiers, XVI [1958], 41–146).

7. The modern name is variously given as Kunya-Urgentch, Küne Urgentch, and Ürgenj. See Canard, p. 59, n. 71, and Blake and Frye, p. 30.

8. Or rather, the site of Bulgar. The town of Bulgar was not in existence when Ibn Faḍlān visited the king of the Bulgars; it seems to have come into existence partly as a result of his journey, when the king of the Bulgars got money from the Calif of Bagdad to make his encampment permanent by building a fort. See Zeki Validi (ZV), *Exk.* § 78a (pp. 221–26), and Czeglédy, "Zur Meschheder Hs.," p. 221.

9. For details of this route see, besides the above, ZV's notes to the text of his translation, *passim*; Canard's Introduction and his maps on pp. 55 and 80; and especially Blake and Frye, "Notes on the Risāla," pp. 29–31. For the trade routes of the Rūs, see Holger Arbman, *The Vikings*, trans. A. Binns (London, 1961), p. 94 and Fig. 15.

10. The portage between the Volga at what is now Stalingrad and the Don is only a few dozen miles long and links the Caspian and the Black seas. Today there is a canal.

11. "Jewish" because their dominant class had accepted Judaism. This now-vanished people occupied lands west of the Caspian and lower Volga. Their hostility to Islamic power may well be the reason—or a reason—why the Calif's embassy took the route it did, far east of the lower Volga. It has been suggested that the Khazars played a role in the east comparable to that of the Franks in the west in putting a terminus to Muslim expansionism. See D. M. Dunlop's excellent *History of the Jewish Khazars* (Princeton, N.J., 1954).

12. ZV, § 48; Canard, pp. 90–95. "Abū Bekr" is evidently the *kunya* of Ibn Faḍlān. A *kunya* is a cognomen in which the *Abū* usually means "father of" and the accompanying name is usually that of the eldest son. It is most respectful to call a man by his *kunya*. See *Encyclopedia of Islam*, s.v. *kunya*. At the beginning of the *Risāla* IF's patronymics are given as far back as his great-great-grandfather, but no *kunya* is given.

13. P. 29.

14. P. 48.

15. P. xix.

16. "Zum Text von IF's Reisebericht," p. 100. See also Canard's review of Kovalevsky, *Arabica*, V (1958), 299–300.

17. In the portions of the *Risāla* with which we are concerned, it happens that variants offered by ZV and Canard from the twelfth-century Persian cosmographer Ahmed Tūsī (also known as Nājib Hamadhānī) prove to be of no moment. Similarly I do not find variants from the thirteenth-century Arab Qazwīnī to be worth mentioning even if, as ZV thinks, Qazwīnī may have known a version older than Yāqūt or a better version of Yāqūt than the one we have.

18. ZV, pp. XI–XIII; Canard, n. 348 and elsewhere. This is also the opinion of Kovalevsky, who attaches importance to AR in the reconstruction of the original: see Canard's review of Kovalevsky's second edition, in *Arabica*, as cited above.

19. For evidence that AR may also

have known Yāqūt, see his reference to duelling in the var. to § 91 and compare Frähn's edition and translation of Yāqūt, p. 3.

20. For a biographical sketch of Amīn Rāzī, see Charles Schefer's Introduction to the excerpts, published in his *Mohammed Nerchakhy: Description topographique et historique de Bokhara* (Paris, 1892).

21. Zeki Validi's observation that AR has the *two* nearest of kin (rather than one) light the pyre is somewhat impressive, though we do not have very clear warrant for believing that this was the Scandinavian custom: Carl Weinhold, whom ZV cites, was evidently thinking only of the funeral of Balder in the *Ynglinga saga*, where Thor consecrates the pyre and Odin lays a magic ring on it. A second evidence offered by ZV, that of the smoke of the funeral pyre, I shall discuss below (p. 113). Notable is the fact that AR alone speaks of playing musical instruments at the funeral festivities, though he, unlike Meshed and Yāqūt, does not mention a musical instrument among the grave goods (var. to § 87). Note also his mention of the use of sables as a medium of exchange at a point where the texts of Meshed and Yāqūt are cloudy in such a way as to suggest that some discussion of currency has been misunderstood (var. to § 82). Such details, too, as the "loud voice" with which a kinsman addresses to the slave girl a statement which should be overheard by the dead man (second var. to § 89), and the use of a (bridal) veil to strangle the girl are perhaps too apt merely to have been thought up. See also Canard's notes 302, 318, 326, and 331. In this connection, it should be noted also that AR, rationalist or not, omits the true kernel at the beginning of § 93; see var. to § 93 and see also page 102 and the following pages.

22. Coins of the Mohammedan lands.

23. The *Risāla* elsewhere shows that the Rūs themselves made this drink. It was strongly intoxicating, as we see later (§ 87), but it cannot have been brandy, for no kind of distilled liquor was yet known to Germanic people, according to George Sarton, *Introduction to the History of Science*, I (Baltimore, 1927), p. 534. See also ZV, p. 86, n. 2, and Moriz Heyne, *Fünf Bücher deutscher Hausaltertümer* (Leipzig, 1901), II, p. 380. That Norse ale or beer could be highly intoxicating if drunk with perseverance is copiously attested in Norse literature – see, for example, *Hóvamól*, 12–19. The absence of distilled liquors makes the more baffling those tiny gourd cups found in the Sutton Hoo ship. See Bruce-Mitford, *The Sutton Hoo Ship Burial: A Provisional Guide* (London, 1954), p. 30 and pl. 13.

24. "Stakes" (*ces pieux de bois fichés en terre*) in Canard; ZV has "stake" and a note interpreting the passage to mean that the heads are hung on the big idol.

25. Some sort of ceremonial formulas, Frähn suggests. See Canard, n. 317.

26. Canard (n. 318) explains that the Persian word *gunbādh* (which ZV transliterates here parenthetically as *kunbad*) corresponds to the Arabic *qubba*. In the next excerpt, AR uses the Arabic word *qubba*. Both words are translated alike by both Canard and ZV as respectively *pavillon à coupole* and *Kuppel*.

27. So Canard; ZV: *aus romäischem Dibag*.

28. The word here translated "pandora" is given by ZV as *tanbura* and by Canard as *ṭunbur*, and translated respectively as "Mandoline" and "pandore." Canard refers the reader to an article by Farmer in the Supplement to the *Encyclopedia of Islam*, s. v. *ṭunbur*. He takes issue with Kovalevsky's translation as "lute," which is also the translation of Frähn – *Laute* – in his German version of Yāqūt, p. 15, pointing out that a different work (*'ūd*) is used to designate a lute. Both instruments had a "belly" sound-chest but, like the harp, were strummed without use of a plectrum. The *ṭunbur*, which differed from the lute in having a smaller sound-chest and longer neck, rivaled the lute in popularity among the Arabs of the early tenth century.

29. This datum – that the dead man did not smell bad – is in Canard alone.

30. The first reference in Meshed to a grave chamber (*qubba*).

31. This sentence is omitted by Canard.

32. The sweating of the horses is evidently a relic of torturing of sacrificial animals (or human beings) to enhance the value of the sacrifice to the god. See ZV, *Exk.* § 90d.

33. When Canard differs from ZV he often adduces the Arabic word of the Meshed text (or Persian word of AR), and sometimes justifies his translation in a footnote. In such cases I tend to follow him. Here he has "kinsmen" vis-à-vis ZV's "companions" (*Genossen*) and *plantes odiférantes* (twice) as opposed to ZV's *Blumen, Rosen*, respectively. Perhaps these latter "fragrant plants" correspond to the bracken strewn over the floor of the grave chamber of the Sutton Hoo ship, as noted by Bruce-Mitford (*Provisional Guide*, p. 33). Cf. A. W. Brøgger and H. Shetelig on the moss and juniper bushes used to line the grave chamber of the Tune ship (*The Viking Ships*, trans. K. John [Oslo, 1951], p. 81).

34. "In a loud voice" so as to be overheard by the dead man, as Canard points out (n. 331). See above, n. 21.

35. The Persian word (*haqq*) has either meaning, "duty" or "right"; see Canard, n. 331. ZV translates *Pflicht*.

36. "And seek to escape death with their masters" is not in ZV but is in Yāqūt (Frähn: *und abgeneigt machen könnte*) and Canard.

37. Canard corrects the text to read "re-entered" rather than "entered" on the authority of Yāqūt, holding that the Angel of Death had stepped out of the pavilion while the kinsmen were having intercourse with the girl.

38. So Canard. ZV: "this duty of fellowship" (i.e., with the deceased).

39. "Arrives"–so Canard; ZV: *geht*, to which ZV supplies a parenthetic *in die Kuppel hinein*. This AR reading is thus the basis for Canard's revision of Meshed to indicate that the Angel of Death has stepped out of the pavilion while the six men are having intercourse with the girl. See above, n. 37.

40. ZV has "a tent-cord," "the cord of the pavilion," in place of "veil," a substitution which Canard professes himself unable to understand. See the discussion of this passage on p. 111.

41. The parenthetic phrase "(toward the people)" is a conjecture of ZV's which also appears in Canard. See ZV, p. 96, n. 1, and Canard, p. 133.

42. In § 91 I have so far followed Canard rather than ZV, who has made what seems a needless transposition of sentence order. See his p. 95, n. 3.

43. The datum about the cities, like an occasional other datum in AR, is to be found in a later source. See ZV, p. XII.

44. Characteristically, a considerable part of the exaggeration has to do with sex. In a masterful excursus on the exaggerations indulged in by writers describing the sexual practices of peoples other than their own (*Exk.* § 93b), ZV amply demonstrates that "Die Semiten zeigen in ihren Erzählungen über fremde Völker ein besonderes Interesse für deren sexuelle Verhältnisse und übertreiben dabei häufig."

45. See ZV's *Exkurse* to § 93, esp. § 93e. The length of time that the Rūs had been in contact with oriental peoples is a moot point; ZV thinks it greater than do other authorities. See, for example, D. M. Dunlop, "ZV's Ibn Faḍlān," *Die Welt des Orients*, I (1949), 307–12.

46. AR's version of this section is quite useless.

47. *Scandinavian Archaeology*, trans. E. V. Gordon (Oxford, 1937), pp. 148, 340–42.

48. (Christiania, 1919), pp. 188–89.

49. *Scand. Arch.*, pp. 340–42.

50. It may be that these three words designate the same garment.

51. For excellent and superbly documented descriptions of the *kyrtill*, see Falk's *Kleiderkunde*, pp. 147–53; and for *mǫttull* and *skikkja*, the same, pp. 178–85.

52. P. 118. See, however, ZV, p. 82, n. 5, where ZV rejects Frähn's statement that the sword of the passage is "patterned" (rather than "grooved"). Two-edged swords had

a shallow depression down the center of either side. Perhaps the sword of the Sutton Hoo find was of this latter sort: the sword and scabbard are fused by time, but Bruce-Mitford says that "There seems to have been a groove running down the scabbard for some four inches from the cross-guard" (*A Provisional Guide*, p. 58). Mrs. H. R. E. Davidson suggests that the sword in Ibn Faḍlān was like the one in Sutton Hoo, but as we have seen, the former has "grooves" (in the plural—*Rinnen*) (*Swords of the Anglo-Saxons* [Oxford, 1962], p. 114).

53. Holger Arbman, *The Vikings*, trans. A. Binns (London, 1961), Plate 29 and pp. 67, 200.

54. H. M. Chadwick, *The Cult of Othin* (London, 1899), pp. 40 ff.

55. So ZV, who refers to W. J. Raudonikas, *Die Normannen der Wikingerzeit und das Ladogagebiet* (Stockholm, 1930), p. 53. I have not been able to see this, but Professor Margaret Schlauch has kindly summarized for my use the pertinent passages in the copy in the Historical Institute of Warsaw.

56. See ZV, *Exk.* § 82a, and also Shetelig and Falk, *Scand. Arch.*, p. 276; Peter Paulsen, *Studien zur Wikinger-Kultur* (Neunmünster, 1933), pp. 22 f., 45, and Pl. xv, xvi, xvii, and esp. xxix; Oscar Montelius, *Kulturgeschichte Schwedens* (Leipzig, 1906), p. 301 and Fig. 492.

57. Arbman, *The Vikings*, p. 35.

58. In quoting *Beowulf*, I use the normalized text of F. P. Magoun, Jr., *Béowulf and Judith* . . . (Department of English, Harvard University, Cambridge, Mass., 1959).

59. *De Arabum Persarumque commercio cum Russia et Scandinavia medio aevo* (Copenhagen, 1825), p. 35. For a somewhat different and shorter list, see the *Norse Mythology* of P. A. Munch, rev. Magnus Olsen, trans. S. B. Hustvedt (New York, 1927), p. 10. See also E. A. Philippson, *Die Genealogie der Götter in germanischer Religion, Mythologie, und Theologie* (Urbana, Ill., 1953), p. 52.

60. See ZV, *Exk.* § 85c and Cleasby-Vigfusson, s. v. *trémaðr*.

61. Shetelig and Falk, p. 422.

62. A single boat burial in Denmark, with the boat inverted over the body, is Swedish. See A. F. Major, "Ship Burials in Scandinavian Lands and Beliefs That Underlie Them," *Folk-Lore*, xxxv (1924), p. 119.

63. The striking find of a cremation ship burial on the tiny Isle de Groix off Lorient, which had been the stronghold of a Viking pirate, is perhaps the most notable exception. See, e.g., Arbman, *The Vikings*, pp. 82 ff.

64. See Haakon Shetelig, *Viking Club Saga Book*, iv (1906), 328; T. D. Kendrick, *A History of the Vikings* (London, 1930), p. 49; ZV, *Exk.* § 87b, who cites K. Weinhold as authority that there are 100,000 cremation graves in Sweden; and Major, "Ship Burials," pp. 113–50, esp. 121 ff. I think the last article uncommonly fine, as my repeated uses of it attest. Major holds that the numerous references to ship burial in Icelandic literature are due to the fact that such burial was alien to Icelanders and therefore noteworthy; he observes that, on the other hand, Snorri's *Heimskringla*, which covers all the heathen period of Norway, mentions only two ship burials.

65. The story is translated from Ibn Miskawaïh by Clément Huart, "L'expédition des Russes de 943," *Comptes rendus* of the Académie des Inscriptions (Paris, 1921), pp. 182–91.

66. See n. 28, above.

67. As we have noted, it is only AR who tells us (twice) that music was a part of the celebration during the ten days, though in his condensation he omits mention of the grave goods in the temporary grave. See above, n. 21.

68. See, for example, Major, "Ship Burials," and Brøgger and Shetelig, *Viking Ships*, p. 87.

69. ZV: *kunbad*. Here, as sometimes elsewhere, ZV and Canard differ in their transliterations of Arabic and Persian words.

70. Major, "Ship Burials," p. 119.

71. Major, "Ship Burials," p. 145; A. W. Brøgger *et al.*, *Osebergfundet* (Christiania, 1917), i, 396 ff; Bruce-Mitford, *A Provisional Guide*, p. 36.

For a description of what an actual ship's tent must have been like as deduced from its framework, of which specimens have been found in graves, see Brøgger and Shetelig, *The Viking Ships*, pp. 137–43.

72. It will be noted that Canard associates the *anābīr* with the four posts: around the posts have been built great scaffoldings of wood. It is perhaps worth mentioning that Major describes a Swedish boat burial in which the grave chamber was built to rest on stone walls beside the ship rather than against the insides of the ship (p. 122) and that the grave chamber of the Tune ship is erected at the stern of the ship on planks driven vertically into the ground near the gunwales (see Brøgger and Shetelig, *The Viking Ships*, p. 81).

73. "Vilka mann trauþan né torbónan/ of óra sǫk aldri týna" (*Lieder der Älteren Edda*), ed. Hildebrand-Gering [Paderborn, 1922], p. 358; see also ZV (with citation of Meissner and Graf) *Exk.* § 87d; Chadwick, *Cult of Othin*, pp. 41 ff; and Canard, n. 312.

74. "Traces of the Custom of 'Suttee' in Norway during the Viking Age," *Saga Book of the Viking Club*, VI (1910), 180–208; see esp. p. 196.

75. Brøgger and Shetelig, *The Viking Ships*, pp. 88 f.

76. See Chadwick, *Cult of Othin*, pp. 47 f., and H. R. Ellis, *The Road to Hel: A Study of the Conception of the Dead in Old Norse Literature* (Cambridge, 1943), pp. 69–73 and *passim*.

77. Ellis, *Road to Hel*, pp. 50 f.

78. Ellis, *Road to Hel*, p. 172. See Oliver Elton's translation of the *Gesta Danorum* (London, 1894), I, 31 (pp. 37 f.).

79. See p. 103. Arbman refers to Ibn Faḍlān in connection with this "bird."

80. *The Vikings*, p. 32.

81. "Ship Burials," p. 141.

82. Major, "Ship Burials," pp. 141 f. See also Chadwick, *Cult of Othin*, pp. 47 f.

83. Canard points out that both the door frame and the way of palms may have been in the original *Risāla*.

84. See Edward Westermarck, *The History of Human Marriage*, 5th ed. (New York, 1921), II, pp. 535 ff.

85. The idea that cries could date back to a ceremony with stabbing but without strangulation of course occurs to one, but there seems no reason to suppose that the strangulation is a later addition to the ritual. If orientals were addicted to using the bow-string, Germanic people were also addicted to strangling, by hand-drawn cords as well as by hanging, as Chadwick's examples make clear.

86. Chadwick, *Cult of Othin*, p. 20.

87. ac him wæl-benda   witoda tealde
    hand-ʒewriðena.   Hræðe siþþan
                        wæs
    æfter mund-gripe   méce
                        ʒeþinged
    þæt hit scáden-mǽl sciran
                        móste,
    cwealm-bealu cýðan.

88. Edition of the *Germania* (Heidelberg, 1937), pp. 248 f.

89. At this point I relegate to a note what seems to me a possible, if very faint, parallel between Beowulf's funeral and that of the Rūs. In Ibn Faḍlān we note that the master of each tent on the shore had intercourse with the slave girl before she mounted into the ship. In *Beowulf*, when Wiglaf gives orders to the Geats about the preparation of Beowulf's funeral pyre, he directs them not *en masse* but by *households*: he orders "many warriors, many householders, that they, chiefs, should bring wood for the funeral pyre" —
(Hét þá ʒebéodan   byre Wíh-stánes,
hæle hilde-déor)   hæleða manigum,
bold-ágendra, þæt híe bǽl-wudu
feorran fereden,   folc-ágende,
(gódum toʒeaʒnes).   [ll. 3110–14a]
It must be noted, however, that after the nearest of kin has lighted the pyre in Ibn Faḍlān, it is not heads of households but each of "the people" who in turn adds his faggot to the blaze.

90. Ellis, *Road to Hel*, p. 32; *Heimskringla*, trans. with notes by Erling Monsen and A. H. Smith (Cambridge, 1932), p. 6. Cf. ZV, *Exk.* § 91c.

Some *Beowulf* Readings

KEMP MALONE
Emeritus, Johns Hopkins University

In PREPARING a facsimile edition of the Nowell Codex (the name I use for the second MS. of the volume catalogued in the British Museum as Cotton Vitellius A.xv), I have been led to suggest a certain number of new readings and interpretations of the text of *Beowulf*. I present some of these here for what they are worth, in the hope that they may prove of interest to our jubilarian and to students of English poetry generally.

i

> 1228 Her is æghwylc eorl oþrum getrywe,
> modes milde, mandrihtne heol.

According to C. L. Wrenn (ed., p. 126), "some other letter was originally written before the *e*" of *heol* but I find no signs of this letter in MS. or facsimile and Zupitza noted none in his *Autotypes*. Some medieval emendator, however (hardly our scribe himself), crossed out the *e* of *heol*, thus making a form *hol*. In so doing, he presumably had in mind the *hōl* of his own speech, a later form (with rounded vowel) of *hāl* 'whole.' In this context *hāl* or *hōl* would mean "undivided (in loyalty)." Thorkelin in his edition of the poem emended this *hōl* to *hold* and his reading has been accepted throughout the history of *Beowulf* studies. In itself *hold* is well enough, since it makes better sense than the *hol* it replaces. But an emendation that does not account for the *Beowulf* scribe's *heol* is in the nature of the case unsatisfactory (not to say unsound), and I prefer to disregard the medieval cross-mark and take *heol* for a case of scribal metathesis: I conceive that our scribe copied as *heol* the *hleo* of his *vorlage*. The queen here is telling Beowulf that every *eorl* in the Danish dright is a protection to the liege lord (that is, is a tower of strength to Hrothgar).

ii

> 2223 . . for þreanedlan þ(eow) nathwylces
> hæleða bearna heteswengeas fleoh,
> ærnes þearfa, ond ðær inne feal(h,
> secg synbysig. Sona mwatide
> 2227 þæt (gehðo) ðam gyste, gryrebroga stod.

Here the *mwatide* of the MS. is "hopelessly corrupt," according to Klaeber, but it makes excellent sense if read as three words: *in þa tid(d)e* 'inside then it came to pass.' We may reasonably think that the scribe mistakenly wrote *m* for *in* (so Thorpe), that he failed to double his *d* (so Wyatt), and that he actually wrote "thorn," though the letter now looks like "wynn" because its ascender has faded away. So many letters and letter parts are faded on this page of the MS. that my reading here seems acceptable enough. As for my restoration *gehðo* 2227, this fits the space in the MS., provides the needful alliteration, and gives a meaning suitable to the context.

iii

> 2339   wisse he gearwe
> þæt him holtwudu he(lpan) ne meahte,
> lind wið lige. Sceolde ::þend daga
> æþeling ærgod ende gebidan,
> worulde lifes, . . .

In the MS. the second line of folio 185^r now ends with *sceolde*, the final *e* of which is not whole. The Thorkelin transcripts show that more has been lost here: A has *sceolde* and a blank space and B has *sceolde* . ., his dots indicating that two letters are wanting or illegible. A's blank space usually signalizes illegible letters, but here it comes at the end of his line and we therefore cannot be sure that in this instance it has its usual meaning. In the original state of the MS. there was plenty of room here for two or three more letters, and the obvious restoration is *li*, since the next line begins with *þend* and *liþend* 'seafarer' makes a good epithet for Beowulf, the noted swimmer and voyager, to say nothing of the metaphorical voyage of life with which the present passage is concerned. I therefore read *liþend* and translate lines 2341b−43a thus: "the seafarer, the prince good from of old, was destined to face the end of his days, the end of his earthly life." Oddly enough, nobody until now (myself included) seems to have taken into account the evidence given above. Grundtvig's drastic emendation of *þend* to *læn* has been generally and uncritically accepted; so far as I know, it has never even been questioned.

iv

3150 Swylce geomorgyd (G)eat(isc) meowle
(Beowulfe brægd), bundenheorde,
(so)ng sorgcearig. Sælde geneahhe
þæt hio hyre (here)gangas hearde (ondre)de,
wælfylla worn, (wer)udes egesan,
hyðo ond hæf(t)noð.

Here I accept, though with misgivings, Pope's *Geatisc*. My restoration
of line 3151a may be described as a blend of Bugge and Pope. The reading
song (l. 3152a) is Bugge's. The off-verse here begins with what looks
like *sælðe* in the MS., but the cross-stroke of the supposed ð is of dubious
authenticity, according to N. Davis (EETS 245.xi), and I read *sælde*
with AB. In line 3153 Mackie's *heregangas* best fits the context; Bugge's
ondrede is generally accepted. In *worn* (l. 3154) the first down stroke of
r is only a trifle longer than the second, and AB mistook the letter for
n but we have here only an extreme example of the second scribe's
habitual *r* and Zupitza's reading *wonn* is to be rejected. In reading
werudes (l. 3154) I follow A. H. Smith. The reading *hæftnoð* (l. 3155) is
my own; the usual reading is *hæftnyd* but since the last letter is clearly
ð in the MS. the letter next before ought to be *o* and I think it is. I translate the passage thus: "Likewise a bounden-haired Geatish maiden wove
a lament for Beowulf, a song of sorrow and care. It would happen often
that she would dread cruel invasions, a multitude of deaths on the battlefield, army terror, plundering, and captivity." For some strange reason
editors and commentators have not hitherto put a full stop after
sorgcearig, nor have they taken *sælde* for what it surely is, a form of
sælan 'happen.'

v

3174   hit gedefe bið
þæt mon his winedryhten wordum herge,
ferhðum freoge, þonne he forð scile
of lichaman, (life) weorðan.

The MS. has what looks like *lachaman* in line 3177, but the reading
lichaman is now generally accepted. As Ker says, "the upstroke of the
l . . . cannot be interpreted as part of an *a* . . ." (EETS 245.xii–xiii).
At the head of the MS. line before *weorðan* there is room for only four
letters, and presumably the word that the scribe wrote there was of that
length. But this word is now illegible and must be supplied by conjecture.
To alliterate with *lichaman* it must begin with *l*, of course. Kemble's
restoration *læne* fits the space and alliterates but otherwise it is obvi-

ously an unhappy solution. Holthausen's *læded* is equally unhappy
besides being too long. I suggest *life*. Note the ellipsis *forð* for *forð
gewiten*; compare line 1179, where *forð* is elliptical for *forð gewitan*.
In the present passage, *lichaman* and *life* are parallel objects of *of*, and
the clause *þonne . . . weorðan* means "when he shall be gone forth
from the body, from life."

The "Thryth-Offa Digression" in *Beowulf*

NORMAN E. ELIASON
University of North Carolina

No PASSAGE in *Beowulf* has proved more vexing to editors and to critics than lines 1925–62, which begin by describing the court of Hygelac, mentioning first his royal hall, then the king himself, and then Hygd, his admirable queen. Through line 1931a, nothing the poet says is at all unclear, and his intent is quite plain. Having earlier ·described the Danish royal hall at considerable length, as was necessary and proper, he evidently chose to be very brief here about the Geatish hall (1925a), and he is equally brief about Hygelac (1925b), whom he had already told much about and is to tell more later on. It is the queen on whom the poet centers attention. This is obviously fitting, for as Hygelac's consort she demands notice and nowhere else in the poem does she receive it in any significant way. Hence it is here that we expect to learn something about her and, in view of her position, something of consequence.

This expectation is heightened by the way the poet proceeds with the account. He begins by describing her as stately, young, wise, and fortunate, but quickly abandons such conventional generalities in favor of more specific details, stating that Hygd, the daughter of Hæreth, has been at court only a short while and that there she is not at all niggardly. These details might not attract special notice were it not for the manner in which they are mentioned. The comment about her short stay at court (1927b–29a) implies obviously that she had been married to Hygelac only recently. We naturally wonder why the poet puts it so obliquely and hence anticipate an explanation. Similar anticipation is aroused by his remark about her lack of niggardliness (1929b–31a). If intended as praise of her generosity, it falls ludicrously short. As a queen, generosity is to be expected of her—just as it is of the gracious Wealhtheow, Hrothgar's queen, of whose generosity the poet leaves no doubt. His remark about Hygd is evidently not a superfluous and inept compliment but rather a pointed though tantalizingly brief reference to the unwonted kindness she displays towards the Geatish retainers.

Our expectations are not fulfilled, however, for with line 1931a the account of Hygd abruptly stops, and without warning or apparent reason the poet begins to tell of an altogether different woman, "Thryth," the wife of Offa. This sudden shift from one queen about whom we expect to hear more to another about whom we hardly expect to hear at all presents a serious problem for which there seems to be no satisfactory solution. The only choice we are offered is a true Hobson's choice – between the utterly unconvincing pronouncement that the shift is not unwarranted and the despairing conjecture that the text is corrupt.[1] There is another solution, and though modern scholars rarely if ever even mention it, it deserves reconsideration. Up to about a hundred years ago, the passage was commonly construed as referring to a single queen. I think there is something to be said in its favor. Accordingly, I propose to reexamine the objections to it and to see if the passage cannot legitimately be read thus.

I shall begin with the passage itself, which, though long, we need before us.

>   Bold wæs betlīc,   bregorōf cyning,   1925
>   hēa[h on] healle,   Hygd swīðe geong,
>   wīs wēlþungen,   þēah ðe wintra lyt
>   under burhlocan   gebiden hæbbe,
>   Hærebes dohtor;   næs hīo hnāh swā þēah,
>   nē tō gnēað gifa   Gēata lēodum,   1930
>   māþmgestrēona.   Mōdþrȳðo wæg,
>   fremu folces cwēn,   firen' ondrysne;
>   nænig þæt dorste   dēor genēþan
>   swæsra gesīða,   nefne sinfrēa,
>   þæt hire an dæges   ēagum starede;   1935
>   ac him wælbende   weotode tealde
>   handgewriþene;   hraþe seoþðan wæs
>   æfter mundgripe   mēce geþinged,
>   þæt hit sceādenmæl   scȳran mōste,
>   cwealmbealu cȳðan.   Ne bið swylc cwēnlīc þēaw   1940
>   idese tō efnanne,   þēah ðe hīo ænlicu sȳ,
>   þætte freoðuwebbe   fēores onsæce
>   æfter ligetorne   lēofne mannan.
>   Hūru þæt onhōhsnod[e]   Hemminges mæg:
>   ealodrincende   ōðer sædan,   1945
>   þæt hīo lēodbealewa   læs gefremede,
>   inwitnīða,   syððan ærest wearð
>   gyfen goldhroden   geongum cempan,
>   æðelum dīore,   syððan hīo Offan flet
>   ofer fealone flōd   be fæder lāre   1950
>   sīðe gesōhte;   ðær hīo syððan well
>   in gumstōle,   gōde mære,

līfgesceafta   lifigende brēac,
hīold hēahlufan   wið hæleþa brego,
ealles moncynnes   mīne gefrǣge   1955
þone sēlestan   bī sǣm twēonum,
eormencynnes;   forðām Offa wæs
geofum ond gūðum,   gārcēne man,
wīde geweorðod,   wīsdōme hēold
ēðel sīnne; —   þonon Eomēr wōc   1960
hæleðum tō helpe,   Hem[m]inges mǣg
nefa Gārmundes,   nīða cræftig.²

   If one queen (not two) is referred to here, then Hygd, the wife of
Hygelac, must formerly have been the wife of Offa. If so, the abrupt shift
in line 1931 is eliminated, along with other smaller textual vexations.
The account, as I read it, may be briefly summarized thus: Hygd, the
admirable wife of Hygelac and not long married to him, is now unwont-
edly kind toward the Geatish courtiers.³ This renowned folk-queen
(*fremu folces cwēn*⁴, 1932a) had been guilty of haughtiness (*mōdþrȳð
ō wæg*,⁵ 1931b) and of a great wickedness (*firen' ondrysne*,⁶ 1932b)
[an instance of which the poet then cites]. No man at court dared to
look at her even — except her own lord (*nefne sin frēa*,⁷ 1934b) — and
if one did, he was cruelly put to death. This kind of behavior, however
(which the poet righteously condemns [1940b–43]), was stopped by
her father (*þæt onhōhsnode Hemminges mǣg*, 1944 — see p. 131f.) or,
by another less reliable account (*ealodrincende ōðer sǣdan*, 1945),
by the young and valiant Offa, to whom she was given in marriage — an
event arranged or instigated by her father.⁸ As Offa's wife she behaved
well for the duration of their marriage⁹ and bore him a son, Eomer.
   Thus read, the passage contains an account of Hygd properly begun,
continued, and completed — something the poet's audience or readers
would naturally expect. It concludes, moreover, with something an
English or more precisely a Mercian audience¹⁰ would be especially
interested in — the early history of the Mercian royal line. To this the poet
gives brief but proper attention, succeeding both in complimenting the
Mercian royal house and in explaining an obscure detail in its early
history. The poet's adroitness here merits notice. His singling out of
Offa seems only natural, of course, for as the former husband of Hygd he
is part of the story and it is only as such that the poet first treats him.
The fact that he is king of the Angles and thus a progenitor of the
Mercian royal line is clearly brought out only at the conclusion, when by
naming Offa's father (Garmund) and son (Eomer) the poet identifies him
and establishes his place in the lineage. His resounding praise of Offa
seems intended as praise of the whole royal line — at any rate this is its
effect. Eomer thus needs and receives no special praise, and with him

the poet stops, since this brings him to the terminal bounds he had set for his work (c. 550).[11] But if about Eomer he is content to mention only his pedigree, he takes pains to make it especially clear, citing Eomer's maternal as well as paternal ancestry and thus effectively underscoring the fact that Eomer is the son of Offa, king of the Angles, and Hygd, queen of the Geats.

Thus, as I interpret it, the conclusion (1955–62) skillfully succeeds both in bringing the account of Hygd to a fitting end and in giving proper recognition to the reigning family of Mercia. As usually interpreted, however, neither the conclusion nor the passage as a whole is satisfactory. The obvious irrelevancy of the "Thryth-Offa" story has to be attributed to scribal bungling or regarded as a singularly inept digression, and the compliment to the Mercian royal house serves only to raise the unwarranted suspicion that the passage is a later interpolation or the daring speculation that the poem is of later date than generally believed. But when the passage is read as an account of Hygd throughout, telling how this haughty and wicked girl had become an admirable woman and that before her marriage to Hygelac she had been the wife of Offa and had borne him a son who was the ancestor of the royal line of Mercia, it all fits together quite well.

In the description of her as the admirable young wife of Hygelac and then as the wicked girl she once was, the transition (1931b) is abrupt, to be sure, but no more so than many other transitions in the poem, especially those involving contrast or sudden change in a person's character, for example, the two passages concerned with Heremod (898–915, 1709–24), a good man who turned bad. But it is really not the abruptness of the transition here that is bothersome so much as the lack of any forewarning of it. Describing Hygelac's queen as very young (*Hygd swīðe geong*, 1926b) is, in view of what follows, anything but felicitous.[12] The lapse is not unique. Hygelac too is described as young (1831), despite the fact that by an earlier marriage he has a grown daughter. The resulting discrepancy is inconsequential, for it is obvious that Hygelac's age is poetical (designed to enhance the contrast between Hygelac and the aged Hrothgar) rather than biological. Having made Hygelac young, the poet probably felt it appropriate that his wife also should be young. Moreover, "very young" is a relative term, applicable in some circumstances to virtually anyone this side of dotage. It does not make a child-bride of Hygd.

Her age no longer figures prominently in the "Thryth" controversy, as it once did. Grundtvig, the first scholar to detect both Hygd and "Thryth" in the passage, insisted it was ludicrous to suppose that someone as young as Hygd could previously have been married to anyone, least of all Offa, who was of a much earlier time.[13] Kemble, whose understanding of the passage was even more fantastic than Grundtvig's, thought the passage was concerned with but one woman, the unnamed widow of Offa and therefore extremely old or, if young, his daughter-in-law.[14]

With the publication of Grein's famous essay[15] in 1862, the presence of both Hygd and "Thryth" in the passage was firmly established, together with the reasons for thinking this must be so. In ridding the passage of most of the fantastic explanations that it had had, Grein performed a notable service, and the lucidity of his explanation lent weight to the reasons he gave. These were very simple. Offa, he maintained, lived in the mid-fourth century and Hygelac at the beginning of the sixth, and therefore Hygd could not possibly have been the wife of both. Her name too argued against it, for Offa's wife was named "Thryth" or something like it,[16] a fact which he claimed was supported by the St. Albans account. Of these reasons of Grein's, the first (Offa's date) was and remains by all odds the more important, the second (his wife's name) being more or less incidental. Neither seems ever to have been effectively challenged. In current scholarship both are accepted without serious question or essential modification.

Let us take up first the name of Offa's wife. Our concern is not whether it is Modthryth or Thryth (see n. 5) but whether it is anything of the kind. The only warrant for thinking so is the *Vitae Duorum Offarum*, a Latin work written by an anonymous monk at St. Albans (c. 1200), concerning Offa I (the Angle king told of in *Beowulf*) and Offa II (the famous Mercian king who reigned 757–96, presumably after *Beowulf* was composed). His account need be rehearsed only in part and very briefly here,[17] where it will suffice to note that the wife of Offa I is depicted as an innocent, long-suffering creature, cruelly wronged by her father who has incestuous designs on her, is set adrift in the sea but finally happily reunited with her husband. The wife of Offa II, on the other hand, is a wicked girl who is set adrift in punishment for her wickedness, but is rescued and then succeeds in deluding Offa and marrying him, remaining wicked, however, till her death. It is this woman, the wife of Offa II, who is named *Drida*.

It would seem obvious, I should think, that this story told by the St. Albans monk about two queens, one good and one bad, derives ultimately from a story essentially like that in *Beowulf*[18] about one queen who had changed from bad to good. It is usually maintained[19] that the story of Offa II's wife (rather than Offa I's) is particularly similar to the story in *Beowulf*, but this ignores their basic dissimilarity (the girl's continued wickedness vs. her change from wicked to good). The only real reason for insisting on its particular similarity is that Offa's wife in *Beowulf* is thus provided with a name. *Drida* certainly resembles "Thryth" closely enough to be an acceptable variant, and the resemblance can hardly be construed as accidental. But *Drida*, the name in the St. Albans account, is not one that was handed down from Germanic tradition. Offa of Mercia had a wife whose name indisputably was *Cynethryth*, which is inscribed on coins. This one historical detail the St. Albans monk managed to get right—or almost right, altering *Cynethryth* in his Latin to *Quendrida*, from which by bad etymologizing (*id est regina Drida*) he abstracted the name *Drida*. It is this name, derived as it demonstrably is from the name of the historical Cynethryth who lived some time after *Beowulf* is thought to have been composed, that provides the only basis[20] for supposing that the wife of Offa told about there was named "Thryth."

Thus the crux of the whole matter is the date of Offa's life. If he antedated Hygd by a century or more—as Grein insisted and as has been confidently reiterated ever since—it is impossible that she could have been his wife. If the evidence bears this out, my reading of the passage is wrong. I could, of course, argue otherwise, blaming the poet or his source for the anachronism. Instead of resorting to anything so shabby, I prefer to let the evidence settle the issue. If it does not place Offa significantly earlier than Hygd, then the passage, I insist, is concerned with her alone and not also with "Thryth." With "Thryth" disposed of, there is no longer a "Thryth-Offa" digression to vex critics and editors.

Before turning to the evidence itself, we need to recall what we are seeking and may reasonably expect to find there. The occasion with which we are concerned in the poem is the return of Beowulf to Hygelac's hall and the description of Hygd there. This, by Klaeber's dating, occurred in 515. Since Hygd has not long been married to Hygelac, we may date her widowhood, that is, Offa's death, as about 510. Taking into account Klaeber's admonition about the approximateness of these dates (see n. 11) and also the nature of the evidence to be examined, as well as the inexact results to be expected of it, I should think it fair to conclude that any date for Offa's death as early as 400 would rule him out, but any date from 450 or later would not.

The evidence consists essentially of only two things—the Mercian pedigree, which is said to indicate that Offa lived in the fourth century, and legendary accounts placing Offa three generations earlier than Hygelac. The Mercian pedigree[21] simply lists, without dates, the royal line back from Penda (d. 655) and from Offa of Mercia (d. 796). Reckoning back eight generations from Penda's death, and allotting thirty years for each generation, as is regularly done,[22] gives us 415 as the date of Offa's death, and reckoning back similarly twelve generations from Offa of Mercia's death gives us 436. Although both dates are obviously and comfortably within the fifth century, Offa is nevertheless regularly assigned to the fourth on the basis of precisely this same evidence.[23] For a reason I shall explain below, the Mercian pedigree errs by including at least one generation too many, and hence the date of Offa's death becomes 445 or 466. In view of the rough system of reckoning,[24] this would seem close enough to 510 so that Offa cannot be ruled out as being about contemporary with Hygelac. Indeed, ruling him out on the basis of the Mercian pedigree seems to me inconceivable.

The other kind of evidence,[25] which places Offa three generations before Hygelac, is very complex and confusing. Fortunately, it has been thoroughly explored by Malone[26] and therefore need not detain us long here, especially since our concern is with only one of the many puzzling genealogical confusions involved.[27] For us the essential problem is the discrepancy between the genealogy preserved in English tradition (that is, in *Beowulf* and in the Mercian pedigree) and that preserved in Scandinavian tradition (as found in Bk. IV of Saxo) and how this discrepancy can best be explained.[28]

Our first and most crucial step is to resolve the discrepancy between the *Beowulf* and Mercian genealogies. In the former the pedigree is *Garmund*[29] – *Offa* – *Eomer*, but in the latter it is *Garmund* – *Offa* – *Angeltheow* – *Eomer*. Angeltheow, I believe, does not properly belong in the Mercian pedigree. In some versions[30] he is designated as *Ongengeot*. The difference ought not be dismissed as a mere instance of scribal carelessness (thus Sisam, p. 298), for it seems significant and can be explained as significant (thus Malone, p. 169). The fact that one form of the name (*Angeltheow*) contains the element *Angle* and the other (*Ongengeot*) contains the element *Geat*[31] provides the clue for resolving the discrepancy between the *Beowulf* and Mercian genealogies. According to the *Beowulf* account (as I read it), Eomer was the son of Offa, the Angle king, and Hygd, a Geatish princess.[32] Under the circumstances, it would be very natural that their son would acquire the two by-names *Geat* (in reference to his maternal nationality) and *Angle* (in reference to his paternal nationality). The existence of these two by-names, together with the fact that his mother later became queen of the Geats, evidently led to genealogical confusion, Eomer's by-names being construed as the name(s) of Offa's son(s) and then acquiring a second element, Angel*theow* and Ongen*geat*. If the discrepancy between the *Beowulf* and Mercian genealogies ought not be ignored, as it usually is, the explanation I have suggested would seem a plausible way of resolving it.

Its plausibility is strengthened when we turn to the genealogy found in Bk IV of Saxo, where the pedigree is *Garmund*[33] – *Offa* – [   ] – *Hygelac*. In reconciling it with the pedigree preserved in English tradition, we must of course assume that the latter, being recorded much earlier and representing unbroken Angle tradition, is the more accurate. The problem, then, is to find a reasonable explanation of how Saxo's strange and obviously incorrect pedigree might have derived from the

probably correct pedigree preserved by the Angles. The process was
presumably something like this: (1) With the erroneous addition of
Angle and *Geat* as explained above, these names came to be construed
as eponyms. (2) *Geat* was accordingly provided with appropriate Geatish
descendants, that is, [   ] and Hygelac. (3) To *Angle* and *Geat*
a third eponymous brother *Dan* was added, who alone was then kept in
Danish tradition.[34] Thus Saxo's genealogy, though utterly at variance
with the genealogy preserved by the Angles, supports the view that the
latter is correct except for the addition of *Angeltheow/Ongengeot*. This
addition, which was due to confusion about Eomer's parents, gave rise
to confusion about Offa's descendants. This latter confusion has led to
the erroneous belief that the evidence of Germanic legend indicates that
Offa lived three generations before Hygelac.

There is, then, no solid basis whatever for the confident assertion
that Offa lived too early to have been Hygd's husband. In our brief examination of the genealogical evidence, another striking fact has
emerged. Reflected there, in the English as well as the Scandinavian
accounts, is a fusion of the Angle and Geatish royal lines. This is obvious
in Saxo, whose patent error in putting Offa and Hygelac in the same
royal line underscores the fact, but only obscurely in the Mercian
pedigree, where *Angel*theow and Ongen*geat* reflect it faintly. The fusion
of the two lines may of course be due simply to error, which has clearly
entered in. But if due only to error, it seems odd that the fusion reflected
in both as occurring at about the time of Offa should conform so remarkably with the *Beowulf* version, which (as I read it) provides a fairly
clear account of how the fusion occurred. Reduced to tabular form, the
Beowulf genealogy is this:

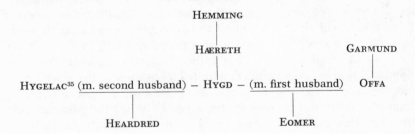

Even in so simplified a tabular form, the matter seems rather complicated, and hence the poet cannot be severely blamed for failing to explain all the details clearly and fully. About some of them he was
evidently unsure. Besides his uncertainty about the relationship of
Garmund and Offa,[36] he was also unsure of the relationship of Hemming
and Hæreth, and so of course are we. I list Hemming as Hæreth's father

because this is the simplest solution, because their names alliterate properly, and because it does not conflict with the poet's account. He speaks of Hæreth as Hemming's kinsman. (To construe *Hemminges mæg*, 1944b, otherwise, that is, as referring to Offa, is quite unwarranted in view of the lines that follow.) He also speaks of Eomer as Hemming's kinsman (1961b), which is logical enough but at first glance rather odd. Since in Eomer's pedigree the parental grandfather Garmund (1962a) is cited, we would expect the maternal grandfather Hæreth to be cited too instead of the maternal great-grandfather Hemming. I suspect that the poet deliberately refrained from citing Hæreth because of his unsavory reputation. In citing Hemming and Garmund, the poet's intent is to make clear that Eomer, the son of Hygd and Offa, was the offspring of two royal lines, the Geatish one about whom his poem was concerned, and the Angle line, in whom his audience were especially interested. If he failed to be as clear about this as he might have been, he deserves some consideration in view of his highly compressed account. After all, to describe Hygd and her checkered career, marital and otherwise, and to set straight how and when the Angle and Geatish lines were united is not a mean feat to accomplish in thirty-seven lines.

If his account of the union of the Angle and Geatish dynasties is essentially correct (as I take it to be), it may be thought strange that the event which marked it, the marriage of Offa and Hygd, is recorded nowhere else. But the very tale the *Beowulf* poet tells suggests why. Memory of the event had faded, as it naturally would in oral tradition. There the principals got separated, Hygd—because of her subsequent marriage to Hygelac—being remembered only as a Geatish queen and thus not as the mother of Offa's son. Only in *Beowulf* was this memory of her still preserved, and there, as the poet's uncertainties about some of the details reveal, the memory had already become somewhat clouded.[37] Hastening the process, I suspect, was the story itself, involving something about Hygd herself or her father that was evidently more disreputable than the poet wants to admit. Two or three of his cryptic references suggest that he is suppressing something unseemly, as he naturally would out of respect for Hygelac or for the Mercian royal line. For this he hardly deserves censure.[38] Certainly in telling as much as he does about Hygd's wicked past, he adds to the credence of his tale.

If, as is generally recognized, the poet's information about Danish, Swedish, and Geatish history is essentially sound, it is surely reasonable to suppose that his information about the history of the Angles, his own people, is equally trustworthy. His account of Offa is certainly not to be regarded as mere fiction. From other sources we know that Offa's legendary reputation rested not only on the notorious woman he married but also on a famous duel he fought as a young man. This is briefly recounted in lines 35–44 of *Widsith*, a poet older than *Beowulf*,[39] and also in much later works, both English and Scandinavian, where it is greatly expanded and fictionalized. Since the *Beowulf* poet is concerned with Offa as husband and father, not as warrior, he merely alludes to this youthful exploit,[40] but enough to reveal his familiarity with the old legend.

Although as history his tale of Offa and his marriage to Hygd may not be unimpeachable, it is legitimate to accept it as trustworthy—just as we accept other matters recorded in *Beowulf* but not elsewhere, provided they seem circumstantially true and are not contradicted by any other equally credible evidence.

Whether we accept it as history or not, we ought to accept it as it stands (that is, without conjecturing that something significant has been inadvertently omitted) and to interpret it as we naturally must when disabused of the notion that Hygd cannot conceivably have been the wife of Offa before she married Hygelac. The tale he tells is then a fairly simple one—of a girl married first to one man, by whom she has a child, and then to another—and as such hardly one to strain the bounds of credulity. The poet's narrative plan requires that the tale be told not from its beginning but from near the end, that is, after Hygd has married Hygelac. The scene is Hygelac's court and it is of his wife that the poet tells. Had it been his purpose to tell of "Thryth," the long-dead wife of a long-dead king of another people, we would expect him to put the tale into the mouth of another, for example, a scop, as he commonly does when inserting stories of the distant past—of Heremod, Sigemund, or Finn.[41]

But the tale he tells involves much more than a tale of tangled marriage and means much more than that. Hygd was a renowned queen, the former consort of Offa, king of the Angles, and the mother of Eomer, ancestor of the Mercian kings—a fact not only intensely interesting to the poet's audience but gratifying even to us today. The presence of Offa is, as Wrenn declares, "the one certain link of the poem with English history."[42] Displacing Offa as Hygd's husband and Hygd as Eomer's mother, as scholars for the last hundred years have insisted on doing, has removed this "one certain link" that would be so gratifying for us to have and that is so vital in the poet's design. One of his chief concerns is the Geats, a people whose greatness he celebrates and whose decline he foretells. After their eclipse, memory of them gradually faded, their once-famous kings and queens being all but totally forgotten. But in his tale of their renowned Queen Hygd, the *Beowulf* poet preserved one cherished memory—the fact that the royal line of Mercia was descended from the illustrious Offa, king of the Angles who were destined to have a glorious history, and Hygd, queen of the Geats at the time of their great glory.

NOTES

1. Wrenn provides a good, up-to-date appraisal of the problem and of the critical and textual proposals for solving it. (Supplement to Chambers, pp. 540–43, See n. 2 below). Professor H. C. Matthes in *Festschrift zum 75. Geburtstag von Theodor Spira*, edd. H. Viebrock and W. Erzgräber (Heidelberg, 1961), pp. 14–31, argues, as I do here, that the passage is concerned with Hygd alone. In all other respects our views are different.

2. Fr. Klaeber, *Beowulf and the Fight at Finnsburg*, 3d ed. (Boston, 1951). Other standard editions and commentaries consulted and similarly cited are E. V. K. Dobbie, *Beowulf and Judith* (New York, 1953); C. L. Wrenn, *Beowulf with the Finnesburg Fragment* (Boston and London, 1953); *Heyne-Schückings Beowulf* neubearbeitet von Else von Schaubert, sechzehnte Auflage (Paderborn, 1946–49) (cited as "Schaubert"); R. W. Chambers, *Beowulf: An Introduction to the Poem with a Discussion of the Stories of Offa and Finn*, 3d. ed. with a Supplement by C. L. Wrenn (Cambridge, 1959); Johannes Hoops, *Kommentar zum Beowulf* (Heidelberg, 1932).

3. *Swā þēah* (l. 1929b) implies that her kindness is in some way or other exceptional, and so too, I think, does *Gēata lēodum* (1930b) since *Gēata* seems rather pointed in view of the fact that only Geats were present there. *Lēodum* does not of course imply that her kindness was directed toward all her subjects—that she went about in the slums or hospitals dispensing royal charity and cheer. The poet is depicting a sixth- (or eighth-) century queen, who, judging by the immediate context as well as by the behavior of Wealhtheow, showed kindness and was expected to show it only to the favored few gathered about in the king's hall.

4. The phrase is appropriate only if it refers to Hygd, who as consort of Hygelac and formerly of Offa is properly designated as a *folces cwēn*, and since she has just been described as *wīs* and *wēlþungen*, another laudatory adjective *fremu* 'admirable, renowned' is fitting. If it refers to the wicked "Thryth," however, *fremu* is odd and *folces cwēn* odder still. See Klaeber's attempt to justify the phrase as applied to her (p. 199) and note his puzzled query, ". . . was she married twice?"

5. The MS. reading is *mod þryðo wæg*, which editors usually alter in one way or other. Here *wæg* may have perfective or past-habitual force (as the preterite often has in OE). If so, *ō* is best construed as an adverb (= *ā* 'ever') used to mark and reinforce the perfective sense of the verb (see n. 6). Its object is *mōdþrȳð* (fem. acc. i-stem noun) meaning "haughtiness" or something of the kind. For alternative interpretations of *mōdþrȳð* and sound objections to them, see especially Wrenn, pp. 215 and 275, and his further comments in Chambers, pp. 541–42. For a good survey of the various interpretations, see Dobbie, pp. 214–15.

6. Since *ondrysne* may have either a good or bad sense, the safest rendering I think is "great." Whether or not *firen'* (for *firene*) is a variant of *mōdþrȳð* is a nice question, answerable only if we could be certain about the precise meaning of the two terms. Since their meaning is somewhat similar, I take it as an instance of variation and conclude that the poet uses the variant in anticipation of what is to follow. (That the poet uses variation thus is pointed out by F. C. Robinson, "Variation: A Study in the Diction of *Beowulf*," Univ. of North Carolina doctoral dissertation, 1961, pp. 147 ff.). Where, as here, a verb takes two objects *mōdþrȳð* and *firen'*, the sense of the verb may depend more upon the first or fit it better than the second (cf. *feorh ālegde, hǣþene sāwle*, ll. 851–52, where *ālegde* fits perfectly with *feorh* but not so well with *sāwle*, and accordingly is trans-

lated as "he *laid down* his life, *gave up* his heathen soul.") Similarly, here *mōdþrȳð . . . wæg . . . firen* may be translated as "she *possessed* haughtiness, *was weighed down* by a wickedness," thus obviating the need for construing *wæg* as having perfective force.

7. This seems the safer MS. reading and rendering. The more doubtful alternative (*sinfrēa* = "husband") derives mainly from the assumption that the context requires it (see Hoops, *Kommentar*, p. 213, for a survey of the arguments).

In using *sin* (the reflexive posses-sive rather than the more usual geni-tive form *hire*) and giving it metrical heightening (both stress and allitera-tion), the poet is referring, I suspect, to her father's incestuous attentions, but in using the ambiguous term *frēa* 'lord' he is either indicating his doubts about this unsavory detail or trying to play it down.

8. The poet's uncertainty seems to be due to the two different accounts he has heard of the affair but may actually be due to his reluctance to reveal the worst he has heard. Lines 1947b–49a suggest simply that her father gave her in marriage to Offa, but lines 1949b–51a suggest that his role was not so conventional nor so creditable, for in the poet's cryptic words there is the hint that her jour-ney across the sea to Offa was invol-untary on her part and involved something nefarious on the father's part—a hint borne out in the St. Albans account (see below).

9. This is the clear implication of *līfgesceafta . . . brēac* (1953). It also implies, I think, that the mar-riage ended with Offa's death, for *līfgesceafta* would be quite inappro-priate if it had ended otherwise. The term implies nothing about the length of time they were married.

10. *Beowulf* is certainly of Anglian origin and probably of Mercian. I assume the latter here merely to simplify the discussion. Northum-brian origin would not weaken the argument.

11. See Klaeber, pp. xxxi ff. His dates, we should remember, are "at best . . . approximate dates only,"

designed merely "to show the se-quence of events in such an order as to satisfy the probabilities of the narrative." An additional reason for stopping with Eomer is that he, if Schütte can be trusted, was the first of the line to rule in England: ". . . he being an emigrant, already belongs to Britain. With Offa the true continental Angles come to an end. . . ." (Gudmund Schütte, *Our Forefathers*, II [Cambridge, 1932], p. 316). I suspect, however, that Schütte is merely guessing about this, for his discussion of Offa (pp. 310 ff.) is not reliable, revealing an unfamiliarity with modern *Beowulf* scholarship on this passage. Among modern scholars, he and Matthes (see n. 1 above) are the only ones who do not subscribe to the usual inter-pretation of it. Like me, he adheres to the view prevailing before Grundtvig and Grein, but unlike me, he clings to the manifestly impossible notion that Hygd was Hygelac's widow rather than Offa's.

12. Hence it is tempting to explain it as an instance of scribal correction, the original being *gēong Hygd swīð̄e*, meaning "Hygd went about briskly," or, if this seems stylistically unac-ceptable, *gēong Hygd swīð̄e wīs/ond wēlþungen*. But, as I go on to in-dicate, emendation is not really necessary.

13. N. F. S. Grundtvig, *Beowulfes Beorh eller Bjovulfs-Drapen* (Copen-hagen, 1861), pp. 156 ff. and p. XLV. In its anticipation of Grein's argu-ment and conclusion, Grundtvig's discussion of the passage is of some historical interest. Otherwise it is quite worthless now.

14. J. M. Kemble, *Beowulf*, 2d ed. (Lon-don, 1835–37). Kemble did not know what to make of *Hygd*, evidently taking it as a by-name of Hygelac (II, 78). He thought Offa's widow, if it was she rather than his daughter-in-law presiding in Hygelac's hall, must be old since Offa preceded Hrethel, Hygelac's father, on the throne (I, xii). Like Grundtvig, he thought the text must be badly defective—a notion that still persists.

15. C. W. M. Grein, "Die historischen Verhältnisse des Beowulfliedes,"

Jahrbuch für romanische und englische Literatur, IV (1862), 260–85. The pertinent part of his paper begins p. 278.

16. Grein took *Mōdþrȳðo* (1931b) as her name, rejecting Grundtvig's *Thrytho* on the excellent grounds that it lacks the necessary alliteration. Grein was obviously none too happy about Mōdþrȳðo, but was practically forced to accept it because he felt her name ought to be found in the text. Later scholars, who reject Mōdþrȳðo as a name (in whole or part) and accordingly leave her nameless in the text, nonetheless speak of her as "Thryth."

17. It is summarized briefly by Klaeber (pp. 196–97) and more fully by Hoops (pp. 208–12). Chambers' discussion (pp. 31–40), with which I cannot fully agree, is valuable, and he includes long excerpts of the original (pp. 217–43).

18. And hence the St. Albans account may be relied on – though only cautiously of course – to supply details cryptically referred to in *Beowulf*, e.g., the father's role and especially his incestuous proposal.

19. For example, by Klaeber (p. 197), Hoops (pp. 210–12), and Chambers (36–37). In discussing the supposed greater similarity between the St. Albans account of Offa II's wife and the *Beowulf* account, Chambers finds a striking parallel in the names *Drida* and *Thryth*, and though recognizing that Offa II's wife was in fact named *Cynethryth*, he regards this only as a coincidence, which he then tries to explain away. The question, however, is not the "coincidence" of *Drida* and *Thryth* but whether there is a *Thryth* at all.

20. Saxo's *Hermuthruda* (the second element of which corresponds to *þryð*) is often cited as evidence, but it obviously is irrelevant. She was not Offa's wife but his grandmother. Even Chambers, who does his best to wring from her name some sort of support for "Thryth," must lamely conclude, "It may well be that there is some connection between the Thryth of *Beowulf* and the Hermuthruda who in Saxo weds Offa's ancestor" (p. 40).

21. The pedigrees as found both in the Anglo-Saxon Chronicle (626 and 757) and elsewhere are most readily available and conveniently arranged in Chambers (pp. 195–98). The relationship of the several versions of the pedigrees is discussed by Kenneth Sisam, "Anglo-Saxon Royal Genealogies," *Proceedings of the British Academy*, XXXIX (1953), 287–348.

22. Grein is the only exception I have noted. He takes 4 generations = 130 years. In comparison with the rough guess (30 years per generation) usually used, the basis of Grein's computation (4 generations = 130 years) looks impressively accurate. But, as he notes, he got it from P. E. Müller, who arrived at it by simply subtracting 626 (the date when Penda began his reign) from 757 (the date when Offa II began his reign four generations later). Thus Müller's formula, derived as it is from this single instance, is even less reliable than the usual rough guess. Its accuracy is also questionable, for, as Miss Whitelock notes (*The Anglo-Saxon Chronicle* [1961], p. 17), the date 626 for Penda's accession is doubtful.

Karl Müllenhoff (*Beovulf: Untersuchungen über das angelsächsische Epos und die älteste Geschichte der germanischen Seevölker* [Berlin, 1889], p. 85), who explained the slender basis of Müller's formula and pointed out its unreliability, was guilty of a similar inaccuracy in arriving at Offa's I's date, one that keeps persisting in spite of admonitions about it by Chadwick and others – who themselves fail to heed their own sage advice. The inaccuracy consists in using a base date that is doubtful or wrong, in this instance taking 576 as the date of Penda's birth to arrive at 336 as the date of Offa I's birth. The date of Penda's death (655) is certain, but not the date of his accession or birth, and therefore 655 is obviously the proper base date and the others are not.

The rough guess (30 years per generation) commonly used in historical reckoning (*OED*, see *generation* 5) is probably as satisfactory as any other. Worth noting, however, is the definition of *generation* 1 b (3) given in *Webster's Third New International Dictionary,* "the average span of time variously computed and varying according to cultural and other conditions between the birth of parents and that of their children," and the illustration cited there, "among primitive peoples twenty years may make a generation." In the present instance, thirty years – though acceptable enough – seems to me rather high. If twenty-five years (which is hardly an inordinately youthful age for parenthood) were used instead, the date of Offa's death, reckoned above (p. 129 f.) as 445 or 466, would become 480 or 521.

23. Grein, mid-fourth (p. 281); Klaeber, latter half of the fourth (p. 196); Hoops, c. 400 (p. 210); Wrenn, fourth century (Chambers, p. 539).

24. That is, thirty years per generation, which is hardly so meticulous as to preclude all possibility of error (see n. 22). Nor is the evidence itself completely reliable. As Sisam has observed: ". . . the Anglo-Saxon genealogies are not primitive documents. Counting their generations will not lead us back safely to Continental chiefs or kings of the fourth or fifth centuries . . . . all the genealogies in their early parts fail because fact, fiction, and error cannot be distinguished" (pp. 328 – 29).

25. The WS genealogy is often cited also as providing corroborative evidence, but I am dubious about both the reliability of the evidence and its pertinence. What is regarded as pertinent there are the names *Wig* and *Freawine* (Wig's father), who in Scandinavian tradition are represented as contemporaries of Offa (i.e., his brother-in-law and father-in-law respectively, who play roles in Offa's youthful exploit, the famous duel he fought – see pp. 132 f.). It is questionable whether they were originally in the story of this famous exploit or were later put into it, and it is also questionable whether their inclusion in the WS pedigree is due to this story. Sisam (see n. 21) thinks there is no doubt of this, attributing their insertion into the WS pedigree (where they do not belong) on this account. "English literary sources do not mention Wig or Freawine, and they could not be expected to appear in incidental references like those in *Beowulf* and *Widsith.* But it can hardly be doubted that they had a prominent part in the full story as it was told at the Mercian court, and I regard Cerdic's pedigree as evidence for it. A West Saxon embellisher of pedigrees would not dare to claim Wermund and Offa of Angle while Offa of Mercia and his pedigree were fully remembered" (p. 307). Even if Sisam's conjecture is right, there is still the question whether their position in the WS pedigree reflects the correct chronology or the incorrect chronology resulting from Offa's being shifted back three generations (see pp. 130–131). Aside from this, the reliability of the WS genealogy is not to be counted on. Taking it at face value, however, and reckoning back four generations from Cerdic (d. 534), we get 414 as the date of Wig's death.

26. Kemp Malone, "Humblus and Lotherus," originally published in *Acta Philologica Scandinavica,* XIII (1939), 201–14, but reprinted in his *Studies in Heroic Legend and in Current Speech* (Copenhagen, 1959), pp. 168–80, which is cited here.

27. Especially in Bk. 1 of Saxo and in the *Hervararsaga,* which Malone explains.

28. My explanation, though heavily dependent on Malone, differs from his.

29. In *Beowulf,* Offa is not specifically said to be Garmund's son, but Eomer (Offa's son) is designated as *nefa Gārmundes* (1962a), i.e., Garmund's grandson (see n. 36).

30. Notably in Vespasian B. vi. See n. 21 and Sisam's discussion referred to there.

31. On *geot* for *geat* see Malone, p. 169, n. 2.

32. Whether a Geat by birth or by virtue of her later marriage to Hygelac is immaterial.

33. For the sake of simplicity I use the English name-forms.

34. This is essentially the same as Malone's explanation (pp. 170–172).

35. Omitted as irrelevant here are Hygelac's ancestors, his first wife, and his daughter.

36. Reflected in his designating Offa's son as the *nefa* of Garmund. This is now regularly and properly construed as meaning "grandson" here, but only on the basis of genealogical evidence outside of *Beowulf*.

37. That is, by the eighth century.

38. Much of what is blamed as obscure in the passage is due, I think, only or mainly to this.

39. Though the Offa passage may be a later addition, there is no good reason to suppose it postdates *Beowulf*.

40. In lines 1957b–60a, where the allusion is pretty vague, and more specifically in lines 1948b–49a, where *geongum cempan* seems clearly to refer to the youthful exploit (thus Klaeber, p. 200) and where I think *æðelum dīore* is a variant of *geongum cempan* rather than of *goldhroden* (i.e., I construe *dīore* as a substantive use of the adjective *dēor* and translate the phrase as "to the noble fighter.")

41. This observation, a very sound one, is made by J. R. Gaskin, "Structural Principle and Device in *Beowulf*, Univ. of North Carolina doctoral dissertation, 1952, pp. 16 ff. He does not apply it to this passage (ll. 1925–62). It is ignored here by scholars who conjecture that some portion of the text has been omitted before 1931b.

42. Chambers, p. 539. Wrenn's whole comment is worthy of thoughtful consideration.

Anglo-Saxon Heroic Attitudes

G. N. GARMONSWAY

King's College, London

THE THEMES and character shapes that make up the world of Teutonic epic are various. Many different attitudes and types of valor and heroic self-assertion are graded before our eyes, exhibited as personifications of the ideal hero, the aged wise king, the young reckless warrior, the tyrant, the crafty councilor, the faithful retainer — and others that are readily apparent.

Although it would be a bold man nowadays who would attempt to prove that *Beowulf*, say, was written for the edification of a particular Heptarchy monarch, or that this or that portrait in the poem was drawn as the caricature of a contemporary,[1] nevertheless, taken as a whole, the story with its episodes and digressions does form a kind of eighth-century *Mirror for Magistrates* or *Book named the Governor*, wherein those in authority might have seen pictured their obligations and responsibilities, and from which they could have gleaned political wisdom had they so desired, and learned some useful lessons about current moral sanctions governing behavior in general, and heroic conduct in particular.

Perhaps, in fact, too much emphasis has been placed on the contextual value of the poem's episodes and digressions, which interrupt the flow of the narrative as effectively as the breaks in the interlacing zoomorphs of the period. While there is no doubt that as *exempla* they reveal by comparison or contrast some trait or quality of a protagonist, they serve above all to vary the pattern of the poetic tapestry and to throw into prominence those bright threads of narrative which depict the lustre of the young hero's triumphs. Set beside the exploits and reputation of the great heroes of the past, Beowulf's valor and demeanor can be gauged; stories reflecting a warrior culture become the subplot, and lend verisimilitude to fables of monster slayings.

Of the famous figures of the Germanic past which appear in *Beowulf*, each represents a crystallization of a general heroic figure specifically developed along lines appropriate to the poet's purpose and intention. To suit the design of his plot he will magnify the reputation of one hero and diminish that of another. In Norse tradition, Hrothulf is the idealized hero in his exploits against the Swedes, and in his fight to the death in defense of his hall, but in *Beowulf* he is completely subordinated to his uncle Hrothgar, and his forthcoming part in the defense of Heorot against the Heathobards not even hinted at. Nor can one imagine that Unferth had always appeared in heroic tradition as he is depicted in the poem. No doubt some original lay presented him with partial, if not complete, glorification by providing motivation for the slaughter of his kindred, as adequate and as sympathetic as that received by Hildebrand, or Hæthcyn or the followers of Cynewulf and Cyneheard. However that may be, it is important to remember, when considering the part he plays in the poem, that the guilt of fratricide appears to have been no barrier to a hero's successful career, if we are to judge from the cases of King Penda or those members of the royal families of the Franks and the Swedes whose infamies rivaled those of the house of Pelops. But the poet lays considerable emphasis on Unferth's guilt, and he is cast for an unsympathetic role at the Danish court.

As Cedric Whitman has so ably demonstrated for the *Iliad*, many and various become the "elaborations upon the heroic norm":[2] to obtain variety even minor differences of character may require emphasis to obtain the effects of contrast required. The first to appear in the Beowulf poem are the least complex. The aggressive Scyld employed a policy as old as Caesar's Suebi—"It was their greatest glory to lay waste the frontiers of their neighbors for as wide a distance as possible, considering this to be the real evidence of their prowess."[3] Scyld is set in contrast to the sage Hrothgar, whose boast was that he had kept his realm in peace against all foreign aggression. Heroic types range from individualists like Sigemund—"he that kills me some six or seven dozen monsters at a breakfast"—to more complex characters like Hengest, who has to endure with impatience the slow passage of a bloodstained winter before he can take vengeance for the slaying of his lord. Of Sigemund, the poet speaks with some reticence, and with a hint of disapproval of his "warfare and deeds of violence";[4] like Saxo's Starcatherus, he becomes the prototype of the more ruthless type of Germanic hero, with a touch in his make-up of the berserk or ruffian. Second only to Beowulf, Hygelac's character comes nearest to the heroic ideal. The imagination is stirred by the bravura of his trumpet call at Ravenswood and by the bravado of his last foray into Frisia. Arthur G. Brodeur has eloquently reminded us how the poet returns again and again to speak of him. In the relationship of Beowulf and Hygelac, the man-lord theme finds its happiest and most typical expression. The firm affection of the comitatus for its lord, and of the lord for his comitatus, becomes not only a recurrent theme of song but also compels the notice of early historians. To the succinct statement of Tacitus that the Teutonic chief fights for victory and the thane for his chief, Caesar adds information about the Celtic *soldurii*, the comitatus of ancient Gaul, — "in the event of a lord meeting a violent death all his men fall together with him or else commit suicide; there is no case on record," says Caesar, "of a man refusing to die with his leader."[5] In later days Bede[6] testifies to the devotion of the followers of the sons of Æthelfrith of Northumbria who share their exile, and sixty years after the Battle of Maldon the retinue of Earl Ælfgar of East Anglia follows him into banishment. It is the *Andreas* poet, however, who gives the most poignant expression to the despairing attitudes of faithful thanes who face separation from their lord: "Whither can we turn if we desert thee? Heavy of heart, bereft of happiness, separated from our lord, we shall have to face the hatred and contempt of people everywhere." Rarely in fact do we hear of lords who were betrayed or slain by their personal followers, and it was left to a Biblical poet to exploit the unusual situation of a thane in open rebellion against his former lord, and to depict Satan as hurling heroic defiance against his God from the very depths of Hell.

Many are called to the heroic trial but only a few attain to the standards of nobility which the Greeks called *arete*, which Cedric Whitman defines as "nobility, a value composite of personal, social and military features, the implicit cultural aspiration universally accepted without definition."[7] The *Beowulf* poet, more than any other Anglo-Saxon, keeps us in mind of the universal acceptance of such standards, and introduces several pointers of sententious comment to indicate approbation or censure. As for example, "So ought a young man to bring it about by good and ready gifts of treasure, while he is young, that willing companions will stand by him in aftertimes when war comes and help their chief" — adding, perhaps as the minstrel's hint — "Generosity is the condition of success in every community." Heremod fell short in this respect, and for that reason, among others, lost his throne. He did not distribute treasure *æfter dome*, which implies, I think, "as the standard of kingly honor requires," *not* "to gain glory," which is the meaning proposed by Kaske[8] and others. The much debated *woruld-rædenne* in the Finn story appears to me of similar import. Hengest, says the poet, did not reject the course "suggested by public opinion," when he girt upon himself the sword which had once been Hunlaf's. Again, Beowulf, after his return to Hygelac's court, *dreah æfter dome* 'lived honorably.' He presented his trophies to his lord as he was expected to do, and flushed with success as he was, did not entertain ambitious thoughts of supplanting his uncle nor did he behave arrogantly to his fellows in the hall. "This is what one ought to do," says the poet, "not to lay snares for one's relative, or compass a comrade's death by treachery."

In the presentation of character the Anglo-Saxon poets are constantly exploring the significance of heroic deeds and the meaning of heroism; and it is one sign of the maturity of this literature that we are enabled to see how heroic attitudes appeared to others who, though sometimes involved in the action, serve in the role of chorus, to remind us of the world of common sense and nonheroic norms. Just as the members of Arthur's court deplore the departure of Sir Gawain on his perilous quest and speak of it as foolishness to allow one so worthy to risk his life for a Christmas game, so too the *Beowulf* poet draws our attention to Hygelac's cautionary words to the hero who, egged on by the elders of the court, is about to embark on perilous adventures overseas. Moreover, his prowess in swimming against Breca is made more credible by Unferth's first depreciatory references to it. Garulf's valor to the death, in leading the attack against Hnæf and his men in the hall, is conveyed to us in the cry of his comrade Guthhere, who entreats him not to imperil his life on the first onslaught since a doughty champion guards the door. Nor is criticism of Byrhtnoth shirked by the *Maldon* poet: "The earl in his overmastering pride actually yielded ground to the enemy, as he should not have done." Significant, too, are the words with which Hildegyth endeavors to restrain the impetuosity of her lover Waldhere: "Thou didst ever strive to press thy martial suit *ofer mearce*, beyond the limits of safety, pressing the attack up to the spot where the advantage was rather to thy foe than to thyself." Such conduct would not have won the approval of the poet of *The Wanderer*, who counsels warriors not to be headstrong or too rash, but Waldhere cared nothing for his safety, and his heroism hinges upon "a certain excess, an ability to outdo not only everybody else, but especially himself."[9] In this he resembles the Greek heroes Achilles and Ajax, each of whom was in possession of a "standard which becomes a kind of fatal necessity that drives toward self-destruction. . . . It seems excessive and culpable only if one's standard is life and common sense; if one's standard is *arete*, it is an inevitable course."[10] As W. H. Auden has said, "The code by which the hero lives is a code of honor which is not a universal requirement like law, but an individual one, that which I require of myself, and that which in view of my achievements I have a right to demand of others."[11] This assessment of heroic attitudes is particularly relevant to Beowulf's last action against the dragon. The hero's mandate to his followers, "This is not your affair, nor anyone's responsibility but mine, to put forth his powers against the monster, to do heroic deeds," is put into sharp contrast to the common sense criticism of Wiglaf: "Often must many an earl suffer misery through the will of one, as has happened to us: the beloved prince would not listen to our advice not to attack the keeper of the gold."

The comitatus failed to perceive that man does not live by common sense alone. The hero's decision to fight was not the expression of selfish or misguided individualism which lightly put the realm in jeopardy, but sprang from a consuming desire for that *arete* characteristic of the hero and not easily understood by lesser men. "You will find the aspirations of men utterly unreasonable," says the prophetess to Socrates, "unless you understand how they are stirred by the love of an immortality of fame which all men long for, and long for the more, the worthier they be."

Yet lines 2419–20 of the poem, which describe how Beowulf sits contemplating the dragon's mound, are usually interpreted as reflecting a shift in Beowulf's mood from confidence in victory to a state akin to feyness.

> Him wæs geomor sefa,
>   wæfre and wælfus. . . .

That is: "His spirit was gloomy within him, wavering and ready for death." Professor Brodeur would interpret the passage as an example of the pathetic fallacy as the hero contemplates the solitary mound by the sea.[12] The potency of fate is described in the following lines, but is not this simply the usual dramatic foreshadowing of the issue of the struggle? Are physical manifestations of danger likely to daunt a hero who has just been described as journeying to the headland "swollen with anger," and "storming in his rage"? This surely is no Hector "in a panic blinded by a god-sent infatuation."[13] Greenfield has shown that the half-line *him wæs geomor sefa* is totally formulaic—it appears three times in the poem—and Beowulf's sadness, if this is the meaning, may derive from his suspicion that he has bitterly offended against natural law, to adopt Bloomfield's phrase. But must *wæfre* be interpreted as "wavering"? The *vafrlogi* around Brynhild's dwelling might well have been a flickering magical fire, sufficiently dazzling to stop a hero's steed, but the Old English word *wæfre* has also the meaning "nimble" or "active," just as the word *quiver* once had the sense of "nimble" or "rapid." *Wæfre* appears in the Old English *Daniel* to translate the "burning, fiery furnace," *fornax ignis ardentis*, and in each of its three occurrences in *Beowulf* the meaning of the word could well be "furious," "raging." It is used to describe Grendel's mother as *wælgæst wæfre*, usually translated as a "wandering, murderous spirit"; surely in the context "wandering" is a most inappropriate adjective (despite Fr. Klaeber's attempted justification)[14] to describe a monster striding across the moors bent on revenging her son's death. The poet emphasizes both the suddenness of her attack, and the rapidity of her departure.

The second appearance of the word appears in a passage usually taken as referring to Finn: "his flickering spirit could not keep its footing in his breast"—in other words, "Finn was killed." But it has been pointed out that it was more in accordance with Old English style that

the following lines should be parallel in meaning.[15] Hence several of the
older scholars took the phrase to mean "the furious spirit of the attack-
ing party (Guthlaf and Oslaf) could no longer restrain itself." Such an
interpretation, at least, would mean that we are told only twice, not
thrice, within a few lines that Finn has been slain. Finally, why should
wælfus (which only occurs here) be twisted from its natural meaning of
"eager for slaughter" to one of "ready for death," a meaning deduced
to fit the supposed mood of the passage, but which does the hero an
injustice?

   Beowulf's sadness, the disquiet and unease in his heart before combat, is something many of us can understand, but it is kept under control
by a fierce, masterly resolution to wage battle to the death. Hamlet
before his rapier fight with Laertes experiences something of the same
kind, though it is usually explained as a presentiment of treachery:[16]

HORATIO: You will lose this wager, my lord.
HAMLET: I do not think so; since he went to France I have been
           in continual practice. I shall win at the odds. But thou would'st
           not think how ill all's here about my heart. But it is no matter.
HORATIO: Nay, good my lord.
HAMLET: It is but foolery, but it is such a kind of gain-giving, as
           would perhaps trouble a woman.
HORATIO: If your mind dislike anything obey it. I will forestall their
           repair hither, and say you are not fit.
HAMLET: Not a whit: we defy augury.

   I should like to believe that Beowulf never succumbs to doubts or
delusions; rather does his pent-up rage hide a deadly efficiency. Like
Hamlet, he never doubts the issue, and "in a long 'vaunt' boasts that his
many victories have relieved him of fear."[17] He makes hardly any preparations for the fight. As Tolkien says, "He will not deign to lead a force
against the dragon as wisdom might direct even a hero to do. He will
only use a sword on this occasion since wrestling single-handed with a
dragon is too hopeless even for his chivalric spirit." He rejects by his
actions Hrothgar's cautionary words of many years before: "Entertain
no feelings of arrogance or over-confidence; a time will come when
death shall overpower thee, noble warrior as thou art," advice not
unlike Athena's to Ajax: "If rich in power you seem superior, be not
insolent, for know one day suffices to exalt or depress the state of mortal
man." But the heroes of the world are not guided by the cautionary precepts of old men or divinities; they are driven forward by their personal
integrity and, as Werner Jaeger has said of the Homeric hero, "by an
insatiable thirst for honor, a thirst which is itself a moral quality."[18]
Brodeur rightly says "Beowulf is a hero without a tragic flaw,"[19] but it

is superfluous to introduce the notion of hamartia, when perhaps the majority of scholars, following Werner Jaeger, would now agree that "the variety of experience on which the whole effect of tragedy depends—*catharsis* to use Aristotle's term—does not rest on the faults but on the virtues of men."[20] Beowulf's decision to fight is not pride, but a moral act which his honor compels him to undertake: he cannot suffer to let the immense strength with which God has endowed him rust in him unused.

In the realistic world of the Icelandic sagas, in contrast, considerable credit is given to those heroes who make firm preliminary estimates of danger ahead. Caution and foresight become cardinal virtues, yet this calculating circumspection is but the prosaic preliminary to demonstrations of fearless courage once the issue is joined. The first stanza of the *Hávamál* sets the tone: "Before making your way up the hall you should observe and note all the doorways, for you can never be certain when you will find enemies present."

Sigurth prepares to fight *his* dragon by digging several pits in the ground and waits for the monster to crawl over one of them, relying on his knowledge that dragons are especially vulnerable in the soft underbelly.[21] Seated in one pit he can stab from below with perfect safety, and escape being drowned in the dragon's blood, which will conveniently drain off into the other pits he has prepared. Ragnarr Lothbrók prepares for a similar encounter by making cowboy trousers for himself and a fur cape; these he boils in pitch and rolls himself in sand.[22] In the *Saga of the Sworn Brothers*,[23] one of the pair when facing his enemies weighs up the heavy odds against him, and makes the sensible decision to seek a temporary truce: "Now I would ask of you," he says to them, "that we do not let our valor and hardihood become foolhardiness and enmity." Yet the next day when treacherously surprised on his ship he "made such a stand, as had never been seen before," as the sagaman testifies.

Unlike King Frodi, who was advised by Odin[24] to cover his shield with bulls' hides and to protect his body from the venemous poison of the dragon's blood, Beowulf makes hardly any preparations. To the common sense view of his comitatus all this is incomprehensible, even perverse. Yet even at this level of evaluation they can appreciate the *arete* in his conduct. As the Pastor in Wordsworth's *Excursion* maintains, contemplating the graves in the village churchyard:

> Strength to persevere and to support
> And energy to conquer and repel—
> These elements of Virtue, that declare
> The native grandeur of the human soul—
> Are oft-times not unprofitably shown
> In the perverseness of a selfish course.

To the *Beowulf* poet there is nothing selfish in the hero's death. One might perhaps have expected him to draw the moral that a hero must endeavor to find the point of balance between love of *lof* and fear of *ofermod*—between love of men's praise and fear of excessive high-mindedness. But not so. In the last lines of the poem he praises the hero's virtues, the kindest to his people and most eager for fame, and finds

> no weakness, no contempt,
> Dispraise or blame;   nothing but well and fair
> And what may quiet us in a death so noble.

NOTES

1. See Dorothy Whitelock, "Anglo-Saxon Poetry and the Historian," *Transactions of the Royal Historical Society* (Fourth Series), XXXI, 74–79.
2. *Homer and the Heroic Tradition* (Cambridge, Mass., 1958), pp. 163 ff., and *Sophocles* (Cambridge, Mass., 1951), pp. 59–80 and *passim*. To both of these books I am much indebted.
3. *De Bello Gallico*, IV.3.
4. *Beowulf*, l. 879.
5. *De Bello Gallico*, III.22.
6. *Historia Ecclesiastica*, III.1.
7. *Homer and the Heroic Tradition*, p. 163.
8. *PMLA*, LXXIV (1959), 493.
9. Whitman, *Sophocles*, p. 60.
10. *Ibid.*, p. 73.
11. *The Portable Greek Reader* (New York, 1955), p. 17.
12. *The Art of Beowulf* (Berkeley, 1959), p. 65.
13. G. S. Kirk, *The Songs of Homer* (Cambridge, 1962), p. 374.
14. *Anglia*, XXXV (1911), 256.
15. For references, see R. W. Chambers' edition of *Beowulf*, l. 1150.
16. V.ii.197–210.
17. J. R. R. Tolkien, "The Homecoming of Beorhtnoth," *Essays and Studies*, N.S., VI (1953), 14.
18. Cf. Whitman, p. 76. "Ajax slays himself to rectify his position for all time, to let his *arete* appear untrammeled by the outrages of his last days. The grief of the chorus when his body is found, Teucer's gallant defence of his right to burial . . . should be a caution to those who prefer to find the 'fault,' or hamartia, of Ajax, instead of seeing his greatness. His suicide is a moral act in defence of his *arete*, a fact which we are in a better position to recognize than his own companions were."
19. P. 105.
20. Peter Alexander, *Hamlet, Father and Son* (Oxford, 1955), p. 113.
21. *Vǫlsunga saga*, Ch. XVIII.
22. *Ragnars saga*, Ch. II.
23. Ch. XVI.
24. Saxo Grammaticus, *Danish History*, Bk. II.

Wulf and Eadwacer:
A Noninterpretation

ALAIN RENOIR

University of California, Berkeley

T. s. ELIOT once remarked that he was in love with French poetry long before he could understand a word of it. The statement is not nearly so preposterous as it may sound at first, for most of us have had the experience of being profoundly moved by poetry which we should be hard put to interpret. For the student of English literature, the nineteen-line Anglo-Saxon poem *Wulf and Eadwacer* is a case in point.

Wulf and Eadwacer was probably composed in the tenth century or earlier and is recorded in the Exeter Book; the term "poignant," which Charles W. Kennedy used in his account of the poem,[1] best describes the emotional impact it has on the reader. In recent years, George K. Anderson has called our attention to its "true passion [which] comes to the surface in an unexpected manner";[2] David Daiches has praised its "intense romantic passion in a way quite uncharacteristic of Anglo-Saxon poetry as it has come down to us";[3] and P. J. Frankis has likewise commented on its "intensity of passion which is rare in OE poetry."[4] We may thus say that both sides of the Atlantic seem in essential agreement concerning the quality and high emotional appeal of the poem.

There is no such agreement, however, concerning the meaning. Benjamin Thorpe, who printed the poem in his 1842 edition of the Exeter Book, gave up any attempt at translating it and excused himself with the summary comment, "Of this I can make no sense,"[5] and the divergences of subsequent interpretations more than justify his scholarly reluctance to commit himself. The poem has been interpreted, for instance, as a metrical riddle for the name Cynewulf and various other things,[6] a "fragment of a dramatic soliloquy spoken by a woman,"[7] a translation from the Old Norse in which Signy, the heroine of the *Vǫlsunga saga*, laments her conflict in allegiance toward Siggeir and Sigmund,[8] and even a touching story about dogs.[9] Wulf and Eadwacer have shared the honor of having both been considered lovers and husbands to the speaker,[10] while their names have tempted scholars into trying to identify the former with Wolfdietrich[11] and the latter with Odoaker.[12] In short, we may say that, like Mr. Eliot with French poetry, a great many professional students of English literature have fallen in love with *Wulf and Eadwacer* without understanding it; and the number of studies to which the poem has been subjected since Thorpe's edition bears ample testimony to the enduring fascination it holds for the modern mind.

The purpose of the present essay is not to offer yet another interpretation, but rather to try to isolate the elements which make the poem an equally effective work of art for critics who completely disagree about its meaning. We know that many a valid literary utterance is subject to the individual reader's interpretation. Anyone who has attempted to translate poetry, for instance, has probably found that his translation often depended on his own interpretation of the text and that this often differed from those of others equally familiar with the original document. Marie Borroff has aptly reminded us that some of the most effective lines in Shakespeare lend themselves to widely divergent interpretations,[13] and the disputes of textual scholars more than bear out the general validity of her specific examples. All readers of Homer supposedly agree that Helen is a beautiful woman, but we may reasonably doubt that any two of them would draw her alike. This element of subjective interpretation is perhaps at the root of the enduring effectiveness of great nondramatic literature.

Whether we interpret *Wulf and Eadwacer* as a riddle, a dramatic monologue, or a dog story, each of us has a fairly clear idea of the action that is taking place, and the poet has presented us with enough effectively suggestive details to insure a similar reaction in a majority of readers independently of their respective interpretations. Each reader, of course, arrives at this reaction through a slightly different road, depending on his notion of what the text is about. From this point of view, the only serious difference between modern readers and the original audience of the poem is that the latter was presumably equipped with the information necessary to place it within the appropriate context and to know for sure whether it was a dog story or a clever riddle, but the former must rely on purely conjectural information and guess at the basic meaning while supplying the details. Kemp Malone, who is fully cognizant of the problem,[14] sums it up in one neat sentence: "This poem is based on a tale familiar to the poet's audience but unknown to us."[15] This lack of context, however, need not prevent us from appreciating the artistry, for the text of a riddle may have a high emotional appeal of its own, and Jack London has amply demonstrated that a whole era may be entranced by stories about dogs as well as by stories about

human beings—it all depends on the kind of dogs or human beings the
author chooses and what he has them do.

The key to the poignancy of *Wulf and Eadwacer*, I believe, may be
found in its concluding statement:

> Þæt mon eaþe tosliteð   þætte næfre gesomnad wæs,
> uncer giedd geador.[16]

The sentence is composed of a series of semantically contradictory
phrases which, even out of context, convey a sense of hopeless struggle.
Clearly, one cannot tear apart (*mon . . . tosliteð*) something that *never*
was put together (*þæt . . . þætte næfre gesomnad wæs*); and, literally
speaking, that which never was together cannot be the song of two
people *together* (*uncer giedd geador*). Yet, the total statement assures
us that this is the case and that under the circumstances it can be done
easily (*eaþe*); furthermore, the binding force of the union that never was
is emphasized with the dual pronoun (*uncer*). It is significant that the
pronouns *þæt* (that [which never was united]) and *uncer* ([the child] of
the two of us) both begin the lines in which they occur, so that the very
syntax of the statement emphasizes the firmness of the connection between the contradictory concepts of separation and union. This oxymo-
ronic relationship must have seemed even more striking to the original
audience of the poem than to the modern reader, for recent investigation
by Francis P. Magoun, Jr., and other scholars suggests that Anglo-Saxon
poetry was delivered orally in a rhythmical manner which emphasized
individual metrical units.[17]

We must note that the statement analyzed above is self-contradictory
only when considered on a single level. If we reconsider it on two different levels, it immediately becomes semantically cogent. I have already said that no two people can be both united and separated; but this
is true only on the physical level, since one can be at only one place at a
time. If we consider the emotional level as well, we realize that two
people may be both united and separated, for the mind can easily wander
away from the body, especially to escape an unpleasant situation. The
speaker of *The Wanderer* illustrates this phenomenon when he shows a
solitary exile fondly dreaming of the days when he would embrace his
lord in the warmth and friendliness of the great hall:

> Þinceð him on mode   þæt he his mondryhten
> clyppe ond cysse,   ond on cneo lecge
> honda ond heafod,   swa he hwilum ær
> in geardagum   giefstolas breac.[18]

Thus, in the concluding statement of *Wulf and Eadwacer*, the persons
concerned may be either physically united but emotionally separated or

vice versa. In any case, things are not as the speaker would want them, and the tension created by this rhetorical union of disunion is, I believe, the key to the passionate poignancy which critics have admired in the poem.

I have said above that various readers may follow different roads to arrive at a similar evaluation of a given work of literature. In the case of a poem whose meaning is as controversial as that of *Wulf and Eadwacer*, each reader is necessarily entitled to great freedom of interpretation as long as he can support his views with objective evidence, but he must exercise the utmost caution before yielding to the temptation of imposing his own interpretation upon others who may have widely different but equally valid views. For the purpose of the present study, I shall disregard the canine theory because such a statement as *leodum is minum swilce him mon lac gife* (l. 1) and such a question as *gehirest þu, Eadwacer?* (l. 16) suggest concepts and activities not normally associated with animals, except in rather special contexts, such as the *Roman de Renard*, *The Jungle Book*, or *Uncle Wiggly*. I shall take for granted that Wulf and Eadwacer are men, for their very names imply the masculine sex. I shall further assume that the speaker is a woman: otherwise the statement *mec se beaducafa bogum bilegde* (l. 11) would suggest a behavior suspiciously verging on homosexuality — and this topic is, to my knowledge, nonexistent in early Germanic poetry.

The interpretation of *Wulf and Eadwacer* most in favor today assumes that Wulf is the speaker's exiled lover whom her people would gladly kill if he came among them, and that Eadwacer is her abhored husband. In Anderson's words, "The speaker is a woman, and probably a captive in a foreign land; she yearns for Wulf, her lover, and bristles at the thought of Eadwacer, her unloved and possibly brutal husband."[19] Because they differ from this interpretation, as well as from that implicit in my own analysis, I am quoting in their entirety two recent and widely divergent translations.

The first one is by John F. Adams, who ingeniously solves the problems of Eadwacer's identity and of his relation to the speaker by assuming that there is no Eadwacer at all and that the poem is "an appeal to Wulf to settle down":[20]

> Our fate like a gift's,   by the giver unvalued:
> Friends will assist him   if hardship should threaten;
>   It is not so with us.
>
> Wulf is on one island,   I on another:
> His island held safe   by a bordering mire;
> Warriors dwell there,   in battles his comrades —   5
> Friends will assist him   if hardship should threaten;
>   It is not so with us.

Wulf's days of wandering   were my days of torment;
I wept for Wulf   when the weather was rainy.
Yet when he clasped me   fast in his arms,   10
My joy was great,   but they held grief, too.
Wulf, my Wulf,   hoping for you,
For your seldom visit,   has brought on me sickness:
The longing of heart,   not my hunger for food.   15

Do you hear, Cradle-Watcher,   the lank wolf
Carries our eaglet to the woods. —
Easily a man tears apart   what was never joined:
  Our bond is this riddle.

My analysis will largely disregard this interpretation, not because I wish to reject its potential validity, but rather because it forces the student to rely on the translation rather than on the original text. To illustrate, the Anglo-Saxon text has no counterpart for such words and phrases as "by the giver unvalued" (l. 1b), "friends [will assist him if hardship] should threaten" (ll. 2, 7), "days [of wandering]" (l. 9a), "the lank [wolf]" (l. 16b), and "our bond" (l. 19); and even the justification that "Bosworth and Toller define the noun *eadwacer* as 'a watchman of property' "[21] does not permit one to discuss the interpretation "Cradle-Watcher" and pretend to be analyzing the poem recorded in the Exeter Book.

The second translation is by Kemp Malone,[22] and the most cursory comparison with Adams' text will illustrate the disparities in interpretation which have plagued scholars to this day:

It is to my people as if one gave them a gift: they will take him in [i.e., welcome him as they would a gift] if he comes into peril; it is otherwise with us. Wulf is on an island, I on another; fast [i.e., a fastness] is that island, surrounded by the fen; fierce men are there, on the island; they will take him in if he comes into peril; it is otherwise with us. I was mindful of my Wulf in his wanderings, his expectations [i.e., hopes and fears]: when it was rainy weather and I sat weeping, when the doughty man wrapped me in his arms, it was a joy to me so far, but hateful too. Wulf, my Wulf, [vain] hopes of thee, thy rare visits, have left me sick; a mourning heart, not want of food. Hearest thou, Eadwacer? Wulf bears our poor whelp [i.e., son] to the woods. One easily tears asunder that which was never joined, our song together.

Like Adams — though not so radically — Malone departs from the interpretation favored by most scholars, and he supports his own with such thorough philological annotations that no serious study of the poem may henceforth fail to take them into consideration. I shall accordingly indicate, both in my text and in the notes, such differences between us as are clearly relevant to my analysis. I would not be thought, however, to impugn his formidable arguments, but rather to take advantage of his own statement that his "interpretation of the text depends, of course, on [his] translation"[23] in order to justify my views on such points as remain open for discussion.

My analysis of the concluding two lines of *Wulf and Eadwacer* has called attention to the themes of separation and union, and the three interpretations discussed above indicate that a similar observation may be made about the entire poem. Again on the basis of the lines already analyzed, we may add the themes of hostility, suggested by *þæt mon . . . toslite∂* (l. 18), and of suffering as the logical result of an unwelcome separation. Examination of the Anglo-Saxon text will show that these four themes permeate the entire poem, which I am printing here according to the following scheme: italics indicate the theme of separation; small capitals indicate the theme of union; a solid underline indicates the theme of hostility; and broken underlining indicates the theme of suffering. A fifth theme—that of happiness—which does not occur in the concluding lines, is indicated by an asterisk.

> Leodum is minum   swylce him mon lac gife;
> willa∂ hy hine aþecgan,   *gif he on þreat cymeþ.*
>   UNGELIC IS US.
> *Wulf is on þæt eglond,   ic on oþere.*
> *Fæst is þæt eglond,   fenne biworpen.*   5
> Sindon wælreowe weras   *þær on ige*;
> willa∂ hy hine aþecgan,   *gif he on þreat cyme∂.*
>   UNGELIC IS US.
> *Wulfes ic mines widlastum*   wenum dogode;
> þonne hit wæs renig weder   ond ic reotogu sæt,   10
> þonne MEC SE BEADUCAFA   BOGUM BILEGDE,
> wæs me wyn to þon,*   wæs me hwæþre eac la∂.
> Wulf, min Wulf,   *wena me þine,*
> seoce gedydon,   *þine seldcymas,*
> murnende mod,   nales meteliste.   15
> Gehyrest þu, Eadwacer?   UNCERNE EARNE HWELP
> *bire∂ Wulf to wuda.*
> *Þæt mon eaþe toslite∂*   *þætte næfre gesomnad wæs,*
>
> UNCER GIEDD GEADOR.

Some of the themes indicated here are, of course, detectable only within context. For instance, the statement *ungelic is us* (ll. 3, 8) carries no intrinsic implication of union or separation; it merely indicates a contrast with whatever precedes it. I take the preceding statement—*gif he on þreat cymeþ* (l. 2b)—to mean "if he comes among [this] people," in other words, if he comes here.[24] Malone's choice of "peril" as a translation for *þreat* is justified by Bosworth-Toller's listing it as a choice;[25] but it is there listed last in the second of two entries for the Anglo-Saxon word, while the first entry reads, in this order, "a troop, band, crowd, body of people, swarm, press, throng." My choice implies a further difference between my reading and Malone's. Since the context gives no ground for supposing that anyone around the speaker feels particularly friendly toward Wulf, I must reject the possibility that he will be welcome there if he comes into peril. Bosworth-Toller's translation of *aþecgan* by "to receive" unquestionably bears out Malone's "they will take him in," but the explanation "i.e., welcome him" is by no means the only possible interpretation, for one can receive an enemy as well as a friend and prepare the reception accordingly. Indeed the entry in Bosworth-Toller's *Supplement* reads "substitute: to take *food*, to consume," thus suggesting that the connotation of *aþecgan* to an Anglo-Saxon ear may not necessarily have been exclusively friendly. Then there is a question of logic: if Wulf has a secure place among friends with the speaker's people, we wonder why she seems so worried about him. For these reasons, although I do not reject the intrinsic validity of Malone's interpretation, I prefer to base my analysis on the view that Wulf may expect a hostile reception if he dares visit the people with whom the speaker lives. Thus, since one cannot come unless one be elsewhere in the first place, and since the term *ungelic* implies a contrast with whatever precedes it, the sentence *ungelic is us* has to mean that the antecedents of the pronoun *us* are together in a way or another. Conversely, the proper name Wulf may not necessarily imply hostility each time it appears in the poem, but its connotation to an early Germanic audience would surely have suggested an element of hostility which no context could completely erase.[26]

As it is printed above, the poem reveals nine lines that express the theme of separation (2b, 4, 5, 6b, 7b, 9a, 13b, 14b, 17, 18), ten lines that express the theme of hostility (2a, 4a, 6a, 7a, 9a, 11a, 12b, 13a, 17, 18a), five lines that express the theme of suffering (9, 10b, 12b, 14a, 15a),[27] five lines that express the theme of union (3, 8, 11, 16b, 19), and only one line that expresses the theme of happiness (12a). It is significant that this single expression of happiness—*wæs me wyn to þon* (l. 12a)—is immediately qualified with a contrary statement: *wæs me hwæþre lað* (12b). Since the speaker states unequivocally on two different occasions that her separation from Wulf is painful to her (ll. 9, 13–14), and since Wulf is the object of the theme of separation, the themes of suffering and separation become associated within the context, as does the theme of hostility whenever Wulf is the potential victim (ll. 2a, 6, 7a). The theme of suffering thus occurs seventeen times throughout the nineteen lines, so that suffering through separation looms to the fore as the fundamental theme of *Wulf and Eadwacer*.

We must not forget that the theme of suffering through separation

recurs frequently in Anglo-Saxon poetry. In one form or another we find
it in such commonly studied poems as *The Wanderer, Deor*, and *The
Wife's Lament*, as well as in certain sections of *Beowulf* (e.g., ll. 2213b
ff. and 2444a ff.). In a way it lies behind such pieces as the Old High
German *Hildebrandslied* or the Old Norse *Oddrúnargrátr*; it is implicit
behind the emotions which in the *Waltharii poesis* push Hagen and
Walther to flee the court of Attila and return to their own nations; and
the mere prospect of enduring it is what prompts Gunnar to seal his
doom by defying his sentence of exile in the *Brennu-Njáls saga*. We may
accordingly conclude that the theme is common to early Germanic literature in general. This observation is of some importance, for it suggests
that, even if the passionate tone of *Wulf and Eadwacer* is as "uncharacteristic of Anglo-Saxon poetry" as Professors Daiches and Frankis have
pointed out, its principal theme is on the contrary quite characteristic.
Because of the pitifully diminutive size of the surviving corpus of
Anglo-Saxon poetry, we cannot tell how anomalous the poem really was
in its own time; at most we can say that it may have been a variation
on a theme for the benefit of an audience familiar enough with that
theme to appreciate such variations as the poet might wish to produce.

The theme of a poem may lend itself to various treatments, but it
does not in itself guarantee effectiveness unless it be effectively
organized and presented with the right imagery and tone from an
appropriate point of view. To be effective, the theme of suffering must be
presented in such manner as to make the audience share in, or at least
sympathize with, the sufferer's emotions. I believe that *Wulf and
Eadwacer* does just that.

It is surely no preposterous generalization to say that human pity
and sympathy are easily aroused by passive suffering, and we have such
a situation in our poem. Without question the unseen and unheard Wulf
has his share of troubles, but he is by no means a passive victim. Presumably to escape whatever dangers might befall him if he remained
at the speaker's side, he wanders far away (l. 9), and his occasional
visits (l. 14b) imply the sort of daring which we find in Tristan when
he visits Isolde in King Mark's garden or in Romeo when he crashes a
dinner party at the Capulets to catch a glimpse of the fair Rosaline.
Such deeds arouse our admiration but not our pity. Even if Wulf falls
into the hands of his enemies, the chances are that he will not prove an
easy capture; at any rate the word *lac* in the opening line may not unlikely give grounds for thinking so, for the gloss "gift" appears only in
the third entry in Bosworth-Toller, while the first entry lists "battle"
and "struggle" in this order, thus justifying the possibility that the
speaker thinks someone may be about to present her people with some
show of violence — as Wulf indeed does at the end of the poem.[28] She,
on the other hand, suffers passively as a result of the hostility between

Wulf and Eadwacer. The statement *ic . . . dogode* (l. 9b), with which
she describes her own behavior, aptly sums up the picture she draws of
herself: her *murnende mod* (l. 15a) and the rarity of Wulf's visits — *wena
me þine seoce gedydon, þine seldcymas* (ll. 13b – 14b) — are the things
that hurt her; and the very grammar of the latter utterance emphasizes
her passivity, for Wulf's activities are the subject of the active verb
gedydon, while she herself is merely the object expressed by the pronoun
me. Whereas the men about her seem poised for action (ll. 2, 7) and
Wulf wanders far and near, the visual image she draws of herself is
symbolic of utter inactivity: *ic reotogu sæt* (l. 10b). Likewise, the single
instance of physical action in which she takes part shows her as the
passive object of a man's embrace and offers not even the hint of any
return emotion on her part: *þonne mec se beaducafa bogum bilegde.
. . .* (l. 11). Thus, the speaker is unquestionably the passive victim of the
action.

The pathetic situation outlined above is turned into a powerful
statement of despair by the organization and tone of the poem. From the
point of view of time, *Wulf and Eadwacer* is divided into three sections
dealing respectively with present (ll. 1 – 8), past (ll. 9 – 15), and future
(ll. 16 – 19). The first section simply presents the situation as it is now and
uses the verbal forms *is* five times (ll. 1a, 3, 4a, 5a, 8a), *sindon* once (l. 6a),
willað twice (ll. 2a, 7a), and *cymeþ* twice (ll. 2b, 7b). Even the possibility
of future action (ll. 2, 7) is expressed from the point of view of the
present, and the aggregation of ten verbs in the present tense within
eight lines necessarily impresses upon us the actuality of the present.
The second section outlines the actions which in the near and distant
past have caused the speaker's unhappiness. Here, the past is expressed
three times with *wæs* (ll. 10a, 12a, 12b) and four times with *dogode* (l. 9b),
sæt (l. 10b), *bilegde* (l. 11b), and *gedydon* (l. 14a), used only one time
each. The third section is somewhat more difficult to analyze, since it is
addressed to Eadwacer, whose attention it calls in the present tense —
Gehyrest þu, Eadwacer? (l. 16a) — and since it concludes the poem with
a reference to a situation that has begun in the past (ll. 18 – 19). However, the action to which Eadwacer's attention is called is clearly in the
future: *Uncerne earne hwelp bireð Wulf to wuda* (ll. 16b – 17). [29] We
must note that the verbs grow more specifically active with each successive section. We have seen that the verb *beon* is preponderant in the
first section, and the verb *cuman*, which occurs twice, carries no intrinsic
implication of specific action beyond the motion of the subject; only the
verb *aþecgan* has such an implication. In the second section, we find
three verbs of specific action, *dogian*,[30] *sittan*, and *bilecgan*, but *dogian*
and *sittan* carry an implication of passivity. The four lines of the third
section, however, contain three verbs that either request or imply
specific action, and two of these denote vigorous motion: *gehieran*,

beran, and *toslitan*. Thus, the action becomes more specific and vigorous as the poem progresses toward its conclusion, although we are given no indication that the speaker herself does anything except sit and suffer.

Considered apart from the element of time, the poem may be divided into five, rather than three, distinct sections. The first section (ll. 1–3) is a statement of the general situation: an unidentified man will be mistreated by the speaker's people if he should come among them, but things stand differently between her and another unidentified person. The second section (ll. 4–8) clarifies the situation: the potential intruder is named Wulf, and he is on an island surrounded by fen, while she is on another. The third section (ll. 9–15) illustrates the situation with particular instances. The fourth section (ll. 13–15) is addressed to Wulf and introduces us to the speaker's emotional reaction to this situation: her separation from Wulf has hurt her to the point of illness, although he visits her on occasions which she finds much too rare to suit her; and the embraces of a certain man—*se beaducafa* (l. 11a)—are a source of both pleasure and displeasure to her. The fifth and final section (ll. 16–19) is addressed to Eadwacer, whom the speaker threatens with action by Wulf, and it concludes with a summation of the situation: Eadwacer had better realize that Wulf will some day carry off their *earne hwelp*, and the fact is that one may easily tear asunder that which was never united.

The tone of the poem closely follows the organization. The opening three lines are purely descriptive, and even the statement *Ungelic is us* (l. 3) implies no particular emotional attitude. Beside the first-person pronoun in the statement quoted here, the only words that may imply a possibility of personal involvement are *leodum . . . minum*, but even these really suggest nothing beyond a relationship to some of the people involved. We know nothing of these people, except that they stand in a certain relationship to each other. The next five lines (4–8) take on a somewhat more tense and personal tone. With the subject pronoun *ic*, the speaker becomes personally involved in the action, however passive her participation may be; and her emotional attachment to Wulf is suggested by the parallel construction *Wulf is on iege, ic on opere* (l. 4). The tenseness of tone resultant from our realization that the speaker is personally involved in what has already been described as a dangerous situation is increased by the reassertion that Wulf's life would be endangered if he were to come among her people—*willað hy hine apecgan, gif he on þreat cymeð* (l. 7)—as well as by the information that the men who live on his island are by no means of the gentlest sort: *Sindon wælreowe weras þær on ige* (l. 6). The next seven lines (ll. 9–15) further increase the tenseness and the personal aspect of the tone. Here the speaker not only expresses her emotional reaction to the situation and lets us know that Wulf occasionally risks his life to visit her among his enemies, but she uses the first-person pronoun seven times in doing so: *ic* twice (ll. 10b, 11a), *mec* once (l. 11a), *me* three times (ll. 12a, 12b, 13b), and *min* once (l. 13a). The possessive *min* occurs only once in the entire poem, to emphasize the emotional bond which links Wulf to the speaker despite their physical separation: *Wulf, min Wulf* . . . . (l. 13a). The tenseness of tone is likewise the result of an accumulation of words and phrases that imply boldness — *se beaducafa* (l. 11a) — or unhappiness: *ic . . . wenum dogode* (l. 9); *ic reotogu sæt* (l. 10b); *wæs me . . . eac laδ* (l. 12); *wena me þine seoce gedydon* (ll. 13b–14a); *murnende mod* (l. 15a); *meteliste* (l. 15b).

The last four lines (16–19) operate a nearly complete change in tone. Until now the tone has been almost as passive as the speaker's physical behavior, and much of the tenseness has resulted from the contrast between this passivity and the potentially explosive situation. Even verbally, the speaker has remained apart from the action of the poem and contented herself with brooding over her sorrow and its causes, for we are given no reason to assume that Wulf is present to listen to her tale, or that she is addressing anyone in particular. Certainly her address, *Wulf, min Wulf*, is not aimed at inciting any particular action, since it is followed by a preterit account of her frustration rather than by a specific request. In contrast, her address to Eadwacer is a request for immediate action: *Gehyrest þu, Eadwacer?* (l. 16a) We may not assume that Eadwacer is necessarily here to answer; but, even if addressed to an imaginary interlocutor, the question demands at least an imaginary re-action and a prompt one at that: the real or imaginary Eadwacer had better listen to the statement that follows. This statement is, likewise, one that requires action: unless something be done, Wulf will act in a fashion presumably harmful to Eadwacer: *Uncerne earne hwelp bireδ Wulf to wuda* (ll. 16–17). We may thus say that, whereas the speaker remains physically passive throughout the poem, her tone in the last four lines suddenly shifts from passive to brutally active. This shift is marked, not only by the message itself, but also by the verbs of action, *beran* and *toslitan*.

In one respect the tone of the concluding four lines remains a puzzle, for analysis must rely in part on the reader's interpretation of the question, *Gehyrest þu, Eadwacer?* Depending on how it is spoken, such a question may be either a simple warning or an outright threat. Because the speaker has repeatedly contrasted her relationship to Wulf with her relationship to Eadwacer, and because she is obviously very fond of the former, we are tempted to assume her dislike of the latter and hence the threatening tone of her question; but the poet may well have in-tended something quite different. In any case, the shift in tone remains. The concluding two lines of this section, and of the poem as well, have been discussed earlier in the present essay, and I have suggested that they convey a sense of hopeless struggle. One additional observation, however, is in order: with the final appositive—*uncer giedd geador*—we witness a contrast within a contrast as the poem returns for a brief instant to the inactive tone that has marked the first fifteen lines.

If we accept the foregoing observations, we must necessarily note that everything in the poem leads to the explosion in the concluding four lines: the spoken account—however we wish to interpret it—presents a situation which seems to grow more unbearable as the narrative progresses; the tone grows tenser with each section until the final outburst; and the speaker's personal involvement likewise becomes increasingly marked. Thus her address to Eadwacer seems to affect a release of the pressures that have been building throughout the entire poem.

The imagery follows the tonal organization of the poem. The only formal rhetorical image—the simile *swylce him mon lac gife*—is part of the opening statement and occurs in the first line. Just as the tone of the line is indeterminate, so the image is an open simile, which does not tell us in what respect things are to the speaker's people *swylce him mon lac gife*; it merely hints at a potential struggle, the nature of which will become somewhat more precise with the second line. The four subsequent images are purely visual. The first of these shows Wulf on his island populated by warlike men and emphasizes the theme of separation by reiterating three times the concept of insularity—*iege* (l. 4a), *eglond* (l. 5a), *ige* (l. 6b)—and by mentioning the surrounding fen which clearly isolates that island from the rest of the world. The picture of an island *fæst . . . fenne biworpen* (l. 5) likewise brings in the mournful tone that pervades the poem: still today the sight of an island in the fens is likely to prove somewhat depressing, and it must have been even more so at a time that assumed the existence of a weird life in such regions. The next image, that of a woman sitting in sorrow as the rain falls to earth, reinforces the mournfulness of tone. The expression *renig weder* (l. 10a) deserves our attention in this respect, for it does not evoke a brief and lively shower, but rather the sort of lasting drizzle and general greyness which we easily associate with a dismal and inactive scene. It forms the proper background for the immediately subsequent image of a bold man holding the speaker in an embrace which, however intrinsically pleasurable, must under the circumstances be *eac lað* (l. 12b). Just as the visual images discussed above emphasize the mournful aspect of the poem, so the concluding image emphasizes the active tone of the concluding address. The abduction of a child is almost necessarily a violent and shocking affair, and the sight we are asked to imagine emphasizes its wildness. Here the child is a *hwelp* snatched away by a wolf—with a bitterly serious pun on Wulf's name—and taken to the woods (ll. 16b–17). Like his residence in the fens, Wulf's predicted withdrawal to the woods with his prey impresses our imagination with the rugged wildness of his life.

The element of separation which I have discussed at the outset of the present study finds supporting echoes in the various aspects of the poem which have been analyzed above. Wulf's presumably rugged and active way of life, for example, stands in sharp contrast to the speaker's melancholy inactivity; the embraces which she receives produce in her the two opposite reactions of pleasure and suffering; and the tenses of the verbs clearly separate both past and present from the future. Paradoxically, the refrain-like repetition of *ungelic is us* (ll. 3, 8), which first expresses and then reiterates the theme of union in the poem, is itself expressive of contrast and thus provides the reader with the most obvious cue to the theme of separation.[31] The organization likewise emphasizes the dichotomy in the speaker's feelings toward Wulf and Eadwacer respectively: after twelve lines devoted to the speaker's unhappy reminiscences, we are suddenly presented with two juxtaposed direct addresses whose respective tone and content forcefully bring out the difference in her feelings toward Wulf and Eadwacer. By placing these addresses at the end of his text, the poet leaves his audience with the unequivocal realization that the element of separation is indeed the key to the suffering that causes the rising intensity of *Wulf and Eadwacer*.

I have said earlier that my purpose here was not to offer yet another interpretation, and I have accordingly attempted to present an analysis which might suit most of the usual interpretations, except in such particulars as have been indicated. In order to keep true to this plan, I have necessarily shirked several problems which would require a completely arbitrary interpretation. For instance, much more might have been said about the tone if I had followed my own conviction that Wulf is the speaker's lover and that Eadwacer is either her husband or guardian, but nothing in the text makes it possible to determine the exact nature of her relationship to either man. The very fact that the speaker was once identified with the Signy of the *Vǫlsunga saga* shows that Wulf might conceivably be considered her brother as well as her lover — or both, depending where one wishes to locate the poem within the saga. Nor does the text warrant the definite identification of Eadwacer as her husband,[32] and I find no evidence for the common assumption already quoted that he is "possibly brutal." From the poem as a whole, I personally derive the impression that he might prove somewhat ungentlemanly if he were to hold Wulf in his power; but, if he is indeed the speaker's husband and Wulf her lover, we could hardly expect him to stretch the limits of *savoir faire* to the point of offering the latter a cup of mead at the family table. The text likewise makes it difficult to tell whether the man who embraces the speaker is Wulf or Eadwacer. If *se beaducafa*

(l. 11a) refers to Eadwacer, the embrace itself might be physically sat-
isfying but its author repugnant, and we have a situation somewhat
reminiscent of Emma Bovary's allowing Charles an awkward caress
while inwardly loathing the very shape of his back; if it refers to Wulf,
then both the sensation and the man would probably be a source of sat-
isfaction, but the inevitable afterthought that this daring embrace could
cost him his life would surely spoil this fleeting pleasure. I personally
incline toward the latter explanation, and I accordingly find here added
tension which I have refrained from discussing above. The most serious
crux occurs in the interpretation of the lines *Uncerne earne hwelp
bireð Wulf to wuda* (ll. 16b–17a), for the tone of the utterance depends
to a great extent on whether we assume the *hwelp* to be the offspring of
Wulf or of Eadwacer. If we accept the latter interpretation, we may
suppose the tone to be one of intense hatred, and perhaps bitter resent-
ment, since the speaker is in effect willing to predict the murder of her
own child in order to torture his father emotionally; if we accept the
former interpretation, then we may suppose the tone to be one of anticipated triumph, since Wulf will finally get back what belongs to him.

I have similarly shirked various minor problems because they have
only little bearing on my argument. Such is the case of the frequent
assumption already quoted that the speaker is "probably a captive in a
foreign land." I am not saying that she is not, but I find no textual
evidence for thinking that she is any more a captive than any other unhappy woman in a society that had not yet discovered the amenities of
alimony. As for locating her in a foreign land, we should have to assume
against the testimony of both history and literature that all Anglo-Saxon
maidens were betrothed abroad like Freawaru in *Beowulf*. The assumption that the speaker of *Wulf and Eadwacer* lives among foreigners is
of course tempting, since it would add an element of loneliness to the
woes she expresses; but not even her reference to *leodum minum* may
serve as clue in this instance, for she may use it to denote the people
among whom she lives with her husband as well as the people among
whom she was born. A similar argument may be made in respect to the
obscure reading *earne* (l. 16b), which some editors would emend to
eargne and others—including Malone—to *earmne*.[33] Since the former
solution connotes a little more contempt than the latter, we should have
to know whether the *hwelp* thus qualified is Eadwacer's son or Wulf's
before we can make up our mind, and our decision would have no great
effect on the analysis of the total poem.

To return to the point I made at the beginning of this essay, the
important thing for us is that to a point the poem stands apart from its
meaning. Whether or not the speaker is an exile in a foreign land,
whether or not Eadwacer is her husband and the father of her child,
whether or not the man who embraces her is her lover, *Wulf and*

Eadwacer reaches us through the passionate intensification of grief, which it expresses as few poems have done in any language. It moves us through the juxtaposition of powerful emotions and through the sense of tragic separation which it conveys – even if we understand its specific nature as little as Mr. Eliot pretends to have understood French poetry when he fell in love with it.

NOTES

1. C. W. Kennedy, *The Earliest English Poetry* (London, 1943), p. 50.
2. G. K. Anderson, *The Literature of the Anglo-Saxons* (Princeton, N. J., 1949), p. 164.
3. David Daiches, *A Critical History of English Literature* (New York, 1960), I, p. 20.
4. P. J. Frankis, "*Deor* and *Wulf and Eadwacer*: Some Conjectures," *Medium Aevum*, XXXI (1958), 172.
5. Benjamin Thorpe, ed., *Codex Exoniensis* (London, 1842), p. 380.
6. Heinrich Leo, in the Halle program for 1857, concludes his interpretation with the words, "Quae de se ipso Cynevulfus . . . tradiderit." A similar interpretation was proposed by Frederick Tupper, "The Cynewulfian Runes of the First Riddle," *Modern Language Notes*, XXV (1910), 235 ff.; however, Moritz Trautmann, *Anglia*, VI (1884), 158 ff., proposed the solution "riddle"; and H. Patzig, "Zum ersten Rätsel des Exeter Buches," *Archiv*, CXLV (1923), 204 ff., proposed "millstone."
7. Henry Bradley, in a review of Morley's *English Writers*, in *Academy*, XXXIII (1888), 197 f., further argues that Wulf is the speaker's lover and Eadwacer her "tyrant husband." This view, which is discussed by L. Whitebread, "A Note on *Wulf and Eadwacer*," *Medium Aevum*, X (1941), 150 ff., was substantially accepted by Ferdinand Holthausen, "Klage um Wulf," *Anglia*, XV (1893), 188 ff., and by Sir Israel Gollancz, "Wulf and Eadwacer: an Anglo-Saxon Monodrama in Five Acts," *Athenaeum*, (1893), p. 883. It is accepted by a majority of modern scholars.
8. The theory that the poem was an adaptation from the Old Norse was advanced by W. W. Lawrence, "The First Riddle of Cynewulf," *PMLA*, XVII (1902), 245 ff.; the connection with the *Vǫlsunga saga* was argued by Henry Schofield, "Signy's Lament," *ibid.*, pp. 262 ff.
9. W. J. Sedgefield, "Wulf and Eadwacer," *Modern Language Review*, XXVI (1931), 74.
10. Cf. n. 7 above for the theory that Wulf is the lover and Eadwacer the husband; on the other hand, Gollancz, *Athenaeum* (1902), 251 f., makes Wulf the husband and Eadwacer the lover. The former theory is favored by a majority of scholars today.
11. L. L. Schücking, *Kleines angelsächsisches Dichterbuch* (Cöthen, 1919), pp. 16 f.
12. Rudolf Imelmann, "Die altenglische Odoaker-Dichtung," in *Forschungen zur altenglischen Poesie* (Berlin, 1907), pp. 73 ff.
13. Marie Borroff, *Sir Gawain and the Green Knight*: *A Stylistic and Metrical Study* (New Haven, Conn., 1962), pp. 10 ff.
14. Kemp Malone, in *A Literary History of England*, ed. A. C. Baugh (New York, 1948) notes that *Wulf and Eadwacer* "is one of the most obscure poems in the English language" (p. 90).
15. Kemp Malone, "Two English *Frauenlieder*," *Comparative Literature*, XIV (1962), 108, reprinted in *Studies in Old English Literature in Honor of Arthur G. Brodeur*, ed. S. B. Greenfield (Eugene, Ore., 1963), pp. 106 ff. On the other hand, Frankis, *Medium Aevum*, XXXI (1962), 172,

argues convincingly that, short of the improbable assumption that Anglo-Saxon audiences always remembered all the details of their legends, the "references would be to a considerable extent self-explanatory." By arguing a connection between the poem and *Deor*, which precedes it in the manuscript, Frankis works out the following context and interpretation: "Wulf is a warrior-minstrel at the court of the king of the Heodoningas; he loves the king's daughter (probably named Hild), and under the circumstances described in *Wulf and Eadwacer*, ll. 10–12, she conceives a child by him; the king is enraged, and Wulf is forced to flee into exile; Heorrendo receives Wulf's position at court, and also his estates; the king's daughter is kept under guard on a remote island. The fate of the child is not clear: *Wulf and Eadwacer*, ll. 16–17, could refer to an accomplished fact . . . or to an anticipation of the future."

16. All quotations from *Wulf and Eadwacer* are from *The Exeter Book*, edd. G. P. Krapp and E. V. K. Dobbie (New York, 1936), pp. 179–80.

17. The theory of oral-formulaic composition and delivery was developed by Milman Parry in respect to Homeric poetry in "Studies in the Epic Technique of Oral Verse-Making: 1. Homer and Homeric Style," *Harvard Studies in Classical Philology*, XLI (1930), 73 ff., and "The Homeric Language as the Language of an Oral Poetry," *ibid.*, XLIII (1932), 1 ff. F. P. Magoun, Jr., "Oral-Formulaic Character of Anglo-Saxon Narrative Poetry," *Speculum*, XXVIII (1953), 446 ff., was the first to apply Parry's theory to Anglo-Saxon poetry, and he later investigated the actual act of composition in "Bede's Story of Caedman: the Case History of the Anglo-Saxon Oral Singer," *Speculum*, XXX (1955), 49 ff. My own argument is not concerned with composition, since *Wulf and Eadwacer* is not a narrative poem in the strict sense of the word and Magoun's theory is based on the investigation of narrative poetry, and since Malone, *Comparative Literature*, XIV (1962), 110, points

out that "this poem was not done in . . . formulaic style." However, we have no reason to think that the possibility of written composition would seriously affect the general pattern of delivery, for the versification is clearly in the Anglo-Saxon tradition. Additional evidence for my argument concerning delivery may be found in A. B. Lord's most extensive study of the problem, *The Singer of Tales* (Cambridge, Mass., 1961), as well as in T. F. Mustanoja's "The Presentation of Ancient Germanic Poetry: Looking for Parallels," *Neuphilologische Mitteilungen*, LX (1959), 1 ff. I have discussed the presentation of Anglo-Saxon poetry in "Point of View and Design for Terror in *Beowulf*," *Neuphilologische Mitteilungen*, LXIII (1962), 145 ff., and in "*Judith* and the Limits of Poetry," *English Studies*, XLIII (1962), 1 ff. The emphasis placed on individual metrical units by traditional oral delivery may be ascertained by listening to the tape recordings in the Milman Parry Collection of South Slavic Texts of Harvard University.

18. *The Wanderer*, in *The Exeter Book*, pp. 134–37.

19. Anderson, p. 163.

20. J. F. Adams, "Wulf and Eadwacer: An Interpretation," *Modern Language Notes*, LXXIII (1958), 1 ff. His translation of the poem occurs on p. 5.

21. *Ibid.*, p. 2.

22. Malone, *Comparative Literature*, XIV (1962), 108.

23. *Ibid.* Malone's interpretation, one might add, depends also on his evaluation of nearly all previous scholarship on the subject.

24. If we wish to agree with many scholars (e.g., Malone, as above) that Wulf may be an outlaw, we need not even insert "this" before the word "people" since he might be set upon by almost anyone who sees him. This interpretation detracts nothing from my argument, and I have avoided it in my text merely because my purpose is to avoid arguing in favor of any interpretation unless it be relevant to the aims of the present essay.

25. Joseph Bosworth and T. N. Toller,

An Anglo-Saxon Dictionary and Supplement (Oxford, 1898 and 1921), henceforth cited as Bosworth-Toller without further references. My argument likewise implies a difference with R. K. Gordon, whose translation, in *Anglo-Saxon Poetry* (Everyman's Library 794), is the most generally accepted and reads, "Will they feed him, if he should feel want?" (p. 91).

26. Bosworth-Toller notes that the term *wulf* is often "applied to a cruel person"; note also the connotation of *se awyrgda wulf* (the devil) and of the compounds *wulfes-heafod* (outlaw), *wæl-wulf* (warrior), *wulf-heort* (cruel), *wulf-hliþ* (wolf slope), *wulf-hol* (wolf den), *wulf-seap* (wolf pit), *heoru-wulf* (warrior), *here-wulf* (warrior), *hilde-wulf* (warrior).

27. In his edition of the text, Malone emends *ic . . . dogode* (l. 9) to *ic . . . hogode*, as first proposed by F. Hicketier, "Fünf Rätsel des Exeterbuches," *Anglia*, x (1888), 579, and subsequently accepted by W. J. Sedgefield, who printed it in *An Anglo-Saxon Verse Book* (London, 1922) with the remark, "the MS reading *dogode* makes no sense" (p. 195); and he thoroughly supports his choice with additional linguistic evidence. In the notes to the edition used here, however, Krapp and Dobbie retain *dogode* and cite Bülbring's argument that the emendation to *hogode* presumes the improbable infinitive *hogian*; they also point out that the manuscript reading is accepted by Schücking, Holthausen, and Sieper. I have likewise kept the manuscript reading because the present essay is a literary analysis rather than a textual study, and I prefer to analyze the text as it was known to the contemporary readers of the Exeter Book than as modern scholarly investiga-

tion may think it ought to have been. Since Malone's emendation, when considered within context, also suggests suffering, my analysis applies to it up to a point.

28. Boswoth-Toller's introductory statement about the word *lac* is relevant to the present argument: "The idea which lies at the root of the various meanings . . . seems to be that of motion."

29. Unlike Malone, I construe *bireð* as future rather than present. Although Frankis accepts both "Wulf is bearing our wretched son to the forest" and "Wulf will bear . . . ," and both interpretations are grammatically feasible, the use of *gehieran* in the preceding line suggests that the poet intended the speaker to be understood as predicting a future event rather than calling attention to an actual abduction. If the abduction were actually taking place unheard by Eadwacer, he would have to be either deaf or out of earshot, and the speaker would surely ask him to *look* rather than to listen. On the other hand, a future warning or threat may be introduced by appealing to either the ear or the eye: "look here" or "listen here."

30. See above, n. 27, for my acceptance of *dogian*, glossed as "to bear, suffer" in Bosworth-Toller.

31. In reference to *ungelic is us*, Frankis writes, "the refrain of *Wulf and Eadwacer* emphasizes unlikeliness and proclaims a contrast."

32. Frankis (p. 173, n. 34) concludes that "it is most satisfactory to regard [Eadwacer] as either a guardian over the speaker or perhaps as a man who had somehow betrayed the lovers, corresponding to the *træsker Mand* of the Danish ballad *Ribold og Gulborg . . . .*"

33. For a list of scholarly views on this point, see Malone, as above, p. 110.

Dramatic Voices in *The Wanderer* and *The Seafarer*

JOHN C. POPE

Yale University

IN THIS ARTICLE I propose to reconsider the structure and certain aspects of the meaning of *The Wanderer* and *The Seafarer*. *The Seafarer* even more than *The Wanderer* has been the subject of a great deal of interpretation, and much of it has enduring value; but certain very basic issues are still in doubt—largely, I believe, because we have not reached a full understanding of its structure. My view of the structure is only a little different from some others that have been advanced both long ago and recently; yet I think the difference makes the basic idea more acceptable, and this idea itself needs to be brought into relation with what other critics have had to say about the probable meaning of certain passages. *The Wanderer*, by contrast, has seemed a relatively clear and well-organized poem and the usual view of its structure, though in my opinion incorrect, has had only a few undernourished rivals. Hence my interpretation is novel enough to need careful demonstration. But it is not entirely without antecedents, and is really more obvious than the interpretation of *The Seafarer*. Certain parallel features of the two poems strongly suggest the same basic structure, and certain features peculiar to *The Wanderer* seem to point the way to a fuller understanding of that structure. For the sake of clarity, therefore, I shall begin with *The Wanderer*.

i

THE PREVAILING view of *The Wanderer* in its formal aspect has been that it consists principally of a long dramatic monologue, lines 8–110, spoken by a man who is introduced in line 6 as an *eardstapa* or wanderer. This monologue is enclosed by a seven-line introduction and a five-line epilogue spoken impersonally by the poet, and it contains within itself a subordinate speech by a purely hypothetical person, introduced as *se . . . þisne wealsteal . . . deope geondþenceð*, he who deeply considers this foundation.[1] The hypothetical speech, coming at the end of the monologue, is a lament for all that men care for on earth and for the earth itself. It puts what the principal speaker has to say in a grandly objective way. When it is finished the wanderer himself stops talking and the poet adds the epilogue.

But now, at the head of the epilogue, we read,

> Swa cwæð snottor on mode,   gesæt him sundor æt rune.

That is, "So spoke one wise in spirit, sat by himself at counsel." To whom is the poet referring? Those who take lines 8–110 as the wanderer's speech generally assume, as surely they must, that the poet is referring by this new epithet to the wanderer himself. He can hardly mean the speaker of the closing lament in lines 92–110, for that indefinite person is merely a rhetorical figment, and his speech is introduced by the present-future *acwið* 'will say,' to which the preterite *cwæð* here does not properly correspond. It is plausibly argued that the wanderer has spoken not only of his personal sufferings (ll. 8–57) but with philo-sophical breadth of the losses all men must sustain in this unstable world (ll. 58–110). Hence, having appeared to us at first as merely an *eardstapa*, he has earned by his discourse the epithet of a wise man, a *snottor on mode*.

This is roughly the view set forth by Max Rieger in 1869,[2] and very ably reasserted by S. B. Greenfield in 1951.[3] There are some variations of it that are of interest though they do not change the basic conception of the structure. Thus it was assumed by Thorpe in the first modern edition of the poem, and later by Gollancz and others, that the wanderer rather than the poet spoke the first five lines – a very probable inference which will prove to be of some importance.[4] A logical extension, though somewhat less inviting, is a recent suggestion that the last four lines also are spoken by the wanderer, so that only the lines describing the speaker, 6–7 and 111, are the poet's.[5] Real dissent from the prevailing view has been rare,[6] though it should be remembered that some of the most reputable editors have been unwilling to commit themselves as to where the wanderer's speech ends. They put a quotation mark before line 8 for the beginning (or resumption) of his speech, but one looks in vain for a corresponding mark of conclusion.[7]

If one is to object to the prevailing interpretation it must be rather for what it leaves unexplained than for any demonstrable error. It does not openly conflict with the development of meaning in the poem, and it explains plausibly what the poem itself says, in lines 6 and 111, about who is talking. But this explanation is not inevitable, and there are other points at which we may wonder whether we are on the right track. Most notably, there is a sharp cleavage between the first half of the

poem, lines 1–57, and the second, lines 58–115.[8] In the first half the
wanderer is dwelling on the sorrows he himself has endured, general-
izing them only enough to include others whose lot closely resembles his
own. A cold and desolate sea provides the setting for poignant descriptions of the loneliness that attends a friendless and lordless retainer. In
the second half he seems to have put aside his personal sorrows, indeed
all his past experience with its desolate seascapes, in exchange for
thoughts about mankind at large, for images of walls and cities in ruin,
for the sweep of history and the awesome prospect of the end of the
world. And the change comes, not gradually, but all at once. We may
easily begin to wonder whether the speaker is really the same, whether it
is advisable to identify the *eardstapa* with the *snottor on mode*.

    An unsuccessful but nevertheless significant effort to separate the
two characters was made some twenty years ago by Bernard F. Huppé.[9]
His basic feeling, that the poet was making a distinction between a man
hemmed in by his own bitter experience and a man whose mind could
range freely over the universe with philosophic detachment, was
grounded in the contrast to which I have already alluded. Unfortunately
a slip in reasoning caused him to ignore the natural division between
lines 57 and 58 and to assert that the *eardstapa*'s speech extended to line
62a. His reason was that the pronoun *ic*, after giving way to the third
person in lines 30–57, had reappeared in the sentence at 58–62a and

that therefore the *eardstapa* must still be speaking. This was a fatal
deduction, for lines 58–62a are lines that introduce a broad consideration of human life and if they are spoken by the *eardstapa* they mark
him as a philosopher, so that there is no reason to deny him any of the
ideas that follow. Mr. Greenfield, in the article cited above, accepting
as an obvious truth the fallacy in Mr. Huppé's reasoning about the
pronoun, had no difficulty in showing that the latter's analysis of the
structure was inconsistent in itself and much less satisfactory than the
traditional view. Additional trouble was created by Mr. Huppé's effort
to identify the wise man's speech with the concluding lament, lines
92–110, so that he was obliged to designate the lines between speeches,
62b–91, as a bridge passage spoken by the poet. The result of this
analysis could only be general confusion. The important perception at
the root of it was nearly obliterated.

    What did not occur to Mr. Huppé, probably because he had already
assigned lines 92–110 to the *snottor on mode*, was that if there are two
speakers in a poem they can both use the pronoun of the first person.
Suppose we start with the possibility that the *eardstapa* and the *snottor
on mode* are different characters, as the different epithets suggest, and
ask ourselves how much of the poem, in that event, is appropriate to
each. The answer is very clear: Lines 1–5 and 8–57 are appropriate to
the *eardstapa*; lines 58–110 (including the imaginary lament, 92–110)

good

are appropriate to the *snottor on mode*. Lines 6–7, identifying the first
speaker, line 111, identifying the second, and lines 112–15, bringing
down the curtain with a combination of gnomic wisdom and pious
reassurance, may best be left to the poet. The hypermetric form of the
last five lines helps to set them off as an epilogue.

If now we look more narrowly at the two speeches thus distinguished
we shall find that we have replaced one vaguely inclusive character
with two firmly defined ones. The wanderer's speech becomes the perfectly rounded utterance of a person whose own bitter experience has
made him an authority. Having achieved some measure of resignation
to his lot, he is expressing for all who have suffered similar losses just
what this kind of sorrow is made of. His concluding generalization,

> Cearo bið geniwad
> þam þe sendan sceal   swiþe geneahhe
> ofer waþema gebind   werigne sefan,

should not be taken primarily as an appeal for sympathy. It is concurrently, and more importantly, a truth gleaned by suffering. From
beginning to end he is telling us what he has learned about life. His
personal history gives him the right to speak.

And since we have thus limited his speech, it is important to make
sure that it has a proper beginning. The first five lines do not say anything that is beyond the range of such a character, and they say much
that is appropriate to him:

> Oft him anhaga   are gebideð,
> metudes miltse,   þeah þe he modcearig
> geond lagulade   longe sceolde
> hreran mid hondum   hrimcealde sæ,
> wadan wræclastas.   Wyrd bið ful aræd!

The opening clause keeps the consoling possibility of God's ultimate
mercy in view without assuring us that the speaker has already obtained
mercy. He does seem to have reached a state of comparative tranquillity,
but his past sorrows are still vivid in his mind, and they form the substance of what he has to communicate. As he begins to recall them he
thinks of the inexorable power of fate. It is characteristic of him to
generalize out of his own experience, so that his hypothetical characters
are but projections of himself. Thus the word *anhaga* (repeated in line
40) sums up his own loneliness. (We may remember that it is used of
Beowulf in a similar situation, when he swims back to his country alone
after having witnessed the death of Hygelac and all the Geatish host.)
And the image of one stirring the rime-cold sea anticipates the climactic
seascapes of lines 37–57. So long as the wanderer is thought to be
responsible for speaking most of the poem one may toy with the idea that

the poet speaks the opening lines in such a way as to anticipate the
wanderer's own point of view while he adds a bit of piety. But if the
bulk of the poem consists of two complementary speeches, this kind of
introduction is less appropriate. Besides, the wanderer's speech needs
some sort of generalization at the start to hold it together. His words
at line 8 are not a beginning but a development proceeding out of what
has been said in lines 1–5. Thus, although the pronoun of the first person
appears in line 8 for the first time, the sentence is not otherwise comparable to the sentences with which *The Seafarer* and *The Wife's Lament*
begin. And the *Swa cwæð eardstapa* at line 6, though there is precedent
for such an expression (under somewhat different circumstances) as
an introduction to a speech, is much more likely to refer to something
already said.[10]

In the second speech we find just as consistent a characterization as
in the first. The *snottor on mode* proclaims himself at once as a person
who relies, not on direct experience, but on the wide reach of his thought:

> Forþon ic geþencan ne mæg   geond þas woruld
> for hwan modsefa   min ne gesweorce,
> þonne ic eorla lif   eal geondþence,
> hu hi færlice   flet ofgeafon,
> modge maguþegnas.   Swa þes middangeard
> ealra dogra gehwam   dreoseð ond falleð.

Verily[11] I cannot think, within the range of *this* world, why *my*
mind should not grow dark, when I consider all the life of highborn
men, how of a sudden they have relinquished the hall-floor, proud
young retainers. So this world, each and every day, droops and falls.

There are several ways in which this passage gains by being attributed to the second speaker. It was always a little puzzling to find the
wanderer giving reasons for the darkening of his mind, as if it had not
been darkened long ago by the death of his kinsmen. But the thinker,
if he is to feel an answering sadness, must explain the ground for it.
In the second line the possessive *min* now takes on the extra meaning
that explains why it is carrying the alliteration: "why *my* mind should
not grow dark," that is, "my mind also, like the wanderer's." But what
chiefly strikes our attention is the sweeping generalization, so much
greater in range and abstraction than the wanderer's, and so objective,
as having nothing to do with the speaker's personal losses: "*all* the life
of highborn men" (where, as the *modge maguþegnas* more clearly
shows, it is men like the wanderer and his fellow-retainers that are in
view, but collectively and by implication as representatives of mankind). And immediately after we encounter the image of the drooping
and declining world, suggesting on the one hand that men are continually dying and disappearing from the world like leaves from some con-

tinually decadent tree, and on the other that the world is now in its sixth and final age, and resembles an old man on the brink of the grave. We come next to some lines often blamed for irrelevance:

> Forþon ne mæg weorþan wis   wer, ær he age
> wintra dæl in woruldrice.   Wita sceal geþyldig,
> ne sceal no to hatheort   ne to hrædwyrde,
> ne to wac wiga   ne to wanhydig,
> ne to forht ne to fægen,   ne to feohgifre,
> ne næfre gielpes to georn,   ær he geare cunne.
> Beorn sceal gebidan,   þonne he beot spriceð,
> oþþæt collenferð   cunne gearwe
> hwider hreþra gehygd   hweorfan wille.

Verily [or therefore?] a man cannot become wise before he has a share of winters in the world. A wise man must be patient, must not be too hot of heart or too hasty of speech, nor too weak a fighter nor too reckless, nor too fearful nor too sanguine, nor too greedy for money, nor ever too eager to boast before he knows for certain. A fighting man must wait, when he is to speak his vow, until, bold of spirit, he knows for certain whither the purpose of (men's) breasts will turn.

Surely this passage, though it is still a digression from the main course of the argument, looks a good deal more pertinent when it is recognized as part of the characterization of the second speaker. He is no *modig maguþegn* himself, though he may well belong to the warrior class for whose benefit he speaks, but a man schooled in prudential wisdom, and he seems to exhibit this practical aspect of his training at a point where his meditation brings it to mind, partly to show that he knows what is expected of a counselor.[12]

As now his thought carries him forward to the general doom, to its miniature yet impressive prototypes in the ruins that darken the landscape, and to his mournful realization that nothing earthly can endure, he reminds us further of the value he attaches to the intellect. Thus at line 73 he says it is the *gleaw hæle* who must know how terrible it will be when the world is destroyed, and when he introduces his hypothetical elegist in lines 88–90 he defines him as one *frod in ferðe* and requires him to think deeply before uttering his lament. But I need not continue. From first to last he answers to the definition: he is *snottor on mode*.

Once we have made this distinction between the speakers it is difficult to resist it, for it so obviously matches the pattern of theme and image in the poem, and is so direct and simple an explanation for the poet's own words, the *swa cwæð eardstapa* and *swa cwæð snottor on mode*. But we may well hesitate momentarily in the face of the unfamiliarity of the form. Here we have two speeches complementing one another, the second a challenging extension of the first, yet the speakers

are apparently not disputing with one another and the only direct indication that the second has been listening to the first is the vague
implication of his opening *forþon* and the comparison implicit in his
first sentence. This is certainly not an ordinary dialogue in which the
speakers are addressing each other. What is the fundamental conception
that can render such a juxtaposition of two speeches intelligible?

For a time I was inclined to believe that the poem was a meditative
monologue by the thinker in which, after speaking lines 1–5 in his own
character, he introduced the wanderer and quoted his words. Then, at
line 58, the thinker resumed his meditation and proceeded to the end of
it at line 110, after which the poet identified him as the principal speaker.
This notion may need passing attention, because something very like it
has already been suggested for *The Seafarer*; but it is surely mistaken.
Once we recognize that the first five lines are much more appropriate
to the wanderer than to the thinker, we are confronted by two con-
sective speeches of almost the same length, and although the second is
more inclusive than the first and comprehends it intellectually, there is
no good reason why the second speaker should be made to quote the first.
It is much simpler and more intelligible, as well as fairer, for the poet
to quote each of them in turn, acting as a neutral reporter and letting us
make up our own minds about the importance of each.

A much more satisfactory answer to the problem of the two speakers
is suggested by the poet himself when he describes his second speaker,
the *snottor on mode*, and says he was sitting apart at counsel, *gesæt him
sundor æt rune*. Even if we take this expression with Bosworth-Toller
as meaning primarily "sat apart communing with himself," it suggests
that he would normally have been expected to be communing with
others, taking his place *æt rune*. For example, in *Beowulf*, lines 171–72,
we are told that many a man among the Danes *gesæt rice to rune*, and
in *Andreas*, line 1161, that the counselors of the famished Mermedonians
gesæton sundor to rune. The association of the word *run* with the
consultations in hall by a king's trusted advisers is otherwise illustrated
by the description in *Beowulf*, 1325, of the dead Æschere as having been
Hrothgar's *runwita*. It seems possible, then, that the poet is not only
describing the isolation of the thinker but at the same time implying
that the scene is a nobleman's hall where a number of men are
assembled to share experiences and ideas. The topic this time is bereave-
ment, or more broadly, mutability, and two men of vastly different experience and training speak in turn. They are not disputing with one
another but making their separate contributions to the discussion, the
second, of course, speaking with full awareness of what the first has said
and building upon it, but addressing himself, as the other had done, to
the group.

Such, I believe, may well be the dramatic assumption behind these partly corroborative, partly antithetic speeches, though certainly the hall was not the only place where, in everyday life, men might have spoken successively on a topic without directly addressing one another, and it must be admitted that the poet has withheld all but the barest hint of a stage setting. The emphasis, beyond question, is on the speeches themselves, and whatever may be their relation to the patterns of actual discourse, it is clear that these dramatic voices are put in sequence for us in order that the poet may do justice to two different aspects of his theme.

At bottom, in fact, the poet reveals by the contrasting elements in these speeches his consciousness of the rival claims of two schools of thought, almost of two cultures. His love for the old Germanic poetical traditions and his mastery of them are amply revealed in the speech of the wanderer and are not altogether hidden in the speech of the wise man. The opposition between the two characters is by no means absolute. But some of the thinker's ideas in this speech and its whole purport reflect the influence of the Mediterranean learning that became available in the wake of the conversion. The fact that the poet preserves so much of the feeling of tradition in his imagery and his expressions suggests not only his unusual skill but the labor of predecessors in making poetry out of these new ideas and modes of feeling. The author of *The Wanderer*, in a more radical way than the author of *Beowulf*, seems deliberately to juxtapose the new mode and the old, to exhibit both the strength and the limitations of the old, and to suggest a synthesis dominated by the new.

As for the poem itself, it seems to me to gain greatly in precision and richness of meaning by the recognition of its duality. When we consider the relations of the two speeches we see that both characterization and theme have become sharper and have developed additional significance by their interaction in our minds. And the poet himself, in comprehending both his characters and the range of their thought and feeling, has displayed a breadth of understanding far beyond what we could see in the monologue we have grown accustomed to reading.

We must beware of oversimplifying the contrast between the two speakers. Both, we should assume, are nominally Christian, both preserve elements of old traditions, both show some interest in the world and its values. But the wanderer, as a typically loyal retainer, belongs to the conservative aristocratic world in both life and poetry; the thinker, though he recognizes a native tradition of wisdom, has moved into the sphere of Biblical and patristic learning, with some flavor of classical philosophy. And the darkness of spirit that has come over both these characters has different roots and leads to different conclusions. The wanderer's whole-souled devotion to his lord and his fellows of the comitatus is at once the sign of his nobility and the cause of his sorrow.

This all-absorbing passion has been turned by the death of those he loves into the cold fetters of his loneliness. As the recurring images of confinement in the first half of the poem suggest, the wanderer is imprisoned by the sheer unchanging emptiness of his lordless, friendless environment. If he has found some alleviation of his misery it is not because he has learned to see it in a different light.

The thinker, in contrast, is not thus confined, nor has he suffered so personal a loss. His pensive melancholy, beautifully balanced against the other's sorrow, comes from the knowledge of other people's losses and the prospect of the general doom. His mind is constantly moving outward to survey men's history, to look on a landscape sprinkled with ruins, to look *through* life and the world. It is remarkable how often he uses *geond*, meaning variously "over, through, throughout," both as preposition and verbal prefix; it helps to emphasize the notions of penetration and range. The whole oppressive extent of the wanderer's suffering is diminished by his comprehensive view into the image of one disconsolate survivor of a battle saving a dead comrade from the birds and beasts of prey by burying him in the earth—quite uselessly, of course.[13] Thus, although he very movingly laments the passing of all things that seem of value in the world, there is a certain coolness in his attitude toward individual things and persons. His aloofness, as he sits apart, carries very different implications from the other's loneliness. For there is a balance in his thinking between sadness at the instability and waste of the world and the liberating energy of his thought. The elegy with which he concludes his speech expresses this balance with remarkable clarity and power. By its succession of images of good things that have perished it moves from a beginning full of regret and longing to deepening gloom and total disaster. But when, in the closing line, we find it said that "all this foundation of earth shall become void," we can hardly help recognizing that in the relentless completion of his thought the thinker has annihilated the very ground that breeds these vanishing satisfactions. Any expression of grief involves some release, but there is something almost triumphant in the sweep of this vision of dissolution.

Thus I am persuaded that there is more reason than ever to look upon this elegiac poem as having strong affinities with the literary consolation, as has recently been maintained afresh and very ably by J. E. Cross.[14] As Mr. Cross shows, the main reason for listing the poem as a member of this genre is not the brief acknowledgment of God's mercy at the beginning nor the assurance of steadfastness in heaven at the end, though certainly the latter is a significant way of closing the frame. The main reason is that the grounds for lamentation in the second half of the poem are also familiar medicines for a personal grief: in general, the contemplation of other people's distress tends to mitigate our own, and a panorama diminishes the importance of the foreground. With the separation of characters, it becomes evident that the entire speech of the thinker is at one and the same time a lament and an antidote against the sort of misery that had so long engulfed the wanderer. We need not be surprised at the bitterness of the medicine if we remember the methods of Dame Philosophy in Boethius, nor at the tendency toward consolation in a lament if we remember the funeral elegies of the poets.

But certainly what we have in *The Wanderer* is no reversal of mood, nor does the second speaker aim his speech at the first (or even at us) in the manner of a philosopher or a preacher, as if to inculcate a contempt for the world. Rather he assimilates his mood to the other's and seems, as the poet tells us, to be communing with himself though at counsel. He has been following a train of thought and it has ended in a bleak though strangely sublime vision of destruction. If we choose to find it instructive or consoling that is our affair.

Clearly our modern title for the poem does it less than justice. I shall not try to supplant it after more than a century of use, but perhaps I may be allowed to invent, for the sake of summary, one of those generous Elizabethan titles, borrowing a contradiction or two from Peter Quince: "The Wanderer's Lament and the Wise Man's Meditation: Being a Double Elegy and Most Doleful Consolation in Two Voices and an Epilogue, Wherein They that have Lost what they have Loved may Behold the Image of their Sorrow and may Feelingly Know that All Things Earthly Vanish into Night."

ii

THE IDEA THAT there are two speakers in *The Seafarer* emerged early in the modern criticism of the poem and has recently, after a period of disfavor, been put forward again in a significantly modified form. It will appear once more in these pages, this time in a form strongly resembling that which has just been ascribed to *The Wanderer*. But along with many resemblances to *The Wanderer*, *The Seafarer* exhibits some important differences. It is a much harder poem to follow from passage to passage, so that the question of its dramatic form is seriously entangled with other problems of interpretation. We may profitably begin, therefore, by reminding ourselves of certain peculiarities of the poem and of some notable efforts to deal with them.

Under the scrutiny of two sharply opposed interpreters, Kluge and Anderson, who in this one matter agreed, the poem seemed to fall into three unequal sections, with one point of division after the first quarter and another in the middle.[15] I shall follow Anderson in calling the sections A1, A2, and B, although these symbols do not express the relationship that will ultimately emerge. The division in the middle between A and B (l. 64 or 66) is determined by a contrast in ostensible subject matter and style. The first half, A, is lyric and dramatic and contains frequent references to the sea, whereas the second, B, starts with a reasoned attack on the world and its values, ends with precepts and a sermon-like exhortation, and does not mention the sea. There is a transitional sentence (ll. 64b–66a) that preserves a bit of the imagery of A (the reference to *land* in contrast to sea) while it introduces the main theme of B, but otherwise the contrast is clearly marked. The division after the first quarter is determined by what has been interpreted by some as a change of speaker, by others as a shift to a new aspect of the same speaker's character, and to his present purposes as opposed to his past experience. The beginning, A1 (ll. 1–33a), tells in the first person of the hardships endured by a man who has made numerous voyages and remembers the wintry ones with particular vividness. He contrasts his misery with the satisfactions of a landsman, his own knowledge of pain and anxiety and loneliness with the landsman's cheerful ignorance. The remainder of the first half, A2 (ll. 33b–64a), also predominantly in the first person, tells of the speaker's desire to make a voyage to a far country, denies that the satisfactions on land can distract a man from his voyage, and says that all the adornments of the land in its blossoming season urge a man to set out if he means to go far. The cuckoo urges him too and bodes sorrow. In confirmation of this note of sorrow and in accord with the earlier section, the speaker says that the prosperous man cannot know what is suffered by those who go farthest on the paths of exile. Yet the speaker is irresistibly impelled to set forth.

Before Kluge had distinguished these three sections Max Rieger had noted the signs of a change in line 33 and had concluded that there must be two speakers. He regarded the poem as a dialogue between an old man, full of bitter experience, and a young man who longed to make a voyage in spite of the other's warnings. The young man's first reply came at the beginning of A2 and there were further exchanges in the course of which no distinction was recognized between A and B.[16] Kluge, in the article already mentioned, accepted the dialogue theory but pointed out the weakness of the evidence for all the changes of speaker after the first and held that there were only two speeches, the old man's in A1 and the young man's after it. But he limited the young man's speech, as a significant piece of characterization, to A2, because he regarded B as a rather bungling addition to the original poem and was not concerned to reconcile it with A.

To Kluge himself and to other critics the separation of A and B seemed even more important than the question of dialogue within A. According to Kluge, if one accepted B as an integral part of the poem one might feel obliged to read A as an allegory, a reading that he thought incompatible with the internal evidence. By isolating A one could look on it as a purely imitative and secular piece, a lyric and dramatic treatment of men's relations with the sea. On this matter he won the support of W. W. Lawrence, who was concurrently unwilling to accept the notion of a dialogue and tried to show that the contrast between A1 and A2 could be reconciled with the assumption that there was only one speaker.[17]

But Kluge's argument in dismissing B pointed to the means by which it was soon to be defended. Gustav Ehrismann was the first to present an allegorical interpretation.[18] He maintained that the poem was a loosely organized monologue setting forth the nature and claims of the monastic ideal of life. One set of symbols represented ascetic rigor and otherworldly aspiration in terms of a seafarer's life of toil and trouble on the sea and his concern to reach a far country, while another, contrasting set represented the aristocratic ideal of worldly success and pleasure in terms of the prosperous landsman and all the cherished satisfactions of life in the hall. In B the worldly satisfactions were disparaged as perishable, and the true end of a good Christian's endeavor was seen to be the attainment of the Lord's joys in heaven. There is no doubt that the contrasting images of A, when isolated, can be thus simply related to the main thesis of B; but if one considers them in the whole context provided by the formal elaboration of the poem a number of complications arise. Ehrismann made no attempt to explain the sequence of thought from passage to passage. He seems to have considered this a hopeless enterprise, for he described the author as a mere compilator, a clumsy arranger of appropriate passages out of the work of his predecessors, some of whom were skillful poets.

Thus it was left for O. S. Anderson, in the article cited above, to try to read the poem as a coherent and consistent allegory. Since he had followed a number of critics in rejecting the dialogue theories of Rieger and Kluge, he was obliged to explain the supposed allegory in A with respect to the life of its one speaker. He tried (as unsuccessfully, I think, as everyone else) to avoid the implication of a change of speakers at the start of A2, but in other respects he admitted a contrast between A1 and A2. A1, he maintained, was a presentation of the speaker's past life under the figure of voyaging along a dangerous coast in the winter. A2, then, presented the same speaker's longing to set out on a long summer voyage across the deep sea to a far distant country; that is, to take leave of this world altogether and make for the heavenly home.

There are several objections to this interpretation. For one thing, the meaning of the symbols shifts disconcertingly. In A1 the sea represents the vicissitudes of the world; in A2 it represents a passage to the hereafter at the point of death. If the shift were from literal to figurative meanings there would be no difficulty, but the literal meanings of sea and land are (for Anderson) an unregarded element in both sections: the shift is from one figurative meaning to another. Again, there is nothing in A1 to suggest that the speaker means anything beyond what he says. The account he gives of his sufferings at sea, though partly conventional, has seemed to contain so many imaginative touches and to mean so much when taken at face value that many readers are reluctant to take it otherwise. Unless as a secondary interpretation made in retrospect, an allegorical interpretation, having no power to make any of it more intelligible, is merely a nuisance.

It was this last objection that Dorothy Whitelock stressed when she proposed her ingenious and in many ways persuasive interpretation.[19] By assuming with her that the speaker is both a sailor and a religious zealot, a *peregrinus pro amore Dei*, we can come very close to accepting everything in the poem at face value as spoken in character. For such a person would have had firsthand acquaintance with the actual sea (A1), would have reason to plan another voyage, longer and more strenuous, perhaps, for religious ends (A2), and would be ready enough to philosophize and preach (B).

Certainly this interpretation much surpasses its predecessors in refinement and judgment. It does not foist allegory or religious overtones on verses that do not invite them, and yet it permits the positively religious implications of A2 and B to be recognized freely without the suspicion that they are the work of an interpolator. It also provides a historical context within which not only the seafaring *peregrini* but the age in which they flourished can be more clearly understood.

Yet it does not solve quite all the problems. For one thing it does not explain or condone (in terms of dramatic or poetic propriety) the absence of sea imagery in B. A pilgrim who was so deeply aware of the actual sea as to be capable of making the words of A1 his own might, in ordinary life, indulge in moral reflections such as we find in B without once mentioning the sea—in fact if the poem has one author, it is clear, no matter how we interpret it, that he has displayed this versatility. But a poetically conceived pilgrim ought not so to violate dramatic probability. For another thing, though as I have said this interpretation permits the religious implications of A2 and B to be recognized, its literalness nevertheless limits the meaning of A2. For, whereas A1 seems to gain by a literal interpretation, A2 seems to gain by an allegorical one. This peculiarity of A2 has been emphasized by studies more recent than Miss Whitelock's and will be considered in due course.[20]

Above all there is a stubbornly particular difficulty. Like all the theories that have treated the poem as a simple monologue, this theory does not give a satisfactory explanation for the language of the first sentence of A2:

                        Forþon cnyssað nu
        heortan geþohtas   þæt ic hean streamas,
        sealtyþa gelac   sylf cunnige.[21]

If one gives *sylf* the emphasis that its position in the verse demands, there is no good way to avoid the implication that the speaker has not been to sea before. This was pointed out specifically by Wülker,[22] and it was the one firm piece of evidence for the dialogue theories of Rieger and Kluge. If the experienced seafarer of AI is still talking, why does he not say *eft cunnige* instead of *sylf cunnige*? In so crucial a matter the poet would hardly have sacrificed sense to a convenient alliteration. Those who have regarded the poem as a monologue have been obliged to believe that the poet was using *sylf* in a vacuous way and to find translations that would rob it of meaning. Lawrence, who made the first attempt to get around the difficulty, altered and weakened the *sylf* by a free paraphrase in which he inserted "again" for an *eft* that is not in the manuscript: "Even I myself, who have endured so much hardship, am impelled to make trial of the waves again."[23] Miss Whitelock, dealing more exactly with the rest of the sentence, simply leaves *sylf* untranslated: "Therefore my heart's thoughts constrain me to venture on the deep seas, the tumult of the salt waves."[24] One has only to reread the original after any of the translations given by the proponents of the monologue theory in order to feel that the evidence of the text at this point is flatly against them.[25] Yet if they found the older dialogue theories unsatisfactory on other grounds, what were they to do?

An answer of great interest, constituting what seems to me a signal advance, was made a few years ago by E. G. Stanley in the course of his article, "Old English Poetic Diction and the Interpretation of *The Wanderer*, *The Seafarer*, and *The Penitent's Prayer*."[26] He suggested that the poem, though not a dialogue, does in fact have two speakers, one of whom is quoting the other at the beginning. He regards AI as a speech attributed to a typically conceived seafarer and quoted by the principal speaker as a basis and point of departure for his own discourse, which fills the rest of the poem. In order to emphasize the limited reality attributed to the person whose speech is quoted, and perhaps to suggest the direct influence of the rhetoricians, Mr. Stanley borrows the term *ethopoeia* from Mr. Huppé and gives it a more specialized sense than it normally conveyed:[27]

> There are two speakers speaking in the first person, the ethopoeic exile (lines 1–33a), and the wise, pious man eager to go on pilgrimage (33b to the end). The break comes (as it does in the various dialogue theories) in line 33; for the speaker who says (33b– 35b) that he himself is now eager to make trial of seafaring cannot be the man who has just told of the hardships he has experienced in

seafaring. The dialogue theories were advanced in the first place to overcome this difficulty, which is not explained satisfactorily by any of the later theories. The ethopoeic opening is the speech of a man whose imaginary exploits have led to a true view of this world; the poet has chosen this manner of conveying his message because it is the most vivid method of conveying it. The poet then expresses his wish to follow a way of life as contemptuous of the world as that of the ethopoeic Seafarer; he is speaking of himself, but he hopes to urge others to follow the same way of life, for his poem is didactic.

In spite of some dubious features that will be questioned presently, this interpretation marks a real advance because it deals more justly than previous interpretations with the natural implications and relationships of the text. The return to a strict interpretation of *sylf* is only one of its merits. Even if Mr. Stanley is wrong, as I believe he is, in thinking that one speaker is quoting the other, he is right in feeling that the relation between the speakers is not that of an ordinary dialogue. The second speech is not so much a reply to the first as a major declaration of purpose and belief for which the first speech has given the stimulus. There are elements of contrast suggesting rejoinder as the second speech opens, but its main effect is to add another dimension to the imagery and transfer the discussion to another realm. Thus the notion that the second speaker quotes the first (however unsatisfactory in some respects) more nearly accords with the content of the speeches than would the notion of an ordinary balanced conversation or debate such as we usually find in a dialogue. More important, however, is Mr. Stanley's perception that if A1 is set apart, A2 and B can easily be joined together as the speech of a consistent character. For the talk of voyaging in A2 does not, like the talk in A1, reveal any direct experience of the sea, much less any deep subjection to its physical being. Even if we take the voyage literally, as Mr. Stanley, following Miss Whitelock, seems inclined to do, it is a voyage undertaken by the speaker as a part of his effort to disengage himself from the grip of the phenomenal world. With full dramatic propriety, therefore, though still perhaps to our regret, his thoughts move beyond images of the sea to their real center.

Kluge's version of the dialogue theory insisted on a completely secular and realistic interpretation of both A1 and A2, and treated B as essentially a separate, not properly relevant poem. But the allegorists and Miss Whitelock, defending the relevance of B, showed that A2 had strong signs of spiritual if not fully allegorical implications. Since they did not distinguish between the speakers of A1 and A2 they did not see the significance of what they nevertheless helped to establish, that A2 and B have much more in common than A1 and B. Hence Mr. Stanley's return to the notion of two speakers is not a return to Kluge's kind of poem. It involves the acceptance, with Kluge, of a literal and secular A1, but also, with the allegorists and Miss Whitelock, of a religious, possibly allegorical A2 and of a firm union between A2 and the thematically dominant B. In consequence there is opportunity for a more complete release of meaning in the various parts, and a more intelligible relationship between them than ever before.

Yet I think we can profitably modify Mr. Stanley's account of the structure and also his interpretation of the meaning. I shall begin with the structure, and first with the problem already mentioned, Mr. Stanley's notion that one speaker is quoting the other. An obvious objection is that the man alleged to be quoting does not say so. How can we understand what he is doing unless he introduces the other speaker with a *swa cwæð*? If the poem gives us two dramatic characters speaking in turn we can understand the omission of stage directions even if we have been sadly bewildered by their absence; but Mr. Stanley assumes a more or less autobiographical speech made by the poet himself in his own substantial character, at the start of which, without warning, he imitates a seafarer. It does not seem at all likely that the poet, in such a case, would not identify the subordinate speaker. Furthermore, the shadowy character attributed to the imaginary seafarer in contrast to the substantial poet is really not fair to the vividness and power of the speech. Why not accept the simpler view of the old dialogue theory and assume that the two speakers belong to the same plane of dramatic reality: that is, that they are equally fictitious and are speaking in turn? The second speech will still take the first as its point of departure, still overbalance it in length and scope, but will not disparage its authority in its own sphere.

Here at last *The Wanderer* may be called upon to lend its support and at the same time to suggest a further improvement in Mr. Stanley's view of the structure. *The Wanderer*, as described above, and *The Seafarer* show several very striking resemblances, some of which have already emerged and need only be called to mind: (1) Both begin with the speech of a fictitious character. (2) Both introduce a second fictitious character who builds on and enlarges what the first has said. (3) Both introduce the second character's speech with *forþon*.[28] (4) Both make use of the pronoun of the first person at the beginning of the second speech and imply a difference between the "I" now speaking and the "I" who has previously spoken, one of them giving alliterative prominence to *min*, the other to *(ic) sylf*. So much the reader will no doubt have observed for himself. But now there is a further resemblance, one that has often been noticed elsewhere but has not yet been brought to attention here: (5) Both have a passage at the end beginning with hypermetric verses. In *The Wanderer* this passage has already been taken to be an epilogue spoken by the poet. In *The Seafarer* the corresponding passage, though much longer, is probably the same thing.

Hitherto we have not paid attention to the internal structure of the

second half of the poem, called B, since most of the problems could be
treated by assuming its homogeneity. But in fact there is a noticeable
difference between the part that extends to line 102 and the remainder,
lines 103–24. As it happens, these verses begin a new page (actually a
new gathering) in the Exeter Book, and Thorpe, the first editor of *The
Seafarer*, suspected that a leaf was wanting and they were the end of
another poem.[29] There is no supporting evidence for this conjecture
and there are signs of relevance in the lines; but there is excellent
reason for believing that they are not a part of the second speaker's
discourse. In lines 66b–102 this speaker is explaining why he has said
(64b–66a) that he prefers the joys of the Lord to this dead, transitory
life on land, and parenthetically (72–80) maintaining the worth of
virtuous action. He shows the instability of the world and the ultimate
worthlessness of earthly satisfactions, ending at line 102 with the
worthlessness of gold. Then in lines 103–106 we encounter a series of
precepts and gnomic observations that are vaguely pertinent but do not
continue the argument. Six of the first eight of these lines are hypermetric, then the normal form returns. Finally, in lines 117–24, we have
a lucid passage beginning like the closing exhortation of a sermon and
ending with *Amen*.

> Utan we hycgan   hwær we ham agen,
> ond þonne geþencan   hu we þider cumen. . . .

Now the sermonizing conclusion, unlike the gnomic passage, is
obviously relevant to the poem, but neither of them sounds like the
second speaker. He impresses us in the early part of his speech as a man
of intense feeling and compulsive purpose, full of the excitement attending a great personal decision. His reasoned pronouncements from 64b
to 102 can readily be understood as his effort to justify the way of life
he is choosing. The generality and loose sequence of the strongly worded
gnomes form a contrasting boundary beyond which can follow the
sermonizing conclusion with its gentle admonition and encouragement.

It is best, then, to take the precepts with their hypermetric opening
and the cheerfully pious exhortation as an epilogue spoken by the poet
as master of ceremonies. And this view is corroborated by the epilogue
of *The Wanderer*, greatly though it differs in length. The first of its five
neatly balanced hypermetric lines has no counterpart in *The Seafarer*,
being an identification of the second speaker. But its next three and a
half lines correspond in their gnomic style to the first fourteen of *The
Seafarer*, and its last half-line, *þær us eal seo fæstnung stondeð*,
corresponds in the use of the first person plural and in the blend of
admonition and reassurance to the last eight of *The Seafarer*.

Thus it appears that in *The Seafarer*, as in *The Wanderer*, there are
two complementary speeches by sharply differentiated persons, and that

the poet, having presented these speeches, adds a conventional epilogue. This conception of the structure differs from Mr. Stanley's in that it sees both the persons who make use of the pronoun *ic* as dramatic characters clearly distinguished from the poet, and puts both speeches in the same plane of reality. This conception also entails a different analysis of the parts of the poem from that which is implied by the symbols A1, A2, and B. The first speech corresponds to A1, but the second, containing within itself the transition from talk of voyaging to ratiocination, combines A2 with two-thirds of B (ll. 33b–102), and leaves the end of B (ll. 103–24) to be set firmly apart as a mere epilogue to the poet's dramatic vision.

good

– Here

The main structural differences from *The Wanderer* are the absence of *swa cwæð* to identify either of the speakers and the different proportions of the speeches. The first difference may be due to faulty transmission of *The Seafarer* (though it is hard to find a good place in the first speech for an identifying aside), or, more probably, to an attempt to move one step closer to drama. The difference in proportion, however, is closely associated with the radical difference in theme and genre (as Mr. Cross has insisted)[30] between the two poems. For *The Seafarer* presents, in the central character of its second speaker, a man about to commit himself to a fateful course of action. In the early part of his speech he talks of his purpose and reveals the turbulent emotions that impel him toward it; in the later part, after stating the values that govern his choice, he defends it by a reasoned attack on the values he plans to reject. The first speech, insofar as it exists for a purpose beyond itself, is not something to be extended and counterbalanced like the speech of the wanderer, but something whose sensory vitality is to be transferred by the second speaker's thoughts to a different realm of meaning.

That the voyage this speaker contemplates has a spiritual end cannot well be doubted, since he says so clearly that the joys of the Lord are hotter to him than this dead, transitory life on land. And certainly his comparison invests the expression *lif on lande* with a figurative meaning, so that it comes to stand for the life of the worldling. I am not sure, even so, that there is a way to distinguish between the literal voyage that might be contemplated for spiritual ends by the sort of man Miss Whitelock has imagined and the allegorical voyage that might stand generally for the devout life amid the turbulent seas of the world. Yet for a number of reasons I am strongly inclined, now that the first speech in the poem does not have to be included in the same figurative pattern, to regard the voyage as allegorical.

Thus, for one thing, if the voyage is allegorical, the speaker becomes more centrally representative of the religious life, so that both his voyage and his later rejection of worldly values acquire greater scope. Again, if he is not literally concerned with the sea, even as an instrument of purification, it is easier to understand why he never mentions it in the discursive part of his speech. His purpose, which demands a repudiation of the sensory world, merely declares itself openly after the images put into his mind by the vivid discourse of the veteran Seafarer have served their turn. And finally, I think the descriptive part of his speech has the character of the best allegorical composition, in that while it is lifelike and vivid and seems almost right as an imitation of a young man's eagerness for a voyage of ordinary adventure, it suggests, both by its extraordinary intensity and by certain expressions, that it ought to have some deeper import and a more general application. The prospective voyager, when he mentions the anxiety a man must have for his voyage, talks (though not quite explicitly in the negative sentence, ll. 39–43) as if every man that amounted to anything had a voyage to make. And at one or two points I am inclined to accept as secondary implications the meanings that have been proposed by a recent advocate of Anderson's theory.

One of these is *elþeodigra eard*, the destination of the prospective voyage according to line 38. This has usually been interpreted as "the land of foreigners (or strangers)" and taken as a description of a normal seafarer's destination abroad. But G. V. Smithers, in the first part of his study of *The Seafarer* and *The Wanderer*,[31] has argued that the word *elþeodig* here is used with reference to the idea that good Christians are exiles and aliens on earth, destined to travel as *peregrini* toward their *patria* in heaven (as in Hebrews 11:13–16, and in many passages in the church fathers) and that *elþeodigra eard* should therefore be taken as a reference to heaven, the future dwelling place of those who are now strangers on earth. So interpreted, *elþeodigra eard* anticipates and partially explains the speaker's enthusiasm for the joys of the Lord in lines 64b–66a, as Mrs. Gordon points out in accepting it in her edition (p. 9). It helps to explain, too, the ravenous hunger of the speaker's soul (as described in lines 61–64a, a controversial passage of which I shall have more to say in a moment) at the sight of the far-off destination it has scouted on its preliminary flight. I think, therefore, that Mr. Smithers' interpretation, in spite of its riddle-like treatment of the expression, is probably correct. Yet I should prefer to regard *elþeodigra eard* as deliberately ambiguous, like certain expressions that have been pointed out elsewhere in the same speech.[32] The word *eðel* 'homeland' is the usual and less equivocal term for the heavenly home when it is looked upon as the proper dwelling place of sojourners on earth, whereas *eard* is more neutrally taken as whatever country one lives in or is heading for.[33] Hence the ordinary translation, "land of foreigners," will naturally come to mind first, and it should be allowed to do so, for it fits the ordinary idea of a voyage that gives the figure its initial interest. But *eard* is also used for a dwelling place in heaven, and in one of Ælfric's homilies it is used pointedly in that sense, because Ælfric is developing the comparison between the promised land of the Israelites, *þone behatenan eard*, and the heavenly destination of the Christian journey.[34]

A second expression, less central but corroborative, occurs in the lines that describe the approach of summer, enumerating the signs that, as we learn immediately after, admonish the man who plans a long voyage to set forth:

> Bearwas blostmum nimað,   byrig fægriað,
> wongas wlitigað,   woruld onetteð.

The image of the hastening world can be explained, perhaps, as a mere reminder of the swift passage of the seasons provoked by the thought of the earth's activity and change as it bursts into bloom; and once again, as with *elþeodigra eard*, we can welcome this superficial meaning for its relevance to the figure of the voyage. But there seems to be an almost ominous urgency in the expression as it follows upon words so cheerfully evocative of springtime beauty, and the impression is strengthened when we find the cuckoo, as warden of summer, seconding the admonition with mournful speech and foreboding sorrow. The ominous urgency is very well explained if we accept the suggestion, made briefly by Mr. Smithers and more elaborately by Mr. Cross, that *woruld onetteð* is primarily an allusion to the impending though un-predictable end of this world.[35] Not only does the word *onettan* occur in several sermons with reference to the haste with which the world approaches its end, but Mr. Cross shows in detail how Gregory the Great, commenting on the image of the fig tree in Christ's prediction of the end of the world (Luke 21:29 ff.), turns a simple comparison into a paradox by leaving out the middle terms, making earth's fertility and growth into a direct prognostication of its ruin. Ælfric quotes the whole passage from Gregory in his sermon for the second Sunday in Advent,[36] stating the paradox as follows:

Soðlice mid þisum wordum is geswutelod þæt ðises middangeardes wæstm is hryre. To ðam he wext þæt he fealle; to ðy he sprytt þæt he mid cwyldum fornyme swa hwæt swa he ær sprytte.

Immediately afterwards Gregory and Ælfric remind us that the world, having reached its sixth and last age, is like an old man about to die, and the same reminder occurs in lines 81b–90 of *The Seafarer*. I find it hard, therefore, to resist Mr. Cross's conclusion that *woruld onetteð* involves the threat of doom. Thus the prospective voyager has a reason beyond what is usual for setting out while the weather is propitious. No man can know whether there will be other summers after this one, and the voyage means the difference between life and death.

By no means, however, does my acceptance of these secondary meanings involve a commitment to the Andersonian view, now elaborated by Mr. Smithers, that the voyage represents merely the speaker's passage, at death, into the next world. Nor do I agree with Mr. Smithers' suggestion that we should return to the *wælweg* of the manuscript in line 63, with or without the extreme interpretation he has put upon the passage in which it occurs. The passage has caused trouble, however, and must receive some comment before I take up the larger problem of the speaker's death.

The six and a half lines beginning at line 58 form the climactic ending of the descriptive section of the speech. The speaker's soul leaves his breast, goes out over the sea, and comes back to him *gifre ond grædig*, as if hungering for what it has seen across the water.[37] The passage concludes as follows according to the manuscript:

> gielleð anfloga,
> hweteð on wælweg   hreþer unwearnum
> ofer holma gelagu.

In the first of his articles Mr. Smithers argues strongly for *wælweg* as "way to the abode of the dead" instead of Thorpe's almost universally accepted emendation, *hwælweg*. Neither compound occurs anywhere else in Old English, but *hwælweg* has the advantage of conforming to normal alliterative practice and of being obviously pertinent to the context. To make *wælweg* into a *durior lectio* instead of a simple piece of carelessness on the part of the scribe requires too great a strain on both versification and meaning—for although the notion of a violent death as a possible element in the voyage is not necessarily to be excluded even from my own reading of the passage, we must keep pagan associations with Valhalla very far in the background if we are to accept such a word as a description of a devout Christian's transit to heaven. There is an artistic difficulty, too, for such a blunt disclosure of the underlying meaning would shatter the illusion created by the richly figurative language of the passage. The time for disclosure is a moment later, when the images have done their work. Thus I think Mrs. Gordon has made the right choice in preferring the emendation.[38]

Still more emphatically I must protest against a subordinate interpretation by which Mr. Smithers has sought to strengthen the idea that the speaker is about to die. He suggests that the *anfloga* of line 62b, instead of being the bird-like soul (*hyge*) that has been the subject of the preceding verbs, and can very appropriately be described as a "lone flier" (*ānfloga*), is a disease (**andfloga*) ready to give the speaker a quick release into the next world.[39]

This last interpretation represents the extreme to which the Andersonian allegory has been pressed; but even the moderate interpretation of Anderson himself, by taking the prospective voyage as a voyage of death, runs counter to many of the implications of the poem even for those who, like Mrs. Gordon, take it as a monologue. Actually, as Mr. Smithers' own examples from the Bible, the fathers, and the Old English homilists abundantly demonstrate, the usual assumption about the return of the pilgrim to his heavenly home is that it is to be accomplished by a toilsome journey on earth in which death figures merely as a limit; and when the sea is introduced it is primarily associated with the tribulations of the world. Hence the closing sentences of Mrs. Gordon's rejoinder seem to me essentially right:

> The vain and fleeting pleasures and comforts of this world ('life on land') are to be left behind, and the suffering exacted by God from his followers (the *sorge* of the sea-journey) is to be undertaken with eagerness in the quest for eternity. The Seafarer [meaning the speaker of the whole poem, but we may aptly think of the second speaker only] does not choose death; he responds with eager longing to the challenge of that suffering.[40]

An argument for this interpretation within the poem is the passage (ll. 72–80) in which the second speaker concludes that a man should earn the praise not only of those who live after him on earth but of heavenly spirits by fighting against the devil before he dies. This argument is all the stronger if we do not regard lines 1–33a as an account of the prospective voyager's earlier life. By giving these lines to a different person we convert the voyage contemplated in lines 33b–64a into the major adventure of the second speaker's life. We need not insist, with Rieger and Kluge, that he is a very young man, but it is at least appropriate to think that he has not passed the period of manly vigor. This accords well with the imagery of the summer voyage as well as with his ardor, and likewise with his rejection (implicit in ll. 39–47, explicit in ll. 64b–102) of the world and its satisfactions. An old man gains little credit by renouncing what he is obliged to leave. The reasoning here is calculated to persuade those who can still make a choice, and the speaker ought to be such a one himself. He must still *earn* the joys of the Lord, however vividly he imagines them in advance.

The poem that has now taken shape is more complex than *The Wanderer* in spite of the close similarity in structure. By its use of two speakers it sets up a comparison between two kinds of seafaring, and so not only shifts the focus from the natural to the supernatural order but transfers the poignant immediacy of the poetry of sense to the

realm of spiritual action. This aspect of the design seems basic enough
to justify such a modified title as *The Two Seafarers*. But the second
seafarer is the principal character and the essential conflict in the
poem is the conflict that Ehrismann imperfectly discerned between two
ideals of conduct. It begins in the first speech as a mere contrast between life on land and life at sea. It is transformed in the second speech
into a conflict between the secular ideal as defined by aristocratic
standards and the religious, not exclusively monastic, ideal of a servant
of God.

When we look at the second seafarer's speech as now established we
see that it means most at several places if we assume that he himself,
like many a man who took up the cross in those days, is a man of noble
birth who can look forward to the successes and rewards of the
comitatus, the *blæd* and *dream* of the *duguþ* with which he contrasts
the heavenly counterparts in lines 79–80. When he says in the sentence
starting at line 39 that no man on earth is so proud, so liberal (or so
talented?), so youthfully keen, so valiant in his deeds, or so graciously
treated by his lord that he will not always have anxiety for his voyage,
as to what the Lord will bring him to, he is indirectly explaining his own
anxiety and, therefore, implying that he himself has some share of the
endowments he describes. The lures of life on land that he mentions in
line 44, the harp and the receiving of rings, are foremost among the joys
of the hall. He says they cannot keep a man from thinking about the
surge of the waves, but later (ll. 80b–90) he encourages himself to for-
sake all such noble satisfactions by reflecting that the world is getting
old and the glories of the heroic past have grown dim. It is relatively easy
to scorn the soft and sheltered prosperity of the *sefteadig secg* of line 56
(according to Grein's emendation, which Mrs. Gordon accepts), but the
aristocratic ideal includes heroic action as well, and this secular heroism
must also be rejected or at least surpassed. That is what the speaker is
trying to accomplish in lines 72–80. As we know from *Beowulf*, the
military argument was very similar to the religious one: Since death is
inevitable, its hazards must be ignored. *Dom ær deaðe* is all a man can
hope to attain. The second seafarer does not deny this argument, but
carries it a step farther in his effort to establish a new and superior
heroism. By fighting against the devil instead of ordinary enemies he can
hope to receive both the secular hero's reward, the praise of his successors on earth, and something much more valuable, because permanent, the praise of the angels.

I have tried to show that, by attending to the slight indications of the
language and the major implications of the content, we can find ample
evidence for repunctuating *The Wanderer* and *The Seafarer* and treating them as consisting, each in its way, of two dramatic speeches and an
epilogue. The proof, as it seems to me, rests largely on the increased

clarity, dramatic consistency, and richness of meaning in the poems when thus read. But I must not leave wholly unanswered the objection that was often made to the old proponents of dialogue in *The Seafarer*. Why is the point of change in *The Wanderer* so weakly marked? Why has the change in *The Seafarer*, though not quite so unobtrusive in it-self, been left so entirely without the aid of stage directions? And why is the epilogue marked by so slight a hint as a group of hypermetric lines and a change of tone? How could any reader of the Exeter Book when it was new have understood the form any better than a reader of today? To this objection I can only say that I think there has indeed been a me-chanical failure in the written presentation of the poems. So many scholars would not have gone wrong for such a long time if there had been due warning of the changes I have mentioned. But this is an easy mistake for a poet or an anthologist to make when he is recording poems in an age that is accustomed to oral delivery. I do not think, as the dual performance of Widsith and his fellow Scilling might suggest, and as Rieger imagined for *The Seafarer*, that there would normally have been two performers: the epilogues of both poems render this doubtful, and the *swa cwæð*'s of *The Wanderer* preclude it. But before an audience a single performer might have indicated the change by shifting his posi-tion or by a change of tone after a pause, and he might also have given warning of what was coming by a revealing title and a few words of explanation before he began. In the Edda we find dialogue poems introduced by explanations in prose, and it seems as if something of the sort might have been general when poems were recited, though rarely included when they were put on parchment. It is as if *The Wanderer* and *The Seafarer* had been recorded in too nakedly poetical a form with only such explanations (namely, the *swa cwæð* lines in *The Wanderer*) as had all too inadequately been incorporated as orthodox verses. In the dialogue of *Solomon and Saturn* the speakers are identified, but by for-mulas that stand outside the verse. In the dialogue of Joseph and Mary in the *Christ* there are no explicit identifications, and we must judge, as in *The Seafarer*, entirely by what the speakers say (that is, until Mary's carefully introduced speech at the end), though I must add that I do not myself believe in the rapid interchange of speeches ascribed to Joseph and Mary in our editions.

The form I have attributed to *The Wanderer* and *The Seafarer* has no exact parallel either in Old English or elsewhere, so far as I know; but the sharply differentiated dramatic speeches I have outlined, in contrast to the loose and often inconsistent monologues we have been accustomed to reading, are of a sort that is by no means unusual in Old English poetry. From *Beowulf* to the Exeter Book *Riddles* there is abundant evidence that Old English poets took delight in inventing speeches for clearly imagined characters. We have wholly dramatic monologues in *The Wife's Lament*, *The Husband's Message*, the passionate little lyric *Wulf and Eadwacer*, and the brilliant *Deor*. All these poems have their obscurities, to be sure, but not in their dramatic aspect. We have a carefully framed dramatic monologue in *Widsith*. And in what is probably the finest of all the dramatically conceived poems, *The Dream of the Rood*, we have a speech within a speech; for the dreamer is as carefully conceived a character as the rood itself. Thus *The Wanderer* and *The Seafarer*, if we can attribute to them the form I have described, take their places even more securely than before as members of a vigorous dramatic tradition.

One may naturally ask whether these two poems are the work of the same poet or merely closely related products of the same poetic circle. The extraordinarily close resemblances in style, structure, and underlying ideas make it hard for me to resist the conclusion that they belong to the same poet, and the differences I have noted, important though they are, need not be considered an obstacle. Still, there is probably room for doubt. What appears certain is that each of these poems is the work of an accomplished and original poet, one who had full command of the traditional poetic idiom in combination with unusual powers of invention,[41] who understood the ancient feelings and attitudes of his people and also the intellectual and spiritual claims of the new age. If there were two such poets, the age was the richer.

NOTES

1. Quotations are from *The Exeter Book*, edd. G. P. Krapp and E. V. K. Dobbie (New York, 1936), pp. 134–37. Once or twice I have altered the punctuation.

2. "Über Cynewulf," *Zeitschrift für deutsche Philologie*, I, 313 ff.; on *The Wanderer*, 324–30.

3. "*The Wanderer*: A Reconsideration of Theme and Structure," *Journal of English and Germanic Philology*, L, 451–65. Greenfield's analysis has recently been elaborated by Willi Erzgräber, "Der Wanderer, Eine Interpretation von Aufbau und Gehalt," *Festschrift zum 75. Geburtstag von Theodor Spira*, edd. H. Viebrock and W. Erzgräber (Heidelberg, 1961), pp. 57–85.

4. *Codex Exoniensis*, ed. B. Thorpe (London, 1842), p. 286; *The Exeter Book*, Part I, ed. I. Gollancz (EETS 104, London, 1895), p. 287. Their punctuation is briefly supported by W. S. Mackie, *Modern Language Notes*, XL (1925), 92.

5. T. C. Rumble, "From *Eardstapa* to *Snottor on Mode*: The Structural Principle of 'The Wanderer'," *Modern Language Quarterly*, XIX (1958), 225–30.

6. For example, Norah Kershaw (Mrs. Chadwick), in *Anglo-Saxon and Norse Poems* (Cambridge, 1922), pp. 8 ff., limits the wanderer's speech to lines 8–29a, after which the first person gives way to the third; but in her introductory remarks on p. 6 she expresses uncertainty. Emily Doris Grubl, in her *Studien zu den angelsächsischen Elegien* (Marburg, 1948), pp. 15 ff., limits the wanderer's speech to lines 8–57, attributing all else to the poet himself until the

conclusion, 112–15, which she attributes to the *snottor on mode*. Her analysis on p. 31, however, disregards speakers and treats the poem as consisting of prologue (ll. 1–5), Part i (ll. 6–57), Part ii (ll. 58–110), and conclusion (ll. 111–15).

7. The list includes Sweet, Gollancz, Bright, Kluge, and (perhaps unintentionally) Krapp and Dobbie. See Huppé's article, cited below in n. 9, pp. 518 f.

8. Fernand Mossé prints the poem with an extra space between lines 57 and 58, and in his notes calls lines 58–115 the "seconde partie de la poème" (*Manuel de l'Anglais du Moyen Âge*, i, *Vieil-Anglais* [Paris, 1945], pp. 290 and 404.) F. P. Magoun, Jr., setting off the introduction and conclusion, divides the middle section into Part i (ll. 8–57) and Part ii (ll. 58–110) of the wanderer's speech (*Anglo-Saxon Poems . . . Normalized* [Second Corrected Printing, Dept. of English, Harvard Univ., 1961], pp. 18–21). Earlier Ernst Sieper had tried to show that lines 58–110, along with the prologue and epilogue, were not part of the original poem. (*Die altenglische Elegie* [Strassburg, 1915], pp. 197 ff.) Grubl (above, n. 6) and Erzgräber (above, n. 3) observe the same division into two parts between lines 57 and 58 but treat these parts (with prologue and epilogue) as members of a carefully unified whole.

9. "*The Wanderer*: Theme and Structure," *Journal of English and Germanic Philology*, XLII (1943), 516–38.

10. This was Mackie's opinion in the article cited above, n. 4. Greenfield (*op. cit., supra*, n. 3, pp. 455 f.) cited two examples in which *swa cwæð* precedes a quotation and held that Mackie's argument was therefore inconclusive. He chose to attribute lines 1–5 to the poet for the sake of what he thought was the most satisfactory structure. His view is supported by Erzgräber (*op. cit., supra*, n. 3, pp. 77 f.), who nevertheless calls attention (p. 75) to the link between *anhaga*, line 1, and *anhogan*, line 40.

11. This meaning of *forþon* was ably discussed by W. W. Lawrence in his influential though now largely superseded article, "*The Wanderer* and *The Seafarer*," *Journal of English and Germanic Philology*, IV (1902), 460–80; on *forþon*, pp. 463 ff. Fundamentally the word asserts that there is some sort of connection between what has been said and what follows. "As for that" is perhaps as close as one can come to the vague meaning paraphrased here by "verily." I find this vague meaning earlier in the poem at line 37 and probably also at line 64, though this last may be "therefore." The meaning is certainly "therefore" at line 17. The same meanings and another, "because" or "for," appear in *The Seafarer*. The case for an adversative sense, first suggested by Rieger for *The Seafarer*, is strongly supported by Marjorie Daunt, "Some Difficulties of *The Seafarer* Reconsidered," *Modern Language Review*, XIII (1918), 474 ff. Some of her examples are persuasive but a clearly adversative sense does not seem to be demanded in either of these poems. See further n. 28 below.

12. A rhetorically similar passage in Blickling Homily x (ed. Morris, p. 109, ll. 26–30), to which G. V. Smithers has called attention (*Medium Ævum*, XXVI, 140), is by contrast one-sidedly clerical in content.

13. Ll. 80–84. J. E. Cross has shown that at least the *sum*-formula of this passage, and possibly the enumeration of different ways by which the body may be destroyed, can be attributed to the influence of patristic writings. ("On *The Wanderer* Lines 80–84: A Study of a Figure and a Theme," *Vetenskaps-Societetens i Lund Årsbok*, 1958–59, pp. 75–110.) Yet whether this influence is admitted or not, I think we must recognize the basic sense of the passage as something rather different from what the fathers were concerned about. Here the distinction between the accusative plural in *Sume wig fornam* and the following instances of the accusative singular *sumne* should be observed. The thinker has just pictured a military host lying dead by a wall. He says, with understatement, that "some," meaning

"many," had been carried off by war, and he now mentions what happened to the corpses: "One a bird carried off over the high sea, one the grey wolf shared with death, one a sad-faced earl hid in an earth-pit." A very similar interpretation is set forth by Erzgräber, *op. cit.*, *supra*, n. 3, p. 69.

14. "On the Genre of *The Wanderer*," *Neophilologus*, XLV (1961), 63–75. The idea was suggested earlier, with apt comparison to Boethius, by R. M. Lumiansky, "The Dramatic Structure of the Old English *Wanderer*," *Neophilologus*, XXXIV (1950), 104–12. Erzgräber (above, n. 3) presses still further the argument for Boethian influence.

15. F. Kluge, "Zu altenglischen Dichtungen, I, Der Seefahrer," *Englische Studien*, VI (1883), 322–27; O. S. Anderson, "The Seafarer: An Interpretation," *K. Humanistiska Vetenskapssamfundets i Lund Årsberättelse*, 1937–38, pp. 1–49.

16. Rieger's brief exposition forms part of the article cited above, n. 2, *Zeitschrift für deutsche Philologie*, I (1869), 330–32. On pp. 334–39 he printed the entire poem as a dialogue according to his theory. The old man speaks ll. 1–33a, 39–47, 53–57, 72–124; the young man, ll. 33b–38, 48–52, 58–71.

17. *Op. cit.*, *supra*, n. 11. Lawrence's opinion has sometimes been misrepresented, as if he had accepted as original all but lines 103–24. On p. 462 he says, "I believe with Kluge that 64b–124 is an addition," and it is to this entire half of the poem (which Kluge had called homiletic) that he must be referring in his conclusion, p. 480: "There seems no reason to assume that the *Wanderer* and the *Seafarer* are not preserved in essentially their original form, with the exception of the homiletic addition to the latter poem." Doubting the originality of such a large part of *The Seafarer* could seem a small matter to Lawrence because his article was aimed chiefly at the fantastically disintegrative theory of R. C. Boer. It is a wholly different and subordinate problem that Lawrence takes up on p. 471, where

he agrees with Thorpe that lines 103–24 may be, not an addition, but the end of another poem. See below, n. 29.

18. "Religionsgeschichtliche Beiträge zum germanischen Frühchristentum, II, Das Gedicht vom Seefahrer," *Beiträge zur Geschichte der deutschen Sprache und Literatur*, XXXV (1909), 213–18.

19. "The Interpretation of *The Seafarer*," in *Early Cultures of North-West Europe*: H. M. Chadwick Memorial Studies (Cambridge, 1950), pp. 261–72.

20. Mrs. Gordon advances another objection in her excellent edition (London, 1960), p. 6. I do not make use of it here because (properly enough for Mrs. Gordon but disconcertingly here) it draws evidence for the speaker's character indiscriminately from A1 and A2.

21. Ll. 33b–35. My quotations are from Mrs. Gordon's text, though I have sometimes altered the punctuation, and for consistency I spell *forþon* as one word.

22. Richard Wülker, *Grundriss zur Geschichte der angelsächsischen Literatur* (Leipzig, 1885), p. 210.

23. *Op. cit.*, *supra*, n. 11, p. 467.

24. *Op. cit.*, *supra*, n. 19, p. 264.

25. Mrs. Gordon weakens *sylf* partly by a shift of emphasis and partly by a different interpretation of the clause in lines 34b and 35: "And so the thoughts trouble my heart now that I myself am to venture on the deep (or towering) seas." Here she gives partial recognition to *sylf* ("I in person" rather than "I also") but argues that the saving distinction is to be found in the emphasis on the *deep* seas, as if the speaker had made only coastal voyages before – a distinction that would be much clearer if only *sylf* were omitted. Her "now that" further weakens the effect. But this interpretation of *nu . . . þæt* is abnormal (the ordinary idom being *nu . . . nu*) and is rendered very improbable by the seeming parallelism of the clause of purpose in the next sentence. (She is probably right, however, though this does not affect the argument, in taking *heortan* as object of *cnyssað*.)

26. *Anglia*, LXXIII (1955–56), 413–66; esp. 454 f.

27. Huppé discusses *ethopoeia* in the article cited above (n. 9), pp. 517 f. He took the term from Margaret Schlauch, "Prosopopoeia in *The Dream of the Rood*," in *Essays and Studies in Honor of Carleton Brown* (New York, 1940), pp. 30 f., who found it mentioned several times in *Rhetores Latini Minores*, ed. C. Halm. See especially the accounts of it by Emporius (Halm, pp. 561 ff.) and Isidore (Halm, p. 514). It applies properly to any imaginary speech so devised as to characterize the speaker, and therefore to almost all speeches in poetry, to which the rhetoricians resort for models. It seems hardly worth reviving, but it may have served as a catalyst for some good ideas of Mr. Stanley's.

28. At line 33b in *The Seafarer* the meaning of *forþon* may be exactly like that at line 58 in *The Wanderer*, an "as for that" which we may render as "verily" or "truly," or it may be "therefore," referring to the seafarer's statement that the landsman cannot believe what he has endured at sea: therefore the second speaker is impelled to make trial for himself. On the whole I prefer the vaguer sense. I also prefer not to take the *forþon*'s at lines 33 and 39, or those at 58 and 64, as correlatives, as Miss Whitelock suggested in the article cited, pp. 264, 266, because the suspension created by the first *forþon* in the pair weakens the force of the sentence it introduces. Elaborate logical structures are usually hostile to poetry. In both instances the first *forþon* (ll. 33 and 58) can be "verily" or "truly," the second (ll. 39 and 64) "for." See above, n. 11.

29. *Codex Exoniensis*, p. 312, n. The idea was mentioned with at least tentative approval by others, e.g., Lawrence, *op. cit., supra* (n. 11); N. Kershaw, *Anglo-Saxon and Norse Poems*, p. 18; Krapp and Dobbie, *The Exeter Book*, p. xxxviii. W. J. Sedgefield omitted these lines from his *Anglo-Saxon Verse-Book*, saying (p. 32), "We have omitted 22 or 23 lines with which the poem ends in the MS., as they are definitely religious rather than moralizing. It is possible that the latter part of this poem and of *The Wanderer* may have been later 'tailpieces' added by some monk for purposes of edification." Sweet, who first included the poem (as a monologue) in the seventh edition of his *Anglo-Saxon Reader* in 1894, accepted lines 103–108 as comparable to the last four lines of *The Wanderer* but relegated the rest to his notes. The problem is reviewed by Mrs. Gordon on p. 11 of her edition.

30. *Op. cit., supra* (n. 14).

31. "The Meaning of *The Seafarer* and *The Wanderer*," *Medium Ævum*, XXVI (1957), 137–53; continued in XXVIII (1959), 1–22; Appendix, 99–104; the discussion of *elþeodigra eard* is in XXVI, 147–51.

32. Earthly and heavenly meanings of *dryhten* in lines 41 and 43; *dream* in 65, 80, and 85; *blæd*, 79 and 88; *duguþ*, 80 and 85. See S. B. Greenfield, "Attitudes and Values in *The Seafarer*," *Studies in Philology*, LI (1954), 15–20; also Mrs. Gordon's edition, pp. 26 f., and her discussion of "life on land," pp. 4 ff. and 42.

33. See the references under these words in Joseph Bosworth–T. N. Toller, *An Anglo-Saxon Dictionary and Supplement* (Oxford, 1898 and 1921). Mr. Smithers' most persuasive Old English illustration, from Blickling Homily II (ed. Morris, p. 23, ll. 1–7) has *eþel*: ". . . we synd on þisse worlde ælþeodige, . . . and nu eft sceolon oþerne eþel secan, swa wite, swa wuldor, swe we nu geearnian willaþ." Cf. also Ælfric, *Catholic Homilies*, ed. Thorpe, I, 162, ll. 16–20: "Nis ðeos woruld na ure eðel, ac is ure wræcsið; forði . . . we . . . sceolon efstan mid godum geearnungum to urum eðele, þær we to gesceapene wæron, þæt is to heofenan rice."

34. *Catholic Homilies*, ed. Thorpe, II, 214, ll. 25–27: "He gehælð his folc fram heora synnum, and gelæt to ðam ecan earde heofenan rices, swa swa se heretoga Iesus gelædde þone ealdan Israhel to ðam earde þe him behaten wæs." The word *eard* is repeated in the same sense at p. 222, lines 11 and 12; but at line 25 heaven is "ðone ecan eðel." I must add that

the interpreters of the Bible did not feel obliged to adopt the same allegory for every mention of foreign travel. Thus Ælfric, expounding the parable of the talents (Matt. 24:14 ff.), translates "Homo quidam peregre proficiscens" as "sum rice man wolde faran on ælðeodigne eard" or, a little later, "on ælðeodignysse," and then cites Gregory for the interpretation: "Hwæt is se man þe ferde on ælðeodignysse buton ure Drihten, seðe, mid þam lichaman ðe he on eorðan underfeng, ferde to heofenum? Witodlice flæsces wunung is eorðe, and Cristes lichama wæs gelæd swilce to ælðeodignysse ða ða he wæs ahafen to ðære heofenlican wununge, þær ðær næfre ær nan lichama ne becom." (Thorpe, II, 548, 550. Max Förster, *Anglia*, XVI, 3, identifies Gregory's homily as the ninth of the series on the Gospel.) By this line of reasoning we could take *elþeodigra eard* as heaven because it is the land of spirits, who are strangers to the flesh; but certainly the interpretation offered by Mr. Smithers rests on a much more basic and widely diffused concept of the Christian's status on earth.

35. Smithers, *Medium Ævum*, XXVIII, 7; Cross, "On the Allegory in *The Seafarer*—Illustrative Notes," same volume, pp. 104–106.

36. *Catholic Homilies*, ed. Thorpe, I, 614.

37. In his second article, *Medium Ævum*, XXVIII, 14 ff., Mr. Smithers cites evidence to show that behind this vivid passage is the widespread superstition that a man can send his soul out of his body and that it may appear to others in the form of an animal, often a bird. The same point has been made independently by Vivian Salmon, "*The Wanderer* and *The Seafarer*, and the Old English Conception of the Soul," *Modern Language Review*, LV (1960), 1–10. These illustrations seem decidedly pertinent, though there is no need to insist on taking the superstition literally here: it gives imaginative form to a universal psychological experience. Miss Salmon, however, has made it appear likely that related superstitions are responsible for

some of the expressions in *The Wanderer*, ll. 52–55, notably the otherwise puzzlingly redundant combination, *secga geseldan*.

38. E. G. Stanley has renewed the plea for *wælweg* in his review of Mrs. Gordon's edition, *Medium Ævum*, XXXI (1962), 54–60. He proposes (p. 58) a double meaning, both *wælweg* 'oceanway,' first adopted by Grein, and Mr. Smithers' *wælweg*. The meaning "oceanway" would certainly be acceptable if the alliance of *wǣl* and *weg* could be shown to be probable (as I think it cannot), but the demands of alliteration would not be served, for crossed alliteration on *h* and *w* does not seem at all probable with this particular grammatical pattern. Mr. Stanley urges that a scribe would not be likely to change an easily understood compound such as *hwælweg* to anything so difficult as *wælweg*; but a scribe might very well drop an *h* without intending to change a meaning. The scribe of the Exeter Book has omitted initial *h* before a consonant at *Christ* 783 (*leotan* corrected to *hleotan*); *Azarias* 22 (*to worfne* corrected to *tohworfne*); *Phoenix* 126 (*remig*), 137 (*-leoþres*), 197 (*gewæs* corrected to *gehwæs*); *Juliana* 577 (*bi lænan*); *Widsith* 14 (*wala*); *Riddle* 15, 4 (*leorum*); 33, 3 (*leahtor*); 54, 5 (*rand*). Before vowels he has added it wrongly or omitted it on numerous occasions: e.g., *Christ* 615 (*is* for *his*), 885 (*healle* for *ealle*), 1412 (*ingonge* for *hingonge*); *Guthlac* 271 (*hus* for *us*), 950 (*hælmihtiga*), 1215 (*onhæfen* for *on æfen*); *Azarias* 61 (*hofne* corrected to *ofne*); *Phoenix* 477 (*eortan* for *heortan*), 650 (*elpe* for *helpe*); etc. My attention was called to this phenomenon by Miss Whitelock, to whom I am indebted for some very helpful criticism both at this point and elsewhere. I must add that Mr. Stanley says nothing in this review of his earlier interpretation of *The Seafarer* and seems inclined to favor that of Mr. Smithers.

39. *Medium Ævum*, XXVIII, 20–22. Mrs. Gordon's desire to identify the *ānfloga* with the cuckoo (*geac*) of line 53 (edition, p. 9) seems ill advised as soon as we are willing to

grant that the soul itself resembles a bird in flight. The epithets of line 62a, *gifre ond grædig*, accord with the verb *gielleð* of 62b and should refer to the same creature. There is no need to identify the *hyge* with any particular bird, but these words would suit a bird of prey (*ful oft þæt earn begeal*, 24; [ic] *gielle swa hafoc, Riddle* 24, 3) at least as well as a sea gull, a bird that Mrs. Gordon understandably thinks inappropriate. Perhaps in the whole context the eagle supplies the greatest number of relevant characteristics, since he not only flies alone, screams, and has a voracious appetite, but is noted for his powerful flight and his sharp eyes. As a type of St. John the Evangelist he can look at the divine radiance by which others are blinded. But of course the speaker would hardly wish to claim for his soul more than a distant resemblance to so exalted a symbol.

40. Mrs. Gordon's edition, p. 10.

41. The traditional attitudes and expressions are naturally most abundant in the speeches of the two traditional characters, the wanderer and the veteran seafarer. That is probably the main reason for what J. J. Campbell has noted in his study of the distribution of verse formulas and poetic diction in *The Seafarer*: "Oral Poetry in *The Seafarer*," *Speculum*, XXXV (1960), 87–96. That there is a distinction between oral and written composition in different parts of the poem is unlikely on general grounds and is rendered still more unlikely by W. A. O'Neil, "Another Look at Oral Poetry in *The Seafarer*," *Speculum*, XXXV, 596–600.

Old English Riddle No. 20:
Heoruswealwe

LAURENCE K. SHOOK

Pontifical Institute of
Mediaeval Studies, Toronto

Ic eom wunderlicu wiht   on gewin sceapen,
fréan mínum léof,   fǽgre gegyrwed.
Byrne is mín bléofág,   swylce beorht seomað
wír ymb þone wælgim   þe me waldend geaf,
se me wídgalum   wísað hwílum   5
sylfum to sace.   Þonne ic sinc wege
þurh hlútterne dæg,   hondweorc smiþa,
gold ofer geardas.   Oft ic gǽstberend
cwelle compwǽpnum.   Cyning mec gyrweð
since ond seolfre   ond mec on sele weorþað;   10
ne wyrneð wordlofes,   wísan mǽneð
míne for mengo   þǽr hý meodu drincað.
Healdeð mec on heaþore;   hwílum lǽteð eft
rádwérigne   on gerúm sceacan,
orlegfromne.   Oft ic óþrum scód,   15
frécne æt his fréonde.   Fáh eom ic wíde
wǽpnum awyrged.   Ic me wénan ne þearf
þæt me bearn wræce   on bonan feore,
gif me gromra hwylc   gúþe genǽgeð;
ne weorþeð sio mǽgburg   gemicledu   20
eaforan mínum   þe is æfter wóc,
nymþe ic hláfordléas   hweorfan móte
from þám healdende   þe me hringas geaf.
Me bið forð witod,   gif ic fréan hýre,
gúþe fremme,   swá ic gíen dyde   25
mínum þéodne on þonc,   þæt ic þolian sceal
bearn gestréona.   Ic wiþ brýde ne mót
hǽmed habban,   ac me þæs hyht plegan

géno wyrneð,   se mec géara on
bende legde;   forþon ic brúcan sceal   30
on hagostealde   hæleþa gestréona.
Oft ic wírum dol   wífe abelge;
wonie hyre willan.   Héo me wóm spreceð,
flóceð hyre folmum,   firenaþ mec wordum,
ungód gæleð.   Ic ne gýme þæs compes.   35

Riddle 20[1] of the Exeter Book, here newly edited, was first solved as "sword" by Dietrich in 1859,[2] a solution which has since been accepted by all editors except Trautmann, who prefers "hawk"[3] or "hunting falcon."[4] The rejection of Trautmann's solution has been general since Swaen's impressive and learned demonstration that "falcon" or "hawk" (a distinction which he rightly feels irrelevant for the solution of the riddle) is untenable.[5] It might be well to review the Tupper-Trautmann-Swaen exchanges before making a new and, I am confident, correct defense of Trautmann's "hawk," though under a title *heoruswealwe,* which I take to be the precise word which the riddler would expect the interpreter to pronounce.[6]

Tupper presents the case for "sword" very convincingly.[7] He feels that the solution "sword" satisfies all the motives of the riddle, which he lists adequately as follows: the adornments of the warrior, dependence upon a lord, the grim work of death on the battlefield, lack of an avenger, celibacy, hatefulness to women. Moreover, he regards the phrases *wír ymb þone wælgim* 'wire about the gem of death,' l. 4, *hondweorc smiþa* 'handiwork of smiths,' l. 7, and *on gewin sceapen* 'made for battle,' l. 1, to argue powerfully for his solution; *wír, hondweorc smiþa,* and *on gewin sceapen,* he feels, should be regarded as belonging to the recorded terminology of Anglo-Saxon weapon manufacture. He admits that OE Riddle 20 has little in common with traditional sword-riddles,[8] but accepts its originality as typical of many of the Exeter Book riddles. He finds it, as indeed it is, a delightful manipulation of heroic materials, and some of these are clearly related to literary treatment of metal ornamentation which, of course, includes the ornamenting of swords. He has one piece of linguistic evidence on which he relies heavily: OE *awyrged* in the obscure phrase *wǽpnum awyrged* (l. 17) also turns up in the metrical version of the psalter, where it is applied to a sword.[9] Tupper has few comments to offer on lines 17b–35, the second half of the poem, which present the themes he describes as "lack of an avenger," "celibacy," and "hatefulness to women." His position here is a shaky one: he does not ask, for example, why the sword's complaint about having no offspring to avenge his violent death should be qualified with the statement "unless I can stray off, a lordless one, from the master who gave me rings" (*nymþe ic hláfordléas hweorfan móte/*

from þám healdende þe me hringas geaf, ll. 22–23); nor is he disturbed
by the final bathos of an angry woman screaming an insult (*ungód
gæleð*, l. 35) at the heroic weapon, but merely notes that "this is the only
picture of the shrew or scold in Old English poetry."[10]

Trautmann, on the other hand, in his edition of 1915, makes an
impassioned and somewhat bitter plea for his solution, *Der Jagdfalke*,
with a disconcerting blend of good arguments, absurdities, and reckless
textual emendations. His interpretation of the colored coat of mail
(*byrne is mín bléofág*, l. 3) as the falcon's feathers, which really do
gleam like a ringed corslet, and of the welcome slipping of the "travel-
weary" (*rádwérigne*, l. 14) bird from the falconer's fist, and of the
enforced celibacy of the captive hawk,[11] is eminently convincing, but
stands in sharp contrast with his overly ingenious invention of a hood
(his *wirn*, l. 4), of "a murderous eye" (*wælgim*, l. 4), and of miniature
hawks' clothes (*sinc*, l. 6), like those in the children's rhyme "Ich zoch
mir einen valke." Trautmann's case, as presented, is too dependent
upon emendations, too impatient of the force of some of Tupper's arguments for the sword, and too neglectful of the last eighteen lines of the
riddle, which in fact strongly support his solution.

Swaen attempts to dispose of Trautmann's solution by dealing with
the riddle from the point of view of one conversant with the history of
falconry.[12] He properly points out that Trautmann's emendation of *wir*
'wire ornamentation' to *wirn* 'hood' or 'impediment' introduces an
anachronism, since the use of the hood did not reach Europe until the
thirteenth century. He also finds Trautmann's remarks on the adorning
and training of hawks, and especially his suggestion that they were
decked out in clothes, imaginative but uniformed. Swaen admits, however, that most of the poem's thirty-five lines are open to either solution,
hawk or sword, and that lines 9b–15a and 17b–31, which deal with the
king's personal attitude toward the unknown subject of the riddle, and
introduce the notion of its enforced celibacy, suit the hawk or falcon
rather better than the sword. He points to special difficulties in five passages (3b–4b *wir*, 6b–8a *sinc* as expanding *wælgim*, 8b–9a *gǽstberend*, 15b–16a *óþrum scód/frécne æt his freonde*, 32–35 *wífe abelge*,
and so on) which seem to him to be satisfactorily dealt with by Tupper
in the context of the solution "sword." Swaen's knowledgeable approach
to the general subject has left recent editors convinced that "hawk"
is hardly tenable.[13] Without for the present dealing with these five
problematical passages in detail,[14] let me anticipate emphatically that
Swaen's arguments are in no instance decisive, and that although they
dispose of some of Trautmann's absurdities, present no new or positive
evidence for "sword" as understood by Dietrich, Tupper, and others.

The correct solution to this riddle, it appears to me and as Trautmann
claims, is "hawk," but hawk as identified by the recorded OE kenning

heoruswealwe 'sword-swallow.' This solution has the advantage of giving real significance to all clues, whether they refer to the sword or the hawk, and of leaving no intelligible phrase in the poem unaccounted for.

The *heoru-* of the kenning *heoruswealwe* is not undescriptive of the sword-like action of a swooping hawk and conveys, moreover, as a "horrific intensive," something of the terror attaching to a bird of prey. The word appears in the gnomic verses of the Exeter Book in the fowler passage of the poem, now usually called *The Fortunes of Men* (ll. 85–92).[15] These lines have been cited as a sort of *locus classicus* on the training of hawks in Anglo-Saxon England.[16] No one seems to have noticed the particular significance of the figure *heoruswealwe* for Riddle 20. Since there are other possible connections between the two poems, the text on the fowler is worth examining in some detail:

> Sum sceal wildne fugel   wloncne átemian
> heafoc on honda,   oþþæt seo heoroswealwe
> wynsum weorþeð;   déþ he wyrplas on,
> fédeþ swá on feterum   fiþrum dealne,
> lepeþ lyftswiftne   lytlum gieflum,
> oþþæt se wælisca   wǽdum ond dǽdum
> his ǽtgiefan   éaðmód weorþeð
> ond to hagostealdes   honda gelǽred.

The following translation explains my reading of this text: One shall tame the proud wild bird, the hawk on the hand, until the sword-swallow becomes gentle; he puts jesses on it, and so raises in captivity one proud in its wings, feeds the swift-in-flight one with little morsels of food until the slaughtering-one, in what he wears and does, becomes submissive to his feeder and docile on the hand of a boy.

These reflections on the trainer and his hawk record a number of associations which, by art or hap, turn up also in our riddle.

1]   Most significant, it seems to me, is the use in both poems (*Fortunes*, l. 92; Riddle 20, l. 31) of the word *hagusteald* 'young nobleman,' 'boy,' 'unmarried person.' Now the idea that hawking has a particular appeal for boys was certainly a familiar one to Anglo-Saxons of the late OE period. In Ælfric's *Colloquy*, for example, the magister elicits from the boy whom he is interrogating considerable information on this subject. Even more enlightening is the circumstance that the earliest known western European treatise on hawking, the *De Cura Accipitrum* of Adelhard of Bath, is a dialogue with his nephew on hawks. Adelhard chooses the subjects as relaxation from the heavier and more serious matters of the *Quaestiones naturales* which he was taking up with the young man.[17] It is quite in line with this attitude that the gnomic pas-

sage speaks of the trained hawk as "docile on the hand of a boy" (*to hagostealdes honda geláered*). It is precisely this association which I would see behind the lines in the riddle where the hawk, in complaining about not being able to breed, says that it has to use its generative powers *on hagostealde* 'like a boy,' in celibacy:[18]

Ic wiþ brýde ne mót

hǽmed habban . . . .

. . . . forþon ic brúcan sceal

on hagostealde   hæleþa gestréona [ll. 27b–31].

2]   The hawk is described in both poems as wearing something (*Fortunes*, l. 190, *wǽdum . . . éaðmód weorþeð*; Riddle 20, l. 3, *byrne is mín bléofág*, and l. 6, *ic sinc wege*, and *passim*). The author of the gnomic lines seems to have in mind the gear which a good falconer must fit on his bird in the course of training.[19] We cannot be certain what this consisted of during the tenth and eleventh centuries, but we know that the Emperor Frederick in the thirteenth century lists jesses, leash, swivel, bell, "and everything else necessary for the falcon's equipment and care."[20] The riddler seems to have in mind the bird's plumage in line 3 and its ornate gear in lines 3–4, 6–8, 9–10. Both poems show an awareness that a hawk, like a ship or a warrior, must be handsomely equipped.

3]   In the gnomic passage the hawk is specifically said to be equipped with *wyrplas* 'jesses' (l. 87), that is, with straps running from its leg to the ring which slides over the fist of the carrier, and to be a captive (*on feterum*, l. 88). It is held in restraint (*on heaðore*, l. 13), laid in bonds (*bende*, l. 30) in the riddle.

4]   The use of *wæl*- is to be noted in important, if obscure, passages in both poems: *wǽlisca* (*Fortunes*, l. 90) must mean "slaughtering one" rather than "slave," judging from the structural parallel which seems to pattern the passage *seo heoruswealwe wynsum weorþeð—se wǽlisca . . . éaðmód weorþeð*; *wǽlgim* (Riddle 20, l. 4) means "slaughtering gem," referring probably to the hawk's talon.

Collectively, these four parallels, along with the important sword motif, reveal similarities of language which suggest that they have a common subject matter, specifically identified in the one case as *heoruswealwe*, and highly appropriate when supplied as the solution of the riddle in the other.

Riddle 20 of the Exeter Book invites the reader to identify a *wunderlicu wiht*, for which two sets of clues are provided: weapon clues (ll. 1–17a) and celibacy clues (ll. 17b–35); these clues divide the poem into two clearly distinguishable parts. Some would see a third division of the poem, lines 32–35, devoted to the theme of hostility between the *wiht* and womankind, basing their position on what seems to be a doubtful interpretation of the last four lines. The weapon clues, which constitute the first division of the poem, describe characteristics of the *wiht* which point primarily to a sword but which, on reflection, a hawk can be seen to share: it is shaped for fighting, it is decked out in gold and silver ornaments, it kills living creatures, the king is fond of it and praises its excellent qualities before his friends in the mead hall, it is kept in restraint or confinement (in a scabbard if a sword, attached to the fist ring if a hawk). Only twice, (ll. 5–6 and l. 14), do there appear clues which, at least as I read them, suit the hawk rather than the sword: the *wiht* is trained by its master (*waldend* 'falconer') in such a way that it can be sent into battle by itself (*me . . . sylfum to sace*), and the king sometimes permits it to fly at large (*on gerum sceacan*), especially when it is weary of riding on the fist (*rádwérigne*). In the case of one clue, *oft ic óþrum scód, frécne æt his freonde* (ll. 15b–16a), there seems to be a personal reference: some friend of the king, possibly the poet himself, perhaps even several of the king's friends, have been injured by this particular *wiht* which seems to be no respecter of persons. The final clue in this part of the riddle has never been satisfactorily read and may be unreadable: I render *fáh eom ic wíde, wǽpnum awyrged* (ll. 16b–17a) as "I am hostile over a wide area, outlawed by weapons." What the words mean is that the *wiht* does not battle within a narrow compass but over an extended area and is not strictly speaking a weapon at all.[21]

The second part of the riddle, lines 17b–35, is devoted to a series of clues based on sexual and marital relations which the *wiht* perforce forgoes: (1) I am childless and go unavenged if slain; (2) I have no family unless I leave my master; (3) I do not breed with a mate because my master will not let me; (4) I am a boy in what concerns the begetting of heroes; (5) near a formel on my perch, I bate and scream but fight rather than breed. This series of five clues on the celibacy of the *wiht* is fittingly rounded off with the simple statement that the *wiht* has nothing to do with this kind of battle – and the *compes* of line 35 establishes an artistic return to the *gewin* of line 1, the kind of battle for which it has actually been trained.

The final clue in the second series, the fifth in the above list, which I take as continuing the celibacy motive, has in the past been understood very differently. Tupper and Trautmann both suppose that we have here to deal with a new theme: enmity between women and the subject of the riddle. Tupper would have it that Anglo-Saxon women must have been unsympathetic toward war and all its symbols, and he thinks that the poet here depicts a scene in which some aggrieved woman hurls insults at a sword which has attracted her notice. Trautmann with no less ingenuity suggests that women as well as men tried their hand at falconry in Anglo-Saxon England, sometimes, as here, unsuccessfully. These suggestions are without relevance to the first thirty-one lines of the riddle.

This closing passage, however, is best interpreted as continuing the theme of celibacy. Hawks and falcons, when not being carried on the fist, were attached to their perch. Their behavior both on perch and fist was often marked by bating, that is, an intermittent beating of the wings as though trying to fly off. When more than one hawk was placed on the same perch, they were always fastened far enough apart so that they could not injure their wings when they bated.[22] The birds were not mated or bred. These last few lines seem to describe the unfriendly and unnatural attitudes existing between tercels and formels in captivity. The tercel is, the poet has him say, *wírum dol* 'foolishly preoccupied with his ornaments,' a statement which rationalizes his abnormal sexual behavior.[23] He has as a consequence little or no desire for relations with the formel: *ic wonie hyre willan* 'I count as little the enjoyment of her.' He displays a certain hostility toward her, *wífe abelge*, a hostility which she returns in good measure:

> Oft ic wírum dol   wífe abelge;
> wonie hyre willan.   Héo me wóm spreceð,
> flóceð hyre folmum,   firenaþ mec wordum,
> ungód gæleð.   Ic ne gýme þæs compes.

Meanwhile, vainly preoccupied with my ornaments, I am hostile towards a formel, count as little the enjoyment of her. She taunts me, beats her wings, reviles me in words, screams an insult. I don't pay any attention to this battle.

The following translation of Riddle 20 incorporates the suggestions offered throughout this study.

Heoruswealwe

(SWORD-SWALLOW or HAWK)

I am a wonderful creature   shaped for conflict,
dear to my lord,   decked out handsomely.
My corslet is many-colored,   bright too lies
wire around the slaughter-gem   which the falconer gave me,
he who betimes trains me,   a far-wandering one,   5
for battle on my own.   Then I carry treasure,
the handiwork of smiths,   through the bright day,
gold over the dwellings.   Oft I kill living creatures
with my battle weapons.   The king adorns me

with treasure and silver   and honors me in the hall;   10
he does not withhold words of praise;   makes known my virtues
before all   who drink mead there.
He holds me in restraint;   at times he allows [me],
weary of riding [his fist],   again to fly about at large,
skilful in battle.   Oft I have injured others,   15
[been] dangerous to a friend of his.   I am hostile over a wide area,
outlawed by weapons.   I need not expect
that a child will avenge   the life of my slayer
if some hostile one   strikes me down in battle;
nor will the family   be increased   20
by offspring of mine   to whom I have given life,
unless I can stray off,   a lordless one,
from the master   who gave me rings.
It is decreed for me,   if I remain under my lord,
do battle [for him],   as I have hitherto done,   25
pleasing to my prince,   that I shall forego
the begetting of children.   I am not to have
relations with a mate,   because he still denies me
that pleasure,   he who long ago
laid fetters on me;   thus must I use   30
like an unwed boy   [my] power to beget heroes.
Meanwhile, proud of my ornaments,   I am hostile towards a formel,
count as little the enjoyment of her.   She taunts me,
beats her wings,   reviles me in words,
screams an insult.   I don't pay any attention to this battle.   35

NOTES TO THE OE TEXT

l. 1. *on gewin sceapen* 'shaped for conflict,' from the heroic language of weapon manufacture; cp. below, l. 35, *þæs compes*, and note that the *wiht* of 1a is very differently prepared for the two conflicts.

l. 3. *Byrne is mín bléofág*, for full sense render "my plumage is like a many-colored corslet." See, on the many-colored plumage of birds of prey, Frederick II's *De Arte*, II, xx; *Art of Falconry*, ed. Wood and Fyfe, p. 121, etc.

l. 3. *seomað* for MS. *seo mad*, adopted by all editors since Grein.

l. 4. *wir ymb þone wælgim* 'wire [i.e., ornamentation] about the slaughtering-gem [i.e., talon]': (1) *wir* is another term from the language of weapon and metal manufacture; it regularly implies ornamentation; cp. l. 32 below and Riddle 26, l. 14, Riddle 14, l. 3, Riddle 17, l. 2. Trautmann's emendation, *wirn* 'hood' is anachronistic and unacceptable; (2) *-gim* is best taken as "talon"; however, in *Phoenix*, l. 300, the beak of the phoenix is said to gleam like a gem, and the possibility of *gim* referring here to the beak of a hawk is attractive, especially if it implies, compounded with *wæl-*, that the beak is dangerous, for example, to the eye of the falconer or others; if so, this may explain ll. 15b–16a.

ll. 5–6. *wísað hwílum sylfum to sace* 'trains me betimes for battle on my own,' retains the true meaning of *wísian*, construes *hwílum* with *wísað*, and makes *sylfum* taken along with l. 14b the major clue of the riddle.

l. 6. construe *sylfum* 'on my own' with *me wídgalum*, not with *se* as Trautmann does.

l. 6. *sace* is less desirable metrically than *sæcce* would be.

l. 8. *ofer* is significant in a hawk solution.

l. 8. *gǽstberend* is best taken as an accusative plural and applies with equal validity to the victims of both sword and hawk; since it can also be construed grammatically with *ic* it creates a kind of triple ambiguity dear to riddlers.

ll. 13–14. *hwílum lǽted eft/rádwérigne on gerúm sceacan* 'at times he allows [me] again, weary of riding [his fist], to fly about at large.' The word *eft* is given real significance in this translation, suggesting that the slipped hawk is returning to a former freedom. Cp. ll. 5–6: the falconer has trained the bird for flight on its own, and now the king too permits it to fly free. The two passages, which together constitute the most inportant clue in the riddle, are curiously connected by the use of *hwílum* in each. The motive also recurs in the second division of the riddle, ll. 22–23.

ll. 15b–16a. This teasing passage can only, in the context of the solution "hawk," mean something like this: "Oft I have injured other beings, as I said above [ll. 8b–9a], but I have even injured a friend of my king's." Such a rendering turns this passage into a personal reference, always a dubious procedure. I have, however, some supporting evidence for tentatively introducing this motive here; I hope in another article on the Exeter Book riddles to demonstrate that several of these poems appear to deal with an injury inflicted on a court poet by a bird of prey.

ll. 16b–17a. No editor has been satisfied with *fáh eom ic wíde/wǽpnum awyrged*. The note supplied by Krapp and Dobbie, p. 332, calls attention to the following guesses: a line is missing between ll. 16 and 17 (Holthausen, *Eng. Stud.*, LI [1917], 185); Psalm 143:10 calls a sword "malicious," OE *awyrged*, so a sword could very well be meant here (Tupper, p. 113); an emendation, e.g., *wordum awyrged* or simply *awyrded*, cp. Grein, is necessary (Trautmann, p. 82, and *Anglia*, XLII [1918], 130). The following translation is as satisfactory as any: "I am hostile over a large area, by weapons I am outlawed"; i.e., I am not eligible to be regarded as a weapon because I cover such a wide area in my attack.

ll. 17b–31. The lines are admitted by all to be entirely devoted to the theme of celibacy; they are in every detail applicable to the hawk. Swaen writes as follows: "17b–31 zouden, indien de voortreffelijk in het kader passen: de gevangen valk die in 'celibaut' moet leven, beklaagt zijn lot, maar troost zich met de gedachte dat hij *brúcan sceal hæleþa gestréona*" (p. 262). Somewhat lamely, he proceeds to reject this position on the strength of Trautmann's bad guesses and by granting that, after all, the same kind of thing can be said of a sword.

ll. 22–23. This statement reintroduces the important clue used in ll. 5–6 and 13–14, thus constituting an important link between the two divisions of the poem. See above, note to ll. 13–14.

l. 29. *géara* for MS. *gearo*, all recent editors.

ll. 30b–31. *forþan ic brúcan sceal/on hagostealde hæleþa gestréona* is rendered by all "therefore I have to use in celibacy the treasures of heroes." This is satisfactory in that it points back to the various treasures (*e.g.*, the *sinc* of l. 6) mentioned in the first section of the poem. The sentence, however, may carry another meaning which seems to me to render more accurately *on hagostealde*, which may well not mean precisely "in celibacy" but "after the manner of an unmarried person." If so, the whole passage means: "therefore I have to enjoy the begetting of heroes like a boy," i.e., not at all. For *hæleþa gestréona* 'the begetting of heroes,' cp. above, l. 27, *bearn gestréona* 'the begetting of children.'

l. 34. *flóceð hyre folmum*. All captive hawks bate from time to time. See Frederick II, *De Arte*, II, lvi; *The Art of Falconry*, ed. Wood and Fyfe, pp. 175 ff.

l. 35. *ungód gæleð* 'scream an insult' from OE *galan*. It is interesting to note that OE *giellan* is also used for the cry of a hawk: *gielle swá hafoc* (Riddle 24, l. 3).

NOTES

1. The numbering is that found in G. P. Krapp and E. V. K. Dobbie, edd., *The Exeter Book* (New York, 1936), pp. 20–21. In Trautmann and Swaen it is Riddle 18, in Tupper, Riddle 21.
2. Franz Dietrich, "Die Rätzel des Exeterbuchs," *ZfdA*, XI (1859), 465.
3. Moritz Trautmann, "Die Auflösungen der altenglischen Rätzel," *Anglia Beiblatt*, V (1894), 49.
4. Moritz Trautmann, *Die Altenglischen Rätzel* (Heidelberg, 1915), p. 81.
5. A. E. H. Swaen, "Het 18ᵉ Oudengelsche Raadsel," *Neophilologus*, IV (1919), 258–62.
6. OE riddles are not properly solved by a modern equivalent but only by a precise Old English or, occasionally, Latin word.
7. Frederick Tupper, *The Riddles of the Exeter Book* (Boston, 1910), pp. 110–13.
8. *Ibid.*, pp. 110–11.
9. See *The Paris Psalter*, Psalm 143:11: *of þam awyrgedan wraðan sweorde*. G. P. Krapp, ed., *The Paris Psalter and the Meters of Boethius* (New York, 1932), p. 142.
10. Tupper, p. 113.
11. The early treatises do not speak of falcons bred in captivity. All hunting falcons dealt with by the Emperor Frederick II of Hohenstaufen in his *De Arte venandi cum avibus* are either eyeases (taken as nestlings) or branchers (taken shortly after leaving the nest). See C. A. Wood and F. M. Fyfe, edd., *The Art of Falconry of Frederick II* (Boston, 1943), and cp. Juliana Barnes (or

Berners), *The Boke of Saint Albans*, ed. William Blades (London, 1901).
12. Dr. Swaen is an authority on falconry as cultivated in Holland since 1771; he is also editor of Adelhard's *De Cura Accipitrum*. See *The Art of Falconry*, edd. Wood and Fyfe, p. 560.
13. Krapp and Dobbie, p. 332.
14. See "Notes to the OE Text."
15. Krapp and Dobbie, p. 156.
16. Johannes Hoops, *Reallexikon der germanischen Altertumskunde* (Strassburg, 1913–15), II, 5–9, s. v. "Faukenbeize."
17. This treatise provides us with the interesting information that Harold, last of the Anglo-Saxon kings, was the possessor of a number of books, including writings on the subject of hawks. Harold, incidentally, is depicted on the Bayeux Tapestry with a hawk on his fist. See C. S. Haskins, *Studies in the History of Mediaeval Science* (Cambridge, Mass., 1924). For Adelhard's text see *De Cura Accipitrum*, ed. A. E. H. Swaen (Gronigen, 1937).
18. See "Notes on the OE Text," ll. 30b–31.
19. It is quite proper to speak of falconry as having its own language. This is especially true of the noble and gentle art as seen in later texts like the *De Arte* or *The Boke of Saint Albans*. Many of Juliana's headings in the latter work indicate her constant preoccupation with proper terminology, e.g., "And we shall say that hawkys doon draw when they bere tymbering to their nestes and

nott they beld ne make ther nestes. And in the time of their love they call and not kauke. And we shall say that they trede." *The Boke of Saint Albans*, ed. William Blades, p. aii.

20. *De Arte*, II, cxxxviii; *The Art of Falconry*, edd. Wood and Fyfe, p. 138.

21. See "Notes to the OE Text" for further discussion.

22. Frederick II, *De Arte*, II, lvi ff.; *The Art of Falconry*, edd. Wood and Fyfe, pp. 175 ff.

23. Lest one think that this statement reflects a strictly contemporary preoccupation with analysis, let me point out that although the Emperor Frederick has nothing to say about the vanity of trained birds of prey, he does insist that their training reduces their normal instincts by overdeveloping tolerance of the senses of taste, hearing, and touch with corresponding distortion and imbalance of the sense of vision (*De Arte*, II, liii; *The Art of Falconry*, pp. 170–71). This would disturb normal sexual behavior, which is related to all the senses.

Problems in the Dating of *Deor* and its Allusions

FREDERICK NORMAN

King's College, London

THERE ARE many puzzling problems that remain to be solved and unfortunately are unlikely ever to be solved in the difficult, perplexing,
and beautiful poem we call *Deor*. Form, style, possible antecedents,
relevance, and even meaning of the heroic references: all these have
tempted students again and again. My old friend Frank Magoun has
argued a possible stylistic and formal connection with an elegiac Edda
poem[1] tersely and imaginatively. In my re-examination of some aspects
of *Deor* I am not concerned with the interesting and thought-provoking
parallels to which he has pointed, as my main business is the various
arguments that may help us toward a less indefinite date; I hope he will
allow me to present to him some further reflections, inevitably dry, on
this ever fresh and ever lovely poem.

It is naturally important that we should be able to date a literary
product and the closer we can get to the original date of composition the
better, not only from the point of view of the text itself but also in view
of all other related texts. We can judge neither the literary antecedents
of a work nor its successors unless we can evolve a reasonably fool-proof
relative dating scheme. This can be a difficult process where there exists
a great deal of literature; where we have, owing to actual paucity or to
regrettable loss, few literary remains, the problem becomes well-nigh
insoluble.

We have to be content with such relative dating in most cases in
the early medieval field. Absolute dating usually depends on outside
evidence. Where we know the name of an author, and have independent
evidence of the time at which he lived, we are in the fortunate position
that we can fix, more or less, dates for his work. We can then attempt to
build other work round it, though this is a dangerous and conjectural
proceeding. Where the poem refers to a datable event or even celebrates
such an event as in the poem on the battle at Brunanburh (937), we can

get very close to a definite date, which clearly cannot be too long after
the event which is commemorated. Similarly, the poem on the battle at
Maldon (991) cannot have been produced very much later than the
actual battle. In the case of the Old High German *Ludwigslied*, we are
even more fortunate. The poem celebrates the victory of Louis III over
Scandinavian raiders at Saucourt on 3 August 881. There is no doubt
that Louis is alive when the poem is produced; it would be most natural
to assume that it was recited before him. As the king died on 8 August
882, we are presented with a very narrow limit for the time of
composition.

The bulk of Old English poetry is anonymous, and the bulk of it is
contained in late manuscripts. Some of the poetry, even substantially
in the form in which we have it, is well over 300 years earlier than the
written evidence. Where such poetry refers to characters whom we cannot prove to have been historical the traditions are lost in the mist of
time: even where we are dealing with personalities known to have
existed we are sometimes taken back hundreds of years beyond the
putative date of first poetic composition. Thus Ermanaric the Ostrogoth
died c. 370–375; the earliest reference to him in Old English verse
should be in what has been conjectured to be the oldest part of *Widsith*,
where he occurs together with Attila, who was born some time after the
death of Ermanaric.[2] We do not know the age of this line; it could have
been composed well before 700. The manuscript, however, which preserves *Widsith* and also *Deor*, where there are further references to
Ermanaric, is assumed to have been written between 970 and 990.

As we go back in time our appreciation of the time scale fore-
shortens. We have no great difficulty in assigning a work either to 700,
800, or 900. It is very difficult for us to imagine that the gap between
800 and 900 can be just as important as the gap between 1850 and 1950.
If we are dealing with a line of poetry first written down, as far as we
were able to trace, in 1950, that for various reasons we thought might
have been first composed in 1650, and if, furthermore, that line contained a reference to somebody who we knew had died some time
before the middle of the fourteenth century, we should be getting near
to the real time scale which distance tends to obliterate.

Where we are dealing with a fragment like the *Battle of Finnsburh*,
the manuscript of which has vanished so that we can give a latest date
merely on linguistic and not on paleographical grounds, there is room for
a certain amount of speculation even in the dating of our lost, unique
copy. While most scholars would agree that the fragment must have
been an early eleventh-century one, this does not help either with the
original date of the poem or with the date of possible versions. And a
comparison with the famous report of the recital of the scop in *Beowulf*

helps no further; nor does the statement in *Widsith* that Fin Folcwalding was the ruler of the Frisians give any chronological information.[3]

Strictly speaking, the only extant example of heroic song in Old English is the *Battle of Finnsburh*. Even with this fragment we could well argue – and it has been argued – that the poem must have been of a length that would have burst the confines of the normally accepted span of a Germanic heroic song. Whatever else the other poems in Old English embodying heroic material may be, they are not heroic songs. *Beowulf* is an epic constructed on Virgilian lines though, apart from a few Biblical references, on heroic and heroicized historical material; *Waldere* likewise must have been of epic proportions; *Widsith* and *Deor* are each the only surviving example in Old English of a different class.

No certainty can be obtained in the relative dating even of these five works. *Widsith* is normally regarded as the oldest, though there must be different layers incorporated in the poem,[4] *Beowulf* is considered earlier than *Waldere*, which very likely it is but it cannot be proved, *Deor* defies us at every turn, and our present fragmentary version of the *Battle of Finnsburh* remains equally difficult, though what is generally accepted to be the oldest catalog in *Widsith* knows of Finn.

The earliest historical events referred to in *Beowulf* must lie at least a century and a half before the composition of the epic even if we accept a date before 700, which is unlikely, anyway. Similarly, *Waldere* mentions a context connecting Theodoric the Ostrogoth with Widia and adventures with giants. As such stories may well have been current not long after 600, they are clearly no use either. The father-son relationship, Wayland-Widia, mentioned in *Waldere* and implied in *Deor*, cannot have been original. Widia is a Gothic hero whose exploits were known among the Langobards, who also took over traditions of Theodoric the Ostrogoth, probably in the late sixth century. Wayland seems to have belonged to the more northern parts of southern Germania, possibly Continental Saxony, more probably Continental Anglia. The family connection may have been constructed for purely alliterative reasons, just as Wade became the father of Wayland and thus the grandfather of Widia, a tradition still known to the upper Bavarian epic of the late thirteenth century. We cannot say where this relationship was first postulated. We may guess that it took place on the Continent not long after 600.

The *Battle of Finnsburh* contains no recognizable historical context, and as for *Widsith*, the latest historical character mentioned is King Alboin the Langobard, murdered by the paramour of his wife in 572, again a date far too early to be of any use.

There is no reliable method of establishing even the approximate date of composition of *Deor* – not an heroic poem and yet of paramount interest to students of Germanic heroic tradition. The Exeter Book, our only source for the poem, was probably written between 970 and 990, which would supply us with c. 950 as the latest possible date. Schücking argued[5] a tenth century date for reasons which can be neither proved nor disproved, for the postulated connection with the didactic elegies – whose date we do not know, alas, though they must be fairly late in the preserved corpus of Old English poetry – is extremely doubtful not to say improbable; interest in the fate of Beadohild (and, we should add, Mæðhild) need not be a late feature; the references to characters in heroic story are indeed not simple, but they are nevertheless a perfectly intelligible development of allusive technique abundantly attested in heroic poetry. Nor need we assume that earlier poets were "simple." As for an earlier date: here again we are merely dealing with the opinion of scholars. A date before 700 would seem to be extremely unlikely, a date as late as 900 need not be assumed.

There are, for such a short poem, quite a number of traces of possible Anglian origin. If the poem was Anglian, and the heroic references would seem to point to Anglia originally rather than to the Saxon part of England, then we must reckon with a good deal of manuscript trans-mission. For an Anglian poem, orally transmitted to the south, might show Anglian words, but it could hardly show traces of Anglian phonological features when written down from oral tradition by a West Saxon scribe. Anglian origin, particularly on account of the disturbed condition of the realm in the Anglian parts of the country due to Danish inroads, would point to earlier rather than later times, and one would think then of an Anglian Christian, most likely a cleric who, steeped in heroic traditions and familiar with stanzaic form in the learned tongue, produced his melancholy and elegiac verse, possibly at a court but possibly also at a monastery; for we know that monastic communities were not averse to listening to heroic songs as primitive in their notions and as bloodthirsty as the lay of Ingeld. We must, therefore, if we regard the poem as originally Anglian, operate with a date not later than 850, though there is nothing against a considerably earlier date.

Arriving at a satisfactory date for *Deor* is conjectural enough in all conscience; we are faced with far greater difficulties when we attempt to deal with the possible provenance and date of the individual stories, and, in one case in particular, the actual content of the story. The only characters mentioned whom we know to have been historical are Theodoric the Ostrogoth[6] (d. 526) and Ermanaric (d. 370–75). We cannot say whether any of the others ever had any real existence.

In 1937 I tried to prove that there was a scheme in the mind of the *Deor* poet according to which he arranged his heroic material.[7] Details in the scheme have frequently been attacked, some with a show of reason. What no commentator has done is to argue against or refute the existence of such a scheme, and that is the only point that really matters.

The poet began with the misfortunes of Wayland, who ultimately succeeded in revenging himself. This led on to the fate of the wronged Beadohild. Her triumph came because she bore a famous son, Widia. We then come to the enigmatic Mæðhild, of whom we merely know what we are told here.[8] She was clearly unfortunate, otherwise she would not have occurred in the list. Also, her lot improved later. She is coupled with an equally unknown Geat, who presumably outlived his misfortunes as well — just as Wayland and Beadohild did, though for different reasons — and thus we have a scheme in which the stories of two couples are referred to. We begin, naturally enough, with the man, Wayland, go on to the woman, Beadohild, then carry on with a mention of the second woman,[9] Mæðhild, followed by the second man, Geat. Since Mæðhild follows on Beadohild and Geat is succeeded by Theodoric we may conjecture that the fate of Mæðhild was in some ways similar to that of Beadohild, and that there were features in the story of Geat that linked him with Theodoric. In view of the *sorglufu* (whether we take this as a reciprocal feeling or refer it to either of the characters) which deprived them (or him, or her) of sleep, there was presumably some trouble with her clan, and Geat was an exile.[10] It would not be profitable to speculate further, in the present context, on this unknown story. The next person mentioned is Theodoric, by common consent the Ostrogoth and not the Frank. We know that he was an exile, in heroic tradition, for thirty years,[11] and that this exile ended ultimately in his triumph. Theodoric leads on, naturally, and inevitably, to his wicked uncle Ermanaric.[12] The ultimate triumph here is not that of the named Ermanaric but of his people who rejoiced when at long last the cruel tyrant was dispatched.[13] This really completes the scheme, and one might imagine that the general reflection on adversity which follows, and which very properly leaves out the refrain *þæs ofereode; þisses swa mæg*, was interpolated at a later date for, to our feeling, the final verse would follow on far more naturally after the reference to the treacherous Ostrogoth. There seems, however, to be no obvious break in style, and the thought of God the inscrutable who rewarded or failed to reward in such an incomprehensible manner may well have presented itself to the author when he was puzzling over the unaccountable behavior of kings. However that may be, the last verse is an integral and essential part of the whole structure and the real reason why the poem was composed at all.[14]

We are told: "I, Deor, was the court poet of Heoden for a very long time. I have now been supplanted by Heorrenda, a powerful singer to whom Heoden has granted the property that I formerly held. That passed; so may this." Apart from the general theme of misfortune outlived there is no link between Ermanaric on the one hand and Heoden and Heorrenda on the other, nor can we from the reference itself tell much about the story that lies behind the Heoden/Heorrenda reference, since in this case the example of misfortune outlived – by gaining another master at whose court he is reciting through the power of his song? – refers to the fictitious Deor himself, not an heroic character.

Before we consider this final heroic reference it would be well to consider the scheme as a whole. There is no need to assume that the acquaintance of the *Deor* poet with heroic material is confined to the references he utilizes. It would be most odd if he happened to know nothing but tales with a happy end. After all, in this particular context stories were no use to him unless they did end happily. That cut out much of the tragic background constantly hinted at in *Beowulf*; it removed Ingeld, Finn, Sigmund, Guðere, Ælfwine, the Herelingas, and much besides.[15] On the contrary, the poet must have been steeped in heroic material if he managed to find so many examples of misfortune outlived, including the Geat-Mæðhild episode, the content of which can merely be established conjecturally.

The last stanza, with its surprising personal reference and immediate relevance, real or imagined, to an actual situation, is one of the freshest and most original conceits in Old English poetry. While it is totally isolated, the theme is readily intelligible. A poet who has to please his patron in order to make a living must be ready to solicit good will in a variety of ways, and the Scandinavian skalds developed this art most successfully. The personal reference is, of course, of frequent occurrence in Old English poetry, and a normal feature of the poems classed together, somewhat summarily, as elegies. Reference to personal performance is, however, not restricted to the elegiac lay. We also find it in *Widsith* when the putative author and his companion sing before their lord and when, according to the singer, everybody present judged it to be a most magnificent performance. The particular point of interest in *Deor* is the reference back to an heroic age, the assumption that the singer in the heroic age was and still is a real person, and the knowledge of the actual poet that such a conceit would be readily understood and readily appreciated by a discriminating and reflective audience.

For us, who have less knowledge, the reference to *Heorrenda*, the *Heodeninga scop*, does raise some problems. The only other place where Heoden is referred to in Old English is in the oldest catalog in *Widsith*, line 21: *Hagena weold Holmrygum and Heoden Glommum.*[16] The two references, in themselves, tell us very little, though they are extremely helpful when we attempt to reconstruct the original story and its later development.[17]

The original story is simple enough. It is the later development that causes all the bother. Heoden elopes with Hild, daughter of Hagene.[18] Hagene pursues the couple. There is a clash, and there are four possible ends: (1) reconciliation, (2) Hagene killed, (3) Heoden killed, (4) both killed. (1) is unlikely at this stage, the others are all possible endings, and it is conceivable that there were variant versions with different endings. We cannot tell. At this stage not more than three characters were involved. The story is located east of Continental Anglia, and at a very early stage there was an Anglian poem on the subject. Later, still on the Continent, another character was added: Heorrenda. In Scandinavia, Hjarrandi is a shadowy person who has no real business in the story and who, in some accounts, masquerades as the father of Heoden. He does not sing. We need not accept all the notions of F. Panzer, though his contention that originally Heoden and Heorrenda were one and the same person makes sense and solves many problems. If that was so we can postulate that Heoden, a *leoðcræftig monn*, beguiled Hild with his song, and fled with her during her father's absence. King and singer were later separated; the singer still beguiled the lady, though now on behalf of his lord. This version remained totally unknown in Scandinavia, which developed mythological notions that do not concern us in our present context. Since *Deor* knows Heorrenda as a singer among the Heodenings, this later version must have been known in England. Heorrenda has no other function; in German tradition (*Kudrun*, *Dukus Horant*) he is also a fighting man but that must be a later development.

A third character is then added to the story: Wada. This is a fairly late development since Wada does not appear in Scandinavia at all; it must, however, have still happened when there were some Anglians on the Continent. These Anglians then brought Wada to England, where we know very little of any actual story or stories in which he may have been involved—but where he was a popular character, some knowledge of whom survived right to the end of the Middle Ages. We cannot say whether the *Deor* poet knew him in connection with the Heoden-Heorrenda tale, nor can we be absolutely positive that, in the old catalog in *Widsith*, he is in fact to be connected with Hagena and Heoden, since there is not only a syntactic break, but another name intervenes.[19] On the Continent he avenges the death of Heoden (Hetel) by slaying Hagena (Hagen).

We cannot enter any further here into the ramifications of this famous story. We must, however, keep later developments in their proper place. All the *Deor* passage can tell us is that Heorrenda was a scop at Heoden's court. He must have known the same story, in essence, that we know; that, however, does not solve our problem, for how are we to imagine an heroic poem in which a powerful singer abducts a lady on behalf of his lord?[20] Hagena may well have slain Heoden; there is never any suggestion that Heorrenda was killed in battle. It remains a puzzle, and perhaps it is fitting, in such a poem, that it should remain so.

NOTES

1. F. P. Magoun, Jr., "*Deors Klage* und *Guðrúnarkviða I*," *Englische Studien*, LXXV (1942), 1–5.
2. *Widsith*, l. 18: *Ætla weold Hunum, Eormanric Gotum.* . . .
3. *Beowulf*, ll. 1068–1159; *Widsith*, l. 27.
4. The details cannot be discussed here. Cf. Kemp Malone, *Widsith* (London, 1936), and *Widsith*, *Anglistica*, XIII (Copenhagen, 1962). Both editions should be consulted. R. W. Chambers, *Widsith* (Cambridge, 1912), retains its value and can still be read with great profit.
5. Levin Schücking, *Kleines angelsächsisches Dichterbuch* (Cöthen, 1919), p. 30: "Was die Abfassung angeht, so weist das Gedicht einerseits eine gewisse Verwandtschaft mit der lyrisch-epischen Einkleidung des Widsith, andererseits mit den lehrhaften Elegien auf. Ein christlicher Verfasser zeigt auch hier eine lebendige Anteilnahme an der heidnischen Sagenwelt und gleichzeitig gesteigertes Interesse an seelischem Erleben auch der Frau. Der Kunstgriff, in einem Gedicht die Helden aus anderen Gedichten auftreten zu lassen, verrät nichts weniger als altertümliche Einfalt. Auf späte Entstehung deutet weiterhin die kunstvolle Knappheit in der Wiedergabe des Wesentlichen an den Situationen. Man wird deshalb gut tun, die Entstehung des Gedichts nicht weit von der anderen Lyrik anzusetzen."
On p. 30 Schücking also remarks: "Der Kehrreim ist dem Abschluss nach Art des Volksliedes noch einmal mechanisch angehängt." This seems to be a rather unfortunate remark. "Nach Art des Volksliedes" is not of course meant in any exact way by Schücking but it may well mislead people. He knows very well that there is no question of folk songs at that stage. There is, however, a more serious objection to this interpretation of the Kehrreim and that is that there is little doubt that the poet was using this particular poem as a method of gaining either a livelihood for good or a temporary position or a present, and that the last verse, which brings in the fabulous Heorrenda, is in fact the starting point for the whole poem and the reason why the whole poem was constructed. Therefore it is far more likely that the Kehrreim is invented for the very last verse and that then all the other heroic examples of misfortune outlived were collected. If we interpret in this fashion, then we may be pretty certain that the poet was successful and knew he was going to be successful and that he was well received by the patron before whom he recited.
6. Even if with Kemp Malone we assume that the person referred to is the Frankish Theodoric, the son of Clovis, the dates are not materially affected. The Frank died in 534. However, I cannot accept the Frankish king in spite of the difficulties of Mæringaburg.
7. "*Deor*: A Criticism and an Interpretation," *MLR*, XXXII, 374–81.
8. I am aware that that is a simplification of the issue, for the language can be held to be so obscure that many different interpretations become possible. Particularly L. Whitbread, off and on, has been remarkably subtle. In "The Third Section of *Deor*," *Modern Philology*, XXXVIII

(1941), 382, after much argument about it and about, he arrives at the following translation: "Many of us learned this [affair, case] of Mæðhild [namely]: her passion for Geat grew boundless [i.e., so great] that this sad love deprived her of all sleep." I still prefer to translate *wurden grundlease Geates frige* 'Geat's passion for Mæðhild became overpowering,' though I am ready to admit that the passage remains difficult. The difficulty does not, however, affect the present argument. I hope to return to the Mæðhild-Geat argument in another context. F. Klaeber, *Archiv f. d. Studium d. neueren Sprachen*, C (1948), 126, also took *monge* in the very general sense of "affair," which is perfectly satisfactory.

9. In this second story it is rather remarkable that the woman should be named first. But that is part of the scheme of reference.

10. Women frequently play a central role in Germanic heroic song: The Burgundian Guðrun, the Gothic Swanhild, the Frankish Brunhild, Hildeburh in the Finn story, the unnamed wife in the Ingeld lay, and many more. Not that they are important as women; but they are, by their marriage or other association with a man, the link between two clans, and thus help to spark off the trouble.

11. This is known to the *Hildebrandslied*, preserved in a manuscript written a little after 800. The poem itself must have been produced c. 600 among the Langobards. Cf. F. Norman, "Das Lied vom alten Hildebrand," *Studi Germanici*, I (Rome, 1963), 19–44.

12. We do not know how early, in heroic tradition, Ermanaric displaced Odoaker, the Old English Eadwacer. It has been argued that even in the *Hildebrandslied*, Odoaker is merely the leader of the army, and is acting on the order of King Ermanaric, who certainly supplanted Odoaker at an early date.

13. L. Whitbread, "More Text-Notes on *Deor*," *Modern Language Notes*, LVIII (1943), 369: "The men of Eormanric are in like case with those of Heremod in *Beowulf*, ll. 901 ff., or of Mezentius in the *Aeneid* (viii, 481 ff.): they were driven to wish their cruel and treacherous king overthrown."

14. J. H. W. Rosteutscher, "Germanischer Schicksalsglaube und angelsächsische Elegiendichtung," *Englische Studien*, LXXIII (1938), 11: "Die Grundsituation der Klage bildet die Vertreibung eines Sängers durch einen anderen Sänger."

15. It is not easy to think of other lays with a happy end. *Waldere* could have been such a poem; it need not have been.

16. MS.: *holmrycum* and *henden*, which Kemp Malone accepts with the meaning "prince, ruler." Since he also holds that the *henden* mentioned is in fact Heoden this makes no odds.

17. There is no evidence at all that Mæðhild is really Hild, and Geat another name for Heoden. This was a frivolous and unnecessary suggestion. Even if it were true, which it cannot be, it would merely tell us that Heoden and Hild ran away together, and thus got themselves into trouble. Elopement and pursuit are common enough themes; all that can be of interest is manner of treatment and new motives.

18. The Old English names are used for convenience.

19. *Widsith*, l. 22: *Witta weold Swæfum, Wada Hælsingum.*

20. In *Widsith* the scop accompanies a princess. We have, however, a scop talking about a scop. Is that evidence?

Wulfstan at York[1]

DOROTHY WHITELOCK

Newnham College, Cambridge

Wᴜʟꜰꜱᴛᴀɴ ᴡᴀꜱ bishop of London from 996 to 1002, when he was
translated to the sees of York and Worcester. He was the third successive
archbishop of York to hold this see in plurality with that of Worcester.
In 1016, Leofsige, abbot of Thorney, was made bishop of Worcester, but
perhaps only as a suffragan to Wulfstan.[2] Wulfstan died at York in 1023,
and was buried in Ely. As well as an important political personage, he
was a prolific writer, and there have survived several manuscripts containing his work and collections of sources which he used. It is perhaps
too readily assumed that any manuscript connected with him emanates
from Worcester. The purpose of this paper is to consider the evidence
for his activities in his see and province of York.

There is no reason to suppose that he spent most of his time in
Worcester. The English kings chose their northern archbishops with
care, for it was a difficult province. After the death in 956 of Archbishop
Wulfstan I, who had been suspected of disloyalty to the English kings,
the choice fell on men of southern origin who had had some experience
of the eastern Danelaw.[3] Such men would be in a better position to
understand the problems of the Anglo-Scandinavian north than would
men of purely West Saxon or Kentish experience. This policy would
have been defeated if the men appointed spent most of their time in
Worcester, leaving their northern province mainly to its own devices.
They were allowed to hold Worcester in plurality, partly because the see
of York was so poor, partly no doubt in order to anchor their loyalty more
firmly to the English king, but hardly as a permanent place of residence.
It is reasonable to assume that after the appointment of Leofsige as
bishop of Worcester the aging archbishop's visits to Worcester would
be less frequent than before. The reason why we do not find many references to him in the north is that our sources of evidence from this area
are scanty. He was at any rate there a fortnight after the death of Swegn
Forkbeard at Gainsborough at Candelmas, 1014, for it was at York that
he consecrated Ælfwig as bishop of London on 16 February.[4] He was
there also on an undated occasion, when he witnessed King Ethelred's

confirmation of a grant of Darlington by a York citizen, Styr, son of Ulf, to St. Cuthbert's at Durham.[5] Possibly this was in 1014, for after Easter in that year King Ethelred had come as far north as Lindsey,[6] so this may have been the occasion of a further journey north to York. It was at York that Wulfstan died.

On general grounds there is nothing against the view that Wulfstan did some of his reading and writing at York. He would have to produce sermons for specific occasions and draft laws by fixed dates, and could not have relied on doing all his work at one only of his sees. He must surely have had secretaries available at both places; probably some traveled with him. He puts *bocweorc, ræding oððon rihting, lar oððon leornung*[7] as part of every bishop's daily work; and he stresses the need for those in a bishop's following to be suitable persons with some special skill.[8]

It is obvious that a scribe's skill would be welcome both *æt ham* and *on siðe*. We may compare the glimpse we get of Bishop Ælfsige of Chester-le-Street, accompanied on a journey south by his scribe Aldred, who entered for him some prayers into the manuscript of the Durham Ritual in his tent at Oakley Down in Wessex.[9] A later bishop of Worcester, St. Wulfstan, is shown by William of Malmesbury's *Life* of him to have traveled with several clerks on his journeys, including Coleman, the author of the vernacular *Life*, which William was using.[10] Archbishop Wulfstan was no doubt similarly accompanied, and hence one should not expect to find linguistic differences between a work first written down at Worcester and one first written down at York.

Several manuscripts connected with Wulfstan are shown by glosses in them or by mention of them in catalogs to have been at one time at Worcester. More than that, we can see that Wulfstan used manuscripts in the possession of that church, if we agree with Mr. Ker that a hand which makes entries in several manuscripts is very probably his own.[11] This hand is found in Hatton 20, the copy of Alfred's translation of the *Cura Pastoralis* which he sent to Worcester; it also annotates the early-eleventh-century part of Tiberius A.xiii, a Worcester cartulary;[12] and it is found in Hatton 42, a book of canons which once belonged to Dunstan and presumably was brought to Worcester by him when he became bishop there.[13] Certain later manuscripts containing Wulfstan's works, Hatton 113, Hatton 114, and Junius 121, were written at Worcester in the second half of the eleventh century, and one manuscript of the collection of Latin texts and excerpts which Dr. Bethurum has named his "Commonplace Book,"[14] that is, C.C.C.C. MS. 265, of the mid-eleventh century, is assigned by Mr. Ker to Worcester on account of its script and its containing a reference to St. Wulfstan.[15] It does not follow that the exemplars of these manuscripts of the generation after Archbishop

Wulfstan were themselves written at Worcester, though they may have been.

Glosses in the "tremulous" hand[16] prove Harley 55, ff. 1–4, to have been at Worcester by about 1200. These four half-sheets contain some medical remedies for hemiplegia, the code known as II and III Edgar, and a set of memoranda relating to lands alienated from the York estates of Otley, Sherburn-in-Elmet, and Ripon, followed by a list of lands acquired for York and Beverley by Archbishop Oscytel, which has notes in the "Wulfstan" hand.[17] York would seem the most likely place where these memoranda would be added, and it may be that the manuscript reached Worcester because Wulfstan, who made a lot of use of II and III Edgar, found it convenient to carry round with him a little manuscript containing it.[18] Yet it is of course possible that he sometimes had copied for him at Worcester matter concerning only his northern see. One may note that the code called IV Edgar relates to the Danelaw,[19] and yet it has come down to us in two manuscripts only, C.C.C.C. MS. 265, from Worcester, and Nero E.i, probably from this same church; however, there is no evidence that the latter manuscript, of about 1000, was actually written at Worcester, and it could have been brought from the north.

There are, however, some manuscripts connected with Wulfstan which supply no evidence of a Worcester provenance. A reluctance to consider the claims of York may arise from a belief that the destruction of St. Peter's at York after the Norman Conquest makes the survival of any of its manuscripts unlikely. The D version of the Anglo-Saxon Chronicle, written in this section by a man of strong York sympathies, records that in 1068 King William "made St. Peter's minster an object of scorn" and that in 1069 the Frenchmen "had thoroughly ravaged and burnt the holy minster of St. Peter." Yet this cannot have been as completely stripped and destroyed as this suggests, for the same authority tells how in 1075 the Danes broke into St. Peter's minster and captured a large amount of property there. If the church had been completely denuded in 1069, it would hardly have recovered much wealth in the troubled years before 1075. One can admit that the chances of survival of York manuscripts and documents were not very good; but the York Gospels have been preserved, and some other books may have escaped. Moreover, some manuscripts produced at York in Wulfstan's time could have found a home elsewhere before the Conquest. One cannot dismiss out of hand a York origin for a Wulfstan manuscript.

The York Gospels[20] afford one clear example of a York manuscript connected with Wulfstan. This was probably written in England about 1000, and has Old English entries on its last six leaves. These are: surveys of lands attached to Sherburn-in-Elmet, Otley, and Ripon, belonging to the see of York;[21] three short Wulfstan sermons, Napier Nos. LIX, LX, and LXI, of which the first is headed *Sermo Lupi* and the last has interlineations in the "Wulfstan" hand; Cnut's Old English letter of 1019–20;[22] a list of service books and plate at Sherburn-in-Elmet;[23] some bidding prayers; and a list of the sureties for a certain Ælfric, many of the names being Scandinavian.[24] Mr. Ker assigns the Wulfstan homilies, the Cnut letter, and the prayers to a single hand of the first part of the eleventh century, and the survey of York lands to three hands of about this time. There is no reason to doubt that the manuscript was at York when the Wulfstan entries were made. It has remained there ever since.

The next manuscript to be considered is Claudius A.iii., ff. 31–86, 106–50,[25] that is, the part of this composite manuscript which consists of a pontifical written in caroline minuscule about 1000[26] preceded by eight preliminary leaves. On the verso of the first of these is a metrical inscription[27] recording that a certain Thureth had had this *halgungboc* beautifully bound; then follow one bifolium and five half-sheets (ff. 32–38) containing the Latin and Old English versions of the code called VI Ethelred. The Latin version is expressly said to be by Wulfstan, and the Old English version is in his style. There are interlineations in the "Wulfstan" hand in both versions of the code. A pontifical is part of the necessary equipment of a bishop or archbishop, and includes the order of several ceremonies, such as dedication of churches and confirmation, which often took place away from the cathedral church. If this pontifical was one which Wulfstan took about with him, Ethelred's sixth code may have been added because he wished to have it available. But it is also possible that a book provided, as this one once was, with a rich binding was meant for ceremonial use at the cathedral, and perhaps kept on the altar; in that case the insertion of leaves containing legal texts could be paralleled by many examples of the entry of documents in blank spaces in gospels and fine ritual books, for their safer preservation. We need go no further than the York Gospels for an instance of this practice.[28] The presence in this part of Claudius A.iii of the "Wulfstan" hand makes unlikely the identification of the Thureth mentioned in the poem with Thored, a landowner who gave an estate at Horsley, Surrey, to Christ Church, Canterbury;[29] it is more tempting to accept the suggestion that he was the earl of Northumbria of this name. He is last heard of in 992, when he was one of the leaders of a disastrous campaign.[30] His successor Ælfhelm signs in 993, but Thored may have lived some years longer and have been deposed from office. If the donor mentioned in Claudius A.iii is this earl, one would expect his generosity to have been directed toward York rather than Worcester; yet, even so, the book might have been removed to Worcester by one of the archbishops who held both York and Worcester. Thus one cannot establish for certain that it was York where the leaves with VI Ethelred were written, though this place has at least an equal claim to Worcester's.

Vespasian A.xiv, ff. 114 – 70, of the first half of the eleventh century, is another manuscript with Wulfstan connections which shows no sign of having been at Worcester. It has a set of verses which Mr. Ker thinks are written in the "Wulfstan" hand, and which show that he was responsible for having the texts in this manuscript compiled. All are in Latin. Among them is a letter written to Wulfstan when he was bishop of London.[31] Several items in this manuscript are of northern interest and likely to have been available at York. These include a letter from Pope Paul I to Eadberht of Northumbria and his brother, Archbishop Ecgberht,[32] a letter from a northern anchorite, Alchfrith, to Higlac,[33] and a letter from Eanbald, before he became archbishop of York, to his predecessor, Archbishop Eanbald I.[34] There is also a collection of twenty-seven of Alcuin's letters, mainly to recipients in England;[35] only two are to continental recipients, and of these, one was written in England.[36] There is also a letter from Arno, bishop of Salzburg, to Alcuin's pupil, Cuculus, who was probably in England at the time.[37] It is of interest to compare this collection with that contained in Harley MS. 208, a ninth-century Continental manuscript which was at York in the Middle Ages. One cannot prove that it was there already in Wulfstan's time, though it was certainly in England by about 1000.[38] What is remarkable is that there is so very little overlap between the collections in Harley and Vespasian. Only two letters occur in both, and one of these has in the Harley manuscript lost its beginning and been run on to the preceding letter, so that its presence in the manuscript has been concealed.[39] In neither case has the Harley manuscript served as the exemplar for the text in Vespasian A.xiv, for the latter sometimes gives superior readings.

This slightness of overlap is not to be explained on the assumption that each compiler is selecting on a different principle. The compiler of the Harley manuscript was not avoiding letters to England; he includes twenty-six letters to persons in England, some of them important letters to Northumbrian kings and prelates. His collection, which has ninety-one letters, seems to have been made abroad: Continental letters predominate, but it avoids the correspondence between Alcuin and Charles the Great, except for three letters, and seems, therefore, to have been drawn up at some house that possessed, or was in process of compiling, a separate collection of these.[40] The absence from the Vespasian manuscript of those letters in Harley which are of English interest is easiest to explain on the assumption that the Vespasian collection was made by someone who had access to the Harley collection, and wished to supplement it. In that case, the inclusion, from some other source, of two letters which are in Harley would be by inadvertence; and the fact that an error in the Harley manuscript has concealed the presence of one of these suggests that the Vespasian compiler used this very manuscript.[40a] The collection as it stands in the Vespasian manuscript need not first have been made by the writer of this; he could have drawn on one made at any time after the Harley manuscript was brought to England. Since we know that this manuscript was at York at a later date, and since York is a place most likely to be interested in the letters of Alcuin, it is a reasonable surmise that it was there that a supplementary collection was made. Whether this was done by the compiler of Vespasian A.xiv, or whether he had access to an existent collection, it seems probable that he was working at York.

Nevertheless, it must not be claimed that Vespasian A.xiv is entirely made up of documents of northern interest. It has several of more southern provenance, for example, Pope Leo iii's letter to Coenwulf of Mercia on the abolition of the archbishopric of Lichfield,[41] the decrees of the synod of Chelsea of 816,[42] the canons of Oda, archbishop of Canterbury,[43] a set of letters written to archbishops of Canterbury in the tenth century,[44] and a letter from Lantfrith to the brothers of the Old Minster at Winchester concerning the miracles of St. Swithin.[45] With the exception of the last, this looks like a set of texts obtained from Canterbury, and it may be that the letters of Alcuin addressed to Canterbury have come from the same source. It would, however, have been easy for Wulfstan to obtain such a set of records, for he was in constant contact with his archiepiscopal colleague. He occurs as legatee and executor in the will of Ælfric, archbishop of Canterbury,[46] and a papal letter to this prelate is included in a set of penitential letters which is found in some manuscripts connected with Wulfstan.[47] Wulfstan's interest in the ecclesiastical history of his nation would cause him to cast his net widely. Yet nothing in this collection has any specific relation to Worcester. If there is anything in the suggestion that Harley 208 was available to the compiler of the collection of Alcuin's letters in Vespasian A.xiv, then York is the more likely place of origin of the latter manuscript.

Entries in the "Wulfstan" hand are prominent in Nero A.i, ff. 70–177, which contains Wulfstan homilies, parts of *Polity*, and several law codes drafted by Wulfstan or used by him. Mr. Ker has pointed out that it has no Worcester marks or glosses, and that scribbles made in s. xiii–xiv suggest that at that date it was not in a monastic house.[48] It contains also an alteration in an eleventh-century hand, which may have a bearing on the question of provenance. When, in a chapter of *Polity*, Wulfstan declares: *Nis nanum weofodþegne alifed þæt he wifian mote, ac is ælcum forboden*, this has been erased and replaced with the state-

ment: *Riht is þæt preost him lufie clænlicne wimman to gebeddan.*[49]
Such an outspoken utterance in favor of priests' marriage would be less
remarkable in York, where we know from the *Northumbrian Priests'
Law* that this was tolerated,[50] than in a monastic scriptorium like that
at Worcester. Yet it would be unwise to build too much on this. A passage
in the *Life* of the later Wulfstan, bishop of Worcester, while showing the
saint's stern disapproval of married priests, shows also that they were
not rare in his diocese;[51] and there is a marginal note by William of
Malmesbury in Oriel MS. 42 which should warn us against assuming
that all monastic writers shared the views of reformers like the two
Wulfstans, for it says, referring to St. Paul: *Posse presbiterum, ait,
potius debere, uxorem habere.*[52] By William's time, however, papal
attempts to enforce rules against priests' marriage had called forth
much opposition, including several treatises in its defense,[53] so that
William's note is not as surprising as is the alteration in Nero A.i.

So far, we have considered only manuscripts written in Wulfstan's
lifetime. Another compilation of Latin texts which has some entries in
the "Wulfstan" hand, namely Copenhagen Gl. Kgl. S. 1595, has, as far
as I know, no indications to help one decide between Worcester or York
as its place of origin. To turn to manuscripts with Wulfstan connections,
written after his time, we have already seen that some were written at
Worcester in the middle and latter part of the eleventh century. His
work was also known further afield. Exeter seems to have had a particular interest in it. Two manuscripts with Wulfstan homilies, C.C.C.
421 and 419 (Napier's A and B), are from Exeter, and some of the Wulfstan matter in A was written there;[54] Cleopatra B.xiii and Lambeth 489,
which Mr. Ker suggests once formed a single manuscript, were probably
written at Exeter, and the first contains Wulfstan's homily on the dedication of a church (Napier LIV, Bethurum XVIII) and that on the con-
secration of a bishop (Napier XXXVII, Bethurum XVII), while the second
has a homily (Napier LVII) with several Wulfstan passages, as well as a
catena of extracts from Napier V (Bethurum VIII c), XIX (Bethurum XIII),
XXIV, XL, and LVII; C.C.C. 190, one manuscript of Wulfstan's *Commonplace Book*, is probably to be identified with the item *.i. canon on leden.
7 scriftboc on englisc* in the list of Bishop Leofric's gifts to Exeter.[55]
Three added quires are written in an Exeter script, but if this is the
book given by Leofric, it is not known where he obtained it. About the
same period a section of Tiberius A.iii was written at Christ Church,
Canterbury, in the mid-eleventh century, and this includes Napier
XIX–XXII (Bethurum XIII), XXIII–XXV, XXVI (Bethurum VII a), XXVII,
XXVI, LI–LIII, and the Latin text Napier IV (Bethurum VIII a). The detailed history of the spread of Wulfstan's influence remains to be written,
but it is clear that one cannot safely assume that a manuscript in some

way connected with him must necessarily come from one of the sees which he held, at any rate when it is later than his time.

Yet it may be worthwhile to examine one such manuscript, of the middle of the eleventh century, namely C.C.C.C. MS. 201, pp. 1–178, which is one of the chief manuscripts of Wulfstan's works.[56] This has been written at two periods about a generation apart. Its first and thirteenth quires are half-filled by a hand of the early eleventh century, and the intervening and following parts by hands of the middle of the century. The earlier hand writes on pages 1–7 a fragment of a translation of the *Regularis Concordia*, with some additions to make it suitable for women's houses as well as men's.[57] The rest of this quire, and most of the next ten, are in a single mid-eleventh-century hand, and contain a miscellany of Wulfstan writings and sources, including the *Northumbrian Priests' Law*. There follows in the same hand the Old English *Apollonius of Tyre*,[58] then a tract on the Kentish royal saints and the resting places of the English saints.[59] A different hand of about the same date then fills the last leaves of quire 11, and the whole of quire 12, with a section of the Old English translation of Genesis, dealing with the story of Joseph. This is the same extract as one which was in the almost entirely burnt manuscript, Otho B.x,[60] and it is interesting to note that there it followed immediately a homily made up of Wulfstan passages (Napier LVIII), and that another part of this manuscript has a set of penitential texts found in Wulfstan's *Commonplace Book*.[61] Hence the only two known copies of this extract from Genesis occur in Wulfstan surroundings. In C.C.C.C. 201 it is incomplete, for two folios have been lost at the end of quire 12. With quire 13, we return to the first hand, that of the early eleventh century. It fills the first half of the quire with an Old English poem based on Bede's *De die iudicii*, and with two other religious poems.[62] The Judgement Day poem was used by the writer of a homily preserved in the Worcester manuscript Hatton 113,[63] a manuscript which includes some Wulfstan homilies, but the author of this homily had a different, and in some respects better, text of the poem than that in C.C.C.C. 201.[64] After these poems, the main mid-eleventh-century hand takes on again, with metrical paraphrases of the Lord's Prayer and the Gloria, that of the latter being the same as the one in Junius 121, where it forms part of the Benedictine office attributed to Wulfstan.[65] Finally, a third mid-eleventh-century scribe has added a Latin text on confession, which had already been entered by the main scribe as part of the Wulfstan miscellany.

It would appear that in the middle of the eleventh century two quires already half-filled with writing of the early part of the century were filled up, with prose following the prose on quire 1, and verse the verse on quire 13, and assembled with other quires at some place where a collection of Wulfstan material was available. It was an important collection, for among other things this is the sole manuscript to preserve Wulfstan's so-called Pastoral Letter with the address: *Wulfstan arcebisceop greteð freondlice þegnas on ðeode gehadode and læwede ealle gemænelice, þa ðe him betæhte sindon for gode to wissianne*;[66] it alone has the version of Ælfric's pastoral letter for him which he revised in his own style;[67] it supplies our only text of the *Northumbrian Priests' Law*; and it contains what appears to be a first draft of Cnut's laws, with a preface explaining that it was drawn up "as soon as King Cnut with the advice of his councilors completely established peace and friendship between the Danes and the English," presumably for the meeting at Oxford in 1018.[68] This suggests that the collection of Wulfstan's writings and sources copied into the manuscript was one not completed until toward the end of his life, after Leofsige had been appointed to Worcester in 1016, with the probable result that Wulfstan could devote more time to his northern see. The *Northumbrian Priests' Law* is a York document, whereas no item is specifically connected with Worcester. York is certainly a possible place for this assembly of material.

Yet it does not necessarily follow that the manuscript was written there. It has no marks or glosses which would place it at Worcester, but the combination of the Wulfstan material with items not apparently connected with him, that is, the parts written in the early-eleventh-century hand, as well as the *Apollonius of Tyre* and the treatises about saints, could have been made at any place which had secured a manuscript of Wulfstan's works and sources. The inclusion of a treatise on Kentish saints is no safe evidence for Kentish origin, for this was a widely known text: the other main manuscript of it was written at Winchester, and the work was used by Florence of Worcester, William of Malmesbury, and Hugo Candidus of Peterborough.[69] The peculiar features in the version of the *Resting-Places of the English Saints* in C.C.C.C. 201 do not point clearly to any place of origin.[70]

It remains to consider whether the language of the manuscript helps to locate it. In the main, all scribes write late West Saxon literary language, but a few features may be noted. Both the main mid-eleventh-century scribe (B) and his contemporary who wrote the extract from Genesis (C) often write *æ* for *e* before nasals, whereas the early-eleventh-century scribe (A) has only two instances, *længra* in the *Regularis Concordia*, *stænt* in a poem. This feature occurs sporadically in most Wulfstan manuscripts, but it should be noted that scribe B uses this spelling also when copying non-Wulfstan texts, and that it is a pronounced feature in the extract from Genesis in the other manuscript of this, Otho B.x.[71] It has been claimed as a sign of southeastern origin, since Middle English evidence shows that it survived in that area; but

Dr. and Miss Sisam have demonstrated its unreliability as a locating feature of Old English manuscripts, concluding that "it was at least tolerated over a wide area of Southern England."[72] It does not seem, however, to have been favored in the Worcester scriptorium: it is very rare in charters from this area or in either the early or the late portions of "Hemming's cartulary." There is, however, no instance of it in the Old English additions to the York Gospels. It is not uncommon in the first two hands of the D version of the Anglo-Saxon Chronicle (Tiberius B.iv), but does not occur after the third scribe took over in the middle of annal 1016; it is, however, by no means certain where this manuscript was written.[73]

A pronounced feature of the B scribe of C.C.C.C. 201 is the writing of *i* for *y* of any origin, including the mutation of *u* even where the surrounding consonants are not favorable to unrounding. There are few instances of this in scribe C, who does, however, write *scridde* (beside *scrydde*) and *pillican*; scribe A preserves *y* as mutation of *u* except in the neighborhood of front consonants, as in *drihten, þince, filige*. Scribe B's strong preference for *i* does not seem to support a Worcester origin, but in the present state of our knowledge it would be rash to try to locate him closely on this feature.[74] The extreme southwest is included among areas with unrounded *y*, as well as large areas of eastern England. Our manuscript shows hardly a trace of the Kentish and southeastern *e* for *y* as mutation of *u*. The C scribe appears to have been a southerner, for he has a striking peculiarity in spelling *u* for initial *f*, for example, *uæder, uerende, uoran, auandod, uætte*,[75] and so on, and this feature seems to have been lacking in the version of the same text in Otho B.x, so is unlikely to have been in their common exemplar.

The C scribe consistently writes a single back vowel, not a diphthong, after *sc*, and this is the usual practice also in the B hand, whether copying Wulfstan texts or others, while the A scribe also affords many examples of a single back vowel in this position. Most Wulfstan manuscripts contain instances of this feature, yet it does not seem to have been normal at Worcester. The Worcester scribe who wrote Hatton 113–14 and Junius 121 prefers diphthongs, but occasionally writes a single vowel, presumably retaining the spelling of his exemplar.

It seems to me that a great deal more study into the practice of scribes of manuscripts which can be located with reasonable certainty is necessary before one can safely assign a manuscript to a definite area on linguistic criteria like the above. It seems reasonable to see scribe C, with his initial *u* for *f*, as a man from the south or from the southwest midlands, but can one assume that he was writing there? There was a lot of movement among Anglo-Saxon ecclesiastics, and it is, for example, very likely that when Aldred, bishop of Worcester, became archbishop of York in 1060, some members of his *familia* went with him. Bearing

in mind such possibilities, and also the varying degree in which individual scribes were faithful to their exemplar, it would be wiser to refrain from an exact location of C.C.C.C. 201, though there can be no
doubt that it had access to a collection of Wulfstan material made at
one of his sees.

Finally, there are two passages in Wulfstan's style added to the
northern recension of the Anglo-Saxon Chronicle.[76] It is unnecessary to
enter into the controversial issue of where the D manuscript was written.
It certainly kept up a close interest in York almost to the end. There is
no doubt that until the northern version split up, soon after 1031, into its
two branches D and E (F), it was in the north, and strong evidence
speaks for York as its home. Into this common ancestor of D and E (F)
a panegyric on King Edgar was inserted in annal 959, and it survives
in both branches; it is in Wulfstan's style, and we have other evidence
for his great admiration for this king.[77] Another Wulfstan passage was
added in annal 975, describing the antimonastic reaction on Edgar's
death; this survives only in D, having been replaced in E by a brief
statement. The presence of these passages points to Wulfstan's activity
in York.

Thus an examination of the manuscripts gives support to the view
that Wulfstan was not a constant absentee from his archiepiscopal see.
His concern with conditions in the Danelaw is shown by his composition
of the so-called *Laws of Edward and Guthrum*, which has a preface
claiming that these ecclesiastical injunctions are no recent innovation,
but were agreed on by King Alfred and King Guthrum, and confirmed by
King Edward.[78] It seems likely that it was Wulfstan's interest in the code
IV Edgar, a Danelaw code, which has preserved it for us, since it survives
only in manuscripts probably from Worcester. In several places in the
codes which Wulfstan drafted, it is said or implied that different rules
and penalties are in force in the Danelaw; in some places, as in Cnut's
laws, it is stated what these are,[79] but elsewhere we merely get the
reservation that a regulation is valid "in the law of the English." Thus
in v Ethelred 30 a man who wishes to clear himself of the charge of
plotting against the king's life must do so by the king's wergild or three-
fold ordeal *on Engla lage*,[80] but in the repetition of this clause in VI
Ethelred 37 the words *7 on Dena lage be þam þe heora lagu sy* are added.
When some clauses from VIII Ethelred are used in one of the Wulfstan
passages added into the York Gospels (Napier LXI), the words *on Engla
lage* are attached to the statement that failure to pay *Romscot* makes
one liable to a fine of 120 shillings to the king, and, similarly, this phrase
is inserted in the clause *and cyricsceat gelæste man to Martines
mæssan*. This implication of a different practice in the Danelaw sug-

gests that the omission of the clause relating to *cyricsceat* from v Ethelred and from the version of Cnut's laws in C.C.C.C. 201 was not necessarily accidental. Another recognition of variety of local custom in the north is the substitution of Christmas for All Saints' Day as one of the terms for payment of *leohtscot* in the passage in the York Gospels.

Since so clearly Wulfstan was familiar with Danelaw legal practices, it is to be regretted that his surviving works do not tell us more about them. It is possible that some laws issued for the Danelaw have failed to survive. Though we are fortunate in possessing a number of manuscripts which can be connected with him, it must not be supposed that we have his whole library. He used some sources, legal and others, which are not contained in any of the surviving manuscripts used by him;[81] and his *Laws of Edward and Guthrum* and one or two of his homilies are not included in any surviving manuscript directly connected with him.[82]

Wulfstan includes Northumbrian wergilds in the collection of texts on status which Dr. Bethurum claims as his.[83] The *Northumbrian Priests' Law* probably dates from his archiepiscopate. As we saw above, it survives only among Wulfstan material in C.C.C.C. 201; it uses sources with which he was familiar, and also his own writings; and on one matter it agrees with an addition which he made to the pastoral letter written for him by Ælfric.[84] A set of canons in the Brussels MS. Bibl. Royale 8558–63, written in an early-twelfth-century hand, has clauses very close to some in this code, along with others from a Wulfstan work, the so-called *Canons of Edgar*.[85] Liebermann's late dating of at any rate the second part of the *Northumbrian Priests' Law* depends on his date for Cnut's laws, which may have been used, that is, later than Wulfstan's death.[86] If, as I believe, this date is wrong, and Wulfstan drafted Cnut's laws,[87] this argument has no validity. One interesting feature of the *Northumbrian Priests' Law* is its evidence that heathen practices were a reality in the diocese of York, for it graduates the fines for them in accordance with the ranks of society. These practices include the worship of heathen divinities (*idola wurðinge*). This code is later than the accession of Cnut, yet one cannot regard this worship as a new introduction by his followers, for Wulfstan has several references to it in works written before 1016, for example, the Latin version of vi Ethelred refers to *idolorum cultores* and *idolatrie* and his homily Napier x (Bethurum x c) says *Ne ænig man idola weorðie æfre*, while a Latin addition to this text in C and E mentions *idolatria*. Napier LIV (Bethurum XVIII), which enjoins . . . *þæt cristene men þæne egesan æfre ne dreogan þæt hy deofolgyld ahwar weorðian*, cannot be closely dated. It seems unlikely that there was worship of heathen gods in southern England before the conquest by Cnut, even though superstitious practices of heathen origin may have continued; but in Northumbria it is possible that the heathen cults introduced in the tenth century by the Norse invaders from Ireland had not been eradicated. Wulfstan may have been speaking from personal knowledge of conditions in the north when, in his *Sermo ad Anglos*, he speaks of the way *gedwolgoda* and sanctuaries are honored "among heathen people." Similarly, the easy divorce and the disregard of the Church's laws on marriage within the prohibited degrees which prevailed in his northern province may explain his vehement fulminations against adultery and incest in this *Sermo* and elsewhere.

The influence of his sojourns in the north is seen in his terminology. While in general he writes a variety of late West Saxon literary language, he uses in some texts words of Scandinavian origin, especially in speaking of the various social classes. He often uses the Scandinavian *þræl*, besides English *þeowa*, *þeowman*, or *þeowetling*; in the codes which he drafted he uses *bonda* in VI and VII Ethelred, and in Cnut's laws, both in the sense of free householder and of husband, though he also uses the English *ceorl*. What is most significant is his preference for *eorl*, which in Northumbria had begun, under Scandinavian influence, to supplant the native *ealdorman*. Wulfstan uses *ealdorman* only in quotation from older legislation; his own word, in homilies, *Polity*, and laws, is *eorl*. This was not the normal practice south of the Humber in Wulfstan's time, though it became so later; except for the poetic use of *eorl* in the poem on the battle of Maldon to apply to Brihtnoth, the holders of the office are consistently called *ealdormen* until one comes to the appointment of Cnut's Danish followers, Hakon, Eglaf, and so on. In the diocese of Worcester, the holders of the Mercian earldom are called *ealdorman* at this time: we get, for example, Leofwine *ealdorman* in the marriage agreement for Wulfstan's sister,[88] and in an Evesham lease which Wulfstan witnessed about 1023, Leofwine is given this title when the Danes, Hacon and Eglaf, are called *eorl*.[89] Wulfstan's consistent employment of *eorl* does not represent the practice of his southern diocese. In Northumbria from the tenth century *eorl* was often used of this official, especially when the holders of the office were of Danish extraction. Oslac of Northumbria is called *eorl* in IV Edgar, when Æthelwine of East Anglia and Ælfhere of Mercia are given the title *ealdorman*. The northern recension of the Anglo-Saxon Chronicle calls Oslac *eorl*, although it refers to his office as *ealdordom*, and both Thored (c. 975–92) and Uhtred (1006–1016) are always referred to as *eorl*. The intervening holder of the office (992–1006) is, however, referred to as *ealdorman*, perhaps because he was a member of an outstanding Mercian family; otherwise the term *eorl* holds the field in Northumbria, and Wulfstan seems to reflect this usage.

NOTES

1. I am indebted to Dr. Peter Clemoes for reading this article and making many useful suggestions.

The following abbreviated citations are used: Bethurum = Dorothy Bethurum, *The Homilies of Wulfstan* (Oxford, 1957); Ker = N. R. Ker, *Catalogue of Manuscripts containing Anglo-Saxon* (Oxford, 1957); Napier = A. Napier, *Wulfstan. Sammlung der ihm zugeschriebenen Homilien* (Berlin, 1883); *Polity = Institutes of Polity, Civil and Ecclesiastical*, best edited by K. Jost (Berne, 1959).

2. This supposition would explain Wulfstan's issuing of leases of Worcester lands in 1017, and his witnessing of documents concerning this diocese after Leofsige's accession. See Dorothy Whitelock, *Sermo Lupi ad Anglos*, 3d ed. (London, 1963), p. 9.

3. See D. Whitelock, "The Dealings of the Kings of England with Northumbria in the Tenth and Eleventh Centuries" in *The Anglo-Saxons. Studies in some Aspects of their History and Culture presented to Bruce Dickins*, ed. P. Clemoes (London, 1959).

4. Anglo-Saxon Chronicle, 1014 D.

5. *Symeonis Monachi Opera Omnia*, ed. T. Arnold, I, p. 83.

6. Anglo-Saxon Chronicle, 1014.

7. *Polity*, ed. Jost, p. 75.

8. *Polity*, ed. Jost, p. 77.

9. See colophon on p. 167 of Durham Cathedral MS. A. IV. 19; printed in A. Hamilton Thompson and U. Lindelöf, *Rituale Ecclesiae Dunelmensis* (Surtees Society, 1927), p. 185.

10. See R. R. Darlington, *The Vita Wulfstani of William of Malmesbury* (London, 1928), pp. xxxvi, 33, 36, 40, 48.

11. See Ker, p. lvi, and Whitelock, *Sermo Lupi ad Anglos*, pp. 29–31.

12. On this see N. R. Ker, "Hemming's Cartulary," in *Studies in Medieval History presented to F. M. Powicke* (Oxford, 1948).

13. It is entered in *Catalogus Librorum Manuscriptorum Bibliothecae Wigorniensis* of Patrick Young, edd. I. Atkins and N. R. Ker (Cambridge, 1944), pp. 48 f. It is No. 4117 in the *Summary Catalogue of Western Manuscripts in the Bodleian Library at Oxford*.

14. D. Bethurum, "Archbishop Wulfstan's Commonplace Book," *PMLA* LVII, 916–29.

15. Ker, p. 94.

16. Ker, p. lvii; *idem*, "The Date of the 'Tremulous' Worcester Hand," *Leeds Studies in English*, VI (1937); S. J. Crawford, "The Worcester Marks and Glosses of the Old English Manuscripts in the Bodleian," *Anglia*, LII (1928).

17. W. de G. Birch, *Cartularium Saxonicum*, Nos. 1278, 1279; A. J. Robertson, *Anglo-Saxon Charters*, No. LIV; trans. D. Whitelock, *English Historical Documents c. 500–1042*, No. 114.

18. For Wulfstan's use of Edgar's laws see Dorothy Whitelock, "Wulfstan and the Laws of Cnut," *EHR*, LXIII (1948). The insertion of the Latin and Old English versions of Ethelred's sixth code into the pontifical Claudius A.iii could also have been for the convenience of carrying it round with him. See p. 215 above.

19. It mentions as responsible for its circulation only the ealdormen in control of Danelaw areas, Oslac of Northumbria, Æthelwine of East Anglia, and Ælfhere of Mercia, whose territory included that of the Five Boroughs. Since one clause says that the king and his councilors have decided what the penalty for an offense is to be "among the English," without specifying the penalty, one suspects that a companion ordinance relating to the English areas once existed.

20. Ker, p. 468; J. P. Gilson, *Description of the Saxon Manuscript of the Four Gospels in the Library of York Minster* (York, 1925).

21. W. H. Stevenson, "Yorkshire Surveys and other Eleventh-Century Documents in the York Gospels," *EHR*, XXVII (1912); Robertson, No. LXXXIV.

22. F. Liebermann, *Die Gesetze der*

Angelsachsen, I, pp. 273–75; trans. D. Whitelock, *English Historical Documents c. 500–1042*, No. 48.

23. Stevenson; Robertson, p. 249.

24. Stevenson; W. Farrer, *Early Yorkshire Charters*, I, pp. 27 f.; E. Björkman, "Die 'Festermen' des Ælfric: eine Namenliste aus York," *Festschrift für L. Morsbach* (Halle, 1913), pp. 1–19.

25. Ker, pp. 177 f.

26. See H. A. Wilson, *The Benedictional of Archbishop Robert* (Henry Bradshaw Society, 24; London, 1903), p. xviii. The Rev. H. M. J. Banting has kindly informed me that the text in Claudius A.iii has many agreements with Sidney Sussex MS. 100, an early-eleventh-century pontifical from Durham, and that both have connections with the so-called *Pontifical of Archbishop Ecgberht* (Surtees Society Publications, 27).

27. Published by E. V. K. Dobbie, *The Anglo-Saxon Minor Poems* (New York, 1942), p. 97.

28. For other examples, see F. Wormald, "The Sherborne 'Chartulary,'" in *F. Saxl, 1890–1948* (London, 1957), p. 106 and n. 2.

29. Dobbie, p. xc, says that the Horsley charter is in the same manuscript as the Thureth poem, but in fact the charter is on one of a group of leaves which Mr. Ker has shown were once part of a different manuscript, the gospel-book, Tiberius A.ii. See N. R. Ker, "Membra Disiecta," *British Museum Quarterly*, XII (1938), 130 f. The Horsley charter is No. LXXXVIII in Robertson, where it is suggested that the donor is a thegn who attests Cnut's charters. Professor Dobbie would identify both the donor of Horsley and the Thureth of the poem with Earl Thored of Northumbria; Mr. Ker also suggests identifying Thureth with this earl.

30. According to the Anglo-Saxon Chronicle, it came to nothing because Ealdorman Ælfric warned the enemy and then deserted.

31. Both the verses and the letter are conveniently printed in Bethurum, pp. 376–78.

32. Birch, No. 184; trans. Whitelock, *English Historical Documents*, No. 184.

33. See W. Levison, *England and the Continent in the Eighth Century* (Oxford, 1946), pp. 297–302.

34. E. Dümmler, *Monumenta Germaniae Historica: Epistolae*, IV, No. 46.

35. Certainly fourteen, perhaps fifteen, were sent to Northumbria, and five to Canterbury. In addition, one (No. 292) is to an English archbishop, and another (No. 70) to an Abbot Wulfheard, who may possibly be a later bishop of Hereford. No. 45 has no address, but the bearer was Eanbald, later to be archbishop of York. Nos. 235 and 274 have no address and cannot be located. One should note that fourteen letters in this collection occur only here and in Tiberius A.xv, which had access to the material assembled in Vespasian A.xiv (apart from a few extracts in William of Malmesbury, who used the collection in Tiberius A.xv, and for extracts in manuscripts of Wulfstan's Commonplace Book, C.C.C.C. 190 and 265). The presence of so many letters not in any Continental collection suggests that the Vespasian collection was made in England. Of the fourteen letters in question, seven were to Northumbria, three to Canterbury, one to an English archbishop, one to Abbot Wulfheard, and two to unnamed recipients.

36. Dümmler, No. 10. The letter written abroad to a Continental recipient is No. 96, to Paulinus of Aquileia.

37. Dümmler, No. 66.

38. Ker, p. 304. A scribble, reminiscent, as Mr. Ker points out, of *Beowulf*, l. 869, was added in the margin about this time: *hwæt ic eall feala ealde sæge*.

39. This is Dümmler, No. 128, a letter from Alcuin to Æthelheard, archbishop of Canterbury, reproving him for leaving his see, and referring to the archbishopric of Lichfield, a matter in which the Vespasian manuscript shows interest elsewhere. The only other letter to occur in both collections is Dümmler, No. 209, addressed to Calvinus, priest and monk of St. Stephen's, on the use of external things and on the difficulties of Eanbald II, archbishop of York. An error in Dümmler's list

(p. 6), by which the 57th item in Harley is given as No. 235 instead of No. 236, makes it appear as if the two collections shared a third item.

40. A separate collection of letters to or from Charles was available to the Troyes MS. 1165, of the ninth century, and the Vatican MS. Reg. Christinae 272, of the tenth century; part of it was used by the ninth-century Lambeth MS. 218. The three letters to Charles which are in Harley are No. 41, which has lost its address, and two of the latest letters, No. 249, written 801–802, which is preserved in Harley alone, and No. 308, of 801–804.

40a. This same error is, however, also in the tenth-century Vatican manuscript mentioned in the previous note, whose last fifteen letters are all in the Harley manuscript, and in the same order.

41. Birch, No. 288; A. W. Haddan and W. Stubbs, *Councils and Ecclesiastical Documents*, III (Oxford, 1878), pp. 523–25; trans. Whitelock, *English Historical Documents*, No. 205.

42. Haddan and Stubbs, III, pp. 579–84.

43. D. Wilkins, *Concilia Magnae Britanniae et Hiberniae*, I (London, 1737), pp. 212–14.

44. W. Stubbs, *Memorials of St. Dunstan* (London, 1874), pp. 380 f., 383–89.

45. W. Stubbs, p. 369.

46. Whitelock, *Anglo-Saxon Wills*, No. XVIII.

47. See most recently K. Jost, *Wulfstanstudien* (Berne, 1950), pp. 16–21, and Bethurum, pp. 374–76.

48. Ker, pp. 211–15.

49. *Polity*, ed. Jost, p. 112.

50. This code in clause 35 merely stipulates: "If a priest leaves a woman (*cwene*) and takes another, let him be anathema." There is no mention of any penalty for a priest who remains faithful to one "woman."

51. Darlington, p. 53 f.

52. See Hugh Farmer, "William of Malmesbury," *Journal of Ecclesiastical History*, XIII (1960), 49. I am indebted to Dom Hugh for sending me the wording of the marginal note.

53. See C. N. L. Brooke, "Gregorian Reform in Action: Clerical Marriage in England 1050–1200," *Cambridge Historical Journal*, XII (1956), 1–21.

54. Dr. P. Clemoes informs me that items from Ælfric's first series of *Catholic Homilies* in the main hand in C.C.C.C. 421, pp. 227–354, are textually very close to the corresponding items in Trinity College, Cambridge, MS. B. 15. 34, a manuscript probably written at Christ Church, Canterbury, since Ker (p. 132) thinks it written by the scribe of Harley 2892 (ed. R. M. Woolley, *The Canterbury Benedictional* [Henry Bradshaw Soc., 1917], and F. Wormald, *English Drawings of the Tenth and Eleventh Centuries* (London, 1952), p. 63, says that the drawing it contains resembles that in the Christ Church manuscripts Royal MS. 1 E. VII and Arundel MS. 155. There is a good chance, therefore, that C.C.C.C. 419 and 421 were written at Canterbury, except pp. 3–96 and 209–24 in C.C.C.C. 421, which were added at Exeter.

55. This is the reading in the version in the Exeter Book, f. 1ᵛ, and is preferable to that in the Bodleian MS., Auct. D. 2. 16, which inserts. *i.* before *scriftboc.*

56. It is called C by Napier, Bethurum, etc., D by Liebermann, Fehr, Jost, etc. Since the time of Wanley, it has often been assigned to Worcester, but solely on the ground of containing Wulfstan's works. L. Whitbread, "MS. C.C.C.C. 201: A Note on its Character and Provenance," *Philological Quarterly*, XXXVIII (1959), 106–12, would assign the collection of Wulfstan material to Worcester, but the manuscript to Canterbury. My account of the manuscript depends largely on that in Ker, pp. 82–90.

57. Printed by J. Zupitza in *Archiv für das Studium der neueren Sprachen und Literaturen*, LXXXIV (1890), 1–24.

58. Ed. J. Raith, *Die alt- und mittelenglischen Apollonius-Bruchstücke, mit dem Text der Historia Apollonii nach der englischen Handschriftengruppe* (Munich, 1956); P. Goolden, *The Old English Apollonius of Tyre* (Oxford, 1958).

59. Ed. F. Liebermann, *Die Heiligen Englands* (Hannover, 1889).

60. See S. J. Crawford, *The Heptateuch* (EETS, 1922), pp. 5 f., 10, 427; J. Raith, "Ælfric's Share in the Old English Pentateuch," *Review of English Studies*, N. S. III (1952), 305–14. Though the extract in C.C.C.C. 201 has lost its last portion, the original identity of this extract with that in the Otho manuscript is shown by many agreements in wording, which differ from that of the complete version of the translation of Genesis.

61. It is possible, however, that this section, which is now completely destroyed, was not an original part of the manuscript.

62. All three poems are edited by Dobbie, *The Anglo-Saxon Minor Poems*, pp. 58–70.

63. Napier XXIX. See Dobbie, p. lxxii.

64. The fact that the version of the poem in C.C.C.C. 201 is an inferior text weakens Whitbread's argument for a Canterbury origin of this manuscript on the grounds that St. Augustine's Abbey had several copies of Bede's Latin poem and hence the Old English poem may have been produced there.

65. Ed. Dobbie, pp. 70–77. See also J. M. Ure, *The Benedictine Office* (Edinburgh, 1957).

66. Napier XIX–XXII, Bethurum XIII.

67. B. Fehr, *Die Hirtenbriefe Ælfrics* (Hamburg, 1914), pp. 68–140.

68. See D. Whitelock, "Wulfstan and the Laws of Cnut," *EHR*, LXIII (1948), 433–44.

69. See B. Thorpe, *Florentii Wigorniensis Monachi Chronicon ex Chronicis*, I (London, 1848), p. 259; N. E. S. A. Hamilton, *Willelmi Malmesbiriensis Monachi de Gestis Pontificum Anglorum Libri Quinque* (London, 1870), pp. 318 f.; W. T. Mellows, *The Chronicle of Hugo Candidus* (Oxford, 1949), pp. 57 f.; W. D. Macray, *Chronicon Abbatiae Rameseiensis* (London, 1886), p. 55. The bodies of the martyred princes Ethelred and Ethelbert were claimed by Ramsey abbey to have been translated to this house in 974; this may have caused the text to spread through the Fenland abbeys, and it

would be likely also to arouse interest in York and in Worcester, since Oswald, who held both sees, was a founder of Ramsey.

70. The version in C.C.C.C. 201 knows that Cuthbert lies at Durham, not at *Ubbanford* (Norham); it adds Osthryth to the saints buried at Bardney, Lincolnshire. She is not regarded as a saint in any other record, but as she was responsible for bringing St. Oswald's remains to Bardney, whence they were later translated to Gloucester, it is possible that her memory was revered in Gloucester. Our text supplies a longer list of saints in the Old Minster, Winchester, and adds Queen Balthild at Romsey, Cwenburg at Wimborne, and Samson at Milton Abbas. It omits Amesbury, probably by accident.

71. No other part of Otho B.x was written by this scribe. Dr. Clemoes informs me that three folios of the *Catholic Homilies* survive in this manuscript, in another hand, and have two instances with *æ* out of six possible occasions.

72. C. Sisam and K. Sisam, *The Salisbury Psalter* (EETS 1959), pp. 13 f.

73. On the possibility that it comes from York, rather than the diocese of Worcester, see D. Whitelock, *The Peterborough Chronicle* (Early English Manuscripts in Facsimile, IV, Copenhagen, 1954), pp. 29–31; *idem*, with D. C. Douglas and S. I. Tucker, *The Anglo-Saxon Chronicle*: *A Revised Translation* (London, 1961), pp. xiv–xvi.

74. This question has most recently been considered by P. Gradon, "Studies in Late West-Saxon Labialization and Delabialization," *English and Medieval Studies presented to J. R. R. Tolkien* (London, 1962), pp. 63–76. Her study confirms that Devon was an area of unrounding. She concludes with a plea for more detailed investigation.

75. Middle English evidence shows that this voicing of initial *f* took place in the south and in the south-west midlands. Apart from the C scribe of C.C.C.C. 201, it is only slightly evidenced in Old English manuscripts. Even as late as the

post-Conquest entries in the Leofric Missal and on leaves of a gospel now bound up with the Exeter Book initial *f* is normally retained, though the latter entries have two examples of *u, ureode* and *Quikeuot.*

76. This was first pointed out by K. Jost, "Wulfstan und die angelsächsische Chronik," *Anglia,* XLVII (1923), 105 ff.

77. See D. Whitelock, in *EHR,* LXIII (1948), 442 f.

78. *Idem,* "Wulfstan and the so-called Laws of Edward and Guthrum," *EHR,* LVI (1941), 1–21.

79. E.g., II Cnut, 15, 15.1a, 15.3, 45.3, 46, 48, 71.3 ff.

80. In the version of V Ethelred in C.C.C.C. 201, the clause *7 gif he ladigan wille, do þæt be þæs cynges wyrgylde oððe mid þryfealdan ordale on Engla lage* is replaced by *buton he hine ladige be þam deopestan, þe witan gerædan.*

81. Among legal texts, he knew the laws of Kent, which survive only in the *Textus Roffensis,* and probably II Ethelred, which is only in the twelfth-century manuscript C.C.C.C. 383. He knew the report of the legates of 786 (Dümmler, No. 3), though no text of this has come down in Anglo-Saxon manuscripts, and a letter of Alcuin which is in none of the collections of his correspondence (see Levison, pp. 245 f.). The range of his reading shows that he had the use of an ample library. See Bethurum, p. 61.

82. *The Laws of Edward and Guthrum* are preserved only in the twelfth-century collections, C.C.C.C. 383 and the *Textus Roffensis.* Among his authentic homilies Bethurum VIII b is only in C.C.C.C. 302, which does not otherwise appear to be connected with Wulfstan, and Napier LIV (Bethurum XVIII) is complete only in Cleopatra B.xiii, an Exeter manuscript.

83. D. Bethurum, "Six Anonymous Old English Codes," *JEGP,* XLIX (1950), 449–63.

84. See Whitelock, *English Historical Documents,* pp. 434 f.

85. Ker, pp. 8–10.

86. Liebermann, *Die Gesetze der Angelsachsen,* III, pp. 220–22. There are agreements with Cnut's laws, but it is not easy to tell which was the borrower.

87. See article cited in n. 68 above.

88. Robertson, No. LXXVI.

89. Robertson, No. LXXXI.

The Strange History of Caradoc of Vannes

ROGER SHERMAN LOOMIS
Emeritus, Columbia University

IN ALL THE Arthurian cycle it would be difficult to find a narrative more bizarre and barbaric than that incorporated in the First Continuation of Chrétien's *Perceval* and often referred to as the *Livre de Caradoc*.[1]

We are told that King Caradoc of Vannes[2]—not the hero, but his putative father—married Isaive of Carhaix, a niece of Arthur's. But the new queen's paramour, the enchanter Eliavres, contrived on three successive nights to place in the king's bed, instead of the queen, a greyhound bitch, a sow, and a mare, each metamorphosed by magic into the shape of the bride. Eliavres himself took advantage of the opportunity to lie thrice with the queen and begot on her a son, who received at birth the name of his supposed father, Caradoc. Young Caradoc's first exploit was the successful passing of the so-called Beheading Test, familiar to readers of *Gawain and the Green Knight* as the major theme of the English masterpiece.[3] In fact, as Laura Hibbard Loomis[4] and others have noted, there are marked resemblances between the French and the English versions. But the Caradoc version ends quite differently, for the challenger revealed himself to the young hero as his true father, Eliavres. Young Caradoc then hastened to Vannes and told the king of the deception practiced upon him. Whereupon King Caradoc imprisoned his adulterous wife, and forced the adulterer, Eliavres, to lie successively with a bitch, a sow, and a mare, thus fitting the punishment to the crime. From these monstrous unions were born three animals, of which the boar was named Tortain[5] and the colt, Levagor or Loriagor.[6]

To avenge herself and her paramour, the queen concealed a snake in a cupboard and bade her son open it. The serpent leaped out, fastened itself on Caradoc's arm, and began gradually to suck out his life. A friend, learning of his plight, forced the treacherous queen to disclose a remedy. Caradoc, accordingly, took his place in a vat filled with vinegar. Beside it was set a vat of milk, in which stood a pure maiden who had volunteered to save Caradoc's life. When she exposed her breast above the rim of the vat, the snake released Caradoc's arm and sprang toward her. Caradoc slashed at the reptile with a sword, but, alas, cut off the maiden's nipple. The wound, however, promptly healed, and when, soon after, King Caradoc died, young Caradoc, on succeeding to the throne, married his beloved benefactress. However, his arm had shrunk and hence he was called Caradoc Briebras[7] – a cognomen meaning, of course, "Short Arm"; and his wife's breast lacked the nipple. When, after the lapse of some time, he received as a gift the golden boss of a shield endowed with marvelous curative virtues, he applied the golden boss to his wife's breast and it adhered to the flesh, replacing the missing nipple.

The last episode in the *Livre de Caradoc* is concerned with the somewhat farcical theme of the chastity-testing horn.[8] When on a visit to Arthur's court, Caradoc, because of his wife's perfect fidelity, was able, alone of all the husbands there present, to drink from the horn without spilling a drop. Fearing Guenevere's hatred, he dispatched his paragon of a spouse for safety's sake back to Vannes.

This sensational and somewhat scabrous history, particularly the portion relating to the snake, the short arm, and the golden breast, was in 1899 the subject of two articles in *Romania*, by Gaston Paris and Ferdinand Lot, respectively (XXVIII, 214–31 and 568–78). They offered different solutions to the genetic problem and the subsequent migration of this complex of adventures, but, with all due deference to their erudition, a better hypothesis may, I believe, be found. So, after the lapse of sixty-six years, let me undertake the untangling of the threads of a fascinating story.

To Paris goes the credit of first assembling all, or nearly all, the pertinent evidence. It is also to his credit that he claimed no more for his conjectures about the transmission of the story than a measure of plausibility; for, under critical examination, these conjectures prove to be mainly mistaken. He suggested Irish origin for the story of the serpent, the self-sacrificing maiden, and the golden breast, perhaps because he had previously discovered the Irish origin of the Beheading Test (*Histoire littéraire de la France*, XXX, 71–78). But there are no Irish analogues for the serpent story. Paris argued further that the tradition crossed at a remote period from Ireland to Scotland (*Romania*, XXVIII, 227), but though there are two clear Scottish analogues (of which more later), neither is recorded until the nineteenth century. There is, therefore, no evidence that anything like the story of Caradoc and his deliverance from the snake by his self-sacrificing wife-to-be existed in Ireland at any period, or in Scotland till modern times.

Paris also surmised that another branch of the tradition passed from Ireland directly to Brittany. This hypothesis was properly criticized by

Lot in his *Romania* article, but the critic offered an equally baseless proposal – namely, that the serpent story and its sequel, originating in Scotland, passed thence to Wales. But Caradoc, the protagonist, was not, as Lot asserted (p. 576), renowned in the North,[9] and it is only when we look to Wales that we find any traces of him in the early Middle Ages. A manuscript in the British Museum,[10] dated c. 1200, contains a Latin life of the historic St. Paternus, bishop and founder of the church of Llanbadarn Fawr near Aberystwyth in the first half of the sixth century. This *Vita*, according to Tatlock (*Speculum*, XIV [1939], 349), must have been composed before 1136; it celebrates Caradoc Brec[h]bras (Armstrong) as a generous benefactor of the saint.

The hero of the *Livre de Caradoc*, then, was a historic personage of Wales, and it is in Wales that we find certain elements of his legend. His wife, Tegau, was famed for her chastity. Her mantle was listed among the Thirteen Treasures of Britain:[11]

> It would not serve anyone who had violated her marriage or her virginity. For the woman who remained true to her husband it would reach to the ground, and to the one who had violated her marriage it would not reach to her lap, and for this reason there was envy against Tegau Eurvron.[12]

Though the description of the mantle is found in no manuscript antedating the sixteenth century, an English poem, *Annot and Johon*,[13] proves that even as early as the thirteenth century Tegau's reputation for truth had spread across the border to England.

The nickname or epithet attached to Caradoc's wife, Eurvron, signifies "Golden-breast," but it is doubtful whether this means that she was supposed to have a breast made of the precious metal. For *aur* in Welsh usage, as well as the word meaning "golden" in other languages, was often used metaphorically as a complimentary term.[14] In a sixteenth-century tale, *Ystoria Trystan*, Essyllt refers to her handmaid as a "golden mistress," *gordderch aur*,[15] which certainly does not mean that the maid was an image cast in gold. Presumably, then, Tegau was renowned not only for her virtue but also for her physical charms.

Not only did the Welsh Caradoc possess a paragon in his wife but a Welsh manuscript of the late twelfth century, the Black Book of Carmarthen, attests the excellence of his horse: among the three bestowed coursers of the Isle of Britain was Lluagor, the steed of Caradoc Breichbras.[16]

That this Caradoc of Welsh tradition is identical with the hero of the French *Livre de Caradoc* is obvious. The former acquired an epithet Brech-Bras and possessed a wife (nicknamed "Golden-breast") famed for her fidelity, and a horse named Lluagor. The latter, hero of the

Livre de Caradoc, acquired an epithet Briebras, possessed a wife famed for her fidelity, and had for a half-brother a horse named Levagor or Loriagor.

How did this Welsh Caradoc Brechbras become the Caradoc Briebras of Vannes? To this question Lot provided the answer in his *Romania* article of 1899. Correcting Paris's wild hypothesis that the legend had come from Ireland via Brittany to Wales, Lot showed how the legend had been transmitted from Wales to Brittany. It appears that three saints of the Dark Ages were named Paternus.[17] One was appointed Bishop of Vannes c. 465. Of him nothing more is really known, but in the Middle Ages ignorance seldom prevented the growth of a saint's legend. Today a church dedicated to St. Paternus stands in a suburb of Vannes, and there his relics were formerly venerated.[18]

The second Paternus was a historic bishop of Avranches in Normandy (562–65). The third has been mentioned above as the founder of the church of Llanbadarn Fawr. About this Welsh Paternus, as already stated, was composed a typical *Vita*, recounting his missionary labors and telling how he found a patron in King Caradoc Brec[h]bras, who made large grants of land to the church of Llanbadarn.

In this *Vita* of the Welsh Paternus Lot recognized an interpolation, composed in Brittany by a Breton author, who confused the Welsh St. Paternus with Paternus, Bishop of Vannes (*Romania*, XXVIII, 571). In this interpolation we read that Caradoc, surnamed Brec[h]bras, enlarged his dominions even beyond the borders of Britain. Coming to Letavia (that is, Armorica), Caradoc brought it under his sway. It was this Caradoc who, if we may believe the *Vita*, persuaded Paternus to leave Wales for Brittany, and it was Vannes which the saint chose for his episcopal see. At Vannes too, according to the *Vita*, Caradoc built a palace.

So much for the interpolation. Lot's comment is as follows:

> L'auteur a lu dans la Vie insulaire que Caradoc Brechbras avait fait de grandes donations à Saint Padarn et à son église. Ne sachant rien de l'histoire du Vannetais au Ve siècle et voulant à tout prix s'expliquer l'origine de l'église de Vannes dont il croyait Patern le fondateur, il a inventé de toutes pièces ce gauche roman du roi Caradoc étendant son pouvoir au delà de la Manche, sur la Letavia et la ville de Vannes, où il possède un palais. [*Romania*, XXVIII, 574]

There can be little doubt that Lot was right, and that because of a mistaken identification of the two saints who bore the name Paternus, the benefactor of the one was assumed to be the benefactor of the other, and so Caradoc Brechbras came to be regarded as a king of Vannes. This bit of pseudohistory was soon accepted as fact, and a Latin sermon on the subject of the relics of St. Paternus at Vannes refers to the palace

of Caradawc, *cognomento Brech Bras*, and to the church which
Caradawc had built at his own expense.[19]

It was not only the name of Caradoc Brechbras and his reputation
for liberality toward the clergy which were transferred to Brittany. As
we have seen, there came with him his epithet, his wife's renown for
fidelity, and the name of his horse, Lluagor. There were other traditions,
hundreds of them, which are known to have crossed the Channel from
Wales to Brittany, among them the tale of Twrch Trwyth, the boar son
of a prince, whose ravages are narrated in *Culhwch and Olwen*, and who
is recognizable in the *Livre de Caradoc* as the boar Tortain, son of
Eliavres (*Romania*, XXVIII, 217, 578). All these Welsh tales about
Caradoc were evidently adopted by the people of Vannes as a part of their
earliest local history; and coming to the attention of the professional
conteurs excited their imagination and their ingenuity.

How much of the scabrous tale about the begetting of the three
animals by the enchanter Eliavres rests on an earlier Welsh tradition,
how much was invention, it seems impossible to say. But the episodes
connected with the serpent seem to be a deliberate invention, demanded
by the curiosity of French audiences. The *conteurs* who exploited these
traditions for profit were mainly bilingual; and so presumably were most
of their patrons, the aristocracy. But as years passed, fewer understood
or spoke Breton. *Brechbras* became a meaningless epithet. Could it not
have been *Briebras*, French words meaning "short arm"?[20] This is the
substitution we find in Chrétien's *Erec*, where Caradoc is mentioned
among the knights of the Round Table (ed. W. Foerster, vs. 1719). Once
Briebras came into vogue in place of *Brechbras*, questions arose. Why
did Caradoc have a short arm? Likewise, the epithet of Caradoc's wife,
translated into French and interpreted literally as "Golden-breast,"
called for an explanation. How did she come to have a breast of gold?

Faced with the problem of accounting for Caradoc's short arm and
his wife's golden breast, a Breton storyteller, we may assume, drew on
his imagination and invented the tale of Caradoc's vengeful mother, the
snake, the vats of vinegar and milk, the self-sacrificing maiden, and
the golden boss which took the place of her nipple. Thus ingeniously the
descriptive epithets of Caradoc and his wife were explained, and the
narrative was thus neatly adapted to the tradition that Caradoc's wife
was a nonpareil of connubial devotion.

This entertaining tale passed, as we know, into the *Livre de Caradoc*,
and was incorporated in the compilation which formed the First Continuation of Chrétien's *Perceval*. The same tale appears in a late Breton
life of St. Budoc.[21] Here it is the saint's mother who displayed her filial
piety by releasing her father from a serpent which had fastened itself
on his arm, and it was God who rewarded her sacrifice by giving her a
golden breast. This borrowing of the serpent story and its sequel by the

author of the *Life of St. Budoc* seems to show that it continued to enjoy a vogue in Brittany for some time.

But what is one to make of the fact that a tale tied, as we have seen, to Vannes and originating in the attempt to explain the epithet *Briebras* to French auditors, turns up in nineteenth-century Scotland, first as the conclusion to a ballad entitled the *Queen of Scotland* and localized at Edinburgh,[22] and secondly in the repertoire of a Gaelic-speaking tinker (*Romania*, XXVIII, 219 f.)? It was doubtless this fact (first pointed out by the American scholar Carrie Harper, see *MLN*, XIII [1898], 417 ff.) which led Lot to postulate a Scottish legend of Caradoc Vreichvras and the serpent anteceding the Welsh and Breton traditions of the same hero. But there is no reason to believe that our Caradoc was ever a Scottish hero, and the explanation of his short arm by the story of the snake could only have been devised after he had come to be known to the French as *Briebras*.

How account for the transference of the serpent story with its sequel concerning the golden breast to Scotland from Brittany? The answer is not difficult. Though few Arthurian scholars have recognized the fact, there is ample evidence that Breton *conteurs* were welcomed in southern Scotland as early as the reign of David I, who ascended the throne in 1124.[23] We possess three Breton *lais*: *Doon*, *Desiré*, and *Gurun* (the last preserved in Norse translation), which evince some knowledge of Scottish geography. We have testimony that *histriones* were telling stories of Ewen, son of Urien, in twelfth-century Scotland.[24] This Ewen is, of course, identical with Chrétien's Ivain, son of Urien, who married the daughter of Duke Laudunet, that is, Lothian.[25] In fact, the ballad of the *Queen of Scotland* furnishes its own proof that it was derived from Arthurian traditions of the twelfth century. It not only concludes, as scholars seem to agree, with what is substantially the tale of Caradoc and the serpent (though the name of the hero has been changed) but it also opens with an incident drawn from sources close to the Vulgate cycle.[26] The queen of Scotland had a painted chamber in Edinburgh castle. It was the scene of a vain attempt on her part to seduce the young hero. Turning to the Prose *Lancelot* we read that Queen Morgain la Fée vainly attempted to seduce young Lancelot in her castle.[27] In the *Mort Artu* we learn that her castle, the scene of her attempt, was not far from Edinburgh and was adorned with mural paintings.[28]

We are justified, then, in concluding that the two Scottish analogues to the story of Caradoc and the serpent were not indigenous to Scotland and do not represent the sources of the French romance. They are, on the contrary, the late survivors of a Breton tradition transmitted to Scotland in the twelfth or thirteenth century by the French-speaking *conteurs*.

Is it necessary to stress the important part which misinterpretation and mistaken ingenuity have played in the development of this legend of Caradoc, his shrunken arm, and his wife's golden breast? At any rate, it is surely relevant to recall that precisely the same factors, misinterpretation and mistaken ingenuity, best account for the sanctification of the originally heathen Grail legends, for the conversion of Bran's drinking horn, which provided the drink and the food one desired, into the Corpus Christi, the Body of Christ.[29]

To summarize: The strange history of Caradoc of Vannes had its origin not in Ireland or Scotland but in Wales. There in the sixth century flourished a chief Caradoc, surnamed Brechbras, "Arm-strong." He was a benefactor of St. Padarn or Paternus. His wife Tegau came to be renowned as a model of fidelity, and also, it would seem, for the beauty of her figure; hence her nickname, meaning "Golden-breast." Because of a confusion between St. Padarn of Wales and St. Paternus of Vannes, the Bretons adopted Caradoc as the traditional benefactor of their own saint, hence, as a former ruler of Vannes. The French *Livre de Caradoc* retains certain Welsh elements, such as a corrupt form of the name Lluagor, which belonged to Caradoc's horse; a French misinterpretation of the surname Brechbras as meaning "Short-arm"; the concept of Caradoc's wife as a nonpareil of fidelity. The tale of the serpent represents an ingenious attempt to combine this last tradition with incidents explaining why Caradoc was called Briebras, and how his wife came to have a golden breast. This combination could hardly have crystallized before the twelfth century; and either in the same or the next century Breton *conteurs* transmitted it, along with other stories of the Arthurian cycle, to Scotland. There as an oral tradition it lingered on into the nineteenth century in both Gaelic and English forms.

NOTES

1. It is found in all three versions, ed. W. Roach (Philadelphia, 1949–55). The following résumé is based on MS. L (Brit. Mus. Add. 36, 614), which seems closest to the original. See Roach's edition, III: 1, 130–204. Professor Hélaine Newstead most obligingly read an earlier version of this paper as my proxy at the Vannes Congress in 1960.

2. Some MSS. substitute *Nantes* for *Vannes*.

3. See G. L. Kittredge's *A Study of Gawain and the Green Knight* (Cambridge, Mass., 1916).

4. *Arthurian Literature in the Middle Ages*, ed. R. S. Loomis (Oxford, 1959), p. 531.

5. This form occurs in MSS. T, V, D of the Long Version and MS. E of the Mixed Version.

6. These are the forms given respectively by MS. L and the printed text of 1516. Variants include *Lorigal*, *Loriagort*, and *Lorzagor*.

7. Other forms of the epithet are given by Gaston Paris in *Romania*, XXVIII (1900), 222 f.

8. On the horn test, see T. P. Cross in *MP*, X (1913), 289–99; O. Warnatsch, *Der Mantel* (Breslau, 1883); *Speculum*, IX (1934), 38–50.

9. A Caradoc, to be sure, is mentioned several times in the *Gododdin*, a lament (composed c. 600) for the warriors of British stock who fell in

the Battle of Cattraeth. But Caradoc was a fairly common name among Britons, and there is no reason to identify the northern Caradoc with Caradoc Breich Bras.

10. Vespasian A. xiv; ed. A. W. Wade-Evans in *Vitae Sanctorum Britanniae et Genealogiae* (Cardiff, 1944). See *Studies in the Early British Church*, ed. N. K. Chadwick (Cambridge, 1958), pp. 157–59, 183–200.

11. See R. S. Loomis, *Wales and the Arthurian Legend* (Cardiff, 1956), pp. 158–61, and Rachel Bromwich, *Trioedd Ynys Prydein* (Cardiff, 1961), pp. cxxx–cxxxv, 240–49.

12. Trans. F. N. Robinson in *Lyrics of the Thirteenth Century*, ed. Carleton Brown (Oxford, 1933), p. 226.

13. Robinson, p. 138.

14. D. Silvan Evans, *Geiriadur Cymraeg*, i, 409: "As a prefix in composition, *aur* signifies (a) *gold, golden*; and (b) *precious* as *gold . . . splendid, brilliant, illustrious.*"

15. T. P. Cross, "A Welsh Tristan Episode," *Studies in Philology*, xvii (1920), 97, 106.

16. Bromwich, pp. ciii–civ, cvi, 97 f. In the Black Book, *Breichbras*, not spelled out, is implied by initial B.

17. S. Baring-Gould and J. Fisher, *Lives of the British Saints* (London, 1907), iv, p. 43.

18. G. H. Doble, *Saint Patern* (Long Compton, 1940), p. 31.

19. A. le Moyne de La Borderie, *Histoire de Bretagne* (Rennes-Paris, 1896), i, p. 307 n.

20. In *Rev. Celt.*, xiii (1892), 494, J. Loth maintained that Fr. *Briebras* could have arisen only as the result of misunderstanding a written, not an oral, version of the legend, since in Wales the cognomen *Breichbras* had long ceased to be pronounced as such, mutation having substituted *v* for *b*. H. Zimmer, the Celtist, though admitting that this is true if the misinterpretation took place in Basse-Bretagne in the twelfth century, argued that in Haute-Bretagne the mutation must have occurred after the story of Caradoc Brech Bras had been transmitted to the French; see Chrétien's *Karrenritter*, ed. W. Foerster (Halle, 1899), p. cxxiv.

21. G. H. Doble, *Saint Budoc*, 2d ed. (Long Compton, 1937), pp. 1, 2; Baring-Gould and Fisher, iv, p. 331.

22. F. J. Child, *English and Scottish Popular Ballads* (Boston, 1883–98; repr. New York, 1956), v, pp. 176–78. First published by P. Buchan, *Ancient Ballads and Songs of the North of Scotland* (Edinburgh, 1828), i, pp. 46–49.

23. R. S. Loomis, *Arthurian Tradition and Chrétien de Troyes* (New York, 1949), pp. 17, 109–14, 272, 301–305.

24. *Studies in the Early British Church*, ed. N. K. Chadwick, pp. 281–84.

25. Loomis, *Arthurian Tradition*, pp. 302 f.

26. *Proceedings of the Society of Antiquaries of Scotland*, 1955–56, pp. 9 f.

27. H. O. Sommer, *Vulgate Version of the Arthurian Romances* (Washington, 1909–13), iv, pp. 123–28; v, pp. 91–93, 215–18.

28. *Ibid.*, vi, 234–35.

29. Loomis, *Arthurian Tradition*, pp. 170–75; *The Grail, From Celtic Myth to Christian Symbol* (Cardiff-New York, 1963), pp. 25 f., 59–61.

Welsh *chwarddaf, chwerthin,* and *gwên*

E. P. HAMP
University of Chicago

> *. . . it was a good sort of beer, a drink good for the righteous.*
> *It set women to laughing, put men in a good humor,*
> *the righteous to making merry, fools to joking.*
> · · · · ·
> *The women all wreathed in smiles, the men in good spirits listened,*
> *kept marveling at Frank's flow of song which was a*
> *miracle to the listener,*
> *a marvel to those present, and no wonder.*
> —*With apologies to* Kalevala 20:418 *ff.,* 21:370 *ff.*

J. VENDRYES has given us a penetrating study of the words for "laugh" in Celtic.[1] The only respect in which his treatment, so far as it goes, is superseded, to my knowledge, is in the matter of standard references which have since appeared. Thus, for example, the attestation of the Old Irish verb *tibid,* which we might gloss "break with a crashing sound," is now conveniently assembled in the relevant fascicule of the *Contributions* to the *Royal Irish Academy Dictionary.* As a result of his study, the background of the phrase *tibid gen* is tolerably clear. But although he makes a good case for a similar structure in the phrase *chwerthin gwen,* the precise background of all the Welsh elements is left somewhat unclear. I believe it is possible to go on to remove a large part of the ambiguity.

Vendryes (40) and others have correctly seen that *chwerthin* and *chwarddaf* are two separate formations. But I think one can show that they are even less related than has generally been implied. For example, Pokorny in his new *Indogermanisches etymologisches Wörterbuch* (Bern, 1948) (1040) lists under **suard-* 'lachen' (?) (Pokorny's praiseworthy question mark) σαρδάνιος, σαρδίζειν, and then "cymr. *chwarddu,* corn. *hwerthin,* mbret. *huersin*"; under 2 **suer-* 'surren u.dgl.' (1049) we find only *chwyrnu* 'brummen' from Welsh.

The role of *chwerthin* has been to serve as a noun, or verbal noun:

ny chwardaf y chwerthin (Canu Aneurin 12.9–10); *Sef a wnaeth
hitheu chwerthin (White Book Mabinogi* 97. 12–13). Let us then start
by positing this as a noun parallel to *gwên* and meaning something like
"laugh" in Proto-British. It is hard to be precise about its etymology, but
it is perhaps not so ambiguous as Vendryes (40) has it. On principle, I
think it unlikely that any Welsh *chw-* can go back to **sk-*; therefore
*sqer(d)-, OHG *scern*, cannot be considered. One could argue for **skʷ-*
or **skw-*, but I think that neither necessary nor likely here, and we need
not delay by pursuing the question. The base **swer-/swor-* mentioned
by Vendryes seems eminently fitting, as such things go, and we may
compare Skt *svárati* (IEW 1049). The suffix could well be what Lewis
and Pedersen in *A Concise Comparative Celtic Grammar* (Göttingen,
1937) (314) write **-tijen-* (I should reconstruct **-tiXn-*, with a laryngeal,
in the case at hand), and the earlier, perhaps pre-Celtic, meaning would
have been "a (re)sounding, roaring" or the like.

When we come to *chwarddaf* the case is much different. First, we
note the valuable form in the Juvencus englyn *guardam*/gwarðaṽ/. As
Vendryes remarks (41), the alternation *gw-~chw-* may be purely orthographic, though it is surely not in this word. As he remarks too, *gwarae
~chwarae* is more than orthographic, but I cannot agree that this is an
analogy on the "laugh" words. Vendryes accepts Pedersen's etymology
*worigo- for *gwarae* (that is, **worigami>gwaryaf*; H. Pedersen,
Vergleichende Grammatik der keltischen Sprachen [Göttingen, 1909–
1913, I. 434); however the reconstruction may be, considering the
troubles encountered in **VgV* sequences (see K. Jackson, *Language and
History in Early Britian*, pp. 440–60, 469–70, and *Bulletin of the
Board of Celtic Studies* (1956) 16.277–79, the comparison with Irish
fuirech, fo-rig- seems to me less than likely. If we place *chwarae~
gwarae* beside *chwith~gwith, mor guanauc BA* 36, 9*~chwannog* (I.
Williams, *BBCS* 6.107) and *damwain~damchwain*, we have what
appears to be a continuation of the IE alternation **w-~*sw-*, an alternation whose status is well established. Moreover, the survival of this
alternation in Celtic is paralleled in **st~*t (sefyll : tá-)*. We then have
no need of *chwarddaf* as a model for a supposed analogy.

It is possible, too, to view *chwarddaf~guardam* in the same framework as the survival of an old alternation, but I think another view
preferable once we put the forms in the context that Vendryes has un-
folded for us. The fixed phrase *tibim gen*, in its alternate Welsh forms
chwarddaf gwên or *chwarddaf chwerthin*, shows considerable alliteration, even apart from metrical uses such as *am gwymp hen chwerdit
gwen gwas*.[2] If the original form was simply *gwarddaf chwerthin* (or,
more precisely, its ancestor phrase) we may see how the by-form in
chw- was generated.

The *-dd-* is of course ambiguous; Lewis and Pedersen (314) take it to be *-j-, and that seems as reasonable as is possible in the face of such uncertainties. Therefore, we have *worjami, or *worijami (see Hamp, *Evidence for Laryngeals* [Austin, Texas, 1960], p. 208), which in the formula *tibim gen* should mean something like "emit (a laugh)" or "sound forth (a laugh)." Among all the possibilities for an etymology, the likeliest seems to be *(s)wer->Lith. sveriù, Welsh chwaru, Cornish wharfos.³ The phrase would then have been "let fall, let go a laugh." In any event, *worðaũ hwerθin⁴ was not a cognate accusative, and the first word was not "laugh."

Once we note the alliterative shape of this phrase, we can approach a further problem. There is a notorious list of words showing Welsh gw-: Irish g-; the main offenders are given by Lewis and Pedersen (§§34.3 and 38). Osthoff's equation (except for suffix and ablaut) of gweddi with Irish foigde (feminine ia-stem) and Thurneysen's of gwayw with Irish foga (accusative plural fogau), accepted by Jackson LHEB, 357, are highly convincing. Perhaps we may add yet another to this class of explanation: Against Cornish gwels Welsh gwellt,⁵ Breton is clearly inconsistent on this point. There is not only the OBret. gueltiocion and Ouessant guelt, as usually listed,⁵ᵃ but at the other end of the speech area we find in the *Atlas* (map 221) at point 75 in eastern Vannetais, gẅiyóẅ. Thus, Breton has well distributed and clear traces of both *gelt and *(g)welt. Since the OBret. form precludes simple syllabic loss in an earlier *wogelt-, we may suppose a cross of this latter with *gelt- to produce *welt-. And the direct cognate of the supposed compound formation is actually attested in Irish fogelt (feminine), fo·geil 'grazes.'⁶ Thus there is probably no need to look, with Pedersen and Lewis, for an analogy on gwair.⁷ When we come to gwên : Irish gen, a similar explanation seems not to be forthcoming. But now, taking the alliterative phrase structure into consideration, a new avenue is open. We may presume, since in Cornish and Breton wh and c'hw have won out, that the alliterative adjustment to hw- . . . hw- was early; it could even have occurred before the nonlenited *sw- was totally eliminated in favor of *hw-. Similarly then, when we consider that British initial /w/ must early have had an allophone [γʷu̯], and when we recall the frequent lenition of the direct object, an earlier sequence of *worjami and *gen- could easily have developed as *worðaũ en, i.e. [γʷu̯orðaũ γen], > *worðaũ wen, i.e. [γʷu̯orðaũ γʷu̯en], the delinited equivalent of [γʷu̯orðaũ u̯en].

In summary, when we take into consideration the structure of the idiom *tibid gen*, it seems likely that chwerthin is an old noun of the form *swer-tiXn-, that chwarddaf is an old verb of the possible shape *wor(i)jami not meaning "laugh," and that gwên is an alliteratively reshaped descendant of *gen-, and thus an unexciting direct cognate of Irish gen.

NOTES

1. *Études celtiques*, III (1938), 3.38–45.
2. Jackson, *Early Welsh Gnomic Poetry* (1935), p. 28 (v. 7. 3).
3. See H. Lewis, *BBCS*, IV (1928), 136–37, and XIII (1949), 72–73, where J. E. C. Williams specifically discusses forms representing **wer-* beside **swer-*. Lewis, *BBCS*, XVI (1952), 285–86, has attempted to relate *tywallt* to *hollti* as reflexes of *gw*: *chw*. I intend to deal with *hollti* elsewhere, but if this alternation were true here, then *hollti* would have to reflect **sw-*, which I doubt.
4. *LHEB*, 526.
5. But beside this, Lewis has interestingly suggested (*BBCS*, VIII [1936], 229) that in the name *Buallt*, earlier *Buellt* (variant *Buell* in the Book of Llandaf), we have **bow-gelt-*, originally "cow-pasture." If so, this would confirm the variation within Welsh. There is, however, a further problem not dealt with by Lewis, namely, the age and precise constitution of this compound. If the compound were common British we might reasonably expect **beuellt* < **bowo-gelt-* on the lines of *beudy*, OBret. *boutig*, which is precisely what seems to underlie *Bouelt*/*Pouelt* the name of the *Polden Hills*, in Somerset (on which see A. G. C. Turner, *BBCS*, XIV [1951], 117). It is of course possible, but scarcely likely, that this compound would be chronologically on a par with *bugail*; in light of βουκόλος, Mycenaean *quokoro*, this last goes back to IE. **gʷōwkolós*. On the other hand, we could have a late compound of *bu* + *gelt*, dating from late British times. I see too that Loth (*Revue celtique*, LI [1943], 17) has also reconstructed **Bou-gelt* for this, with no further elucidation of the vocalism. But at least the consonantism seems agreed. This argument remains unaffected by the existence, even if true, of the semantically unlikely compound *aeth-wellt* '*after-grass' > 'aftermath,' alleged by R. A. Fowkes, *Lingua Posnaniensis*, VI (1957), 91–92.
5a. See most recently L. Fleuroit, *Dictionnaire des Gloses en Vieux breton* (Paris, 1964), s.v. (*guelt*), pp. 187–88.
6. The weakness in sense of Celtic **wo-* is easily illustrated by Irish *guin* : *foguin* 'wounding.' I have dealt with this and allied questions at some length in a paper for the 2nd International Congress of Celtic Studies, 1963, to be published elsewhere.
7. But a derivation from, or cross with (via *gwallt*), the base **wel(X)-* (see *IEW*, 1139) is still not ruled out, though I think it less than likely.

Havelok and Anlaf Cuaran

CHARLES W. DUNN
Harvard University

IN THE COPIOUS scholarship devoted to the Middle English romance of *Havelok the Dane* and its related versions,[1] attention has often been drawn to G. Storm's identification[2] of the hero with Anlaf Cuaran Sihtricson[3] (a Dane who became king of York in 941, spent most of his life in Dublin, and died in 981). Professor Magoun has always been a sympathetic but exacting critic of arguments of this sort, and it therefore seems appropriate in the present volume to attempt a clarification of the numerous unresolved difficulties raised by Storm's hypothesis.

In summary, Storm reasoned as follows. The wandering Viking king was variously called "Olaf" in Norse, "Anlaf" in English, "Amlaib" in Irish, and "Abloyc" in Welsh; and these names are virtually identical with the name "Havelok." Also, Anlaf's nickname was "Cuaran," and Havelok's alternate name was "Cuaran," according to the Anglo-Norman versions of the legend. Therefore, the name and the story of Havelok (alias Cuaran) are derived from the career of Anlaf. (Curiously, the same argument had been advanced earlier by K. Køster in a little-known work entitled *Sagnet om Havelok Danske*,[4] but it evidently did not attract Storm's attention any more than it achieved later recognition.)

Storm did not, however, make clear whether the name "Havelok" was etymologically related to the counterparts which he adduced or was merely similar to them. This question raises a number of perplexing side issues, but it can be answered satisfactorily. The second question, as to why Havelok bears the alternate name of Cuaran, cannot be answered with equal certainty, but recent research (particularly that of Alexander Bell) into the chronology of the various versions of the Havelok legend provides guidance unavailable to Storm.

The dates of appearance and the forms of the two names are as follows. In Gaimar's Anglo-Norman *Estoire des Engles*, composed c. 1135–40, we find (*Reis*) *Havelocs* (nom.), *Haveloc, Aveloc*; and, as the hero's alternate name: *Cuarans* (nom.), *Cuaran, Cuheran, Cuarant, Cuherant, Cuharant*. In the Anglo-Norman *Lai d'Haveloc*, composed c.

1200, we find *Haveloc, Aveloc; Cuaran, Coaran, Curan, Cuarant, Coarant*.[5] In the anonymous Middle English *Lambeth Interpolation*, composed after 1338 as an addition to Robert Mannyng's *Story of England*, we find *Hauelok* and *Coraunt*.[6] In the anonymous French *List of Lays*, compiled in the thirteenth century, we find *Rey Haueloch* recorded as a title (without, of course, mention of any other name).[7]

In what may be called the native English folk tradition in contradistinction to Gaimar's Anglo-Norman antiquarian tradition, the alternate name Cuaran seems to be unknown. The Middle English romance *Havelok*, which in its extant form represents a version recorded c. 1280, has only *Hauelok* and *Haueloc*.[8] The Grimsby town seal, cut before 1272, has *Habloc* or possibly *Hauloc*.[9] Robert Mannyng in his uninterpolated *Story of England*, composed in Middle English in 1338, has *Hauelok*.[10]

As a first step in clarifying Storm's hypothesis, it can be definitely proved that the name "Havelok" is not related etymologically to the Old English name "Anlaf" or its Norse counterpart "Olaf." "Olaf," according to the most convincing etymology,[11] is derived from Primitive Norse **anu-laibaR* 'successor of the ancestor.' The Old English "Anlaf" was presumably adopted from this Norse original at a time after the unstressed *u* in the prefix *anu-* had been lost but before the resulting *an-* had, as is usual in the development of Old Norse, become *ǭ-*. (In the time of the historical Anlaf Cuaran in the tenth century, doubtlessly the bilingual residents within the area of Viking settlement in England would still have recognized the identity of the two divergent forms.)

The corresponding Old Irish "Amlaib," pronounced [ã:laiv] (later spelled "Amhlaibh"), must have been adopted from the same Norse source **anu-laibaR* during the Viking invasions of Ireland at a time when the prefix *anu-* had been reduced to an open vowel which still retained nasal coloring. (The *m* in "Amlaib" has orthographic rather than etymological significance.)

Unlike the Norse, English, and Irish forms which we have just discussed, the Welsh name "Abloyc" does at least have some superficial resemblance to "Havelok," but a closer scrutiny of its history proves that even it cannot serve as an etymological link. The Latin *Annales Cambriae*[12] and the Welsh *Brut y Tywysogyon*[13] happen to apply the name "Abloyc" to a Norse-Irish king Amlaib (Olaf Godfreyson,[14] who died in 941), but the chroniclers were merely providing a native Welsh substitute for a similar but unrelated foreign name.

The origin of the name "Abloyc," pronounced [avloig], is obscure. According to the *Old Welsh Genealogies*, Cunedda Wledig (fl. A.D. 450), the traditional founder of the north Welsh kingdoms, had a son named Abloyc. One manuscript of the *Genealogies* refers to him as "Abloyc map Cuneda" and another, more specifically, as "Afloch yn Aphlocyawn map Cuneda Wledic" (Afloeg in Aflogion, the son of Cunedda the

Leader).[15] The etymology of the name is thus closely connected with that of the commot Aflogion in the Lleyn peninsula. Most of Cunedda's offspring bear eponymous names (such as "Ceredig of Ceredigion"),[16] but in "Abloyc's" case it is impossible to decide whether the personal name gave rise to the place name or was derived from it. For our purpose, however, its early and intimate connection with a Welsh place name is sufficient to indicate that "Abloyc," unlike "Amlaib," cannot be derived from the Norse Viking name.

What then is the etymology of the name "Havelok"? P. H. Reaney's *Dictionary of British Surnames*[17] reveals the fact that the name was in use in England, altogether apart from the romance tradition, as early as about 1210, when it appears in the *Book of Fees* for Cornwall. Reaney, who is apparently the only authority to commit himself to an opinion in the matter, suggests that the name is derived from Old Norse *haf-leikr* 'sea-sport.' (His *Dictionary* has "sea-port," but this is clearly a misprint.) This compound is a plausible Norse name, even though it does not happen to be listed in any of the obvious collections of Scandinavian names: but there is a phonetic objection. The Old English counterpart would be *haef-lāc*, and the Middle English derivate would consequently be the disyllabic *havlok*. Yet in all the occurrences of the name listed above (except the Grimsby seal), "Havelok" is unquestionably trisyllabic, just as it still is in Modern English.

A more likely explanation is that the name is a native English noun compounded of the two elements: Old English *hafa* (Middle English *have*) 'possession,' and Old English *lāc* (Middle English *lok*) 'gift.' The compound *have-lok*, which would mean "a gift or offering from one's possessions," is unrecorded in Old and Middle English as a common noun. However, the adjectival compound *haveles* 'possessionless,' based on the first element, is of frequent occurrence; and the Old English compound noun *aelmes-lāc* 'alms-offering,' based on the second element, illustrates an exact semantic parallel to the hypothetical *have-lok*. In one of the late *Old English Homilies*, moreover, the two elements occur in such close conceptual relationship as to make the coinage of the compound seem entirely predictable:

> Man hoh . . . , of þan þe god him haueð lend, *loc* to chirche bringen and wurðin þermide godes bord alse his *haue* beð.[18]
> (One should . . . bring to church a *gift* from that which God has lent him and honor God's table with it in porportion to what his *possession* is.)

There seem to be no phonetic objections to this proposed etymology. The modern English pronunciation of "Havelok" corroborates the three syllables; the first stressed vowel -*a*- has remained short, as is to be expected in a trisyllabic word; the unstressed second vowel -*e*- survives as a schwa vowel; and the final long vowel -o- has predictably become short because it has only a secondary stress in the compound.

Havelok's name, then, is entirely unrelated to any form of the name "Anlaf"; but we must still explain the coincidence that, both in Gaimar and in the *Lai*, the legendary hero bears the same unusual name, "Cuaran," that had once been conferred upon Anlaf Sihtricson. There can be little doubt about the source of the name. The word *cuaran*, still familiar in modern dialects of Irish and Scottish Gaelic, means "a covering for the foot and lower leg, legging," etc. The name must have been given to Anlaf in Ireland to differentiate him from numerous other Vikings bearing the same first name, just as his father Sihtric Caoch had been given an Irish cognomen (*caoch* 'squint-eyed' or 'blind'). Presumably "Cuaran" referred to the distinctively Norse style of his leggings.

A simple explanation for the transfer of the nickname to Havelok can be supplied by the following conjectural sequence. The legend of Havelok the Dane evolved in Lincolnshire among people familiar with the Viking settlements. Some storyteller with an antiquarian turn of mind thought he would add a touch of verisimilitude by attaching to the hero a nickname made famous by Anlaf Cuaran. Gaimar learned of the legend of Havelok when he made his journey to Lincolnshire in the retinue of Ralf and Custance Fitz Gilbert, but, as an outsider to the locality, he did not understand the association of the name "Cuaran." He had already referred to Anlaf in his *History* (l. 3544), but he had called him "Anlaf Quiran," following the form of the name, "Cwiran," which appears in the *Old English Annals* (E, A.D. 849). It probably never occurred to him, therefore, that the name "Cuaran," which his informants gave him as an alternate name for Havelok, was the same as the "Cwiran" which he had seen in the *Annals*.

Appreciating the narrative value of the Havelok story, Gaimar arbitrarily used it to fill out his account of the obscure period in the sixth century following the death of King Arthur. Not knowing what to do with the hero's extra name, he adopted a somewhat awkward expedient. Havelok as an unknown Danish refugee is called "Cuaran" by the people in England who are unaware of his origin (ll. 100 ff.) but still goes by the name of "Havelok" within the family circle of his protector Grim (ll. 339 ff.).

The author of the Anglo-Norman *Lai*, ignorant of the reason for this discrepancy, provided an ingenious motivation for it. Inspired by Marie de France, whose Breton lays he was imitating, he boldly invented an etymology for the redundant name. "Cuaran," he asserts, is the name "which the Bretons apply to a scullion." His invention is transparent. There is no record of any word in Breton remotely like *cuaran*. The Modern Breton term for "scullion" is *paotr-kegin* (kitchen boy); and the

French word *quistrun* (from Late Latin *(co)quistro-n-*) used by the poet for "scullion" could not possibly have been converted into anything like *cuaran* even if, by chance, it had been borrowed into Breton.

The English popular tradition, understandably, shows little interest in the extra name. The composer of the Middle English *Havelok*, unlike Gaimar, was more fascinated by the dramatic, human qualities of the legend than by its antiquarian value. If he knew anything of the name "Cuaran," he did not see fit to mention it. When Mannyng tried to discover the native English oral tradition concerning Havelok, he apparently found no mention of the name "Cuaran." Mannyng's later interpolator does, it is true, tell us that Havelok, while serving as *quistron* (scullion), was called "Coraunt," but the very spelling of the name suggests that he had compiled his information from the Anglo-Norman *Lai*. Similarly, the anonymous translator who compiled the Middle English prose *Brut* at some time after 1377 refers to "Curan," but he gives this as the name of the son of "Hauelock."[19] Obviously he is a confused redactor of misunderstood information and not an authority on the living English tradition.

A final question still remains unexamined. Despite the severe limitations which must evidently be imposed upon Storm's thesis, is it not possible that the *career* of the historical Anlaf Cuaran gave rise to the *legend* of the fictitious Havelok? There seems to be no need, however, to re-examine the numerous proposals and counterproposals in this much-debated matter. Skeat summarized the outcome trenchantly when he wrote: "If these divergent views point to any result, it is that the *Havelok* story corresponds to no history at all."[20] In short, then, Havelok owes Anlaf Cuaran nothing except perhaps the temporary loan of a nickname.

NOTES

1. I have limited note references to a minimum because I have prepared an exhaustive bibliography of *Havelok* for the first fascicule of the revised edition of J. E. Wells' *Manual of the Writings in Middle English*, which is now at the press.
2. "Havelok the Dane and the Norse king Olaf Kuaran," *Forhandlinger i Videnskabs-Selskabet i Christiania*, Aar 1879, no. 10; repr. *Englische Studien*, III (1879–80), 533 ff.
3. *DNB*, s.v. "Olaf Sictricson"; *Handbook of British Chronology*, edd. Sir

F. M. Powicke and E. B. Fryde (London: Royal Historical Society, 1961), p. 27.
4. (Copenhagen, 1868), pp. 77–79.
5. The variant spellings in Gaimar and the *Lai* have been compiled from the following editions: *Lestorie des Engles*, edd. Sir T. D. Hardy and C. T. Martin (London: Rolls Series 91, 1888–89), I, i ff. (Gaimar); 1,290 ff. (*Lai*); *Le Lai d'Haveloc and Gaimar's Haveloc Episode*, ed. A. Bell [Publications of the Univ. of Manchester, French Series 4] (Man-

chester, 1925); and Geffrei Gaimar, *L'Estoire des Engleis*, ed. A. Bell [Anglo-Norman Texts 14–16] (Oxford, 1960). Bell is the authority on the dating.

6. As printed in *Havelok the Dane*, ed. W. W. Skeat, rev. K. Sisam (Oxford, 1915), pp. xvii–xix.

7. G. E. Brereton, "Thirteenth Century List of French Lays," *MLR*, XLV (1950), 41, 42 (no. 20).

8. *Havelok*, ed. Skeat.

9. *Havelok*, ed. Skeat, photographic frontispiece. The inscription has always been transcribed as HABLOC, but the reading HAULOC is a possibility, for the letter in question looks very like the U in COM̄UNITATIS. Since V is elsewhere used for U (SIGILLVM, GOLDEBVRGH), U may here, conversely, have been used for V. Despite the vigor of the design, the seal cutter was not a very consistent draftsman (he uses two distinct types of capitals for M and for T).

10. *Havelok*, ed. Skeat, p. xvi.

11. J. de Vries, *Altnordisches etymologisches Wörterbuch* (Leiden, 1961), p. 418. A. Johannesson, *Isländisches etymologisches Wörterbuch*

(Bern, 1956), pp. 24, 738, provides a different analysis of the name.

12. Ed. J. W. ab Ithel (London: Rolls Series 20, 1860), p. 17 (s.a. A.D. 942).

13. *Brut y Tywysogyon: Peniarth MS. 20*, ed. T. Jones (Cardiff, 1941), p. 8; *idem*, trans. T. Jones (Cardiff, 1952), p. 7; *Brut y Tywysogyon: Red Book of Hergest Version* (Cardiff, 1955), ed. and trans. T. Jones, pp. 12, 13.

14. *DNB*, s.v. "Olaf Godfreyson."

15. A. Anscombe, "Indexes to Old-Welsh Genealogies," *Archiv für celtische Lexicographie*, I (1900), 191; III (1907), 63. See also E. Phillimore, "The Annales Cambriae and the Genealogies," *Cymmrodor*, IX (1888), 183.

16. J. E. Lloyd, *History of Wales* (London, 1911), I, 117, and his article, "Cunedda Wledig," *Dictionary of Welsh Biography* (London, 1959), pp. 87–88.

17. (London, 1958), p. 157.

18. *Old English Homilies, Series II*, ed. R. Morris [EETS LIII] (London, 1873), p. 217.

19. *The Brut*, ed. F. W. D. Brie [EETS 131, 136] (London, 1906–1908), p. 92.

20. *Havelok*, ed. Skeat, p. xxvi.

Chaucer's *Manciple's Tale*, LINES 311-13

TAUNO F. MUSTANOJA

University of Helsinki

THE MORALIZING comments at the end of Chaucer's *Manciple's Tale* have received some attention from Chaucer scholars, and several attempts have been made to discover sources for them. A good idea of the present state of research can be obtained from the notes to F. N. Robinson's edition.[1] E. Koeppel believed that Chaucer took many of them from the Latin treatise *De Arte Loquendi et Tacendi* by Albertano da Brescia.[2] His opinion has not been shared by other scholars, and D. S. Fansler is on somewhat safer ground when he quotes parallels from the *Roman de la Rose*.[3] It is unlikely, however, that a single source for the final, nonnarrative, part of the tale will ever turn up, for it seems that Chaucer took his wise sayings and rules of moral conduct from a great many sources, oral and literary alike. As J. A. Work points out, "sententious utterances concerning the impossibility of 'destreyning' nature, the affinity between words and deeds, and the wisdom of bridling the tongue are commonplace in the proverbial wisdom of many peoples and times" and that "in almost all the didactic writings of the Middle Ages, both prose and verse, were repeated admonitions against speaking too much, which leads to jangling and backbiting, which in turn lead to quarrels and lack of peace."[4]

On the other hand, the repeated use of the vocative *my sone* (ll. 318, 319 ff.), preceded by the statement *thus taughte me my dame* (l. 317), suggests that Chaucer may have had in mind those popular collections where proverbial sayings and rules of moral conduct are presented in the form of a parent's advice to a child, as remarked by J. S. P. Tatlock;[5] the fact that in medieval works of parental advice it is normally the father who instructs a son and the mother who instructs a daughter (*The Wise Man Taught his Sone, The Good Wife Taught her Daughter*, and so on)[6] is perhaps not a serious objection to this theory.

Strangely enough, no close parallel has so far been quoted for the piece of worldly wisdom expressed in lines 311–13 of the *Manciple's Tale*, which reads

> Ne telleth nevere no man in youre lyf
> How that another man hath dight his wyf;
> He wol yow haten mortally, certeyn.

G. Stillwell,[7] who has studied the relations of the *Manciple's Tale* to Guillaume de Machaut's *Voir Dit* and an early fourteenth-century moralized version of Ovid in French verse known as *Ovide Moralisé*,[8] finds that the story of Phoebus' white raven in Guillaume's work has the same moral as Chaucer's tale, though it receives less emphasis. In *Ovide Moralisé* the moral derived from the same raven story shows even more conspicuous points of contact, and Stillwell believes that the following passage in that work provides quite a striking parallel to the three lines quoted above from the *Manciple's Tale*:

> Bien puet chascuns apercevoir
> · · · ·
> Que nulz ne doit autrui amie
> Devant son ami diffamer.
> Nulz ne vaudroit oïr blasmer
> Devant soi s'amie ou sa fame,
> Et s'aucuns est qui la diffame
> Devant lui de riens qu'ele face,
> Il se tault s'amour et sa grace,
> Autresi com fist li corbiaux,
> Qui jadis estoit blans et biaux,
> Puis nercist a sa deshonnour.
> Nulz homs, por plere a son seignor,
> Ne doit de sa dame mesdire.
> Et s'ele voult faire avoultire,
> Il ne s'i doit pas consentir
> N'encuser la. Mieux doit mentir
> Ou taire soi, pour pais avoir,
> Que mal souffrir pour dire voir [ii, 2530–48].

Although one has to admit that the story of Apollo's telltale raven in the *Manciple's Tale* often comes remarkably close to that in *Ovide Moralisé* and that it is not altogether impossible that Chaucer had read the raven story in the latter work,[9] the resemblance of this French passage to lines 311–13 of the *Manciple's Tale* can hardly be considered to be a particularly close one, in the light of the evidence to be discussed later in the present article.

The failure of Chaucer scholars to quote a reasonably close parallel

to lines 311–13 of the *Manciple's Tale* is apt to create the illusion that
Chaucer obtained this sententious comment from the proverbial stock
of oral popular tradition or that it is his own invention. The former
alternative might be true, of course, but that Chaucer did not invent the
remark himself is clear from the fact that a remarkably close parallel
is to be found in medieval didactic literature. It occurs in a twelfth-
century Latin poem, a paternal instruction which its modern editor,
B. Hauréau, prints with the title *Carmen ad Astralabium Filium* and
which, he believes, was written by Peter Abelard to his son.[10] The saying
occupies lines 179–80 in Hauréau's edition; for the reader's convenience
I quote also some of the lines following it:

> Nolo virum doceas uxoris crimen amatae,
> Quod sciri potius quam fieri gravat hunc.
> Opprobriis aurem propriis dat nemo libenter,
> Nec te nec quemquam talia scire volet.
> Cuique viro casto conjux sua casta videtur,
> Semperque incestus suspiciosus erit.[11]

Unfortunately I have not been able to trace the origin of the saying
beyond this poem. Jeremy of Montagnone, writing at the end of the
thirteenth century, quotes the passage twice in a compilation entitled
Compendium Moralium Notabilium, preserved in the fourteenth-
century manuscript Bibl. Nat., fonds latin, 6469, fols. 3 recto to 143
verso — a not very carefully executed copy, to judge from the numerous
scribal blunders in it. The quotations from the *Carmen* are to be found
on fol. 80 verso, col. 2, and 115 recto, col. 2. The text is practically the
same in both passages:

> Auctor libri qui incipit Astrolabi: Nolo virum doceas uxoris crimen
> amate;[12] quod sciri potius quam fieri gravat hunc. Opprobriis aurem
> propriis dat nemo libenter; nec te nec quemquam talia scire volet
> (fol. 80 verso).[13]

It is impossible to say, of course, by what channels and exactly in
what form the sententious saying on which lines 311–13 of the *Manciple's Tale* are based reached Chaucer. It is equally impossible to say
whether the ultimate source is the poem attributed to Peter Abelard,
though the possibility of any direct borrowing from that poem seems to
be out of the question. That the *Carmen ad Astralabium Filium* was
known and read in the Middle Ages is suggested not only by the numerous quotations from it in Jeremy of Montagnone's *Compendium* but by
the fact that half a dozen manuscript copies of it are still extant, two
of them in the British Museum.
An analysis of the passages in the *Carmen* and Chaucer's tale is
instructive. In both poems the tone of the advice is undoubtedly cynical.

The former work calls attention to a typical feature of male behavior
in a situation like the one described: it is not so much the wife's unfaithfulness as the fact that the unfaithfulness is known to outsiders that
hurts the husband. The author uses the passive form of the infinitive,
sciri 'to be known.' In Ovid's *Metamorphoses*, the basic source of the
various medieval versions of the story of Apollo's white raven, where
the corresponding passage reads

> Odit avem per quam crimen causamque dolendi
> Scire coactus erat (ii, 614–15),[14]

the active infinitive, *scire*, indicates that the reason for the husband's
hatred of the raven was that he himself had to become aware of his
wife's adulterous conduct. It is also to be noted that in *Metamorphoses*
the reference is to one particular case, while in the *Carmen* and the
Manciple's Tale the saying presented as a moral precept is in fact an
aphorism of general validity. Such a discrepancy does not totally exclude
the possibility that sayings of the type *nolo virum doceas uxoris crimen
amatae* are to be traced back ultimately to the lines quoted above from
Ovid, though any statement to that effect must necessarily remain a
mere hypothesis.

Chaucer's Manciple does not specify the reasons for the husband's
mortal hatred. It is, perhaps, justified to assume that Chaucer is playing
on two separate ideas: (1) a man lives happily in his fool's paradise as
long as he is unaware of his wife's unfaithfulness; (2) as it is from an
outsider that he learns of his wife's unfaithfulness, the implication is
that the matter has become known outside his house.

In *Ovide Moralisé* the point seems to be somewhat different: no man
likes to have his wife or mistress blamed by others. Here the motives of
the man's behavior—at least one tends to think so—are to be sought
rather in a chivalrous attitude to women. Whether this interpretation is
correct or not, the moral in the French poem lacks the utterly unromantic
—or perhaps it would be more appropriate to say "Kinseyan"—tone of
the utterance in the *Carmen* and the *Manciple's Tale*. The three lines in
Chaucer's tale illustrate in a striking way the kind of worldly wisdom
which one naturally connects with a "defrauding, cynical rascal who
elects to tell a tale about cheating in love and to repeat solemnly the
moral that silence pays off much more often than truth-telling."[15]

NOTES

1. *The Works of Geoffrey Chaucer*,
2d ed. (Boston, 1957), pp. 764–65.
2. "Chaucer und Albertanus Brixien-
sis," *Archiv für das Studium der
neueren Sprachen und Literatur-
en*, LXXXVI (1891), 44–46.

3. *Chaucer and the Roman de la Rose* (New York, 1914), pp. 200–202.

4. "The Manciple's Tale," in *Sources and Analogues of Chaucer's Canterbury Tales*, edd. W. F. Bryan and Germaine Dempster (Chicago, 1941), p. 700.

5. "The Date of the *Troilus*, and Minor Chauceriana," *Modern Language Notes*, L (1935), 296.

6. The most notable exceptions are some works where a real historical person addresses his or her child (St. Louis, Eustache Deschamps, Christine de Pisan, the Knight of La Tour Landry, etc.). A survey of parental instructions in English and French literature during the Middle Ages has been attempted in the Introduction to my edition of *The Good Wife Taught her Daughter, The Good Wyfe Wold a Pylgremage, and The Thewis of Gud Women*, Annales Academiae Scientiarum Fennicae, Series B, Vol. LXI, 2 (Helsinki, 1948), pp. 29–78.

7. "Analogues to Chaucer's *Manciple's Tale* in the *Ovide Moralisé* and Machaut's *Voir-dit*," *Philological Quarterly*, XIX (1940), 133–38.

8. Ed. C. de Boer in "*Ovide moralisé*": *Poème du Commencement du quatorzième Siècle*, Verhandelingen der Koninklijke Akademie van Weten-

schappen, Afdeeling Letterkunde, Nieuwe Reeks, XV (Amsterdam, 1915).

9. See, e.g., J. A. Work in Bryan and Dempster, edd., *Sources and Analogues*, p. 703.

10. "Le poème adressé par Abélard à son fils Astralabe," in *Notices et Extraits des Manuscrits de la Bibliothèque Nationale et autres Bibliothèques*, XXXIV, 2 (Paris, 1895), pp. 153–87.

11. "Do not tell a husband about the unfaithfulness [crime] of his beloved wife: the fact that it is known hurts him more than that it has happened. Nobody likes to hear about his own shame or wants you or anybody else to know of it. Every chaste man believes that his wife is also chaste, while an unchaste man will always be suspicious."

12. MS. *amare*.

13. The punctuation and capitalization are mine.

14. "He hates the bird through which he had to know of his wife's act of unfaithfulness and the cause of his torment."

15. Earle Birney, "Chaucer's 'Gentil' Manciple and his 'Gentil' Tale," *Neuphilologische Mitteilungen*, LXI (1960), 260.

The Subjects of Chaucer's Poetry

HOWARD R. PATCH

In one's casual reading there is sometimes a special and highly educational value in deciding what artistic effects, what particular set of motifs or situations, engage the interest of this author or that. Thus, one may notice the unerring precision with which Jane Austen selects the descriptive detail that carries an astringent morsel of her humor, as when she tells us in her letters of a certain Mrs. Blount that she has a broad face, "white shoes, pink husband, and fat neck."[1] Or again, while Jaeger said that Aeschylus in general seeks to "justify the ways of God to man,"[2] his plays may seem to others given to a special interest in human beings under the spell of outraged experience – what I believe one critic has called "exacerbated awareness." I notice too that in Aeschylus and in Sophocles, as in Shakespeare, the tragic pattern is vastly richer for the characterization of aggressive, powerful women, like Antigone, Io, Electra, and the rest. With Dante the use of recurrent motifs lends startling effect, as in the case of the circle all through the *Divine Comedy*. Cervantes is after, I suppose, the ironies revealed in the delusions of the dolorous knight; and Chrétien de Troyes enjoys weaving sentiments together in harmony or contrast. Apart from his learned books, Boccaccio's works show him out for fun, fun unrestricted and fun unrefined, with some cracks at the Church because, it seems, religion for him means restraint, and he wants to drink of life in great gulps right from the stream. The pervasive sentimentality of his poems like the *Teseida* and the *Filostrato*, depending on the old formula of "innocence in distress," reveals him in his search for the pleasures of a man of feeling, whether those strictly of joy or pathos. Dante with the intensity of his comparatively brief stories or allusions to stories, and perhaps because of his relentless moral integrity, makes such a writer seem trivial.

Then what about Geoffrey Chaucer, what drew his special interest and set his imagination going? In his earliest important work, the *Book of the Duchess*, we have an elegy for the lovely Blanche, first wife of John of Gaunt, and, as everybody knows, written in the form of a poem in the tradition of Courtly Love but amazingly touched with humor. When Chaucer was in his middle twenties, a young writer was likely to assume that the literary patterns set by Guillaume de Lorris, Jean de Meun, Guillaume de Machaut, and Froissart represented about the last word in literary elegance for the smart new world of fashion. But here, even in the presence of royalty and death, grief is somewhat in abeyance when the reader learns about the featherbed for the God of Sleep, and especially about the good-for-nothing little dog that guides the dreamer. Perhaps details like these, when the comic spirit breaks through in Chaucer's works, are what made Matthew Arnold and some others deny that the poet had the virtue of "high seriousness." Chaucer's humor has been often and ably discussed, but even now certain passages in the *House of Fame*, the *Troilus*, the *Knight's Tale*, and elsewhere, leave some earnest readers uncomfortable, readers perhaps like Elizabeth Barrett Browning who speaks of

> Chaucer with his infantine
> Familiar clasp of things divine.[3]

What are these "things divine" that he clasped in his poetry? First, in the *Book of the Duchess* we notice the elegiac theme of sympathy or pity in the story of Ceyx, in the portrait of the Man in Black, and in the description of the Duchess. Also, we must note that the poet is greatly taken with a remarkable female character, the Duchess herself. There is also a subtle treatment of the theme of love in the conventional apparatus of the dream. Finally, we have of course the motif of death and what it implies. Woman, pity, love, and death, a good beginning for a young poet. But some things are omitted. We do not find the theme of tragedy here, on the one side, or that of religious mysticism, on the other. With the first of these, a poet differently constituted might have written an impressive and morally enlightening poem, bringing in the Great Plague and the meaning of war and traits like fortitude and justice, all in the high style. But it would have meant less as an elegy, and Chaucer did not work that way. Neither did he stress the funereal or the macabre or the supernaturalistic. The Man in Black in no sense is a real picture of the flaming figure we know in history as John of Gaunt; at best he performs adequately as a symbol, but our thoughts move far beyond him to the lovely lady who is gone. Women, lovely women, virtuous, scheming, aggressive, startling or alluring—these we find in abundance in Chaucer's plots; on the other hand, the number of complicated or extraordinarily vital male characters is nothing like so great. There is Pandarus, of course, the Clerk, and the Merchant, perhaps, certainly the Pardoner (a satiric figure just because he represents his class[4]), even the Canon's Yeoman, and certainly the Host. But compare most of these men with the Duchess, Lady Fame, Criseyde, the Prioress, Dorigen,

Alisoun of the *Miller's Tale*, May of the *Merchant's*, and most of all the Wife of Bath, who can take on several men at once with her right hand tied behind her. Why was it that Chaucer was so especially expert about women, whether naughty little girls or great ladies? He writes competently enough about Constance, St. Cecilia, Griselda, and Emelye, but not so well as he does about even Pertelote. Was it because his sense of humor was predominant, or because, as some people think, he was easily suffused with pity? Was not his "favorite line," "pitee renneth soone in gentil herte," or something like it?[5]

Years ago, Theodore Spencer published an article to the effect that Chaucer belonged to the great tradition of sentimentality, and a similar view is held by Professor Aurelio Zanco who, like Spencer, finds evidence in Chaucer's rendering of the story of Ugolino.[6] But one must point out that in the *Monk's Tale* it is the Monk and not Chaucer who is the sentimentalist, as we can see from the description in the General Prologue of the Monk's luxurious pleasure in sensation; and also when his stories are cut short we note how his milk of human kindness goes sour.[7] On the other hand, we may compare Chaucer's version of the story of Palamon and Arcite with Boccaccio's. Chaucer's is rich in detail, but compared with the long pseudo-epic of Boccaccio it is compact. The Italian poem ends in the lacrimose defeat, death, and funeral of Arcite, based on the formula of innocence in distress and extended to release all fountains filled with tears. In the immense condensation offered by the worthy Knight there are moments no less than gay even in the platitudinous oration of old Egeus, and a sparkle too in the poet's comment on the scene in the presence of the slain hero:

> . . . Allas the pitee that was ther,
> Cracchynge of chekes, rentynge eek of heer.
> "Why woldestow be deed," thise wommen crye,
> "And haddest gold ynough, and Emelye?"[8]

As in the case of the *Book of the Duchess*, what lamentation there is escapes morbidity. The only lines of genuine pathos in the English version are in the speech of the dying Arcite:

> Naught may the woful spirit in myn herte
> Declare o point of alle my sorwes smerte. . . .[9]

and so on, at least as far as "And with that word his speche faille gan." This passage is a whole world different from "Shrighte Emelye, and howleth Palamon,"[10] and the lines that follow, and I am certain that Chaucer was fully aware of this fact because his intention was different. All this has to do with what for me is a cardinal principle of Chaucer criticism: namely that Geoffrey Chaucer always knew what he was doing. If in the *Parlement of Foules* it seems to us odd that the summary of the Dream of Scipio precedes the account of the poet's dream of the garden and all the rest of it, this is no accident or trivial mistake (if one is not to underrate the poet), and it is our business to discover exactly what the meaning of this was in Chaucer's mind. Similarly if in the *Troilus* the young hero really becomes at moments funny in the process in Book III whereby he is led "by the lappe" to the room where Criseyde waits, and eventually to union with her, the humor of the scene and the collapse of Troilus in his swoon are important if we are to understand Chaucer's intentions with regard to this important development of the plot, and to comprehend how he himself sees the character of Troilus.

As for the *Canterbury Tales*, it is astonishing how little sentimentality or pathos we find there. The stories of saintly ladies offer little of this; for, as in the case of the little clergeoun of the *Prioress's Tale*, the tribulations of a saint (whether Constance or Virginia or Saint Cecilia) are transmuted into something rich and strange, just as the happy ending of a saint's legend is martyrdom. Even with Griselda the pathos of her unending patience is altered in effect on us by the context of the magnificent controversy with the Wife of Bath, who among many other things said a clerk would not "speke good of wyves."[11] Failure to take adequate account of the implications of this controversy seems to be responsible for Mr. Bronson's finding the Envoy of the *Clerk's Tale* "a genuine, though unconscious, repudiation of the false morality that the poet was forced by the story to espouse."[12] But Chaucer was not forced to tell the story at all. Or if he felt he was because it offers such a ludicrously extreme instance of a clerk speaking well of at least one wife, the opportunity for pity, however "contagious," is somewhat reduced. Mr. Bronson thinks that Chaucer fell into a pitfall in the *Clerk's Tale* and apparently in the *Merchant's Tale* and elsewhere,[13] and was guilty of an "involuntary yielding of principle, weakened by sympathy and by native gifts." We are told, "Chaucer tossed caution aside; and falling into the pit, only dug it deeper. . . ." But is this the Chaucer we know? Might not a fair-minded reader suppose that any critic would have sought much further before accepting such conclusions as valid, or would have returned for a fresh estimate of the humorous impact of the Wife of Bath's Prologue?

If we must have abundant pathos in Chaucer, let us turn to the *Legend of Good Women*. Here is a whole succession of lovely ladies who all their lives were faithful in love, and who all came to grief. The poet himself speaks of the terrible pity he felt about it: "So gret a routhe I have it for t'endite."[14] His heroine Dido, we are told, fainted twenty times and more in her anguish, and all around we find rivers of tears and collapsing ladies. The tone is rather that of the more violent statements of grief we find toward the end of the *Knight's Tale*; and the pit into which Cleopatra, in preparation for her suicide, put "alle the serpentes that she myghte have,"[15] will serve as an example of the way the emotion is pushed. Chaucer seems indeed at moments to write of grief with his tongue in his cheek, as when we are told that Medea cries out in her misery:

> Whi lykede me thy yelwe her to se
> More than the boundes of myn honeste?[16]

The whole idea of these saints of love is of course a matter of humor even if the poet ground out some of the lines. And at least once the familiar smile comes through:

> Be war ye wemen of youre subtyl fo,
> Syn yit this day men may ensaumple se;
> And trusteth, as in love, no man but me.[17]

The impression we get from the poem is that Chaucer did not by nature take easily to this general flow of sentimentality; after all, he was writing under orders. What then about his favorite line regarding "pitee"? The fact is, indeed, we have known for a long time that the line is a fairly close rendering of a line or two in the verses of the poets of the *dolce stil nuovo*, where, however, we find *amore* instead of "pitee." Clearly, Chaucer uses the word to mean not merely compassion but all generous impulses and even love, as we may see in his *Complaint unto Pity*. It is an emotion that according to Ovid as well as Chaucer accompanies nobility.[18] It is the quality indicated in Ovid's account of the magnanimous lion.

What then about Chaucer's treatment of love? This, it might seem, was his main concern in season and out of season, in the whole succession of poems indebted to the tradition of Courtly Love from the *Book of the Duchess* to the *Legend of Good Women*, with a radiant center in *Troilus and Criseyde*; and also many of the *Canterbury Tales*, especially in the Marriage Cycle and the discourse of the Wife of Bath. There is much about love in the *Consolation of Philosophy* of Boethius and in the *Roman de la Rose*, both of which Chaucer translated and from which he borrowed heavily; and also in the *Divine Comedy* of which *amore* is the theme from beginning to end, and from this work he also borrowed. If one may infer a special moral from all this, whether from Chaucer's allegorical works with a personal reference perhaps, or from his narratives humorous or satiric, it is that in favor of faithfulness in love. The traditions of Courtly Love are subjected to serious scrutiny in the *Troilus*, at times in the person of the hero (however winning his charm in discourse or valiant his exploits in warfare) in the delicate ruthlessness with which he is displayed performing the courtly lover to the outrance. Much of this takes place in the extended bedroom scenes in which he discusses with Pandarus his love and his despair. If Mr. Bronson is right in saying "it was Troilus who essentialized the meaning

of his poem,"[19] then we must be certain as to what kind of young man
Chaucer meant to depict. Mr. Bronson finds him "the exemplar of earth's
best values," but to maintain this view he has to add that in this characterization Chaucer has bungled a bit. At least so it seems when Mr.
Bronson refers to the hero's "comparative unreality in the context of his
immediate society" as "possibly the supreme and most significant instance of the collision in Chaucer's work between actuality and ideality."
But all this is to ignore the element of youthful absurdity that is an
essential part of the hero's character all through the story.

To begin with, we must not neglect the important fact that the young
hero who once jeered at love and lovers falls the hardest when he becomes one of love's victims. His almost constant retreat to his bed when
he is stricken with his desperate anguish would not seem to be part of a
reasonable exhibition of "earth's best values." Gawain, Lancelot,
Tristan, Paolo, Paris (according to Ovid), and others beside Diomede,
knew how to go to work in a fashion more direct than this. We note too
that Criseyde is the first to kiss in the meeting at the house of Deiphebus
(III, 182); that Pandarus leads Troilus to his lady by the "lappe" on the
great night at Pandarus's house after saying,

> . . . Thow wrecched mouses herte,
> Artow agast so that she wol the bite?[20]

Such language to the "exemplar of earth's best values," even with a
medieval regard for a sensitive nature? The hero at length is so stricken
by his lady's anger and tears that he disclaims all responsibility for the
meeting and swoons away. Says Pandarus:

> . . . "O thef, is this a mannes herte?"
> And of he rente al to his bare sherte.[21]

And Criseyde, after helping with the massage that brings him back to
consciousness, makes her contribution:

> . . . Is this a mannes game?
> What, Troilus, wol ye do thus for shame?[22]

After the decision of Parliament regarding the exchange of Criseyde
for Antenor, it is the heroine who argues that she must leave Troy and
go to the Greeks. As for Troilus, he comes to about the same conclusion
when Pandarus urges him to show courage and keep his lady by main
force:

> Ris up anon, and lat this wepyng be,
> And kith thow art a man; for in this houre
> I wol ben ded, or she shal bleven oure.[23]

Apparently Troilus needs to have someone tell him to be a man, and the motif goes through the story from the time Pandarus warns him not to commit suicide (I, 823, as Troilus quotes him), where we see the beginning of what Mr. Meech has called his "obsessive mindfulness of death"[24] and also the suicide motif. Psychologically, the weakness (or delicacy or whatever it is) in Troilus that elicits the challenge from Pandarus and even Criseyde regarding his manhood, the recurrent references to death, the theme of suicide (which actually became a threat though it does not come off) are all in harmony with his swooning as an escape motif. But Chaucer has other things to say about his hero that must also receive attention. He is, we learn, a fine warrior; in addition to his love for Criseyde he has a rich understanding of the depth and meaning of love as the force that holds the universe together; he is ennobled by love as well as somewhat weakened. In a word, he is likeable and attractive as well as just a bit absurd, and given less of an emergency he might have continued to hold the affections of Criseyde. As it is, a woman could move on to a different affair subdued by the dynamic effect of a lover like Diomede, who would waste no time on poetry. Under the circumstances, remembering that Troilus acted as he did at the house of Pandarus, keeping the whole picture before us of the nature of the courtship and its climax, few readers, I believe, who are not completely sold out to sentimentality, could say of the bereft hero in Book v that "Our hearts have been wrung almost literally beyond endurance by Chaucer's utter command of our emotional sympathies with Troilus' suffering. His pangs are ours."[25] He is a "nice boy" in modern parlance; but if he "essentialized the meaning" of the poem for Chaucer, then here we see that Courtly Love in Chaucer's opinion is just a bit absurd.[26] The weeping and wailing, care and other sorrow, in Book IV, however poignant for some readers, is not unmixed pathos. One thinks of the grief described in the *Clerk's Tale* as it is changed in quality by the framework of the dispute with the Wife of Bath and her remark about clerks.

Love according to Chaucer has its nobility:

> Plesance of love, O goodly debonaire,
> In gentil hertes ay redy to repaire.[27]

This is about as close as one can get to Guido Guinicelli and the *dolce stil nuovo*. But as the Wife of Bath has observed, love may also be a sin, and of this fact both Troilus and Criseyde and Pandarus too are fully aware.[28] From this point on, I may leave the discussion to Mr. Bennett and Mr. Muscatine,[29] who show some of the complexities involved in these matters.

I turn instead to the fact that we shall be told that in much of this criticism we are reading modern values such as psychological realism into medieval literature. Such an assumption, says Mr. Bronson for example, is "to take for granted in Chaucer an orientation and a technical achievement that we are probably wrong in expecting before the eighteenth century, at the earliest."[30] This is a proposition that leaves out Shakespeare and some other able writers, and it seems inconsistent with some of Mr. Bronson's own critical observations. Psychological realism appears at times in medieval narratives before Chaucer; not to see it, not even at its best, is to miss something of the ironies and the salutary humor of these writings.[31] How else can one really appreciate the full value of the Wife of Bath's Prologue? The truth is we hardly need to "expect" psychological realism in the fourteenth century; because Geoffrey Chaucer understood human nature, we have only to see it there and enjoy it. The modern preoccupation that may really be an obstacle to our estimate of medieval literature is the current obsession with the sexual so that some readers today apparently assume that the significant part of the Troilus so far as Chaucer was concerned was the union of the lovers in Book III.[32] Undoubtedly there was much discussion of sexual love in the tradition of Courtly Love and elsewhere in the Middle Ages, but there was also extensive treatment of love celestial in St. Bernard of Clairvaux's work and notably in the Divine Comedy. The modern reader may find it hard to accept the fact that Chaucer ends the poem on that theme but after all he ends the Canterbury Tales with a moral disquisition. Readers sometimes seem to forget that Father Denomy acknowledges Chaucer's repudiation of Courtly Love "not only in the Palinode but within the very fabric of the [Troilus] itself."[33] The two moralities that Father Denomy indicates lose their inconsistency when we recognize that Courtly Love in the person of Troilus is deprived of just a little of its dignity as a many-splendored thing.

Finally, I come to the last of the subjects that, in our necessarily limited summary, engaged the poet's attention in the Book of the Duchess and elsewhere. That is the theme of death. There is a fairly large number of references to death in Chaucer's works. Virginia suffers a rather uneasy martyrdom in the Physician's Tale. St. Cecilia in the Second Nun's Tale takes on martyrdom almost with gusto. The death of Arcite, almost clinical in detail, is poignant; so too is the release of the little clergeoun in the Prioress's Tale. In the Book of the Duchess, the grief is real, but the motif is important chiefly for what it shows about the characters involved. For Troilus in Troilus and Criseyde, death is at times a threat and at times an escape but mostly in terms of a young man's emotionalism. Death himself makes an appearance in the Pardoner's Tale with that horrible joke of his about being unable to die. Attempts to interpret the character in some other way — as the Wandering Jew or a pitiable old man — miss the drama of the figure and its full irony, as well as the meaning of the wonderful line: "Why artow al forwrapped save thy face?"[34] But even this is hardly macabre. Chaucer does not cultivate the funereal even in the case of Arcite. His attention was too much occupied with affirmations about life and about the problems of life itself. That may be why some readers have regarded him as chiefly the entertainer, pretty much indifferent to meanings and philosophical implications.

NOTES

1. *Jane Austen's Letters*, ed. R. W. Chapman (Oxford, 1932), I, p. 91.
2. Werner Jaeger, *Paideia: the Ideals of Greek Culture*, trans. Gilbert Highet, (New York, 1945), I, pp. 255 ff.
3. "Vision of Poets," *Complete Works of Elizabeth Barrett Browning* (Boston, 1900), pp. 133, 387–88.
4. Cf. Sedgewick in *Chaucer Criticism: The Canterbury Tales* (Notre Dame, Ind., 1960), pp. 203 ff.
5. See the *Knight's Tale*, A 1761, and Robinson's note on it (*The Works of Geoffrey Chaucer*, 2d ed., ed. F. N. Robinson [Boston, 1957], pp. 675–76). I use Robinson's text for the quotations in the present article.
6. Cf. Spencer in *Speculum*, IX (1934), 295 ff., and Zanco's *Chaucer e il suo mondo* (Turino, 1955), pp. 48, 192, 265.
7. B 3996–97.
8. A 2833–35.
9. A 2765 ff.
10. A 2817.
11. D 688 ff.
12. B. H. Bronson, *In Search of Chaucer* (Toronto, 1960), p. 112.
13. Pp. 112 ff.
14. With respect to the complaint of Dido, F 1345.
15. F 679.
16. F 1672–73.
17. F 2559–61.
18. Cf. Ovid, *Tristia* ("et faciles motus mens generosa capit"), III, v, 32. The instances cited, to be sure, show "human wrath turned to milder ends." See ed. and trans. A. L. Wheeler, Loeb Library (London, 1924), p. 122.
19. P. 117.
20. III, 736–37.
21. III, 1098–99.
22. III, 1126–27.
23. IV, 537–39. Cf. also IV, 529.
24. S. B. Meech, *Design in Chaucer's Troilus* (Syracuse, 1959), p. 409.
25. Bronson, p. 21. It would appear that Mr. Bronson's attitude in this and other matters has been conditioned by his inadequate response to what he has called "ill-timed and merely idle facetiousness." It recalls St. Paul's objection to filthiness, foolish talking and jesting, "which are not convenient." Ephes. 5:4.
26. Note also Meech, p. 165, on the "latent absurdity in the system."
27. *Troilus and Criseyde*, III, 4–5. See Robinson's note, *Chaucer*, p. 823.
28. II, 411–13; III, 267–80; III, 911–14.
29. J. A. W. Bennett, *The Parlement of Foules: An Interpretation*, (Oxford, 1957), p. 187; Charles Muscatine, *Chaucer and the French Tradition*, (Berkeley and Los Angeles, 1957), p. 132, on the "two levels of perspective."
30. P. 81; cf. also pp. 77 ff.
31. Cf. my notes on the development of the character of Criseyde in early literature: *The McAuley Lectures*, II, (Saint Joseph College, West Hartford, Conn., 1954), pp. 36–37.
32. An interesting survey of the problem is offered by Dorothy Bethurum in "Chaucer's Point of View as Narrator in the Love Poems," in *Chaucer Criticism: Troilus and Criseyde and the Minor Poems*, edd. R. J. Schoeck and Jerome Taylor (Notre Dame, Ind.,

1961), pp. 225 ff. But cf. p. 228 ("It would have been irrelevant to talk about marriage. . . ."), and note the fact that Criseyde discards the very idea (*Troilus*, II, 750 ff.).

33. *Chaucer Criticism*, II, "The Two Moralities of Chaucer's *Troilus and Criseyde*," p. 156. Any charge that Chaucer was ambivalent in the poem about the doctrines of pagan and Christian morality (p. 158) must be somewhat tempered in view of the fact that Troilus's great song about the love that rules the heavens and earth and seas and binds them in its course is adapted from the *Consolation of Philosophy* (II, m. viii); and the proem of Book III on the ennobling power of love closely echoes Guido Guinicelli and the *dolce stil nuovo* as indeed Dante of course did (cf. *Purg.* XXIV, 49 ff.). But note C. S. Singleton, *An Essay on the Vita Nuova* (Cambridge, Mass., 1949,) pp. 69 ff., and J. E. Shaw, *Guido Cavalcanti's Theory of Love* (Toronto, 1949), pp. 123 ff. For modern emphasis on the sexual see the remarks in the London *Times Literary Supplement* regarding the International Writers' Conference, p. 657, August 31, 1962, Editorial; also the *Commonweal*, LXXVI (1962), review, p. 519.

34. C 718.

The Study of English Medieval Drama

ARTHUR BROWN

University College, London

THE PRESENT-DAY student of English medieval drama is faced with a number of serious problems, not all of which seem to be fully appreciated. It will be the purpose of this paper to draw attention to some of these, and, although many of them appear at the moment to be insuperable, to suggest a few ways in which efforts may be made to improve the situation.

Medieval literature in general has suffered at the hands of critics for the very simple reason that so much of it has been lost, and that there is always a tendency in these circumstances to attempt to deduce too much from what remains. At the end of the second volume of his *Medieval Stage*, Sir E. K. Chambers lists in an appendix the names of those places which, on the evidence of records, are known to have had their own dramatic performances of one kind or another. Some forty different localities are mentioned. Now extant for our examination, however, are more or less complete cycles of mystery plays from York, from Wakefield, and from Chester (the last surviving in five manuscripts), a fragment of what must have once been a complete cycle from Coventry, a group of plays labeled misleadingly *Ludus Coventriae*,[1] and, to complete the cyclic plays, a group from Cornwall which raise very serious linguistic problems. Other single plays are preserved in a number of isolated manuscripts, some of them perhaps originally forming parts of cycles similar to those already mentioned, others (for example, *The Conversion of Saul* and *Mary Magdalene* in the Digby collection), perhaps, examples of a different kind of play on a single Biblical subject. Very little survives of the morality plays; the Macro manuscript contains three of the better-known ones (*The Castle of Perseverance*, *Wisdom*, and *Mankind*), and the best known of all (*Everyman*) is unique in that it survives in a printed form. The introduction of printing in the fifteenth century improved the chances of survival of the "interludes," many of them short morality plays, but the comparative abundance of material in the early sixteenth century does not mean that the picture is a clear one; there has been more than one occasion during the past ten or fifteen years when the existence of a hitherto unknown interlude has been attested by the appearance of a fragment used as part of the binding in a completely different book.

The appalling loss of material, the very large element of chance in survival, should make us very wary indeed of drawing any hard and fast conclusions about the nature of medieval drama. London was just as much the capital of England then as it is now, and its civic and ecclesiastical records have been pretty well preserved. There is no doubt that a series of plays, probably similar to the mystery cycles in other centers, was regularly performed in the city. Yet we have five manuscripts of the Chester cycle, and not a trace of the London one. Of the four full-scale morality plays that survive, three are contained in a single manuscript; it would be absurd to conclude that this represents the entire output of this particular form during the fourteenth, fifteenth, and sixteenth centuries, and it would be rash to assume that what has survived is necessarily typical of the rest.[2] Yet for many years this drama has attracted to itself what might be termed a "scholarship of the background" quite out of proportion to its own bulk; studies of alleged origins and developments, attempts to present some kind of continuous picture, these have proliferated on the basis of what is, after all, very flimsy evidence indeed.

The plays have undoubtedly suffered too from their religious content and purpose. The material consists for the most part of plays dealing with incidents drawn from the Bible, with a considerable admixture of legend and apocryphal stories, those from the Old Testament concerned with the Fall of Man and the prophecies of redemption through a Messiah, those from the New Testament with the life of Christ on earth, the cycle usually ending with a play on the Day of Judgment. The extant morality plays represent allegorically some of the central teachings of Christianity, the struggle for the soul of man between the forces of good and evil, the inevitability of death, and so on. The point is that the whole nature and purpose of this drama is frankly and unashamedly didactic; all its energy is directed to the presentation, as vividly as possible, of the main facts of Christianity and of the Church's teaching to the greatest possible number of people. In an age of widespread illiteracy such purpose and methods require neither explanation nor justification. To the modern reader, however, a confessedly didactic literature is open to suspicion, accustomed as he is to regard literature as something which should entertain rather than teach. This is a factor influencing his literary judgment against which he needs to be always on his guard. Furthermore, the authors of a mystery play cycle, or of a morality play, must often have been in danger of forgetting their art in their anxiety to communicate their messages, and no amount of sound morality will make a play good drama unless the principles of drama have also been borne in mind. We need to be clear in our criticism where the distinction lies; too often our conclusions are colored by misunderstandings of medieval religious notions, and by preconceived ideas of what literature ought to be or to do.[3]

Closely connected with this problem of religious content and didactic purpose is the problem of language. There is no point here in bewailing the fact that Latin is largely lost to our present generation of English students, and that Middle English bids fair to follow it; so much the worse for our students.[4] Nor can we any longer assume in them even the most elementary acquaintance with the Bible. Yet even when we find the odd person in possession of these disciplines, we usually find that his knowledge of the Bible is based on the Authorized Version, and its language and terminology have come to be regarded with an almost superstitious awe.[5] Our medieval plays, however, were written long before the Authorized Version, and in an English not of scholars who had been specially chosen for the task of translation but, more probably, of men intimately connected with the everyday life of common people, men concerned with ensuring that the message of the Gospels was brought home to laborers and craftsmen, peasants and townsmen, in a form and language which they could readily appreciate. Critics of the medieval drama have often pointed out how harsh some of its renderings of Biblical material are to ears attuned to the cadences of later versions. All medieval literature suffers from the disadvantage of being written in an English no longer familiar, or, where it seems to be familiar, only apparently and often misleadingly so. The disadvantage is even greater as far as the plays are concerned, in that those people to whom their subject matter is already familiar have generally become acquainted with it from an early age in a language more polished and sophisticated.

With some notable exceptions, most scholars are now agreed that it is very important to base one's conclusions about a literature upon reliable texts of that literature. The student of medieval drama must face the melancholy fact that no such texts exist as far as he is concerned. As long ago as 1914, Sir Walter Greg pointed out that it was essential to examine carefully the extant manuscripts of the plays, and to decide upon the true nature of each manuscript; until this had been done, it was impossible to proceed with the work of editing them satisfactorily.[6] Yet we are still compelled to rely upon editions produced before Greg had made this point and had himself made a preliminary survey of the ground to be covered. No one, I believe, has yet followed up with any consistency the lines of research indicated by Greg, or has attempted to incorporate them in new editions of the texts. He himself, in collaboration with F. M. Salter, did in fact take matters a stage further for the Chester plays, and in 1935 produced a volume in which they discussed the difficult question of the relationships of the five surviving manuscripts of these plays;[7] yet there the matter rests. The York plays were edited in 1885 by Lucy Toulmin Smith; this has long been out of print and practically unobtainable outside scholarly libraries, and in any case, as I know from bitter experience, is most unsatisfactory from a textual and glossarial point of view.[8] The Towneley plays have been edited twice as a whole cycle, yet even the most recent edition, that of the Early English Text Society, was done in 1897.[9] The same Society's edition of the Chester plays appeared in two volumes, in 1893 and 1914, but could not, of course, take into account the later work on the manuscripts by Greg and Salter. The Society issued an edition of the remains of the Coventry cycle in 1902, but since the manuscript containing the pageant has been destroyed there is no means of telling how accurate a version of this is available. The plays which have taken their name from the Digby manuscript in the Bodleian Library were edited for the Society in 1896, but this was largely a reprint of the Shakespeare Society's edition of 1882, and a new examination of this interesting collection is long overdue. Similar considerations hold good for the other plays. Perhaps nowhere in the whole field of English literature is the basic textual position so unsatisfactory; perhaps nowhere has there been so large a crop of notes and emendations based, for the most part, on sheer guesswork.

I wrote earlier in this paper of the many studies which have appeared of the supposed origins and development of the English medieval drama, and of the many attempts which have been made to make some kind of continuous picture out of the surviving pieces. It is here, I feel, that our greatest danger lies, and it is here that we need to take a fresh look at the evidence. The pioneer work of E. K. Chambers and the more recent studies of scholars such as Hardin Craig and Glynne Wickham[10] have contributed largely to our knowledge, and are broad enough in scope and detailed enough in execution to raise at least second thoughts in the mind of anyone contemplating a new venture into the field. Yet there have been dangers in their approach, and there are problems in the subject which may not only be glossed over by too broad a treatment but to which such a treatment may, all unconsciously, suggest the wrong answers. Toward the end of his great work on the Latin liturgical drama, Karl Young wrote as follows:

> Of all the changes brought about through the secularizing of the plays, the most far-reaching and impressive is the transforming of them from a cosmopolitan product into a variety of national developments. During the period when the religious drama belonged exclusively to the Church, and was written in the ecclesiastical language, it was, like the Church itself, essentially international. Among the Latin plays, to be sure, we have observed a few national and regional

differences, and some achievements of individual talent; but in a survey of the whole body of Church plays one is impressed less by the rise of special forms from particular places than by the international likenesses in form and content. From the fourteenth century onward, however, although a few types of Latin play continued in general circulation, the chief dramatic developments assumed an unprecedented significance nationally. All had a background in the cycle of plays produced by the Church itself, and all drew upon common sources in Scripture, legend, and ecclesiastical exegesis; but the several countries of Western Europe showed significant variations in literary form, in choice of themes, and in methods of performance.[11]

Here Young makes two important points. The first is that, although one may accept a "background" in the Latin liturgical drama for the vernacular craft cycles, there is no firm body of evidence to show a clear line of development between them.[12] The second is that, although the secular religious drama in various countries drew upon common material, each developing national drama drew upon and used this material in its own way; his use of the words "significant variations" cannot be too strongly emphasized. All too often similarities of content or of treatment between plays of different countries, which could arise easily enough as the result of a common background and a common body of basic material, have been seized upon as evidence for the dependence of the drama of one country upon that of another through the medium of translation.[13] Failure to appreciate Young's points fully has led to some grave critical distortions. There have been too many attempts to treat the whole of medieval drama as a single literary kind, exaggerating apparent resemblances and glossing over apparently minor variations. As a result a picture has emerged of a smooth evolutionary sweep in the development of drama from the liturgical plays through the mysteries and moralities to the Elizabethan and Jacobean stage—and even further.[14]

I am inclined to develop Young's points a little more with regard to the plays in this country. We have no right, I think, in view of the amount of material which has been lost, to assume that dramatic representations necessarily followed the same lines in all the localities at which we know they took place. We should encourage students to understand that by reading or hearing broadcasts of a number of individual plays from different cycles they are not thereby reading or hearing a "typical" medieval cycle of plays. There is, perhaps, little to be gained at present from general historical surveys of the medieval drama in England; the evidence is too fragmentary. What seems to be needed now, apart from good editions, a sound linguistic training, and an ability to understand medieval habits of thought, is a series of detailed studies of medieval drama as it appeared in single localities in this country. This kind of study will consider the drama of a single locality not so much from the point of view of its resemblances to drama elsewhere, not so much as a single manifestation of the great spirit of religious drama in Europe in the Middle Ages, but rather as a local product, influenced to a great extent by local circumstances, reflecting local conditions and attitudes, produced and performed by local people, often tradesmen, regarded as a local responsibility. In this connection it is perhaps useful to bear in mind a single entry from the *York Memorandum Book* in 1417: "Quod ob commodum civium ejusdem civitatis et omnium extraneorum illuc veniencium in festo predicto, omnes pagine ludi, vocati Corpus Christi play, sint sustentate et producte suo ordine per artifices dicte civitatis, ad honorem precipue et reverenciam Domini nostri Jesu Christi et comodum civium predictorum. . . ."[15] One is struck over and over again, when reading the records from York, by the notion that the plays were acted, not only for the glory of God but for the honor and glory of the city of York. They were closely bound up with the daily life of the citizens, financed and acted by the trade guilds under the direction and super- vision of the corporation, the arrangements for their production being regarded as part of the normal corporation business and recorded as such in the minute books. Their fate depended very often on the pros- perity, or lack of it, of these guilds, on the settlement of feuds between the guilds, on the occurrence of other events, such as the plague or a royal visit, regarded for the time being as of greater importance. This close connection between the plays and the life of the city should never be overlooked. It is worth mentioning that although the Creed Play and the Pater Noster Play at York were the responsibility of *religious* guilds, there is very little evidence of much participation by the religious authorities in the presentation of the mystery plays until the reformers felt it necessary to deal with them on doctrinal grounds.[16]

The student of medieval drama in York is fortunate in that so much illustrative material has been preserved for him in the city's archives. A mass of corporation and guild records throw light on all aspects of the productions and performance of the plays. Occasionally these records even contain the text of a pageant produced for a special occasion, such as the visit of Henry VII in 1486.[17] They demonstrate the rise and fall of the guilds' fortunes and the effect of these on the plays. In their refer- ence to "Yule and Yule's wife" they show that not all the entertainment was of a religious nature. During the sixteenth century they reflect the growing hostility of the reformers toward the plays, and the efforts made to fill the gap caused by their suppression with dramatic material of a different kind. Many of these documents have been made available in the publications of the Surtees Society and the Yorkshire Archaeological Society, and many more still remain to be searched. But I suspect that the best possible use has not been made of those which are available. It is true that some of them have been printed and discussed, but not always as fully as they should be alongside the plays themselves. When we take the two together, we find that they bear witness to a remarkable local interest in, and encouragement of, different kinds of drama over a long period of time. It is a municipal activity, a municipal responsibility; the ecclesiastical authorities are no longer in control, even though the plays still retain their didactic purpose.[18]

These, then, are some of the problems that a student of medieval drama must face. His texts are unsatisfactory, there are many linguistic difficulties, we are a long way from the Middle Ages in thought, and a great deal of material has been lost. Time and effort have been wasted in treating the surviving material in the wrong way. I suggest that we now need to concentrate our efforts a little more, first on the provision of reliable texts, second on the relating of these texts as far as possible to their immediate background — not particularly the background of Europe, or even of England, but the city, town, or village in which the plays had their being. The plays are not sophisticated academic exercises, but popular in every sense of the word. Their nature will be best realized when we come to appreciate the intimate connection between a popular, religious, didactic drama and the everyday activities of the citizens who produced it.

NOTES

1. The origin and purpose of this particular group are still far from clear. Chambers put the situation well when he remarked that almost the only thing which is certain about it is that it had nothing to do with Coventry.

2. For further evidence about lost plays of this period see R. M. Wilson, *The Lost Literature of Medieval England* (London, 1952), esp. section XI.

3. For a valuable discussion of what he calls "the fundamental question of the relationship between a religious motion and the imaginative or creative excitement," especially as this affects the medieval lyrics and *Piers Plowman*, see George Kane, *Middle English Literature* (London, 1951). The conclusions he reaches are no less important insofar as they apply to the drama of this period.

4. How far the rot has set in is illustrated by an item in *The Times* (London) for 11 November 1963, which quotes a report from the Student Council at Oxford calling for Anglo-Saxon to be made an optional subject and for Middle English to be treated simply as part of the Chaucerian literary period. One is hardly surprised, though none the less perturbed, to find the students welcoming the elimination of Latin, "which contributes nothing to the English course."

5. See R. A. Knox, *On Englishing the Bible* (London, 1949).

6. W. W. Greg, *Bibliographical and Textual Problems of the English Miracle Cycles* (London, 1914).

7. W. W. Greg and F. M. Salter, *The Trial and Flagellation, with other Studies in the Chester Cycle* [Malone Society Studies] (Oxford, 1935).

8. I am preparing a new edition for the Early English Text Society.

9. A new edition is being prepared for the Early English Text Society by Professor A. C. Cawley.

10. Hardin Craig, *English Religious Drama of the Middle Ages* (Oxford, 1955). Glynne Wickham, *Early English Stages 1300 to 1660. Vol. I: 1300–1576* (London and New York, 1959).

11. *The Drama of the Medieval Church* (Oxford, 1933), II, pp. 425–26.

12. Craig, for example, devotes almost a third of his space to liturgical material, and his remark that "the Latin drama of the church became a secular drama in the hands of the laity" (p. 48), raising as it does more questions than it answers, is a basic assumption in his work. W. L. Renwick and Harold Orton, in *The Beginnings of English Literature to Skelton* (London, 1939), comment more wisely that the study of drama at this period "suffers a little from the praiseworthy efforts of scholars to make a connected history out of disconnected documents. The histories make much of the liturgical drama, for it has the advantage of being documentary, but it does not follow that it explains the whole story" (p. 334). Later (p. 335) they point out that the crucial question has not been answered, "why the 'miracles' in England, and in England alone, became the business of the craft guilds. The sequence 'dramatic liturgy—religious guild—secular company' may hold for France, but it cannot be paralleled with the English sequence 'dramatic liturgy—craft custom—his lordship's servants.'" On the same page they remark that "we must recognise the two solutions of continuity in the history of English acting—in the evidence for the formation of the craft custom and for the formation of the sixteenth-century companies of players. These were fresh starts, at some time and somewhere."

13. Craig, (p. v): "I could not fail to take the French religious drama into consideration, since the English religious drama originated mainly in France, and was from time to time influenced by the French." Contrast Renwick and Orton (p. 335): "It follows also that Dr. Creizenach's thesis (e.g., in his useful chapter in *The Cambridge History of English Literature*, Vol. 5) that whereas England possesses the greatest body of medieval drama, it must be derived from other countries for which no such body of evidence exists, is based largely upon the usual assumption that the English could never have any ideas of their own."

14. See, for example, Arnold Williams, *The Drama of Medieval England* (East Lansing, Mich., 1961), who suggests that once impersonation is introduced into a trope "we are safely on the road that leads to the York Cycle, and *Everyman*, Shakespeare and Shaw, and the latest Hollywood epic" (p. 8).

15. *York Memorandum Book*, ed. Maud Sellers [Surtees Society] (Durham-London, 1915 [for 1914]), II, 63.

16. There have, of course, been studies more or less of the kind I am advocating here, as a reference to C. J. Stratman's *Bibliography of the Medieval Drama* (Berkeley, 1954) will show. Two more recent ones, published too late for inclusion by Stratman, are F. M. Salter's *Mediaeval Drama in Chester* (Toronto, 1955) and, in a rather different way, A. C. Cawley's edition of *The Wakefield Pageants in the Towneley Cycle* (Manchester, 1958). But there is room for a good deal more work of this kind.

17. See "A York Pageant, 1486," ed. A. H. Smith, *London Medieval Studies*, I, Part 3 (1948 for 1939), 382–98.

18. It may be of interest to remark that the Malone Society is encouraging research on a local (usually county) basis into civic records with a view to extracting and printing those items which deal with dramatic activities. Inevitably most of these deal with the visits of traveling com-

panies of players, but other material comes to light from time to time. Dr. Giles Dawson's researches in Kent are now at press, and will form a model for this kind of work. Hampshire records are in the process of being examined by Mr. Clive Burch, and other counties are under consideration. By pushing the search well back into the fifteenth century (or even earlier) it may be possible to establish a much more realistic "continuity" of dramatic development than the ones normally assumed.

A Collection of Proverbs in BM Additional MS. 37075

BARTLETT JERE WHITING

Harvard University

INTRODUCTION

ADDITIONAL MS. 37075 in the British Museum[1] is a varied (forty items) and extensive (410 ff.) collection of texts and other educational materials thoughtfully and generously provided for a London schoolboy[2] of the later fourteenth century. Along with Latin grammars, Latin-English vocabularies, an English working of Donatus's *Ars Minor*, the *Liber Urbanitatis*, a vocabulary in goliardic verse, Latin exercises, and a copy of the *Disticha Catonis* (ending "Explicit liber Catonis. a Warrewyke"), there is found on folios 70 and 71 a group of twenty-eight English proverbs, each with a Latin version, and apparently hitherto unprinted.

Medieval collections of vernacular proverbs with Latin equivalents, frequently metrical and often with more than one Latin version for a single vernacular saying, are not uncommon, and were clearly regarded as useful for the learning of Latin, easy rhetorical devices, and the inculcation of common sense. The oldest of such groups is the early eleventh-century *Durham Proverbs*[3] and the most influential that of Serlo of Wilton (c. 1100–81),[4] nearly all of whose vernacular proverbs are Anglo-Norman.[5] Among Middle English collections are the following: (1) Trinity College Cambridge MS. o 2 45 (a1300).[6] The manuscript contains a fairly extensive group of Latin sayings in Leonine hexameters, and it was clearly the scribe's intention to give the English or French originals, for which spaces are left, but vernacular forms are provided for but eighteen of the first nineteen entries, fifteen of which are English. Only two of these have more than one Latin version. (2) Rylands Latin MS. 394 (c. 1450)[7] and (3) Douce MS. 52 (c. 1450).[8] These two collections, though not identical, are very similar in order and content and are clearly related.[9] The English proverbs are given an alphabetical arrangement of sorts, and there are frequently multiple Latin versions, running sometimes to as many as seven in Rylands (Pantin, p. 81), which has many more Latin examples than has Douce.[10] The editors print only a small selection of the Latin. (4) Harley MS. 3362 (c. 1470).[11] In this somewhat disordered manuscript the English proverbs are fitted into the margins and are sometimes left incomplete for want of space. There are sometimes more than one Latin version, but not all have been printed and not all of the English is proverbial. (5) Rawlinson MS. 328 (c. 1475).[12] There is but one Latin version of each English proverb, except that the first is repeated with a new Latin rendering. Three other English proverbs are given twice, but without new Latin. The editor prints both English and Latin. (6) Hill (a1500).[13] Here again only one Latin is given and the editor prints both versions throughout. The manuscript contains other groups of independent English and Latin proverbs.

A study of collections of this kind in their entirety will make a commendable addition to our knowledge of proverbs and of educational tools, especially if the investigation includes the Vulgaria, such as the Arundel[14] and those by John Stanbridge, William Horman, and Robert Whittington. For the immediate purpose little need be said. A number of proverbs in the present collection are found nowhere, at least before 1500, except in other collections of the same sort. Examples are numbers 16, 20, 21, 23, and 27, and another, 9, appears only here and in the *Proverbs of Hendyng* which, though a proverb poem, is allied to the collections. Since other proverbs not found in this collection are recorded only in collections, the inference is natural that some sayings, no matter how popular in origin, survive only because of their inclusion in these academic exercises. We must not forget, however, the role played by chance in the incorporation of proverbs in works of literature and in the continued existence of the literary works themselves. Thus number 9 would seem a "collection proverb," except for its use by Robert Mannyng, since Idley was drawing directly from Mannyng, and the same would be true of number 15 were it not found in one of the *Coventry Plays*. The element of chance survival is emphasized by the appearance in almost every collection of sayings which are not found elsewhere in their precise forms. Examples in the Additional Manuscript are numbers 5, 11, 13, 14, 23, and 26. Of these 11 and 13 are without comparable parallels in English, and for the others only sayings more or less similar can be instanced. The folly, second childhood, of old men (no. 5) is often expressed proverbially, though not as often as their wisdom, but the present phrasing has not been noted, and the saying is set apart from others in the collections by the inappropriate introductory phrase, "Hyt ys a comyn sawe (Est vulgare dictum)." That one should not praise a thing or man before it has been assayed or tried (no. 14) is a familiar sentiment, which combines the senses of such proverbs as "Praise a fair day at night" (Tilley D100) and "Try before you trust" (Tilley T595), but the only parallel (see Commentary) is not very close. The parallels (see Commentary) to number 23 show the saying's affinity, but our saying is quite distinct in pattern. Although number 26 has the same point as the parallel, it might well not be recognized as a proverb if it were found in a Vulgaria rather than in a collection such as this. The copious documentation of number 25 could have been enlarged, but none of the examples is really close, and it may well be that the English represents a rare case in which the vernacular is a translation, here somewhat inept, of the Latin.

NOTES

1. *Catalogue of Additions to the Manuscripts in the British Museum in the Years* 1900–1905 (London, 1907), pp. 344–49.
2. Neither scholar nor school is named, but the compiler of the *Catalogue* observes that "A reference to the practice of making rose-garlands for St. Anthony's day suggests that this may have been the school of St. Anthony, Threadneedle St., at which Sir Thomas More and others were scholars" [*Catalogue*, p. 344].
3. O. Arngart, *The Durham Proverbs: An Eleventh Century Collection of Anglo-Saxon Proverbs edited from Durham Cathedral MS. B.* III. 32, Lunds Universitets Årsskrift, N. F. Avd. 1, Bd 52, Nr 2 (Lund, 1956). There are forty-six Anglo-Saxon proverbs, each with a Latin equivalent, and of the translations Arngart says, "The Latin text is strangely corrupt and not always to be construed or restored with safety" (p. 6). Not all of the Anglo-Saxon sayings seem popular, and only a few turn up in Middle English.
4. Carefully edited from all known manuscripts and with extensive commentary by A. C. Friend, "The Proverbs of Serlo of Wilton," *Mediæval Studies*, XVI (1954), 179–218. Friend's suggestion (p. 180) that Serlo's Anglo-Norman proverbs were translated into English for later compilations is open to some question, since Serlo may have turned English proverbs into Anglo-

Norman, and in any case proverbs are international to a degree that does not always permit verbal closeness to be taken as evidence of translation.
5. For other Anglo-Norman or French and Latin collections, see Joseph Morawski, *Proverbes Français antérieurs au XVᵉ Siècle* (Paris, 1925), pp. vi, vii, ix. Printed examples include Bibl. Nat. MS. lat. 8653A (Ulysse Robert, "Un Vocabulaire Latin-Français du, XIVᵉ Siècle," *Bibliothèque de L'Ecole des Chartres*, XXXIV [1873] 33–46), which gives two or more Latin versions for each vernacular saying, and Tours MS. 438 (for reference, see Commentary), with one or more Latin versions. See also J. Morawski, "Proverbes français inédits tirés de trois recueils anglonormands," *Zeitschrift für romanische Philologie*, LVI (1936), 419–22.
6. Max Förster, "Frühmittelenglische Sprichwörter," *Englische Studien*, XXXI (1902), 1–9. Förster prints both vernacular and Latin forms, as had John M. Kemble in the rare first issue of his *Salomon and Saturn*, pp. 96–98; the Harvard College Library copy has a note in Kemble's hand, dated 29 December 1844, which reads in part, "These are the sheets of a work not exactly cancelled, but remodelled, and now about to appear in the collection of the Ælfric Society." The published edition does not include the Trinity proverbs.
7. For reference, see Commentary.

8. For reference, see Commentary.

9. See Pantin, *Rylands MS. 394*, pp. 85–89, for a discussion of the relationship and a comparative table of the English and some of the Latin proverbs.

10. The present writer's information about Douce is that given by Förster and Pantin, and further examination is needed before a judgment should be ventured as to whether Douce is taken from Rylands or goes back to a common source.

11. For reference, see Commentary.

12. For reference, see Commentary.

13. For reference, see Commentary.

14. William Nelson, *A Fifteenth Century School Book from a Manuscript in the British Museum (MS. Arundel 249)* (Oxford, 1956).

TEXT

FOR HELP in deciphering a photostat of the not too legible text I am indebted to Morton W. Bloomfield and also to Albert C. Friend, who examined the manuscript in the British Museum, and to J. L. M. Gulley of the British Museum Manuscript Room.

FOLIO 70a

1] A gode begynnyng makyth a gode endyng.
Felix principium finem facit esse beatum.

2] Hyt ys as ryȝth as a rameys horne.
Hoc est ita rectum sicut cornu.

3] The blynd etyth many a flye.
Manducat muscas privatus lumine multas.

4] Hyt ys not gold yᵗ shynyth as gold.
Non constat aurum totum quod splendet ut aurum.

5] Hyt ys a comyn sawe that old men dotyth.
Est vulgare dictum quod senes desipiscunt.

6] What yu doyst thynk on ye endyng day.
Nunc quid ages vel agis semper finis mediteris.

7] The nerer the chyrch the further fro God.
Quanto propinquior vir sit ecclesie tanto remotiorus a deo.

8] Nedys must yᵗ ned schall.
Necessarium est illi cui necessarium est oportunum(?).

9] Better be appylys ȝevyn than etyn.
Prestant poma data melius quam dente vorata.

10] Hyt ys harde to lyke hony of thornys.
Labare mel caram de spinis esset amaram.

11] He comyth sone ayene yᵗ fyndyth no frende.
Cito revenit qui nescit invenire amicum.

12] Asay yi frende er yu have nede.
Cum non indigeas rerum tentabis amicum.

FOLIO 70b

13] Thow the gold be now so rede ȝyt yt ys gevyn for brede.
Aurum tam pulcrum pro pane meminento(?) daturum.

14] Preys no man tyll thow have sayd hym.
Collaudes nullum donec probandis ipsum.

15] Who so may not go byfore lett goe byhynd.
Qui non potest esse precessor sit ille scutor (secutor *struck out*).

16] The schorter hosyn ye longer laynerys.
Ad curtas caligas ligulas decet addere longas.

17] Better(?) ys yᵉ byrd yn hond than ij in yᵉ wodde.
Prestat avis una nunc palma quam duo silva.

18] Yong sent olde devyll.
Angelicus ievenus (*for* iuvenis) senibus satanizat in annis.

19] Thow pepyr be blacke hyt hathe a gode smake.
Niger rugosum quamvis piper est preciosum.

20] Gode helpe and have alle.
Deus det auxilium et fiet esse suum.

21] Be hyt better be hyt worse folow hym yᵗ beryth yᵉ purse.
Seu bene seu male qui stat loculum imitate.

22] There may no man all men ples.
Nemo potest vere cunctim perfecta placere.

23] No man prysyth yᵉ byrde for hys fayre federys.
Nemo propter pennas laudat cumuna (? *for* cummune) volucrem.

24] Honger makyth hard bens hony swete.
Dura licet denti faba fit famis esurienti.

FOLIO 71a

25] A tre scheyth what frute comyth ofe.
Qualis arbor erit talia poma gerit.

26] Who wull drynke unbokyll hys purs.
Qui vult potare loculum debet reserare.

27] He yᵗ ys not bedyn he not wher to sytte.
Ignorat sedem non invocatus ad edem.

28] Of a lytyll sparkyll y^{er} comyth a grett fyre.
Ex modica magnus scintilla nascitur ignis.

COMMENTARY

THE COMMENTARY contains other early occurrences of and parallels to the proverbs found in the manuscript, followed by references to certain of the standard collections. The dates, wherever possible, are those assigned to composition by the *Middle English Dictionary*, except that question marks have been omitted. When there is more than one reference to a work, the following short titles are employed:

Apperson: G. L. Apperson, *English Proverbs and Proverbial Phrases* (London, 1929).
Ashby *Dicta, Policy*: George Ashby, *Poems*, ed. Mary Bateson (EETS ES 76, 1899).
Barclay *Ship*: Alexander Barclay, *The Ship of Fools*, ed. T. H. Jamieson, 2 vols. (Edinburgh, 1874).
Chaucer: *The Works of Geoffrey Chaucer*, ed. F. N. Robinson, 2d ed. (Boston, 1957).
Coventry Plays: Two Coventry Corpus Christi Plays, ed. Hardin Craig (EETS ES 87, 1902, 2d ed. 1957).
Dicts: The Dicts and Sayings of the Philosophers: the Translations made by Stephen Scrope, William Worcester and an Anonymous Translator, ed. C. F. Bühler (EETS 211, 1941).
Douce MS. 52: Max Förster, "Die mittelenglische Sprichwörtersammlung in Douce 52," *Festschrift zum xii. Allgemeinen Deutschen Neuphilologentage in München, Pfingsten,* 1906 (Erlangen, 1906), pp. 40–60.
Dunbar: *The Poems of William Dunbar*, ed. W. M. Mackenzie (Edinburgh, 1932).
Fyrst thou sal: Karl Brunner, "Me. Disticha (aus Hs. Add. 37049)," *Archiv für das Studium der Neueren Sprachen und Literaturen*, CLIX (1931), 86–92.
Gower *CA*: John Gower, *Confessio Amantis* in *The Complete Works of John Gower*, ed. G. C. Macaulay, 4 vols. (Oxford, 1899–1902), II, III.
Hali Meidenhad: ed. F. J. Furnivall (EETS 18 [rev.], 1922).
Harley MS. 3362: printed in part in *Retrospective Review*, II (1854), 309, and in part by Max Förster, *Anglia*, XLII (1918), 199–204, both selections supplemented and corrected from a photostat of the MS.
Hendyng O: H. Varnhagen, "Zu den sprichwörtern Hendyng's – Oxford, Bodl. Digby 86," *Anglia*, IV (1881), 191–200.
Heywood D: John Heywood, *A dialogue conteynyng the number of the effectual proverbes in the Englishe tounge* in *John Heywood's Works*

and Miscellaneous Short Poems, ed. B. A. Milligan (Illinois Studies in Language and Literature, 41, 1956), pp. 18–101.

Heywood *E*: John Heywood, *Epigrammes* (as above), pp. 104–248.

Hill: Proverbs in *Songs, Carols, and other Miscellaneous Poems from the Balliol MS. 354, Richard Hill's Commonplace-Book*, ed. Roman Dyboski (EETS ES 101, 1907).

Hoccleve: Thomas Hoccleve, *Works*, ed F. J. Furnivall (I, III) and Israel Gollancz (II) (EETS 61, 72, 73, 1892, 1897, 1924 [for 1897]).

Lydgate *Fall*: John Lydgate, *Fall of Princes*, ed. Henry Bergen (EETS 121–24, 1924–27).

Lydgate *MP*: *The Minor Poems of John Lydgate*, ed. H. N. MacCracken, 2 vols. (EETS ES 107, 192; 1911, 1934).

Oxford: W. G. Smith and J. E. Haseltine, *The Oxford Dictionary of English Proverbs* (2d ed. ed. Sir Paul Harvey, Oxford, 1948).

Proverbia Communia: Richard Jente, *Proverbia Communia: A Fifteenth Century Collection of Dutch Proverbs Together with the Low German Version* (Indiana University Publications, Folklore Series 4, 1947).

Proverbis of Wysdom: ed. Julius Zupitza, *Archiv für das Studium der neueren Sprachen und Literaturen*, xc (1893), 241–68.

Rawlinson MS D 328: S. B. Meech, "A Collection of Proverbs in Rawlinson MS D 328," *Modern Philology*, xxxviii (1940–41), 113–32.

Rel. Ant.: Thomas Wright and J. O. Halliwell, *Reliquiæ Antiquæ*, 2 vols. (London, 1845).

Robbins: R. H. Robbins, *Secular Lyrics of the xivth and xvth Centuries*, 2d ed. (Oxford, 1955).

Rylands MS. 394: W. A. Pantin, "A Medieval Collection of Latin and English Proverbs and Riddles from the Rylands Latin MS. 394," *Bulletin of the John Rylands Library*, xiv (1930), 81–114. Not quoted when virtually identical with Douce.

Serlo: A. C. Friend, "The Proverbs of Serlo of Wilton," *Mediæval Studies*, xvi (1954), 179–218.

Skeat: W. W. Skeat, *Early English Proverbs* (Oxford, 1910).

Skelton: *The Poetical Works of John Skelton*, ed. Alexander Dyce, 2 vols. (London, 1843).

South English Legendary (Laud): *The Early South-English Legendary*, ed. C. Horstmann (EETS 87, 1887).

Taylor and Whiting: Archer Taylor and B. J. Whiting, *A Dictionary of American Proverbs and Proverbial Phrases, 1820–1880* (Cambridge, Mass., 1958).

Tilley: M. P. Tilley, *A Dictionary of the Proverbs in England in the Sixteenth and Seventeenth Centuries* (Ann Arbor, Mich., 1950).

Tours MS. 438: A. Hilka, "Altfranzösische Sprichwörter," *Jahresbericht der schlesischen Gesellschaft für vaterländische Cultur*, xci (1913) Abteilung 4, Sektion für neuere Philologie, 21–38.

Whiting *Drama*: B. J. Whiting, *Proverbs in the Earlier English Drama* (Harvard Studies in Comparative Literature 14, Cambridge, Mass., 1938).

Whiting *Scots* I, II: B. J. Whiting, "Proverbs and Proverbial Sayings from Scottish Writings before 1600," *Mediæval Studies*, XI (1949), 123–205; XIII (1951), 87–164.

Yonge *Governaunce*: James Yonge, *The Governaunce of Prynces* in Robert Steele, *Three Prose Versions of the Secreta Secretorum* (EETS ES 74, 1898), pp. 121–248.

1] c1300 *South English Legendary*, ed. Charlotte D'Evelyn and Anna J. Mill, 2 vols. (EETS 235–36, 1956) I 216.67–68: This was atte verste me thingth a god begynnynge Ther after was the betere hope to come to god endynge.   c1325 *Proverbs of Hendyng H* in K. Böddeker, *Altenglische Dichtungen des MS. Harl.* 2253 (Berlin, 1878) 288.13: God beginning maketh god endying. c1375 John Barbour, *Bruce*, ed. W. W. Skeat, 2 vols. (STS, 1864–65) I 121.263–66: For gude begynnyng and hardy, And it be followit vittely, May ger oftsiss unlikly thing Cum to ful [conabill] endyng.   a1419 *Letter* in *Modern Language Review*, XXII (1927), 75[7–8]: Make a good ende of that they han well bygonne. a1449 Lydgate *Haste* in MP II 764.155–57: A goode begynnynge requireth a good issue, A good preamble a good conclusyon, For vertuous lyff vertuous gwerdon.   c1450 *Douce MS.* 52 55.122: Of a gode begynnyng comyth a gode endyng.   c1450 *Rylands MS.* 394 105.18.26. a1471 Ashby *Policy* 38.824–25: And your matiers shall have goode begynnyng, And consequently come to goode endyng, a1475 *Dicta* 93.1105–1106: So of goode begynnyng is goode endyng, And of shreudenesse comethe Il concludyng.   c1475 William Gregory, *Chronicle of London* in *Historical Collections of a Citizen of London*, ed. James Gairdner (Camden Society, N. S. 17, 1876) 192 [1–2]: Every goode begynnyng hathe the wery goode endynge. *Proverbium:—Felix principium finem facit esse beatum.*   c1475 *Rawlinson MS. D 328* 117.1.2: A good be-gynnyng makyth a god ende. *Bonum principium facit bonum finem. Principium gratum finem facit esse beatum.*   a1500 Hill 129.42: A good beginning makith a good endinge.   1546 Heywood D 37.71: Of a good begynnyng comth a good end, 1555 E 171.141. Apperson 257, 674; *Oxford* 250; Skeat 28; Taylor and Whiting 24; Tilley B259; Whiting *Drama* 127, *Scots* I 137.

2] c1325 *A levedy a(n)d my love* in *Rel. Ant.* II 19[4]: As ryt as ramis orn.   c1400 *Tale of Beryn*, ed. F. J. Furnivall and W. S. Stone (Chaucer Society, 1887) 6.152: And a red [it] also right as [wolde] Rammys hornyd. c1405 *Mum and the Sothsegger*, ed. Mabel Day and Robert Steele (EETS 199, 1936) 77.1725: And redith as right as the Ram is hornyd.   a1449 Lydgate *Ryght as a Rammes Horne* in MP II 461–64, 8, 16, 24, 32, 40,

48, 56.   c1522 Skelton *Colyn* I 357.1201: By the ryght of [MS. Be hyt ryghte as] a rambes horne, *Speke* II 24.498: So myche raggyd ryghte of a rammes horne, 1522 *Why Come* II 29.87: As ryght as a rammes horne. Apperson 531; *Oxford* 543; Taylor and Whiting 303; Tilley R28; Whiting *Scots* II 115.

3]   c1450 *Fyrst thou sal* 90.120: Many a flee etes the blynde.   c1490 *BM Sloane MS. 747* f.66a: The blynde etyth many a flye.   a1500 *Scorn of Women* in Robbins 224–25.7, 14 *etc.* (refrain): Beware, therefore: the blynde eteth many a fly.   c1500 *Trials of Old Men in Love* in Robbins 164.8: Oftyn-tymes and many the blynde etyth many a flye.   c1500 *Of their nature* in John Stowe, *Works of Geffrey Chaucer* (1561) CCXLI^v [2.14]: Beware alwaye the blind eateth many flye, [2.20–21]: But whether y^t ye blind eate flesh or fish I pray God kepe the fly out of my dishe.   1528 Skelton *Replycacion* I 213.151–52: But, as the man sayes, The blynde eteth many a flye, cf. 216.244, 252.   1546 Heywood *D* 77.231: The blynde eate many flies, 1555 *E* 175.165, 191.259.   Apperson 55–56; *Oxford* 50; Tilley B451; Whiting *Drama* 50, *Scots* I 141.

4]   c1200 *Hali Meidenhad* 10.97: Nis hit nower neh gold al ther ter schineth.   c1250 *Hendyng o* 200.46: Hit nis nout al gold, that shineth. c1380 Chaucer *House of Fame* 272: Hyt is not al gold that glareth. c1385 Thomas Usk, *Testament of Love* in W. W. Skeat, *Chaucerian and Other Pieces* (Oxford, 1897) 54–55.47–48: For every glittring thing is nat gold.   c1395 Chaucer *CT* VIII[G] 962–63: But al thyng which that shineth as the gold Nis nat gold, as that I have herd it told.   a1410 Lydgate *Churl* in *MP* II 481.306: All is nat gold that shewith goldissh hewe.   1422 Yonge *Governaunce* 156.23: Hit is not al golde that Shynyth as golde.   a1425 John Wyclif *Sermons* in *Select English Works*, ed. Thomas Arnold, 3 vols. (Oxford, 1869–71) I 224[2–4]: And so men hav taught comunli that men shulden not holde al gold that shyneth as gold, for many thingis ben fourboshid ful falseli.   a1439 Lydgate *Fall* II 547.2707–708: Al is nat gold, to speke in pleyn langage, That shynith briht, 553.2944: Al is nat gold that shyneth briht, III 911.3160: Al is nat gold that is cleer shynyng, a1449 *Amor* in *MP* II 747.77: Al nys nat golde that shyneth bright, *Mydsomer Rose* in *MP* II 781.12: Al is nat gold that outward shewith bright, *World* in *MP* II 847.93: Al is not goold which shynyth cleer and bryght.   c1475 *Prohemy of a Mariage* in J. O. Halliwell, *Selection from the Minor Poems of Lydgate* (Percy Society 2) 43[21]: Sithe not is golde al that as golde dothe shyne.   a1500 Hill 129.26: It is not all gold that glareth.   a1500 *O man more* in *Anglia* XXXI (1908) 393.8: All is not golde that shynes full clere.   a1500 *Scorn of Women* in Robbins 224.18: "All ys nat gold that shynyth!" men, take hede.   a1500 *Thre Prestis of Peblis*, ed. T. D. Robb (STS 1920) 49.1150:

And weil I wait al is not gold that glitters.   a1508 Dunbar *Tretis* 89.202: He had the glemyng of gold, and wes bot glase fund in.   1546 Heywood *D* 38.122: All is not golde that glisters by tolde tales.   Apperson 6; *Oxford* 249; Skeat 86; Taylor and Whiting 154–55; Tilley A146; Whiting *Drama* 122, 134, 215, *Scots* I 179.

5]   Cf. Apperson 464–65: Old men are twice children; *Oxford* 472; Tilley M570.

6]   a1325 *Sarmun* in W. Heuser, ed. *Die Kildare-Gedichte* (Bonner Beiträge zur Anglistik 14, 1904), 94.167: Takith gode hede, men, to yur end.   a1400 *Wars of Alexander*, ed. W. W. Skeat (EETS ES 47, 1886) 182.3094–95: Heves noght your hert up to highe, take hede to your end; It limps noght all-way the last to licken with the first, 196.3297–98: Loke to thine ende, For die the bose, quen all is done and ay thi day scortis.   a1400 *Proverbis of Wysdom* 246.87–8: Where ever thou be, have god yn mynd And al way thynk on thyn end.   c1440 *Prose Life of Alexander*, ed. J. S. Westlake (EETS 143, 1913) 55.36–37: But alway thynke on thy laste ends, 65.33: And thare-fore take hede to thi laste ende.   a1450 *Castell of Perseverance* in *Macro Plays*, edd. F. J. Furnivall and A. W. Pollard (EETS ES 91, 1904) 186.3647–49: To save you fro synnynge, Evyr at the begynnynge Thynke on youre last endynge. 1450 *Dicts* 122.17–18: He is unhappy that is handelinge in his malice and that thinkithe not on his eende.   c1450 *Fyrst thou sal* 89.69–70: What ever thou do hafe god in mynde And thinke ymonge on thi last ende.   a1500 *Ghostly Battle* in *Yorkshire Writers*, ed. Carl Horstmann, 2 vols. (London, 1895–96) II 428 [43–44]: Salomone seyth: "In alle thy werkes thynke one thy ende, ande thou shalt never doo syne."   a1500 *Harley MS*. 4294 in *Rel. Ant.* I 316[1–2]: Men, remember thy end, And thou shalt never be shend.   a1500 *MS. Marginalia* in Hoccleve I 181, n. 3: Before thou pretend any evill in thy harte, Remember the end when thow shalt departe, quod Carter.   Apperson 397:60; Tilley E125.

7]   c1303 Robert Mannyng *Handlyng Synne*, ed. F. J. Furnivall (EETS 119, 1901) 290.9241–42: Tharfor men seye, an weyl ys trowed, "The nere the cherche, the fyrther fro God."   c1450 *Douce MS*. 52 45.15: The nere the chyrche, the fer fro Crist.   c1450 Idley 210.395–96: But the nerer the chyrch the ffarther from God—Yt ys a proverbe.   c1450 *Rylands MS*. 394 96.4.   c1475 *Rawlinson MS*. D 328 126.87: The nyer the cherche the ferder fowre good. *In quanto homo templo propinquior jn tanto est a deo remosior.*   a1500 Hill 130.12: The nere the chirche, the ferder from God. *Ecclesie quanto prope longior est bono tanto.* 1546 Heywood *D* 33.15: The nere to the churche, the ferther from God, 1555 *E* 174.157.   Apperson 438; *Oxford* 445; Skeat 40; Tilley C380.

8] c1330 *Seven Sages of Rome (Southern Version)*, ed. Karl Brunner (EETS 191, 1933) 68.1597–98: O nedes he sschal, that nedes mot, Hit nis nowt mi wille, god hit wot.   a1393 Gower *CA* II 24.698: So soffre thei that nedes mote, 82.1714: Bot nede he mot that nede schal, 235.351– 53: For it is seid thus overal, That nedes mot that nede schal Of that a lif doth after kinde, III 413.1020: Bot nede he mot, that nede schal.   a1500 *Coventry Plays* 47.456: Then nedis muste thatt nedis schall, 68.1140. a1500 *Jeaste of Syr Gawayne* in *Syr Gawayne*, ed. Frederic Madden (Bannatyne Club, London, 1839) 208.43: Nedes must that nedes shall. *Oxford* 447.

9] c1250 *Hendyng O* 195–96.25: Betere is appel iyeven, then al ieten, a1325 *C* 184.14: Betir is one appil iyevin, than twein iyetin.   Apperson 13; Skeat 30–31; Tilley A292.   See Serlo 197.32 for two Latin versions and three others quoted from *Rylands MS. 394*, f. 16 (no English given). Cf. *Tours MS. 438* 26.51: *Mieulx vault oeuf donné que oeuf mengié* (and two Latin versions).

10] c1200 *Hali Meidenhad* 10.95: Ha lickith honi of thornes   a1225 *Lambeth Homilies* in Richard Morris, *Old English Homilies . . . First Series* (EETS 29, 34, 1867–68) 185[17–19]: Nis nan blisse sothes inan thing thet is utewith thet ne beo to bitter aboht, thet et huni ther in beoth liked of thornes.   c1250 *Hendyng O* 195.22: Al to dere is bouht honi, that mon shal liken of thornes.   a1300 *This World's Bliss* in Carleton Brown *English Lyrics of the XIII Century* (Oxford, 1932) 79.35–36: Thu lickest huni of thorn iwis That seist thi love o werldos blis, 81.35–36. c1390 *Talkyng of the Love of God*, ed. Cecilia M. Westra ('S-Gravenhage, 1950) 4.29–30: Nis no blisse otewith, that hit nis to deore a bought, As hony that me likketh on prikkynde thornes.   a1393 Gower *CA* III 192.927–28: And thus, as I have seid aforn, I licke hony on the thorn. c1450 *Douce MS. 52* 50.79: Hit is harde to lykke hony fro the thorne, 51.80: Dere is the hony bought, That on thornes is sought.   c1450 *Rylands MS. 394* 100.3, 7.   Apperson 307; *Oxford* 301; Tilley H554.

12] c1390 *Fy on a faint Friend!* in Carleton Brown *English Lyrics of the XIV Century* (Oxford, 1952) 156.37–40: Or thou have nede, thi frendes a-tast, Whuche be stif and shuche wol bende, And ther thou fynde bouwynde or bast—And ever fy on a feynt frende!   a1400 *Proverbis of Wysdom* 244.30: Ore thow have nede, assay thy frend.   a1449 Lydgate *Amor* in *MP* II 747.85–86: Pref thy friende afore, and thou shalt se Whom thou maist trust, thy journay for to spede.   a1450 *Poems of John Audelay*, ed. Ella K. Whiting (EETS 184, 1931) 26.452–53: Assay thi frynd or thou have nede And of his answere take good hede.   a1450 *Myne awen dere sone* in *Neuphilologische Mitteilungen*, XLIX (1948)

173.758: Or thou hafe nede, thy frende thou prove.   c1450 *Fyrst thou sal* 88.34: Our thou hafe nede assay thy freet frende.   1474 W. Caxton, *Game and Playe of the Chesse*, ed. W. E. A. Axon (London, 1883) 99[6–8]: And hit appertayneth and behoveth a man to assaye and preve his frende er he have nede.   c1475 *Rawlinson MS. D 328* 119.23; A-say thy frynd ar thow haw nede. *Cum' non' indigias rerum temtabis amicum.* a1477 Anthony Woodville, Earl Rivers, *Dictes and Sayings of the Philosophers* (Caxton, 1477; facs., Detroit, Mich., 1901) 15[7–8]: Enforce your selfe to winne frendis and than first preve them, ar ye put to much truste in them.   a1500 *Faythfull frende* in [Joseph Haslewood] *The Book Containing the Treatises of Hawking, etc.* (London, 1810) E5^v[30–31]: Therfore I rede you, syres all, To assaye your frendes or ye have nede.   a1500 *Gest of Robyn Hode* in F. J. Child, *English and Scottish Popular Ballads*, 5 vols. (Boston, 1882–98) III 62.112[3–4]: For it is good to assay a frende Or that a man have nede.   a1500 Richard L. Greene, *Early English Carols* (Oxford, 1935) 389 (refrain): Man, be ware and wyse indede, And asay thi frend or thou hast nede.   a1500 Hill 132.34: Assay thy frend or thow have nede. *Cum non indegias rerum, temtabis amicum.*   a1504 Stephen Hawes, *Example of Virtu* (de Worde, 1510) CC1^r[8–9]: Prove thy frende in a mater fayned Or thou have nede.   1546 Heywood *D* 54.443: Prove thy freende er thou have neede, 1555 *E* 151.27. Apperson 515, 651; *Oxford* 522; Tilley F718.

14]   a1400 *Cato (Fairfax)* in *Cursor Mundi*, ed. Richard Morris, 3 vols. (EETS 57, 59, 62, 66, 68, 99, 101, 1874–92) III 1672.211–13: Be scarske of thi loving Til hit come to proving Of thi gode frende.   Cf. Apperson 515; *Oxford* 522.

15]   c1450 *Douce MS. 52* 52.92: Who-so may not go byfore, com by-hynde.   c1450 *Rylands MS. 394* 102.13.   c1475 *Rawlinson MS. D 328* 117.5: He that maynot goo be-fore moste goye be-hind. *Qui non precessor valet esse sit ille secutor.*   a1500 *Coventry Plays* 58.804–805: That man thatt canot goo before Nedis must cum behynd.   Tilley G156.

16]   c1470 *Harley MS. 3362* f. 2b in *Retrospective* 309[11] and Förster 201.9: Schorte hosin be-howyth longe [*thonges*]. *Ad curtas caligas ligulas decet addere longas.*   a1475 *Rawlinson MS. D 328* 119.24: The scherter the hose the lynger lessys. *At cortas caligas legulas debet addere longas.*   Cf. *Tours MS. 438* 27.55: A courte chauce longe laniere. *Si brevis est caliga, sit tibi longa liga.*

17]   c1450 John Capgrave *Life of St. Katharine*, ed. C. Horstmann and F. J. Furnivall (EETS 100, 1893) 93–95.250–52: It is more sekyr a byrd in your fest Than to have three in the sky a-bove, And more

profytabye to youre be-hove.   c1470 *Harley MS. 3362* f. 4a in *Retrospective* 309[29]: Betyr ys a byrd in the hond, than tweye in the wode.
Plue valet in palmos avis una quam dupla(?) *silvas. Plus valet in
dextera*(?) *volucres quam quatuour extra.*   c1475 *Rawlinson MS.* D
328 119.27: Hyt ys better a byrd yn hon' than iiii with-owyt. *Plus valet
in dextera volucres* [sic] *quam quatuor extra.*   a1500 Hill 128.6: A
birde in hond is better than thre in the wode.   1509 Barclay *Ship* II
74[3-4]: Better have one birde sure within thy wall Or fast in a Cage
than twenty score without.   c1425 John Heywood, *Dialogue on Wit and
Folly*, ed. F. W. Fairholt (Percy Society, 20, 1846) 24[19-20]: An old
proverb makythe with thys, whyche I tak good, Better one byrd in hand
then ten in the wood, [22-25], 26[19-20], 1546 D 46.181: Better one
byrde in hande than ten in the wood, 1555 E 152.40.   Apperson 48;
Oxford 44-45; Taylor and Whiting 27; Tilley B363; Whiting *Drama* 155,
221, *Scots* I 139.

18]   a1400 *An Exposition of Qui Habitat*, ed. Björn Wallner (Lund
Studies in English, 23, Lund, 1954)9.2-3: And callen hem ypocrites or
yong seyntes [and] olde develes.   c1415 *Middle English Sermons*, ed.
Woodburn O. Ross (EETS 209, 1940) 159.37-40: Itt is a comond proverbe bothe of clerkes and of laye man, "younge seynt, old dewell." And
so thei arn disceyveyd. For often tymes sonere thou seyst a younge man
die than an old man.   a1450 *Of the seven Ages* in *Modern Language
Notes* LXXII (1957) 484[7]: Yonge saynt alde devell is ane alde sawe.
a1470 Henry Parker *Dives and Pauper* (de Worde, 1496) C2*v*[1.17-21]:
Dives: And yet it is a comon proverbe/yonge saynt olde devyll. Pauper:
It is a synfull proverbe to drawe men to synne fro vertue/fro god to the
fende.   a1470 *Harley MS. 3362* f. 2a in *Retrospective* 309[1] and
Förster 199[1]: Young seynt, old devyl. *Angelicus juvenis senibus
satanizat in annis.*   a1513 Dunbar *Merle* 135.35: Of yung sanctis
growis auld feyndis but faill.   1546 Heywood D 39.124: Yong seynt olde
devill, 1555 E 155.61.   Apperson 720; *Oxford* 739; Tilley S33; Whiting
Drama 220, *Scots* II 120.

19]   c1450 *In Praise of Brunettes* in Robbins 31.17-19: Peper wyt-oute
yt ys wel blac, Y-wys wyt-inne yt ys not so; Lat go the colur and tak the
smac.   c1450 *Rylands MS. 394* 105.28: Thawgh peper be blac, it hath
a good smak.   c1470 *Harley MS. 3362* f. 5a: Thaw pepyr be blac (*no
more*). *Est peper sapidum quamvis sit corpore nigrum.*   a1500 Hill
128.9: Thowgh peper be blak, it hath a good smak, 130.17: Thowgh peper
be blake, hit hath a good smakke. *Est piper nigrum, quod gratum
prestat odorem.*   1508 (1519) John Stanbridge *Vulgaria*, ed. Beatrice
White (EETS 187, 1932) 23.1: Though peper be blacke it hathe a good
smacke. *Tamen si piper nig*[ri] *coloris sit bene sapit tamen.*   1546

Heywood *D* 68.66: Pepper is blacke And hath a good smacke And every man doth it bye (*in a multiple saying with snow, milk and ink*).   Apperson 584.7; *Oxford* 496; Tilley S593.

20]   c1450 *Douce MS.* 52 45.9: Helpe God and have alle. *Det Deus auxilium, fiat et omne suum.*   c1450 *Rylands MS.* 394 96.28.   c1475 *Rawlinson MS. D* 328 120.35: God helpe and have all. *Deus deus* [for *det*] *auxilium fiet in om[n]e suum.*   Cf. *Oxford* 283: Have God and have all; Tilley G229.

21]   c1450 *Douce MS.* 52 49.64: Do thow better, do thow worse, Do after hym, that beryth the purse.   c1475 *Rawlinson MS. D* 328 120.32: Be hit beter be hit werse folo hym that berit the pursse. *Sive bene sive male qui fert loculum hemtare* [for *imitare*].   a1500 Hill 130.7: Be it better or be it worse/do after hym that berith the purse. *Seu bene sive male, loculum qui fert imitare.*   1546 Heywood *D* 26.27–28: It is saide be it better be it wurs, Dooe ye after him that beareth the purs.   Apperson 29; *Oxford* 25; Tilley P646.

22]   a1500 Hill 132.49: Ther may no man all men please. *Nemo potest vere cunctis omnino placere.*   Apperson 449; Tilley P88, cf. M526. Cf. Whiting *Drama* 156.

23]   Cf. Tilley F153: The feather makes not the bird, F163.

24]   c1450 *Douce MS.* 52 46.29: Hungur makyth harde benys swete. c1475 *Rawlinson MS. D* 328 123.63: Hungger makyth arde benis honi suete. *Dura licet dente faba melle sapit esuriente.*   a1500 Hill 133.55: Hungre maketh harde bones softe. *Dura licet faba denti sic salus esurienti.*   a1549 Heywood *D* 40.173: Hunger makth hard beanes sweete.   Apperson 318; *Oxford* 310; Tilley H822.   Cf. *Proverbia Communia* 72.389 (*two dissimilar Latin versions*); Serlo 186.3.

25]   c1300 *South English Legendary (Laud)* 282.166–67: For ore loverd seide, i-wis: "Bi the fruyt man may i-seo hwat-manere treo it is."   c1390 Chaucer *Canterbury Tales* x[I] 115: And therfore oure Lord Jhesu Crist seith thus: "By the fruyt of hem shul ye knowen hem." a1400 *Pricke of Conscience*, ed. Richard Morris (Philological Society, Berlin, 1863) 19.658–59: Swilk als the tre es with bowes, Swilk es the fruyt that on it growes.   1402 Hoccleve *Letter of Cupid* 1 79.177: For swiche the frute ys as that is the tre.   a1430 Lydgate *Pilgrimage*, ed. F. J. Furnivall (EETS ES 77, 83, 92, 1889–1904) 261.9457–59: For the ffrut (what-evere yt be) Bereth the tarage off the tre That yt kam fro, a1439 *Fall* 1 133.4771: As off the stok the frut hath his tarage, 206.

246–47: Frut and apples taken ther tarage Wher thei first greuh off the same tree, III 969.1782: The frut also bert[h] of the tre witnesse, a1449 *Vertu* in *MP* II 835.17: Frut fet fro fer tarageth of the tre, *World* in *MP* II 844.18: Frute folwith the tarage of the tree.   1449 John Metham, *Amoryus* in *Works*, ed. Hardin Craig (EETS 132, 1911) 3.55: The [s]qwete frute schewyth the gentil tre.   a1449 Reginald Pecock *Repressor of Over Much Blaming of the Clergy*, ed. Churchill Babington, 2 vols. (Rolls Series, 1860) II 321[21–23]: Aftir the sentence of Crist (Math. vii^e c. and Luk vi^e c.) "Such is the tre, which is the fruyt of the same tree."   c1450 *Jacob's Well*, ed. Arthur Brandeis (EETS 115, 1900) 74.26–27: Be the frute, men may knowe the tre.   c1450 *Pilgrimage of the Lyf of the Manhode*, ed. W. A. Wright (Roxburghe Club 91, 1869) 90[19–20]: Riht it is that the tre bere swich fruyt as kynde techeth it.   c1475 *Rawlinson MS. D* 328 124.69: Sygge tre sygge frytte. *Sepe probat fructus de qua fit harborum ductus.*   a1500 Hill 128.18: Often times prowith the frwight after the stok that hit cometh off.   c1515 Alexander Barclay *Eclogues*, ed. Beatrice White (EETS 175, 1928) 151.321: So every tree hath fruit after his kinde.   1528 Skelton *Replycacion* I 214.156–57: For it is an auncyent brute, Suche apple tre, suche frute.   Apperson 607; *Oxford* 670; Tilley T486, 494; Whiting *Drama* 109, *Scots* II 144.

26]   Cf. Tilley M1088: No money no drink.

27]   c1450 *Douce MS. 52* 48.53: Unbodun gest not, where he shall sytte. *Ignorat sedem non invitatus ad edem.*   c1450 *Rylands MS. 394* 98.18.   1546 Heywood *D* 33.22: An unbydden geast knoweth not where to syt.   Apperson 658; *Oxford* 682; Tilley G476.   Cf. *Proverbia Communia* 62.268.

28]   c1300 *South English Legendary (Laud)* 474.425: Ake of[te] gret fuyr and eke stuyrne wext of a luytel spielde.   c1380 Chaucer *House of Fame* 2077–80: And that encresing ever moo, As fyr ys wont to quyke and goo From a sparke spronge amys, Til al a citee brent up ys.   c1395 *The Holy Bible . . . by John Wycliffe and his Followers*, edd. Josiah Forshall and Frederic Madden, 4 vols. (Oxford, 1850) Eccl. 11:34 [III 145]: Fier is encressid of a sparcle.   a1398 Bartholomeus de proprietatibus rerum, trans. John de Trevisa (de Worde, 1495) & 3^r [1.23–5]: For of a lytill sperkyll in an hepe of towe or of tyndyr cometh sodaynly a grete fyre.   a1400 *Gest Hystoriale of the Destruction of Troy*, edd. G. A. Panton and D. Donaldson (EETS 39, 56, 1869–74) I 47–48. 1426–31: A Proverbe. A word that is wrappid, and in wrath holdyn, May feston as a fyre with a fuerse lowe, Of a sparke unaspied, spred under askys, May feston up fyre to mony freike sorow; So lurkes with lordes of a light wrathe, That growes into gronnd harme, grevys full sore.   a1420

J. Lydgate *Troy Book*, ed. Henry Bergen (EETS ES 97, 103, 106, 126, 1906–35) I 34.785–86: And of sparkys that ben of syght[e] smale, Is fire engendered that devoureth al.   1422 Yonge *Governaunce* 164.15–16: As a Sparke of fyre risyth an huge fyre able a realme to brente. a1440 Benedict Burgh *Cato* in *Archiv* cxv (1905) 314.459: Off brondis smale be maad thes fires grete.   a1449 Lydgate *See Myche* in *MP* II 800.22–23: A lytell sparke ofte sette a tonne a-fyre, But when it [brennythe] it is not lyghtely quent.   1450 *Dicts* 274.5: A litille sparke makithe lightly a (grete) fire.   c1450 *Douce MS. 52* 48.55: Of a lytul sparkull comyth a grete fyre.   c1450 *Ladder* in *Deonise Hid Divinite*, ed. Phyllis Hodgson (EETS 231, 1955) 109.2: Howe mych a fyre kendelyth of so litelle a sparkille.   c1450 *Rylands MS. 394* 98.25: sparke.   c1470 *Harley MS. 3362* f. 4a in *Retrospective* 309[24]: Of a lytyl spark ys mad gret feer. *Ex minima magnus sintilla nascitur ignis.* a1475 Ashby *Dicta* 61.426–27: For of a litle sparkel a grete fyre Comyth, displeasaunt to many a sire.   1483 W. Caxton *Cathon* F1ʳ[9]: For a lytel sparcke of fyre kyndleth ofte a grete fyre.   a1500 Hill 130.15: Of a lytill sparkyll, commeth a gret fyre. *De modica magnus scintilla nascitur ignis.* 1509 Barclay *Ship* I 194[1–2]: A small sparcle often tyme doth augment It selfe: and groweth to flames peryllous.   1509 Watson *Shyppe of Fooles* (de Worde, 1509) 13ᵛ[15–17]: The sparcle . . . encreaseth unto a grete flambe.   1528 More *Dialogue concernynge Heresyes* in *Workes* (London, 1557) 285 H[6–8]: The sparcle wel quenched ere it wer suffred to growe to over great a fyre.   1532 Berners *Golden Boke* in José M. Gálvez, *Guevara in England* (Palaestra 109, Berlin, 1916) 325. 6679–80: With a lyttell sparcle, the house is sette a fyre.   Apperson 593; S714. Cf. *Proverbia Communia* 102.731.

Some Linguistic Reflections of a Wycliffite

ANGUS McINTOSH

University of Edinburgh

BRITISH MUSEUM MS. Royal 17. B. 1 is an early fifteenth-century Wycliffite concordance to the New Testament.* Before the concordance itself, which begins at line 3 of folio 7ʳ and ends on folio 170ʳ, there is a preface wherein the compiler considers some of the problems he has had to face and tells how he has dealt with them. This preface, which (apart from endpapers in Latin) is the only text preceding the concordance, runs from the top of folio 3ʳ to line 2 of folio 7ʳ. The whole manuscript is written in one hand in a highly consistent language and with a remarkable degree of orthographic uniformity. The dialect of the text suggests that the scribe was from northeast Bedfordshire or the extreme south of Huntingdonshire. The preface deserves to be better known than it is, and I offer a text of it below. To illustrate the concordance itself, I have printed from folio 7 the opening seven entries.†

Mannes mynde, þat is ofte robbid of þe tresour of kunnyng bi þe enemye of science, þat is forȝetyng, is greetly releeued bi tablis maad bi lettre aftir þe ordre of þe A B C. Ensaumple, if a man haue mynde oonly of oo word or two of sum long text of the Newe Lawe & haþ forȝetyn al þe remenaunt, or ellis if he can seie bi herte such an hool text but he haþ forȝeten in what stede it is writen, þis concordaunce wole lede him bi þe fewe wordis þat ben cofrid in his mynde vnto þe ful text, & shewe him in what book & in what chapitre he shal fynde þo textis whiche him list to haue.

Þis concordaunce sueþ not oonly þe ordre of þe A B C in þe firste lettris of wordis, but also in þe secounde, in þe þridde, in þe fourþe & so forþ; wherfore *Aaron* stondiþ bifore *Abba*, for þe secounde lettre of *Aaron*, which is "a," stondiþ in þe A B C bifore "b," which is þe secounde lettre of *Abba*. And *Abba* stondiþ bifore *Abel*, for þe þridde lettre of *Abba*, þat is "b," stondiþ in þe A B C bifore þe þridde lettre of *Abel*, which is "e." Þus *conferme* stondiþ bifore *confounde*, bi cause þe fifþe lettre of þis word *conferme* stondiþ in þe A B C bifore þe fifþe lettre of *confounde*, þat is "o"; for in þe firste foure lettris of þese two wordis, whiche ben "c," "o," "n" and "f," in no þing þei discorden. Wherfore if þou fynde ony word in þis werk þat is not set in þis forme, vnkunnyg¹ or neglygence of þe writere is in cause, and liʒtly, bi oon þat can, may it be amendid. If it seme to ony creature þat cotaciouns of summe textis be not spoken off in wordis þere þei shulde be expressid, if þei be duly plauntid yn, so myche is þe bettir, so þat þei be not set in ordinatly,[2] aftir þe maner of þis drawyng.

Whanne a text conteyneþ two wordis & þou can not wel perceyue in wheþer of þo wordis þou shuldist seeke it, þou shalt fynde it quotid in oon of hem at þe leeste & sumtyme in boþe. As, if þee list fynde þis text: *Womman lo þi sone*; if þou fynde it not in S in þis word *sone*, þou shalt fynde it in V[3] in þis word *womman*. If þou fynde not þis text: *Tribulacioun worchiþ pacience* in P in þis terme *pacience*, þou shalt fynde it in T in þis word *tribulacioun* & þus of oþere lijk tixtis.

In Englisch as in Latyn ben wordis synonemus, þat is to seie manie wordis bitokenynge oo þing, as *kirke* & *chirche*, *accesse* & *nyʒcomynge*, *clepe* & *calle*, *ʒyue* & *gyue*, *ʒift* & *gift*, *bigyle* & *disceyue* & *defraude*. And sumtyme suche wordis varyen or diuersen al oonly in oo lettre, as *flax* & *flex*, *invie* & *envie*, *lomb* & *lamb*. And oþerwhile haþ þat oon a lettre more þan þat oþer, as *epistle* & *pistle*. Now it may be so þat in sum Newe Lawe is writen in sum text þis word *kirke* & in þe same text & in a noþer book is writen þis word *chirche*, & þus of oþere wordis bifore rehersid & of manye mo lyk hem. If þou þanne seke a text in ony of suche synonemus & if þou fynde it not in oon of hem, loke in a noþir of hem; ʒhe, loke in alle suche synonemus, þouʒ þer be þre or mo of hem, til þou fynde þ[e] text wiþ which þe liste mete. Remissioun is ofte maad in þis concordaunce fro such a synoneme til a noþer.[4] Sumtyme þe formere remittiþ to þe lattere & sumtyme þe lattere remittiþ to þe formere.

Sumtyme þe same word & þe self þat is writen of sum man in oo manere is writen of a noþer man in anoþer manere. As wher summe writen þese wordis *thyng* & *theef* wiþ "th," oþere vsen to writen þoo same wordis with þis figure—"þ." Wherfore alle þe wordis of þis concordaunce of which þe firste carecte is þis figure "þ" bigynnen in þis table with "th," and in T þei stonden aftir þat here ordre axiþ. Summe writen "gh" in summe wordis, whiche wordis ben writen of summe oþere w[t] a yogh þat is figured þus—"ʒ," as sum man writeþ þus þese termes: *doughter*, *thought*, where a noþer writiþ hem þus: *douʒter*, *thouʒt*. But for as miche as þe carect yogh, þat is to seie "ʒ," is figurid lijk a zed, þerfore alle þe wordis of þis table þat biginnen wiþ þat carect ben set in Zed, which is the laste lettre of þe A B C. Also sum man writeþ sum word wiþ an "h" which saame word anoþer man writiþ wiþouten an "h." As is of þe Englisch word which þis Latyn word *heres* signyfieþ, which terme summe writen with "h" þus—*here* & summe þus—*eir* wiþouten "h."

Þese diuerse maneris of writyng ben to be considerid in þis concordaunce. For perchaunce, aftir my manere of writyng, sum word stondiþ in sum place, which same word aftir þi maner of writyng shulde stonde in anoþer place. If it plese to ony man to write þis concordaunce & him þenkiþ þat summe wordis ben not set in ordre aftir his conseit & his manere of writyng, it is not hard if he take keep wiþ good avisement in his owne writyng to sette suche wordis in such an ordre as his owne conseit acordiþ wel to.

In Englisch also as in Latyn ben wordis equiuouse, þat is, whanne oon word haþ manye signyficaciouns or bitokenyngis. As þis word *kynde* bitokeneþ "nature" and also such a man clepen we *kynde* which is a free hertid man & þat gladly wole rewarde what þat men don for hym. An instrument wherwiþ we hewen clepen we an *axe*, & I *axe* God mercy of synnes þat I haue don. Suche wordis in þis concordaunce ben maad knowen bi sum word addid to hem wherby it may be wist whanne þei ben taken in oon significacion & whanne in a noþer.[5] Textis in whiche ben wordis of plurel noumbre ben quotid in þe wordis of singuler noumbre. A word is singuler noumbre þat bitokneþ but oo þing, as *womman, man, foot*; a word of plurel noumbre bitokneþ mo þingis þan oon, as *men, wymmen, feet*. Loke þanne þe textis in whiche ben þese termes *men, wymmen, feet* in her synguleris—*man, womman, foot*. Loke also suche wordis *wakyng, wepyng, fadirheed, wickidnesse*, in wordis þat þei comen of (as *wakyng* in *wake*, *wepyng* in *wepe*, *fadirheed* in *fadir* & *wickidnesse* in *wickid*, and þus of oþere lyk hem) but if it be so þat boþe þe wordis of whiche oþere wordis comen and also þe wordis þᵗ comen of hem ben expresly sett out in þis table as cheef wordis of þis concordaunce, as is of þese wordis: *seruant, serue* & *seruice*, for ech of þese þree is expressid bi hemself. And þus it is of oþere wordis: *kyng* & *kyngdom* & of sum oþere, as þou may conceyue liʒtly in þis table if þou take good heede.

Wher a chapiter spekiþ miche of a mater, þanne is sumtyme shortly quotyd þe sentence & not þe wordis. As in þis word *bischop* is quotyd how, þᵉ firste pistle to Tymothe þe þridde cᵒ, & Titum þᵉ firste cᵒ, ben specified þe condiciouns of a bischop. And in this word *charite* is quotyd how, in þe firste pistle to Corintheis, þrittenþe cᵒ, Poul spekiþ of þe condicions of charite. Whanne þe cheef wordis of þis concordaunce ben þe firste wordis of þe firste textis þat ben quotyd in hem, þanne ben þo wordis not rehersyd aʒen in þe same firste textis, forwhi þei ben parties of þe same firste textis as þou may perceyue liʒtli in þese termes: *absent, abstene, Acaie, accepcioun*, and in manye oþere. And whanne suche cheef wordis ben not þe firste wordis of suche firste textis, þanne stonden þei absolutely & ben sett by hemself oon, to shewe redyly where þo textis þat suen whiche perteynen to such wordis may be liʒtly founden, as þou mai se in þese wordis: *Aaron, Abba, Abel*, & in many mo. Þe cheef wordis of þis concordaunce I clepe alle þo wordis þat goen bi lettre aftir þe ordre of þe A B C in þis present table.

If ony fruyt come of þis concordaunce, to God be onour & doynge of þankyngis now & euere. Amen.

Aaron. Bi þe ordre of Aaron: *Heb., vii cᵒ.*

Abba. Criynge "Abba, fadir": *Galath., fourþᵉ cᵒ.*

Abel. Fro þe blood of Abel: *Mᵗ., þre & twenti cᵒ.* Fro þe blood of iust Abel: *Luc., elleuenþe cᵒ.* Bi feiþ Abel offride: *Hebr., elleuenþe cᵒ.* Sprynginge of blood better spekyng þan Abel: *Hebreis, twelfþe chapiter.*

Abhomynacioun, of discounfort: *Mᵗ., foure & twenti c.; Marc., þrittenþe c.*

Abortiue. He was sen to me as to an abortyue: *Firste Pistil to Cor., fiftenþe cᵒ.*

Abraham. Of þese stoones þe sones of Abraham: *M*ᵗ., *þridde c.* God of Abraham: *M*ᵗ., *two & twenti* c.; *Marc, twelþe* c.; *Luc, twentiþe* c. We ben þe seed of Abraham: *Io., eiȝte* c. Bifore Abraham was maad, I am: *Io., eiȝte* c. Abraham bileeuyde to God: *Roa., fourþe* c. Abraham fadir to hem þat suen þe steppis of feiþ: *Roa., fourþ*ᵉ c. Abraham aȝen hope: *Roa., fourþ*ᵉ c. Abraham bileeuyde to God: *Galath., þridde* c. Biheestis weren seid to Abraham: *Galath., þridde* c⁰. Abraham hadde two sones: *Galath., fourþ*ᵉ c. Þe feiþ of Abraham: *Hebr., elleuenþe* c. God apperide to Abraham: *Act., seuenþe* c. Abraham was iust: *Iames, secounde* c⁰.

Abregge. But þe Lord hadde abreggid þo daies: *Marc., þrittenþe* c.

NOTES

*This concordance contains well over 1200 separate entries. Their average length is five or six lines but some are much longer. The entry for *loue*, for example, occupies nearly five pages.

†With one doubtful exception, no emendation seemed necessary. I have silently expanded all unambiguous contractions other than the ampersand, but I have not otherwise altered the text except to use present-day conventions in matters of punctuation, quotation, and capitalization. The corresponding conventions of the original, representing as they do the practice of a man skilled in these and similar matters, are of course important in themselves. But their reproduction presents typographical difficulties and the text has sufficient interest without them.

For a note on the manuscript, and an excerpt from the preface, see G. F. Warner and J. P. Gilson, British Museum: *Catalogue of Western Manuscripts in the Old Royal and King's Collections* (1921), II, p. 226. The manuscript is also discussed by Anna C. Paues, "The name of the letter ȝ," *Modern Language Review*, VI (1911), 441 ff.

1. *Sic.* On the form *-yg* cf. A. McIntosh, *Review of English Studies*, New Series, II, 5 (January 1951), 70, n. 2.
2. *in ordinatly.* Leg. *inordinatly.* Or delete preceding *not?*
3. *V* (for modern *U* and *V*) and *W* are treated as one letter. In fact only one of the thirty-one pages containing V or W entries is headed with a V; all the rest are headed with a W.
4. The formula is exemplified on f. 161ʳ: **Wirke.** Loke in **Worche.**

5. This alludes to a labeling according to what part of speech the word is. Thus in the concordance *f.* 12ᵛ, the words for "axe" and "ask" are given two separate entries, the head words being followed by the words "noun" and "verbe" respectively. Similarly, f. 81ʳ, we have **Kynde** listed separately as "adiectyf" and "substantyf." Items that are lexically connected are not separated. Thus **Loue** includes instances of both noun and verb.

Dialectal Traits in
Sir Thomas Wyatt's Poetry

HELGE KÖKERITZ

SIR THOMAS WYATT's father, Henry Wyatt, was a Yorkshireman who in 1493 had acquired Allington Castle on the Meadway in Kent. He had married Anne Skinner of Reigate, Sussex, and their elder son, Thomas, was born at Allington about 1503. He grew up in Kent, went to Cambridge when only twelve years old, and later held various posts of trust at court, including important missions to France and Spain; for some time, too, he was Sheriff of Kent. He escaped the fate of many an illustrious contemporary by dying prematurely of a fever in 1542 while journeying to Falmouth to meet the ambassadors of Emperor Charles V.

From a linguistic point of view, then, it appears that the general outline of Wyatt's life differed very little from that of other contemporary men of consequence. Like him they often spent their childhood and adolescence in the country before going to Oxford or Cambridge prior to entering the service of their sovereign. But unlike Wyatt most left behind no record that might provide a clue to the impact of other varieties of English on their own type of speech. Some no doubt followed the example of Raleigh later in the century who never abadoned his Devonshire dialect. Others, however, adjusted themselves to their new linguistic environment, adopting more or less successfully the characteristics of educated or courtly London speech. We can hardly be wrong in suggesting that Wyatt belonged to the latter group. Yet we can discern in his sheaf of poems the survival of certain Kenticisms, even though these would hardly be very conspicuous in the capital, where southeastern features had been part of the linguistic pattern for over two centuries. Notwithstanding a few seeming northernisms, which will be dealt with below, there is no vestige of his father's dialect. This had doubtless been neutralized by his mother's southern idiom and by his own daily contact with Kentish-speaking members of the household; we catch a glimpse of the boy listening to the songs the Allington maids

used to sing "when they did sowe and spynne" (197).[1] Indeed, in the first
two lines of another poem (196) Wyatt affirms his close ties with Kent,
saying:

> But here I ame in Kent and Christendome
> Emong the muses where I rede and ryme.

No wonder that his muse who had "tasted the sweete and stately measure and style of the Italian Poesie" (Puttenham) and affected the
cadences of Chaucer, Skelton, and the Tudor lyricists, would occasionally lapse into her native Kentish idiom.

Wyatt's Kenticisms are principally phonological. The morphological
and lexical evidence is confined to the four southern past participles
yfixed 9, *istricken* 47, *ycharged* 195, and *isene* 197, all archaic, metrical
doublets ultimately derived from Chaucer; to a few instances of the
southern plurals *hath* and *doth*, for example, *there selves hath bene*
102; *wee bothe . . . hathe don* 106; *the hartes of them wich . . . doth
gro* 145; *some men doth say* 148;[2] and to the two words *kant* 'portion' 198
and *wrislye* 'shrivelled' 141. If EDD can be trusted, *cant* 'portion' is
now restricted to K, Ha, Sr, Sx, whereas *wrizzly* survives only in eastern
So; MED cites an apparently nondialectal instance of *cant* from c. 1460,
antedating OED's first example, the Wyatt word. On closer scrutiny, a
few words now labeled northern in the dictionaries, actually prove to
have had a much wider distribution earlier. This is true of *kest* 'cast'
71, which is regular in the Middle Kentish *Ayenbite*;[3] of *bren* 'burn'
(in *brent* 59, *brennyng* 181), formerly common in the south and used by
Chaucer; and of *grame* 'sorrow' 114, another Chaucerian echo. *Sheene*
'shine' (vb) 199, found in Skelton and labeled a Scotticism (OED), has in
fact been recorded also from D, Do, and So (EDD). *Girn* (in *girning* 199),
a metathesized form of *grin*, is today reported from Scotland to Devon
(EDD) and was earlier used by Bokenham, Skelton, Sir Thomas North,
and others (OED), while a similar case of metathesis, *thrust* 'thirst'
211, 229, is well evidenced from early southern texts, including Palsgrave
(OED). *Narr* 'nearer' 181 (< OE *nēarra*) survives in modern Ha *narre*
(EDD). If *heins* in "Ffor that in heins to fle his rage so ryff" (213.16) is
hain 'enclosure' used metaphorically, it is as much a southern as a
northern word; EDD reports it from So, Wi, and as a verb from Ha, Wt.
The exclusively northern word *force* 'waterfall' (<ON *fors*), which is
listed as *forse* in Muir's Glossary (p. 285), does not occur at all in Wyatt;
unglossed *forse* appears in poem 94, where it is clearly the common word
"force." And the past tense forms *chase* 98, *drave* 64, *strake* 64, *wrate*
pp. 248, 249, *smast* B6 (a contracted variant of *smatest*), were formerly
current in the south.[4]

A phonological examination of Wyatt's rhymes and spellings will prove more fruitful. Admittedly, his rhyming sometimes appears to be as casual as his prosody often is, but such cases are so conspicuous as to cause no serious problem. For instance, he tends to rhyme only the unstressed syllables of disyllabic words as in *harbar:baner:suffre: displeasur* 4 and *reason:season:condition:fashion* 10, or a stressed and unstressed syllable as in *lif:pensif* 161, *free:sea:Thylee* 195. This practice, which may well be due to misunderstanding of Chaucer's prosody, makes most of his disyllabic rhymes phonologically unreliable. Thus *chambre:remember:daunger* 37 cannot be adduced as evidence of [ɛ:] or [ę:] in *chamber, danger*, since the three lines in question have exactly ten syllables each, the tenth being [ər], which probably alone constitutes the rhyme. But monosyllabic rhymes are phonologically useful, even though some of them may already have been traditional, for example, *love:prove, most:lost.*

Characteristic of the spelling is Wyatt's vacillation between conventional and unconventional forms. A word may be written in several different ways, even in the same poem, for example, *patience* 39, *paciens, pacience* 40, or it may change its garb for the sake of visual conformity in rhyme as in *spite:nyte* 39, *six:stix* (sticks) 101. Consonants are doubled for no apparent reason as in *rysse:gysse:devysse* 110, or in *lutte* alternating with *lute* 132. Often the suffixes -*id* and -*is* seem to have had no sounded vowel, for example, in *compellis:ells* 158, *kinde:assignid* 164, *wyld:begilyd* B22. Hence it is impossible to determine whether *fleith* in *fleith:appereth:fereth* 4 is monosyllabic or disyllabic; in 73, however, the meter shows it to be monosyllabic. Wyatt's *f* and *ff* denoted both [f] and occasionally [v]. The latter value is obvious in *elefn* 101, *saffry* (savory) 196, *swarfde* 41 (rhyming with *serued: ondeseruid*), *our sellffes* 205, *them sellfes* 207, *belovffd* 99, and probable in *profd:lofd:reprofd:remofd* 87, *carffd* 304.[5] In *effes* (eaves): *dises: ples* 209 we have instead a variant without the medial *v* (OED *ease* 6, pl. *easen*) as in Shakespeare's *ease-dropper* R3 5.3.22, whereas in *deserft* 25 and *deserftes*, rhyming with *partes* 87.2, the *f* is excrescent and pseudoetymological. French variants with *f* account for *saff* (save) 101, and so on, *natyff* 211, and *pensyf* 161, rhyming with *lif*. For *mouth* and *truth* the text has *mowgh* 207, *mowght* 201, 212, and *trowgh* 121, 199, 207, *trowght* 88, 198, 203, 213, *trowghthe* 71, spellings which reveal that *sightes* 28, *syght* 206, *sighting* 12 represent the common dialectal variant *sithe*, with [θ] or [ð], of *sigh*, found from Northumberland to the Isle of Wight and appearing as *sythyng* B1. The most significant orthographic feature, however, is Wyatt's not infrequent use of *i* or *y* mostly, but not exclusively, after historically long vowels. Thus we find *ai/ay* for late ME *ā* of various origin in *baigne* (bane) 206, *cayge* B38 (rhyming with *Rage*), *haist* (hast) 197, *haith* (hath) 39, 66, *tayme* B38 (rhyming with *gayne*), *taisted* 8, *chaing(e)* 132, 147, 209, *strainge* 132, *straynge*

68, which like the inverted *alith* (aileth) B3, *dalye*, B50, *trators* B27, show the leveling of ME *ā* and *ai*;[6] further, and more remarkably, in *mayni'a* (many a) 101, *maynifold* 200 (EDGr reports [e:] from certain Midland counties, and a similar long vowel was used by Cooper, 1685), *laymentte* 217 (a doubtful poem), *trayvell* B29, 32, *vaylye* B43 (perhaps influenced by *vale*) and *payngys*[7] (beside *pang*) B26. ME *ę̄* and *ę* are written *ei/ey* in *bleyr* (blear) 105, *cheyr* (cheer) B51, *Creytour* (creature) B18, *bereyve* (bereave) B18, *feise* (fees) 198, *fley* (flee) B23, *fley* (flea) B28, rhyming with *I, fleith* 73, *freize* 26, *meit* (meet) 48, *steill* (steel) 31, *greiff* 5, 9, *greif(e)* 43, 51, 58, and so on, *releiff* 9, *leist* (least) 79, *theise* 199, 201, 229, *theys(e)* 114, B44, rhyming with *ways* B41 (*theise* may be a compromise between *these* and *thise*), *deiff* 58 (but *deff* 84, *deffh* 205), *weik* (weak) 93, *weyke* 201, *weyne* 129 (wean — not "ween" as glossed by Muir), *eaysyd:apeaysyd* 103; this *ei/ey* may well be an analogical French spelling.[8] Note also *leynght* (length) 172, which may be a ME survival, for which see Jordan, § 103. Similarly ME *ǭ* appears as *oi/oy* in *noyns* (nonce) 198, rhyming with *bones:groyns* (groins), *foys* (foes) B44, and monosyllabic *goi'the*, rhyming with *trothe:grow'th* (p. 200); further in *soinges* (songs) 132, which may have had a long vowel, still recorded from Kent in *song, wrong* (EDGr § 32).[9] And OFr *ü* is spelled *uy* in *reffueys:acuys* 217, *truyse* 32 and *luyster* (lustre) 204, whose vowel may therefore have been long; *uy* is of course an analogical French spelling. Such forms are not uncommon in documents of the fifteenth and sixteenth centuries. They occur in the Cely Papers (Essex), the Shillingford Letters (Devon),[10] in other southern and southwestern letters,[11] and in the Diary of Henry Machyn, a London Merchant Taylor. Because of their frequency in late ME texts of northern provenance they have come to be classified as northern (Jordan §§ 19, 44, 54). Discussing the 1435 spelling *weyrs* (< OE *wera*), Kjerrström,[12] with nice under-statement, characterizes Jordan's delimitation of this graphic device as "not . . . satisfactory." It would clearly be absurd to call Wyatt's usage above northern. Nearly all these spellings are either inverted or analogical forms, with the exception of *oi* for ME *ǭ* and the appearance of *i/y* after an historically short vowel. Whatever was the rationale of this use of *i* as a length mark, its occurrence in southern texts demonstrates the fallacy of taking such spellings as a criterion of northern provenance in early Modern English.[13]

Highly significant, too, is the use of *i* and *y* for ME *ę̄* and *ę* in *nydes* (needs) 197, which should be compared to *indes* 132, obviously a mis-reading of *nides* for *nedes* of MS. E, *nyd, suype* (sweep), *kype* B46, *kypes* B114, *belyve* B47, *unmyt* 198 as well as *mytt* (meet) 10, whose double *t* need not indicate a preceding short vowel (see above), *styre* (steer) B114, *Lya* (Leah) 134, *clyne* (clean) B46, rhyming with *syen* (seen), *glyne* (glean) 197, rhyming with *bene* (bean), *extryme* B114, and *unnysyd* (uneased) B35;[14] *esteme* alternates with *estime*, the original French form, in poem 196. Taken together with the rhymes to be discussed below, these *i* and *y* spellings obviously stand for [i:]. Moreover, Wyatt often writes *ie/ye*, a French spelling, for ME *ẹ̄*, as in *diepe* 52, 93, *hieraufter* B46, *chiere* 196, *chyer* B 181, *fiever* 64, *lieper* (leper) 207, *syeke* (seek) 172, and the above *syen* B46. This *ie* rhymes with *e* as in *diepe:wepe* 52, and with *ei*, another French spelling, as in *myschief(e):greif(e):relief* 51, 58, three words which also appear as *greff*: *mescheff* B25, *greffe:myscheffe* B42, *greffe:relyeffe* B27, *gryff(e):relyff* B4, B20, and in the rhyme *greffe:lyffe* (life) B38.

Wyatt's Kentish background reveals itself first of all in his not infrequent use of *e* for OE *y*. We find it in *bes(s)ye* B35, *besely* 37, *ded* (did) 123, 134, and so on, *kendeld* 87, *kendlid* 96, 200, *knet* 169, *merth* 216, *myrthe:erthe* 229, *shert* 5, rhyming with *smert:hert* (cf. Chaucer's *herte:sherte* LGW 2628–29), *sterred* (stirred) 8, 9, *sech* 214, whereas *buried* 9, though rhyming with *sterred:weried*, is doubtful, since it rhymes also with *greved* and hence is probably a rhyme in *-ed*. Note further *dere:ffyere* (fire) B41, a poem in perfectly regular iambic meter. Instead of *e* we sometimes find *i* or *y*, for example, in *lifft* (left) 204, *shitt* (shut), *shytt* 120, *kit(t)* (cut) 161 (cf. Chaucer's *shette, shitte, cut, kitte*), *bissely* 12, *kyndeled* 87, *siche* 137, 138, and *mych(e)* B4, 5 as well as *mitch* (6×) in Wyatt's two letters; *u* occurs in *me lusteth* 13 and normally in *such*, with the variant *soche* 152, and so on.

Equally important dialectally is the complete leveling in rhyme of ME *ẹ̄* and *ẹ̄* (< OE *ǣ¹, ǣ², ēa*). The following are conclusive cases: *dede* (deed):*blede* 42, 54, *dede:spede:drede* 189, *nede:dede:yede* 205, *rede: crede:wede:spede* 167 (a quadruple rhyme), *spede:rede* 227, *lede:glede* 24, *wene* (ween):*sene:mene* 36, *mene:sene* 192, *free:sea:Thylee* (Thule) 195, *grene:clene:kene* 64, *kene:medecene:unclene* 76, *hede* (heed): *lede* B19, *reche:beseche* 65, *reche:seche* B36, *clyne* (clean):*syen* (seen) B46, *beleve:preve:leve* (leave) 111; further *bene* (bean):*glyne* (glean): *clene* 197 and the striking *I:fley* (flea) B28. Their common sound was clearly [i:] as shown by the above *i* and *y* spellings, and by the inverted forms *peakes* (piques) 146, used also by Nashe in 1592 (OED), and *medecene* 76, which when trisyllabic and with a secondary stress on the final syllable must have ended in [i:n]—cf. L. *medicīna*, and modern German *Medizin*, Swedish *medicin*, both with stressed [i:] in the final syllable. The reflex of ME *ē* < OE *ĕ* in an open syllable is less clear: it rhymes with itself in *wreke:breke*, *speke:breke* 74, with *ǣ¹* in *heate: freate* 190, *hete:meate* B32, and with *ēa* in *frete:grete* 8, *eaten:thretyn* 8; but it is spelled *wryeke* 132 (cf. *syeke, syen* above), *meet* (meat) 197, and *brake* (break) 132, rhyming *brake:sake* 132, *brake:wreake* B24, *make the:betake the:brake the* B28. Two pronunciations, therefore, seem likely, one with [i:], the normal reflex of ME *ẹ̄* and *ẹ̄* in Kentish, the other with [ɛ:] or [ę:] as in contemporary upper-class London speech.[15] The latter variant must be the basis of the rhymes *ffayne:mene*, *theys* (these):*ways* B41, and possibly *ffaythe:breathe* (breath) B34, unless both had a short vowel; [feθ] has been recorded from northwestern Devon (EDGr), corresponding to such early spellings as *feth*, *fethful*, which I prefer to interpret as having *ĕ*.[16] Before *r* ME *ę̄* and *ę̆* may have had both [i:] (cf. *chyer:cleer* B181) and [ɛ:]. The best evidence of the latter vowel is the rhyming of Fr *galere* 78 with *dere* (dear), *fere* (fear), *chiere*, *clere*, as well as the rhymes *kare not: spare not:fere not* 151, *declare*: *bare* (bear) 181, and *ware* (were) *not:here* (hear) *not*, *bere* (bear) *not* 166; *ware* (were) is frequent in Wyatt.

In the treatment of ME *ī* we note first of all the remarkable use of *ay* in *th'ayes:layes* (eyes:lies) 35, whereas *trayed* 45 is probably the past participle of *tray* 'betray,' despite the E variant *tryed*. The digraph *ay* is the more noteworthy since Wyatt had doubtless leveled ME *ai* and *ā* under the latter as [ɛ:] or [ę:]. Influence from *ay(e)* 'yes' might have been reckoned with if the earliest forms of the word (from 1576 on) had not consistently been spelled *I*.[17] For *stryke* 93 MS. E has *streke*, corresponding to modern Devon *streek* (EDD) and comparable to [di:k] for *dike* in K, Sx, and Sf,[18] as well as *leek* (like) in Peele's *beleek:seek* (*The Arraignment of Paris* 3.4.1–2) and in Bullokar.[19] The same development is seen in *greep'the* (gripeth) 176 – cf. modern Devon *greep* (EDD) and OED's anonymous sixteenth-century spelling *greep* – and in the above *sheene*, which is definitely *shine* and not, as OED suggests, a verbal use of the adjective *sheen*; in fact, Thomas Sackville, who was born in Sussex, rhymes *shyne:fyne:seene* as well as *shrike:beseke*, *keele*: *whyle:while*, *wheele:smyle:erewhile*, and *griefe:lief* (life),[20] identical with Wyatt's *greffe:lyffe*. Moreover, OE *wīc* appears as the place-name *Week(e)* in Co, Ha, So, Wt, with *e*-spellings from the fifteenth century on,[21] that is, the time when ME *ę̄* had become [i:]. The simplest explanation, it seems to me, is to interpret these cases as reflecting a dialectal tendency in the south to preserve ME *ī* undiphthongized. Luick (§ 485, Anm. 6) was aware of this possibility though, because of the rhyme *deke:eke* in *Sir Ferumbras*, he limited it to the southwest. Yet he is probably right in regarding *shriek* as a modern survival of this dialectal [i:] for ME *ī*. In *there:desire* 27, if a genuine rhyme, *desire* may have been pronounced with [i:] in imitation of French,[22] whereas *breers* (briars) 59 represents the original form with ME *ę̄*. We note further that *requyre* rhymes with both *desyre* B42 and *aper* (appear) B30 – whether two pronunciations are implied or only one, with [i:], it is impossible to determine. The two rhymes *tre:fly* B22 and *fflee:lye* B36 show the confusion of the two verbs *flee* and *fly*.[23] If *bridill:Idell:myaell* 198 is a disyllabic rhyme, its first two members may have had [ɪ]; Sir Thomas Smith,[24] who was born in Essex, gives *i* in *bridle* (which now survives only in Cumberland, EDGr), while Bullokar has one doubtful instance of *idle* in which, however, the omission of the length mark may be accidental.[25] A probably unstressed *I*, pronounced [i] or restressed as [i:], rhymes with *bee* 123, *me* B1, *be:she* B2, and with *fley* (flea) B28. Spellings like *by* (be) B10, *my thynckith* B11, *my thynckes* B15 and *the selffe* 132 (also *thy selff*) reveal the leveling of the reflexes of shortened ME *ī* and *ē* under [i].

A southern feature is the use of *o* in *bond:stond:lond* 209, *bronds: honds:fonds* 199, *lond* 212, *stond(es,-eth)* 29, 121, 212, and so on, *hande: withstonde* 164. Dan Michel's *Ayenbite* (1340) vacillates between *a* and *o* in *hand, land, stand.*

The leveling of ME *ǭ* and *ou* is shown by rhymes like *ffoo:sloo* (slow) 8, *bestow:wow* 98, *troo:woo:knoo:goo* 167, *owne:mone* 65; *kno(o)* is a recurrent form. A notable inverted spelling is *owre* (oar) 28, which *Tottel's Miscellany* emended to *houre* with the result that Fowell, Hangen, and Rollins misinterpret it as "hour" despite "A ciascun *remo*" of the Italian original.[26] But *doulfull* 69, *dowlfull* 205, and *dulphulle* B8 represent the variant [du:l] (now obsolete though listed as current in OED), whose ancestral OFr diphthong *ue* developed into ME *ui, ē*, and, by analogy, *ō* (Luick, § 415.3). From the rhymes *cause:knowes:clause* 166, *drawen:overthrowen:gnawen* 8, *unknowen:owne:fawne:sowen* B14 and the spellings *chaw* (chew) 198, *awne* (own) p. 249, we learn that ME *ou* had coalesced also with *au*, a feature characteristic not only of Kent but also of Essex, West Midland, and the southwest (Jordan, § 105, Anm.). This coalescence would therefore imply that ME *ǭ*, too, had the antecedent vowel of modern [ɔ:], now found only in *broad* and occasionally for both ME *ǭ* and *ou* in D, Do, So, W.[27] The same thing happened before *gh* as in *doghter:besoght her:lawghter* 198 and *frowght* (fraught) 114.

Very striking are Wyatt's rhymes between ME *ǭ* and *ū* in *foode: allowdd:clowde* 199, *cowd* (could):*lowde:Roode* 197, *lowde:cowld* (could):*Shrowd* B5, *tow* (two):*now* 101, *thereto:now* 108, all of which should be compared with spellings like *howpt* (hooped) 197, *lowke* 75, *lowking* 67, *souner* 8, *prouf* 5, *reprouff:alowff* 8, *drowpith* 200, *stowpeth* 60, *howgy* (hugy) 22, and *avoo* 215 (a doubtful poem), rhyming with *how:now*. A few similar rhymes occur in Spenser.[28] They are not northern, for ME *ǭ* and *ū* do not rhyme in northern English. Unfortunately we know too little about the Kentish dialect of about 1500 to determine whether it was characterized by undiphthongized ME *ū* as a counterpart to the undiphthongized ME *ī* discussed above. The Sx place name *Hove* [hu:v], written *Howffe* 1531 (cf. the above Wyatt spellings), and going back to OE *hūfe* 'hood, covering,'[29] appears to be a unique fossil of southern undiphthongized ME *ū*.

Wyatt's poems contain other interesting spellings and rhymes, though not so significant dialectally as to warrant a detailed treatment.

Thus raising of *e* to *i* is frequent, for example, in *inimis* 141, *sildam* 31, *yett:fitt* 162, *fryndes* 170, *byn* (been) 207 (also *ben* 183, *bene:sene* 186), *thrid* 161, *stydfastly* 109. The opposite tendency, lowering of *i* to *e*, perhaps with lengthening in an open syllable, is illustrated by *ffeckell* 125, *sperit* 8, *hetherto* 13, *wedow* 198, *leve* (live) 106, and so on, *geve: leve:relieve* 199, *geven* 8, 15, *drevyn* 122; *quakynd* (quickened) 122 may be an inverted spelling showing the qualitative similarity of *e<i* in *quickened* and [ẹ:] or [ɛ:] in *quake*. Another type of lowering is the common change of *er>ar* in *marcye* 199, *warte* (wert):*parte* 135, *sar-wyes* (service) 120, *unharde* (unheard):*reward* 157, *unfarme* (unfirm, ME *-ferme*):*harme:charme* 203. Shortening is probably indicated in *lest* (least):*request* 57, *lest:possest* 190, *sesse* (cease):*redresse* 15, and perhaps in *sayth:breth:feith:deth* 77 (a quadruple rhyme), *fete* (feet):*forgett* 155 (both words probably with [ɪ]). Yet Wyatt's erratic doubling of consonants makes it impossible to say whether the vowel was really short in, for example, *esse* (ease) 58, *knelle* (kneel) 196, *incresse:cese* 155; at times he may have rhymed a long and a short vowel of (practically) the same quality, for example, in *nekke:speke* 38 ([ẹ] and [ɛ:] or [ẹ:]), *hele* (hele):*well:fele* 196 ([i:] and [ɪ]), *cloke: moke*(mock):*stroke* 196 ([ɔ] and [ɔ:], for which see above). Contractions of various kinds occur, for example, *En'mye* 8, *watrid* 175, *gadryng* 202, *saffry* (savory) 196, *sprites* 202, *thebrews* 202, *thevyn* (the heaven) 197, *t'assaye* 138; *ainst* (against) 184, unrecorded in OED and elsewhere, looks like an aphaeretic form of southern *a-yainst* (or possibly *to-yainst* – cf. Dan Michel's *to ayens*, *to yans*, *to yens*) with simultaneous loss of [j], though the doublet *ayenst* may have had a rhythmic variant with initial stress which made it liable to syncopation. With regard to Wyatt's consonants we notice the loss of the palatal fricative in *nyte* (night):*spite* 39 and the inverted spellings *wryght* (write) 103, *spyght* 119, *whight* (white) 86; further, the reduction of certain clusters as in *dyst* (didst) B34, *smast* (smat'st) B6, *twist*, *twyst* (twixt) 29, *spen my* (spend my) 104, *Granfather* p. 245, *hepe* (help) B27, *skarce* 149, rhyming with *cace:place*, *reherst:lest* (least) B33, *thou drieves* 189, *thou stondes*, *restes*, *trottes*, *sayse* 198, rhyming with *dayes*. Prosthetic [j] and [w] appears in *yerth* 101, *yerne* B43, *wone* B15, *won* B22, *many whon* B48, a *d* is added in *dismolde* 199 and a *t* in *deptyst* B5, clearly a variant of the shortened superlative *deppest* – it is curious that a *t* appears also in *Deptford* in Kent and Wiltshire, now pronounced without the p.[30] Only one instance of *v* for initial *f* has turned up, *vauore* B43, and only a few cases of *w* for *v*, namely *werely* B21, *dewoyd* B9, *sarwyes* 120. The recurrent *wich* (which) 153 and so on, *wens* 91, and *whete* (wet) 197 show the coalescence of *wh* and *w*. Regressive assimilation accounts for *lenthe* (length) B26 and *optayn(e)* 116, 120; but *turkylles* (turtles) B22 is an inverted spelling indicating the common colloquial change of [kl] > [tl] as in *tlean* for *clean*.

NOTES

1. Kenneth Muir, ed., *Collected Poems of Sir Thomas Wyatt* (Cambridge, Mass., 1950), here cited by number, and the same editor's *Sir Thomas Wyatt and his Circle, Unpublished Poems* (Liverpool, 1961), referred to as *B* plus number; page references are to the two letters printed in the former volume.

2. Such forms are not unknown to Shakespeare; like him, Wyatt has also a few cases of plurals in *-s*, e.g., *suche as sekes* 124, *them . . . that thynkes* 124, *my dayes dekaes* 137 (cf. Wilhelm Franz, *Die Sprache Shakespeares*, § § 155 f.).

3. J. K. Wallenberg, *The Vocabulary of Dan Michel's Ayenbite of Inwyt* (Uppsala, 1923), p. 135.

4. See the respective verbs in OED, where, however, *smate* 'smote' is said to be only northern, clearly because Wyatt's form above was then unknown.

5. For the same scribal practice in southern documents see Max Franck, *Englische Schreibung und Aussprache im Zeitalter der Tudors und Stuarts (nach Briefen)* (Bottrop i.W., 1939), pp. 88 f. They are also typical of Henry Machyn's *Diary*, written in London between 1550 and 1553.

6. In *change, strange,* etc., *ai* appears as early as late ME (Jordan, § 224, Anm.). Many *ai* spellings are listed in Franck (p. 59), as well as *a* for ME *ai* (p. 70).

7. Cf. *haynge, hainge* (hang) in seventeenth-century New England documents, which have also *grain* (grand), *substainshall* (Anders Orbeck, *Early New England Pronunciation* [Ann Arbor, Mich., 1927], p. 23).

8. Surrey's *weyve*, which Tottel respelled *weaue*, is an instance of the same kind and not, as Veré Rubel (*Poetic Diction in the English Renaissance* [New York, 1941], p. 62) seems to assume, an exchange of *weave* for *waive*.

9. R. E. Zachrisson (*Pronunciation of English Vowels* [Göteborg, 1913], p. 65) reports *stroynge* and *cloys* (close) from the Shillingford Letters

(Devon), and similar spellings are cited in Franck (p. 62). The now obsolete verb *groin* 'grunt' (in the above rhyme *bones:noyns:groyns*) had an early monophthongal variant *grone* used, e.g., by the Londoner Palsgrave (1530): "a hogge groneth," which tended to be confused with *groan* (see OED, *groin* 1b and *groan* 2).

10. See Zachrisson, pp. 50, 64 f., Asta Kihlbom, *A Contribution to the Study of Fifteenth Century English* (Uppsala, 1926), pp. 119, 146 f., 153, 159.

11. See, e.g., Franck, pp. 36, 53, 55, 59 f., 62, 66.

12. *Studies in the Language of the London Chronicles* (Uppsala, 1946), p. 237.

13. This is unfortunately done in Axel Wijk's dissertation *The Orthography and Pronunciation of Henry Machyn, the London Diarist* (Uppsala, 1937), pp. 21 f., where Machyn's use of *i/y* as a length mark is said to be an orthographical feature "characteristic of the North generally" and hence taken as evidence of his alleged Yorkshire origin. Few, if any, of the orthographical, phonological, and grammatical criteria adduced by Wijk to substantiate his thesis are conclusively northern, not even *ees* for *eyes* (p. 28), which is reported as a Devon pronunciation in 1701 (see *Anglia*, XXIV [1901], 116, also Kihlbom, p. 37).

14. But *concyle* 124, rhyming with *whyle:gyle*, need not be "conceal" as glossed by Muir, but should probably be identified with *concile* 'reconcile,' which seems to fit the context.

15. See my *Shakespeare's Pronunciation* (New Haven, Conn., 1953), pp. 194 ff. Since *a* appears in *break* (inf.) from the fifteenth century onwards, it may be analogical as suggested by Zachrisson, p. 58.

16. For these spellings see Zachrisson, (p. 68), who, however, takes them to be Anglo-Norman forms.

17. The earliest occurrence of *I* 'ay(e)' is actually in Sir Thomas Smith's

De recta & emendata Linguæ Anglicæ Scriptione, Dialogus (1568), p. 11a, where "I Latina" is said to mean "ego, aut oculus, aut etiam" (Deibel's ed., Halle, 1913).

18. See my *Phonology of the Suffolk Dialect*, § 284, with a reference to *speke* (spike), *streek* (strike) in Edward Moor, *Suffolk Words and Phrases* (Woodbridge, 1823). Note that *drive* is [dri:v] in Gl (EDGr, Index).

19. R. E. Zachrisson, *English Pronunciation . . . As taught by William Bullokar* (Uppsala, 1927), p. 48. However, I cannot subscribe to his theory that the leveling with ME *ē* may have been due to early ME shortening of *ī* with subsequent lengthening in an open syllable to *ē*. For other examples of this type see Kihlbom, pp. 36 ff., and Franck, p. 50. The 1701 list of Devon provincialisms referred to above (n. 13) gives *cheeld*, *bleend*, *neen* (nine), *kee* (cows), *ees* (eyes), which should be compared with the Devon instances cited in A. J. Ellis, *On Early English Pronunciation* (London, 1869), I, p. 291. Thomas Howell (1581) rhymes *seeke:leeke* twice in his "To the Reader" (*The Poems of Thomas Howell*, ed. A. B. Grosart [Manchester, 1879], pp. 171 f.).

20. In his Induction to *A Mirror for Magistrates*, ll. 307–308, 314–15, 471–74, 492–95, 527–30.

21. Cf. A. H. Smith, *English Place-Name Elements* (Cambridge, 1956), II, p. 261, and my *The Place-Names of the Isle of Wight* (Uppsala, 1940), p. xcvi. My suggestion (*ibid.*) that modern [i:] in *Week* is due to lengthening of a late ME *wick* in early Modern English, does not seem compatible with the fresh material adduced here.

22. See Otto Jespersen, *John Hart's Pronunciation of English* (Heidelberg, 1907), pp. 28, 66.

23. This confusion is very old. In fact, it goes back to OE, where the two verbs *flēon* and *flēogan* were identical in all forms except in the infinitive, the first pers. sg. present, the pl. present, and the whole present subjunctive. The *i*-mutated forms of the 2d and 3d pers. sg. present spread to the 1st pers. sg. and the pl., as well as the infinitive in ME, resulting in the doublets *flē(n)* and *flīe(n)* of both verbs. In Northern English *fly* became *flee*. Orr's suggestion (*Words and Sounds in English and French* [Oxford, 1953], pp. 1 ff.) that *flee* became *fly* to avoid unpleasant associations with the alleged homonym *flea*, is totally unfounded. Moreover, until the end of the 17th century, *flea* was pronounced [flę:] in upper-class London speech; only in southeastern dialects did it become [fli:] in the fifteenth century.

24. P. 27a and § 28.

25. Cf. Zachrisson, *Bullokar*, pp. 177, 204.

26. See further my article "Two Sets of Shakespearean Homophones," *RES*, XIX (1943), 360, n. 5.

27. EDGr, § § 121, 123, f., 127 f., 168.

28. Arvid Gabrielson, *Rime as a Criterion of the Pronunciation of Spenser, Pope, Byron, and Swinburne* (Uppsala, 1909), pp. 77 f.

29. *The Place-Names of Sussex* (Cambridge, 1929), p. 293, and *English Place-Name Elements*, I, p. 267.

30. *The Place-Names of Wiltshire* (Cambridge, 1939), pp. 231 f., and Ekwall, *The Concise Oxford Dictionary of English Place-Names* (Oxford, 1960), p. 142.

Hic Jacet Lincoln,
Rex Quondam Rexque Futurus

FRANCIS LEE UTLEY
The Ohio State University

WHAT FOLLOWS is the last chapter from a short book now going the rounds. It is an appropriate tribute to Frank Magoun, who is an expert on oral formulas and themes, and who does not therefore need to keep his counsel on such hypotheses as Lord Raglan has presented to an incredulous world. The earlier portions of the book discuss Raglan's twenty-two archetypal points as outlined in his *The Hero*, first published in 1936 and often reprinted (for a medievalist's review see that by Jess B. Bessinger, Jr., in *Speculum*, XXVIII [1953], 606–11), and then illustrate them up to point thirteen with sections devoted to the Birth and the Initiation of the Hero, called Abraham Lincoln, but according to Raglan's myth-ritual methodology a purely mythical figure who could not have had an historical counterpart. Besides this model there is another, that of R. L. Littledale's "The Oxford Solar Myth: A Contribution to Comparative Mythology," first published in the Trinity College (Dublin) miscellany *Kottabos* and reprinted in *Echoes from Kottabos* (edd. R. Y. Tyrrell and Sir Edward Sullivan [London, 1906], pp. 279–90). The original publication was in 1870, and the article sought to demonstrate that Max Müller, solar mythologist *par exemple*, was himself a sun myth. It is perhaps best known from H. Gaidoz's translation (with introductory comments): "Comme quoi M. Max Müller n'a jamais existé: étude de mythologie comparée," in the periodical *Mélusine*, II (1884–85), cols. 73–90.

The Lincoln myths are all thoroughly authentic, from collections well known and available. Perhaps the most useful of them have been those of Lloyd Lewis, Dixon Wecter, Carl Sandburg, and Roy Basler. Their only flaw is their failure to see the potency of the Raglanite argument, which turns a reputed American president into a ritual myth.

The Hero's Mythic Death

> *And Moses went up from the plains of Moab unto the moun-*
> *tain of Nebo, to the top of Pisgah, that is over against*
> *Jericho . . . . So Moses the servant of the Lord died there in*
> *the land of Moab, according to the word of the Lord. And he*
> *buried him in a valley in the land of Moab, over against Beth-*
> *peor; but no man knoweth of his sepulchre unto this day.*
> DEUTERONOMY

As Raglan perceives, the world of reality is a tragic one, and hence in the world of ritual the hero loses favor with the gods or his subjects (point fourteen) and is driven from throne and city (fifteen).

In Lincoln's early years we saw a single combat with adversaries, the two outstanding ones being Jefferson Davis and Stephen A. Douglas. Now the forces of evil come together in hordes against him, in dramatic anticipation of the end. To describe this *agon* the myth has created a War, as mythical as the siege of Troy. The very vacillation of its naming betrays its fictive quality: men cannot agree, but call it variously the Civil War, the War of Secession, the War between the States. Its unreality is further demonstrated by its strange, unearthly-sounding battles: Antietam, Shiloh, Chickamauga, Manassas Junction, and, in blatant recall of Frazerian myths about fertility god and wasteland, Bull Run and the Wilderness. Though local legend keeps some of these cult names alive, they are obviously derived from the Lincoln myth — modern survivals of nineteenth-century ritual. On the authority of the mythographers Nicolay and Hay, the hero himself gives us the clue to the war's ritualistic nature. Speaking to wounded soldiers of the Sixth Massachusetts in days when the North was finding mobilization difficult, Lincoln said: "I begin to believe that there is no North. The Seventh Regiment is a myth. Rhode Island is another."

An abstraction called the South was opposed to the hero's armies. Students of comparative religion know well that the hell of Northern climates is an icy one and the hell of Southern climates a fiery one. Summers such as those spent by the hero either in prairie Illinois or Washington's foggy bottoms make it clear where the major devils in this myth must come from. But apart from Jefferson Davis, Lincoln's Dioscuric double, the leaders of the South are not much personalized. Lee and his generals have been made into antagonists of Lincoln's generals, and not of the hero himself. The nominal hell is too far off from the Kingdom of the hero; one must seek his most potent or active antagonists nearer home.

Hence Abraham's enemies were not only in the South. There were Copperheads like Vallandigham of Ohio, radicals like Charles Sumner and Thaddeus Stevens in the Congress, generals like McClellan (who is said to have refused even to talk to his commander-in-chief), antagonists even in his own Cabinet like Edwin Stanton and Salmon P. Chase. And, as we have seen, even the wife of Abraham's bosom was a Destroying Goddess. The well-known folktale process of doubling takes on a mugwump quality, with its mug on one side of the Potomac and its wump on the other. The radical Thaddeus Stevens and Alexander Stephens, vice-president of the Confederacy; Frederick Douglass the freed slave and Stephen Douglas the Democrat; Jeff Davis and a certain Judge David Davis who is said to have managed Lincoln's campaign at the Chicago convention—all these are plain doublets, as their names demonstrate. It is on a minor scale with the lesser *personae* of the myth, the same phenomenon as that of Jefferson Davis and Abraham Lincoln themselves, major adversaries born of the same father in the same log cabin and contending for the Richmond throne. Evil, the Antichrist, always masks itself as good. Similar, though a bit more remote, is the name Rutledge: Ann, the White Goddess of his youth, and Archibald, a Southerner who attacked his body after death. Vilification came from his own Western dominion: the La Crosse, Wisconsin, *Democrat* said prophetically: "And if he is selected to misgovern for another four years, we trust some bold hand will pierce his heart with a dagger for the public good." After his death he was attacked symbolically as well as directly by the rebel Miss Fanny, by Rutledge, and in 1939 by unidentified hoodlums who dented his bas relief in Springfield with bullets, rouged the lips, and scrawled on its back the word "sourpuss." Edgar Lee Masters in 1931 exalted his final antagonist, Booth, and declared that his bullet was "the last one fired for States' Rights." These indignities to the Dead or Dying God are of course worship in disguise, a carrying out of the destinies.

Raglan's points seventeen, eighteen, and nineteen, the driving from the throne, the mysterious death, and the location of that death at the top of a hill, are merged by the Lincoln myth. As Raglan says, chronology, which means everything for history, means nothing for myth. Lincoln now meets his most remarkable antagonist, the antigod or antihero John Wilkes Booth. With the relentless repetition of ritual we see once more the basic dualisms of the world: Set against Osiris, Loki against Balder, Modred against Arthur, Judas against Jesus. In his early life Booth's nature is foreshadowed; then he shot with intense interest cats, dogs, and a sow, all of them, as we have seen, Lincoln's totem animals. Like the Oedipal Judas of legend, Booth had a mother fixation, as Lloyd Lewis tells us. To parallel Lincoln's sacred spouse or spouses, Booth had an antiqueen, Mary Suratt. One of his alleged associates in the conspiracy, David Herold, sounds suspiciously like Herod. In a world of good and evil the antigod is essential, for without him the fatal divine tragedy cannot be played out.

At first glance the nineteenth step in the drama, the god's death on a high hill, seems to be Capitol Hill, where Lincoln served as Representative and later dominated as Monarch. But is Capitol Hill a splendid enough scene for the American Mount Horeb, Mount Carmel, Mount Calvary? Raglan puts us right: "There can be little doubt that the scene of the solitary journey and single combat is the stage." The proper scene was a box in Ford's Theatre and a proscenium arch under which the actor-adversary leaped. Reflecting the cultural lag of one whose cult has been replaced, a Baptist preacher of the old school remarked: "We remember with sorrow the place of Lincoln's death. He did not die on Mount Nebo with his eye full of heaven. He was shot in a theater. We are sorry for that. It was a poor place to die in." Or, as another preacher said: "Would that Lincoln had fallen elsewhere than at the very gates of Hell—in the theatre to which, through persuasion, he reluctantly went. How awful and severe the rebuke which God has administered to the nation for pampering such demoralizing places of resort." Wiser men, full of the new faith, saw "that the miraculous hand of God had passed before their very eyes, lifting Lincoln out of the President's chair for the good of the nation." Like Enoch, implies this statement, Lincoln walked with God.

Booth the adversary knew his destined role. From the stage to which he jumped after leaving Lincoln's box he ritualistically waved the bloody knife of the sacrifice and yelled, "*Sic semper tyrannis!*" Or, as an ancient Irish railroad flagman put it, with deep significance and a recognition of the intimate affinities between god and antigod, "I'm sick, sind for McGinnis!"

Nor could the hero himself have failed to see his role—the playing out of the destinies. Dickens told of how on the very day of the assassination Lincoln had related to the Cabinet one of his mysterious dreams. "He was in a boat on a great river all alone, and he ended with the words, 'I drift—I drift—I drift,'" As Lewis says, the magic three of folklore; we can add that this is the ship procession we have already heard of under the name of *River Queen*, the sacred barge of the Nile, Noah's Ark. Once, after the election of 1860, he saw a double image in the mirror, which he rightly interpreted as "an omen that I should not see life throughout the last term." The second image, no doubt, was his *doppelgänger*, Booth, Douglas, Davis. As the Dark Temptress, Mary Todd Lincoln arranged the scene, though he was strangely reluctant to go, and said like any tired husband that he had seen the play before. Like Pertelote in the *Nun's Priest's Tale*, she attacked his faith in dreams. By now it is clear to us that the play was a mere ritual repetition. This is the real meaning of Lincoln's excuse that he had seen it before. Like most husbands in such a box with his wife he argued, and then said something which at the moment seemed mere jest: "All right, Mary,

I'll go, but if I don't go down into history as the martyr President I miss
my guess." A multiple martyr, to a fretful socializing wife, to the chthonic
Mother, to the Judas Wilkes, to and for the Nation. Like his adversary
Jefferson Davis, he was the hanged god of dark pagan superstition – as a
Southern cult poem recorded by George S. Bryan has it:

> Two posts standant;
> One beam crossant;
> One rope pendent
> Abram on the end on't,
> Glorious! splendent.

Of course in so late a myth we cannot expect many such open references as this to the basic ritual. Rather, like most gods and heroes,
Lincoln gathered up echoes from the best-known religious figures of his
supposed time: Abraham, Moses, and Jesus.

His very name is meaningful. Only secondarily does it come from
ancestral Abraham Lincolns or from paternal Abraham Enloes; its true
source is the Old Testament. As the poem just quoted shows, it vacillates
between Abram and Abraham. Of Abraham the First and Abraham the
Second we have already heard. Even more significant is Father
Abraham, enshrined in many songs, which revolve around a refrain like
"We are coming, Father Abraham, three hundred thousand more!" Or
there is the revealing "jest" in which Lincoln, catching up a little girl
who in a game stumbled and fell, said to her, "When you reach home you
can truthfully tell your mother you have rested in Abraham's bosom."
After the 1860 election a Georgia orator declaimed: "The South and the
North are now as widely separated as Abraham from Lazarus."

Though he was compared to many other heroes, Abel, Saul, Samson,
Socrates, and St. Peter, we may confine our direct illustrations to a hero
certified by Lord Raglan: Moses. On the testimony of a Boston preacher:
"Like Moses he died because his work was done." He led his people out
of the Wilderness, and we remember that there was a "Civil War" battle
by that name. Some of the preachers seemed to be rather happy about
the assassination. According to the Rev. John Todd, "Moses may lay
down to die, on the very borders of the promised land, but a Joshua shall
be raised up to lead the people in to possess it." Joshua is obviously an
etymological doublet of Johnson; indeed one C. B. Crane forgot that
Johnson was a John Barleycorn figure and called him the "Joshua whom
God has appointed to consummate the work which our dead Moses so
nobly commenced." Lincoln himself saw his kinship with Moses as he
had with Abraham. One day he symbolically carried a little colored girl
across the streets of Springfield, a ritual act which Emanuel Hertz
describes as "the type and prophecy of Lincoln carrying four million
of the same race over the Red Sea." Yet he is hero enough in his own

right to question the words of Moses. In an interview of 6 September 1864, the Rev. J. P. Thompson spoke to Lincoln about the distinction in the Mosaic Law between domiciliary imprisonment and chattel slavery. Lincoln is reported to have remarked: "I have sometimes thought that Moses didn't quite understand the Lord along there."

Of course the greatest parallel was that of Christ. The time of his death is proof positive that we have no real history before us, but a plain syncretic myth. For the shooting was on Good Friday. As Joseph Medill of the *Chicago Tribune* put it: "On the sacred anniversary of the day made holy by the crucifixion of Him, we mourn another martyrdom." Even more pointedly we have the statement of the Rev. William Ives Buddington: "God needed for his purposes the death of his Son. . . . God needed likewise the blood of Abraham Lincoln." Many of these remarks would seem blasphemy, confusion of the Creator with the creature, were it not for the by now overwhelming evidence that Lincoln himself is numinous, divine. Some of the old order of preachers make the High God of the pantheon a rather jealous God. They declared that Lincoln's death was a punishment for the surrender of Lee on a Sabbath evening, Palm Sunday. One, quoted by Lloyd Lewis, says directly that Lincoln had been converted into "the idol of the people" and that "God will punish idolatry." But most saw him as the Man of Sorrows, the savior. As we have seen, Nancy Hanks was the Madonna of the Backwoods, Hodgenville, the American Bethlehem. The poet Lyman Whitney Allen called Lincoln "the savior of a race" and envisions him ascending to heaven midst "quiring angels." Gamaliel Bradford, by contrast, associates him in *The Haunted Biographer* with the Harrowing of Hell. With his immense compassion Lincoln gets a special permit to visit John Wilkes Booth in "the lower regions." Booth says he did Lincoln a service (one remembers the heretical Russian sects who exalt Judas because he carried out God's plan); Lincoln complains and says that the folks in heaven are too solemn, and fail to understand his jokes. He thanks Booth for putting a halo round him, and pities poor Woodrow Wilson, who would have benefited by such an end. Though this Descent to Hell has somewhat Shavian overtones, it is one more striking parallel to Christian and pagan hero as well.

Biblical language continually surrounded Lincoln. Senator Nesmith of Oregon said that a miracle of the loaves and fishes would be necessary to satisfy the place seekers. A preacher told Lincoln that he had a divine message for him, and the hero replied that it was strange that he had sent it via the wicked city of Chicago. In a Springfield lecture old Jesse Waik said "If our Saviour had ever come to Springfield and was lucky enough to get away, he would be too smart to come again." Lincoln thought he ought to feel that way about the 1864 election. Francis Carpenter painted *The Emancipation Proclamation*, envisaging Lincoln and his Cabinet as a kind of Victorian Last Supper. Though countless politicians superficially have sought the Imitation of Christ or Lincoln, the most striking of these is the painter Picasso, who once arranged his hair to look like Lincoln's and was quite disappointed when Gertrude Stein said he didn't look like him at all. (John Malcolm Brinnin is the source for this last.) We may summarize this long list of parallels in the words of a Duluth Baptist minister close in time to the assassination. "On the same day years before, Christ had suffered death on Mount Calvary. Both lives began in humble huts." Joseph and Thomas Lincoln were carpenters. Both Christ and Lincoln were reformers, abused, meek, patient. "Both were killed as a sacrifice for man." In the words of Julia Ward Howe, "As Christ died to make men holy, he died to make men free."

After the shock of that sacrifice not only Baptists but other sects clambered aboard the procession of the ritual ship. Though the free-thinking Herndon, a close friend, had called him an "infidel," he was claimed after his martyrdom by Catholic, Freemason, Quaker, Methodist, Spiritualist, even Mormon. Perhaps the last was an echo of his many loves. We see Titus Oates and the Protestant Plot of the English Restoration come to life again in the charges that Lincoln was assassinated by a conspiracy of Catholics; Copperheads retorted that he had been a creature of the Jesuits. In truth, like Christ, he was all things to all men.

Raglan's twentieth point is that the hero, not being a part of the historic dynasty, since he is a mere fiction, is not succeeded by his children. Though in a larger sense as Abraham he was father of the tribe, Lincoln had poor luck in his children. His second son Eddie and his third son Willie died early, and the irrepressible Tad, pet of the White House and, as we have seen, a totemic figure, died at a date called 1871. Robert, the one survivor, who wanted much to be president, was not like his "daddy" at all. The myth reports that once he tried to urge on his father a candidate for postmaster from Cambridge, Massachusetts, whereupon Lincoln told him to attend to his studies or he'd take him out of Harvard. Instead of succeeding his father, Robert became the president of the Pullman Company and turned down the plea of Negro porters for higher wages. His only role, thus, is as apostate from his father's gospel, epigone, denier of the myth. He is, however, said by Lloyd Lewis to have had the same girl as Booth—a minor *hieros gamos* gone wrong, identifying him with the antihero.

The *de jure* heir was Andrew Johnson, said by some to be illiterate, a rebel, who was sleeping off a drunken spree when awakened to take the oath as President. (Were this history, we might seek to say kinder words about Robert Lincoln and Andrew Johnson, but since this is myth criticism no redressing of the balance is relevant.) But the true heir, *de facto*, was Edwin Stanton, Lincoln's Secretary of War, who took the helm of the ritual ship when Lincoln abandoned it. He was an "iron-willed giant" in Sandburg's words, who had worked his way through Kenyon College and been employed in a bookstore in Columbus, Ohio. His own youth has its mythical aspects: he was a snake trainer. Lincoln significantly saw that another god would replace him; he called him Mars, and he allowed him the gift of omniscience in the famous words "If Stanton said I was a damned fool I must be one." A complex and ambiguous figure, like the Hagen of the *Nibelungenlied*, Stanton prosecuted the search for the adversary Booth and the trial of Booth's fellow-conspirators. Yet he ignored the *de jure* heir Johnson, was reputed by some to have been the real murderer of Lincoln, and is said to have killed himself after the tide turned and Johnson fired him from the Cabinet. Certainly he was often a thorn in the side of the martyred President, who when once complimented by a Bostonian because he never swore explained: "I don't have to. . . . You know I have Stanton in my Cabinet." After the death of the hero what one of my students called "the edifice complex" always falls apart. Yet Stanton was the one who said the immortal words, "Now he belongs to the ages." Perhaps he is best described as Lincoln's St. Paul, another ambivalent successor.

Raglan's final two scoring points are that the hero's body is not buried but that, nevertheless, he has one or more holy sepulchres. As various localities compete for Lincoln's birthplace, so do they for tomb and shrine. As Lewis says, "New York, which was always New York, urged that Lincoln be buried there in the great metropolis of the land." Washington "had the ideal spot for Lincoln's body, that niche under the Capitol's dome which had been originally made for the corpse of George Washington," but which remained empty when the family chose Mount Vernon. Illinois, however, demanded the dead hero for his real kingdom, Springfield, and apparently it won. Yet even in Springfield there was confusion. A grave was dug on a hill now the site of the State Capitol, but the dark temptress Mary Todd opposed the ritual hill and shifted the body to Oak Ridge Cemetery.

Such, at any rate, are the apparent literalist views of the sepulchre. As true Raglanites we know that the hero has no real tomb. He would have had to have lived to secure one. The folk, always wiser than city masses and elite, know that the so-called tomb is empty. One caretaker made it clear: "From every state in the Union, people come suspecting that Mr. Lincoln's corpse is gone—lost or stolen." Lincoln is of the race of Barbarossa, Moses, Arthur; like the last he is "dozing in Avalon, watched by waiting queens," among them, no doubt, Ann Rutledge and the girl in the covered wagon. Several times the coffin has been moved or reported stolen, perhaps by Confederates with "their oft-repeated threat to scatter what was left of Father Abraham to the four winds." The "wandering-restless corpse" did not decay. In the words of an old darkey cited by both Basler and Sandburg, "Massa Linkum be eberywhere. He walk de earth like de Lord." Or, as Whitman puts it, "Night and day journeys a coffin." A certain "lost history" quoted by Current asserts that he did not die of Booth's bullet, but lived on till 1881. Fictive as this probably is, it shows the mythic process.

Once more we see the conflict of hero and antihero, the conflict through imitation. By the process of inversion the adversary Booth is the one who above all lives on. I have myself seen his purported body in carnival side shows. In spite of the most elaborate attempts on the part of Stanton and the War Department to document the disposition of the body of Booth, captured and killed according to their interpretation in Caroline County, Virginia, on 26 April 1865 (a week after Holy Saturday with its Blessing of the Paschal Candle and *Felix culpa*), the documents have been rightly disregarded. Some twenty men have been said to be the fugitive Booth in disguise, and they have been found as far afield as the American South, Canada, the South Seas, South America. Among them are a black-eyed and raven-haired man named Couce; a Rev. J. G. Armstrong of Richmond, Virginia; a drunken saloon keeper of Granbury, Texas; a suicide known as David E. George, of Enid, Oklahoma; even Charles Guiteau, the assassin of Garfield. Thus the myth of survival is displaced to the antigod, as is his illegitimacy. One version makes Booth the son of Jefferson Davis who, as we have seen, was Abraham's half-brother. This makes Booth Lincoln's nephew, a striking parallel to Modred, sister's son of King Arthur. The madness and drunkenness ascribed to Lincoln-Moses and his heir Johnson-Joshua were likewise ascribed to Booth. From his reputed father, Lucius Brutus Booth, he inherited a host of religions in the manner of his heroic rival—Lucius was an Episcopalian, a Mason, a Baptist, a Jew, a Catholic, even a Moslem. Thus the twin mysteries of tomb and survival are paralleled in Lincoln and Booth, and merely round out the dualistic pattern of god and antigod.

And thus all twenty-two of Raglan's points score for Lincoln. He is not in the humble rank of Robin Hood, who has only thirteen points, but at the heights, with Oedipus, Theseus, and Moses. Our final Raglanite proof lies not in the mere myth but in the ritual of which it is the embodiment. Ritual, of course, revolves around relics. Of these there are many: a lock of Lincoln's hair, a mattress and a coverlet, the draperies on the coffin, some two hundred pistols cited by George Bryan—each of them the murder weapon, a bloodstained playbill, Laura Keene's bloodstained dress. In addition, there are superstitions like the traditional jeweler's watch-sign with its hands pointing to 8:20, the time variously of his entry to the sacrificial arena or theatre, of the shooting, or of his death. At Lincoln's tomb there was a brown thrush which did not sing for a year after his "death."

Yet more positive aspects of ritual affirm themselves. We have heard already of the *Hieros gamos* or sacred marriage with the "girl in the covered wagon" or on the sacred boat the *River Queen*. It is from such imagery that Whitman secured his famous metaphor, "O Captain! My Captain!" The ritual processional is duplicated in the funeral, which wended through New York, Pennsylvania, Ohio, Indiana, and Illinois, to rest at last symbolically in Springfield. It was retracing, of course, the route taken by the hero from his inland kingdom to the capital of empire. There were many ritual aspects to the procession. On Sandburg's testimony the Washington funeral cortege included the "visiting firemen of the Perseverance Hose Company of Philadelphia, . . . the Fenian Brotherhood, the Sons of Temperance," and various German glee clubs. There was a human sacrifice: Charles Johnson heralded the funeral by cutting his throat in New York. As was fitting for Lincoln, hero of many loves, the continental procession was thronged with female hierophants: three ladies in Washington; six ladies with roses in York, Pennsylvania; many women kissing the hero's face in New York; a beautiful lady made up as the Goddess of Liberty in Philadelphia; "the first young ladies of Albany, dressed all alike in black skirts and white bodices"; young ladies in Columbus, Ohio, singing "hymns in praise of the martyr"; three more at Conners, Ohio, "elevated above a crowd singing a patriotic song"; young women dropping "flowers and hearts" at Piqua, Ohio; sixteen ladies and thirty-six little girls at Michigan City laying a floral cross while Miss Hatti Gistine represented the Goddess of Liberty with the wand of justice in one hand and the Constitution in the other; thirty-six high school girls in Chicago strewing flowers on the casket. Not to speak of the National Hook and Ladder Company and P. T. Barnum's Museum, which both joined in the New York solemnities. As Lloyd Lewis says, it was "half circus, half heartbreak"; he fails to realize that any ritual attempts to seek the eternal through the humble mores of its own culture in time and place. Whitman's poetic gesture,

> Here, coffin that slowly passes,
> I give you my sprig of lilac,

is but one of the ways in which men, vulgar as well as exceptional, paid their respects to the Man of the Ages.

And today they still pay their respects. The Lincoln Guard of Honor still watches the violated tomb. Every April at midnight there passes a phantom train over the original processional route, and clocks and watches stop as it goes by. Every Lincoln's Birthday the members of the Sangamon County Bar Association retrace the route of the hearse (the Stations of the Cross, of course) from the old State House in Springfield to the Tomb, reputedly in Oak Ridge Cemetery. Every year New Salemites put on Robert Sherwood's *Abe Lincoln in Illinois*, a Passion

Play. Memorial Day is a second saint's day, a doubling of the day of honor of the kind ascribed only to the highest in the hierarchy, like St. Peter and the Blessed Virgin. Will Herberg in *Protestant—Catholic—Jew* (1960) says Memorial Day provides a cult of the dead which organizes all creeds and all ethnic groups into sacred unity. We should not be surprised at so great a myth arising so late in human history. Madison Avenue provides miracles of the kind every day. And every four years Republicans and Democrats, not to speak of Bull Moosers and the Communist Party of the thirties, hail Lincoln's picture, and demonstrate their own particular reductionist view of the cultus. In 1960 his words were read antiphonally by Lloyd Nolan and Efrem Zimbalist, Jr., at the Republican National Convention in Chicago. The parties have battled over his name as Italian villages battled over the body of San Antonio of Padua; when Franklin Roosevelt threatened to speak at the Tomb in 1932 Springfield Republicans charged him with "sacrilege." Millions come to the shrines in Springfield and Washington, and in the Lincoln Memorial at the latter city many seek numinous contact with the hero by sitting in his marble lap. No semidivine figure, except perhaps Santa Claus, has become so central an American myth, irrespective of race, color, or creed. The myth is not parochial; it is world-wide, as Tolstoi's Circassian chief testifies.

The scientific demonstration in Raglanite terms, then, is complete. Perhaps those many photographs in Sandburg and elsewhere dissuade us for a moment, but they are obviously forgeries, probably the creation of partisan publicists. It is perfectly obvious that if Lincoln had sat for all those portraits he would never have had time to be either president or mythic hero. "Scholars," armed with these and other delusive documents, may haggle over a few points I have scored as elements in the hero cult—the Royal Virgin, the Father Who is a Near Relative, the ambiguity of the Future Kingdom, and the like. But any good theory needs a little forcing. Cavillers merely demonstrate their own worship of the lowly gods of positivism instead of their fidelity to the high cultus of the Dying God. More scientific mythographers will carry on the work of this book and reinforce the points made by Raglan and myself; each is at liberty to use his own special ploy.

The rail splitter Lincoln exists in our hearts, not in forged documents or in historical hairsplitting. As Roy Basler says, "His existence may some day be denied, but his significance never." On that day, when clarity descends on all from Raglan Castle, the existential Lincoln will give way to the essential even among the "scholars" and "Euhemerists." Then, for once and for all, we will learn that ontology recapitulates philology. If there had been a real Abraham Lincoln, he would have been greater than his myth, and that, of course, is impossible.